N INFORMATION SYSTEMS

Video training courses are available on the subjects of these books in the
James Martin ADVANCED TECHNOLOGY LIBRARY of over 300 tapes and disks,
from Applied Learning, 1751 West Diehl Road, Naperville, IL 60540 (tel: 312-369-3000).

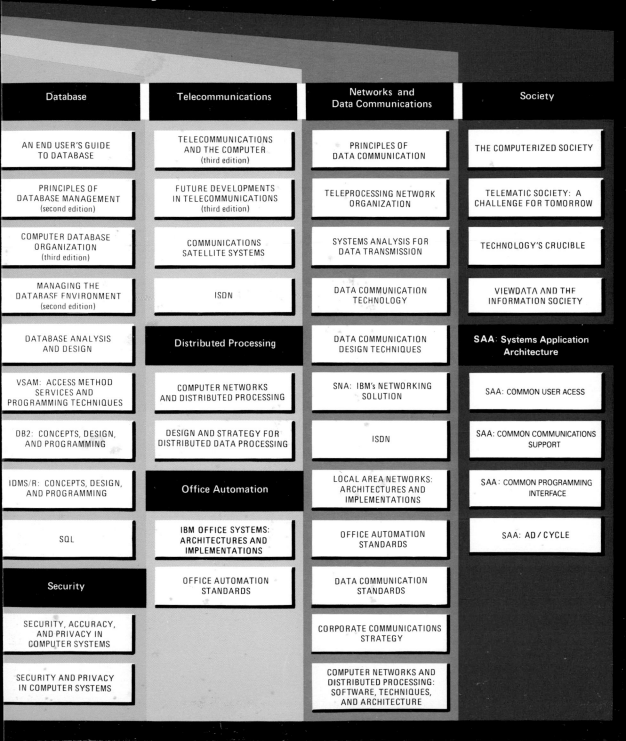

Database	Telecommunications	Networks and Data Communications	Society
AN END USER'S GUIDE TO DATABASE	TELECOMMUNICATIONS AND THE COMPUTER (third edition)	PRINCIPLES OF DATA COMMUNICATION	THE COMPUTERIZED SOCIETY
PRINCIPLES OF DATABASE MANAGEMENT (second edition)	FUTURE DEVELOPMENTS IN TELECOMMUNICATIONS (third edition)	TELEPROCESSING NETWORK ORGANIZATION	TELEMATIC SOCIETY: A CHALLENGE FOR TOMORROW
COMPUTER DATABASE ORGANIZATION (third edition)	COMMUNICATIONS SATELLITE SYSTEMS	SYSTEMS ANALYSIS FOR DATA TRANSMISSION	TECHNOLOGY'S CRUCIBLE
MANAGING THE DATABASE ENVIRONMENT (second edition)	ISDN	DATA COMMUNICATION TECHNOLOGY	VIEWDATA AND THE INFORMATION SOCIETY
DATABASE ANALYSIS AND DESIGN	**Distributed Processing**	DATA COMMUNICATION DESIGN TECHNIQUES	**SAA**: Systems Application Architecture
VSAM: ACCESS METHOD SERVICES AND PROGRAMMING TECHNIQUES	COMPUTER NETWORKS AND DISTRIBUTED PROCESSING	SNA: IBM's NETWORKING SOLUTION	SAA: COMMON USER ACESS
DB2: CONCEPTS, DESIGN, AND PROGRAMMING	DESIGN AND STRATEGY FOR DISTRIBUTED DATA PROCESSING	ISDN	SAA: COMMON COMMUNICATIONS SUPPORT
IDMS/R: CONCEPTS, DESIGN, AND PROGRAMMING	**Office Automation**	LOCAL AREA NETWORKS: ARCHITECTURES AND IMPLEMENTATIONS	SAA: COMMON PROGRAMMING INTERFACE
SQL	IBM OFFICE SYSTEMS: ARCHITECTURES AND IMPLEMENTATIONS	OFFICE AUTOMATION STANDARDS	SAA: AD / CYCLE
Security	OFFICE AUTOMATION STANDARDS	DATA COMMUNICATION STANDARDS	
SECURITY, ACCURACY, AND PRIVACY IN COMPUTER SYSTEMS		CORPORATE COMMUNICATIONS STRATEGY	
SECURITY AND PRIVACY IN COMPUTER SYSTEMS		COMPUTER NETWORKS AND DISTRIBUTED PROCESSING: SOFTWARE, TECHNIQUES, AND ARCHITECTURE	

INFORMATION ENGINEERING

Book II Planning and Analysis

A  TRILOGY

THE JAMES MARTIN BOOKS
currently available from Prentice Hall

- Application Development Without Programmers
- Building Expert Systems
- Communications Satellite Systems
- Computer Data-Base Organization, Second Edition
- The Computerized Society
- Computer Networks and Distributed Processing: Software, Techniques, and Architecture
- Data Communication Technology
- DB2: Concepts, Design, and Programming
- Design and Strategy of Distributed Data Processing
- Design of Real-Time Computer Systems
- An End User's Guide to Data Base
- Fourth-Generation Languages, Volume I: Principles
- Fourth-Generation Languages, Volume II: Representative 4GLs
- Fourth-Generation Languages, Volume III: 4GLs from IBM
- Future Developments in Telecommunications, Second Edition
- Hyperdocuments and How to Create Them
- IDMS/R: Concepts, Design, and Programming
- Information Engineering, Book I: Introduction
- Information Engineering, Book II: Planning and Analysis
- Information Engineering, Book III: Design and Construction
- An Information Systems Manifesto
- Local Area Networks: Architectures and Implementations
- Managing the Data-Base Environment
- Principles of Data-Base Management
- Principles of Data Communication
- Recommended Diagramming Standards for Analysts and Programmers
- SNA: IBM's Networking Solution
- Strategic Information Planning Methodologies, Second Edition
- System Design from Provably Correct Constructs
- Systems Analysis for Data Transmission
- Technology's Crucible
- Telecommunications and the Computer, Third Edition
- Telematic Society: A Challenge for Tomorrow
- VSAM: Access Method Services and Programming Techniques

with Carma McClure

- Action Diagrams: Clearly Structured Specifications, Programs, and Procedures, Second Edition
- Diagramming Techniques for Analysts and Programmers
- Software Maintenance: The Problem and Its Solutions
- Structured Techniques: The Basis for CASE, Revised Edition

INFORMATION

Book I   Introduction
Book II   Planning
Book III   Design

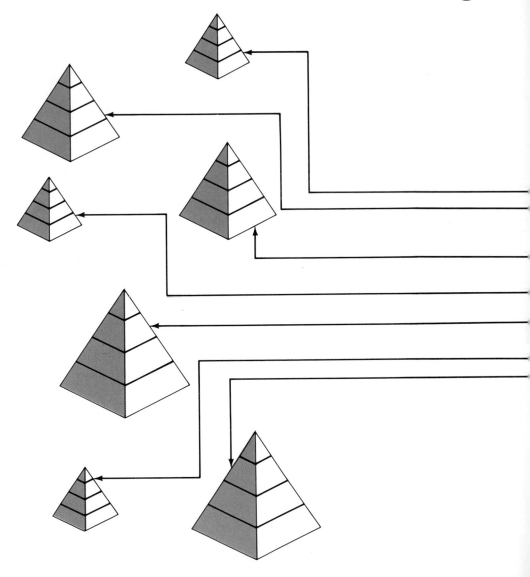

ENGINEERING

and Analysis
and Construction

JAMES MARTIN

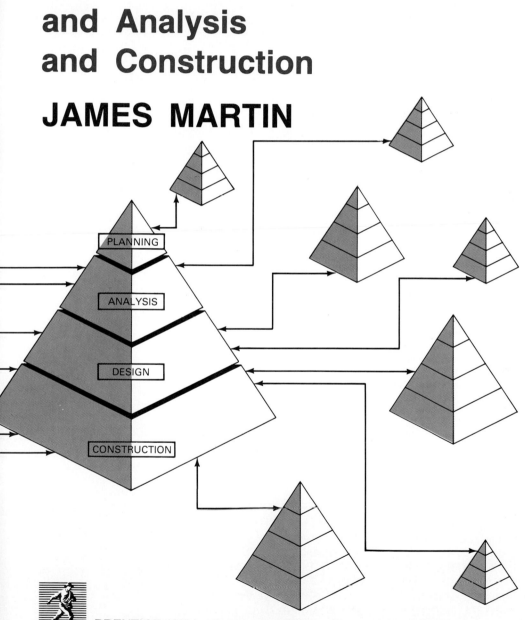

PRENTICE HALL, Englewood Cliffs, New Jersey 07632

Library of Congress Cataloging-in-Publication Data

(Revised for vol. 2)

MARTIN, JAMES (date)
 Information engineering.
 "A James Martin book."
 Includes bibliographies and indexes.
 Contents: bk. 1. Introduction bk. 2. Planning and analysis
 1. Electronic data processing. 2. System design.
I. Title.
QA76.M3265 1989   004   88-39310
ISBN 0-13-464462-X (v. 1)

Editorial/production supervision: *Kathryn Gollin Marshak and Karen Skrable Fortgang*
Cover design: *Bruce Kenselaar*
Manufacturing buyer: *Mary Ann Gloriande*

Information Engineering, Book II: Planning and Analysis
by James Martin
Copyright © 1990 by James Martin

The publisher offers discounts on this book when ordered
in bulk quantities. For more information, write or call:
 Special Sales
 Prentice-Hall, Inc.
 College Technical and Reference Division
 Englewood Cliffs, NJ 07632
 (201)592-2498

Printed in the United States of America

10 9 8 7 6 5

ISBN 0-13-464885-4

PRENTICE-HALL INTERNATIONAL (UK) LIMITED, *London*
PRENTICE-HALL OF AUSTRALIA PTY. LIMITED, *Sydney*
PRENTICE-HALL CANADA INC., *Toronto*
PRENTICE-HALL HISPANOAMERICANA, S.A., *Mexico*
PRENTICE-HALL OF INDIA PRIVATE LIMITED, *New Delhi*
PRENTICE-HALL OF JAPAN, INC., *Tokyo*
SIMON & SCHUSTER ASIA PTE. LTD., *Singapore*
EDITORA PRENTICE-HALL DO BRASIL, LTDA., *Rio de Janeiro*

TO CORINTHIA

Information engineering is defined as:

> The application of an interlocking set of formal techniques for the planning, analysis, design and construction of information systems, applied on an enterprise-wide basis or across a major sector of an enterprise.

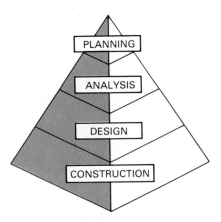

The emphasis is on enterprise-wide planning, modeling, and system design, so sometimes the definition used is

> The application of structured techniques to the enterprise as a whole rather than on a project-by-project basis.

Because an enterprise is so complex, planning, analysis, design, and construction cannot be achieved on an enterprise-wide basis without automated tools. Information engineering has been defined with the reference to *automated* techniques as follows:

> An interlocking set of automated techniques in which enterprise models, data models and process models are built up in a comprehensive knowledge-base and are used to create and maintain data-processing systems.

Information engineering has sometimes been described as

> An enterprise-wide set of automated disciplines for getting the right information to the right people at the right time.

INFORMATION ENGINEERING
A Trilogy by James Martin

BOOK II PLANNING AND ANALYSIS

BOOK **III** DESIGN AND CONSTRUCTION

CONTENTS

Methodologies that Limit Vision 138; Personal Computing 142;
Methodology for Identifying Strategic Systems Opportunities 142;
The Chief Information Officer 145; References 146

8   Tools for Information Strategy Planning   147

Introduction 147; Metadata 147; Matrices 150;
Hierarchies 155; Entity-Relationship Diagram 156;
Analysis 156; Affinity Analysis and Clustering 157;
Clustering Algorithm 159; Summary 160

9   Entity-Relationship Models and Clustering   161

Introduction 161; Entity Subtypes 164;
Entity-Type Decomposition Diagram 168;
Decomposition Shown on an Entity-Relationship Diagram 169;
Avoidance of Too Much Detail 171;
The Entity/Function Matrix 171; Validating the Matrix 172;
Other Matrices 173; Clustering the Matrix 173;
Dependencies among Functions 174; Too Much Detail 181

10   Follow-on from Strategic Planning   183

Introduction 183; Identifying Business Areas 184;
Choice of Business Area(s) to Analyze 185;
Analysis of Current Systems 186;
Top-Level Technology Planning 187;
Who Keeps the ISP Up to Date? 191; Procedure 191

PART II   PHASE II: BUSINESS AREA ANALYSIS

11   Business Area Analysis   197

Introduction 197; Keep It Simple 201; Short Project 201;
Independent of Technology and Organizational Structure 201;
Organizational Changes 202;
Identification of the Business Area 202;
Solving the Communication Problem 204; Reusable Design 205;
Four Types of Diagrams 205; The Initial Diagrams 206;

PART **III**   **APPENDICES**

Appendix I   **Diagramming Standards**   *297*

Appendix II   **Action Diagrams**   *321*

PREFACE

I first used the term *information engineering* in courses conducted in the IBM Systems Research Institute in New York in the early 1970s. The thrust of those courses was that it was necessary to apply top-down planning, data modeling, and process modeling to an enterprise as a whole rather than to isolated projects; otherwise, we could never build a fully computerized enterprise.

Since those days the techniques of information engineering have been greatly refined. Information engineering (IE) is too complex to do with manual techniques. It needs a computerized repository to accumulate and automatically coordinate the mass of detailed information. It needs tools to help in I.S. planning, data modeling, process modeling, and the translation of these models into working systems. The early tools were crude, but provided some early experience that led to the refinement of IE techniques.

The full flowering of IE capability had to await the evolution of CASE (computer-aided systems engineering) tools and the use of these tools to drive a code generator. With these tools we create a repository of planning and modeling information in an enterprise, use this as input to a system design workbench, and generate code from the system design.

The staff of James Martin Associates practiced information engineering, using computerized tools, in many corporations. They steadily refined the methodologies that are described in these three books. As with other engineering disciplines, it became clear that IE needs rigor and professionalism; the computerized tools enforce rigor and guide the professional.

Corporations that have gone from top to bottom in IE, in other words, have done the planning, built the data models, and used these to design systems and generate code, have found that they can coordinate their information systems activities, build systems faster, drastically lower their maintenance costs. Once the data models and process models exist, corporations can make competitive thrusts with computerized procedures much more quickly.

The world is becoming an interlaced network of computerized corporations. As electronic data interchange among corporations grows with intercorporate networks, so the windows of opportunity become shorter. We are evolving to a world of just-in-time inventory control, electronic funds transfer, corporations having their customers and retail outlets online, program trading, a computer in one organization placing orders directly with computers in other organizations, and automation of many business decisions. In such a world the corporation in which data processing is in a mess, with spaghetti code, uncoordinated data, and long application backlogs, will not be able to compete. The techniques of information engineering are vital to the competitive corporation.

The future of computing is a battle with complexity. The complexity of enterprises is steadily growing. The complexity of information processing needed in the military and government is overwhelming. We can win this battle with complexity only with automated tools and automated methodologies. The challenge of every I.S. executive is to evolve as quickly as possible from the mess of old data processing to the building of systems with clean engineering.

Computing needs an engineering discipline with automated tools which enforce that discipline.

James Martin

INFORMATION ENGINEERING

Book II Planning and Analysis

1 PROLOGUE

Book I of this trilogy discussed the principles of information engineering (I.E.). Whereas software engineering applies structured techniques to one project, information engineering applies structured techniques to the enterprise as a whole, or to a major segment of the enterprise. The span of control of information engineering is typically the span of control of the highest I.S. (information systems) executive in the enterprise. In a small, medium-sized, or well-integrated large enterprise, the span of control is the entire enterprise.

Information engineering helps to integrate the separate data processing and decision-support systems built by different teams at different times in different places. It does this by employing a common repository of planning information, data models, process models, and design information. It seeks to maximize the value of the systems built in an enterprise, focusing them on the top-management goals and critical success factors. It seeks to automate the work of building and integrating systems. The cost of building systems is substantially lessened by the identification of common data entities, common rules relating to data, reusable design, and reusable code. It is probably not possible to build the highly computerized corporation of the future, with computer networks going to every desk, without the integration represented by information engineering.

Information engineering is illustrated by the pyramid in Fig. 1.1, which has four basic levels: *strategy, analysis, design, and construction.* The left-hand side of this pyramid relates to data, and the right-hand side relates to activities. There are four levels of tasks in the implementation of information engineering:

- **Information Strategy Planning:** applied to the enterprise as a whole.
- **Business Area Analysis:** in which data models and process models are built for a business area. Different teams may analyze different business areas concurrently.

1

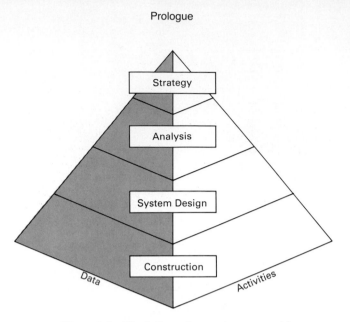

Figure 1.1 The information systems pyramid.

- **System Design:** Systems are designed with the help of automated tools that employ the information stored during the information strategy planning and business area analysis process.
- **Construction:** Systems are constructed with the help of automated tools such as code generators, which are coupled to the system design tools.

The first two of these four levels create a framework within which different teams build different systems at different times. Figure 1.2 illustrates this framework. This book is concerned with the building of the framework: the outer (black) part of Fig. 1.2. Book III of this trilogy is concerned with the design and implementation of systems within the framework: the inner (red) part of Fig. 1.2.

To achieve consistency among separate development activities, the information collected or designed at the four levels of the pyramid is all stored in a repository called an *encyclopedia*. The encyclopedia is an "intelligent" facility that applies many rules to the planning, analysis, and design processes and helps to drive the automatic generation of code. The encyclopedia rule processing helps to ensure the integrity, completeness, and consistency of the information it is given, with a precision far beyond that possible with manual techniques or text specifications. To emphasize that the encyclopedia is an *intelligent* facility, it is drawn with a skull-like icon throughout this trilogy of books (Fig. 1.3). It is this intelligent repository, with its automated coupling to tools for planning, analysis, design, and construction, which makes information engineering practical. The encyclopedias used in practice have grown steadily, acquiring more

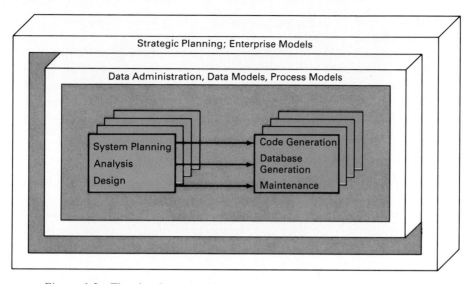

Figure 1.2 The development of individual applications is done within a framework of data modeling and process modeling, which itself relates to strategic planning of how to improve the enterprise with technology. This book is concerned with the red part of this diagram. Book III of the trilogy is concerned with the inner (red) part of the diagram.

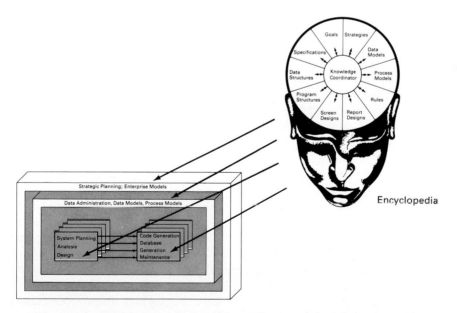

Figure 1.3 The encyclopedia interrelates all parts of the information engineering process.

and more knowledge about the plans, models, and systems in corporations committed to information engineering.

The framework in Fig. 1.2 (the top two layers of the pyramid) takes some time to build. Information strategy planning for the enterprise typically takes six months. Business Area Analysis takes four to six months for one area of the enterprise, with multiple areas being tackled concurrently. Once the framework is in place, individual systems can be designed and constructed relatively quickly using design automation tools and code generators. The plans and models in the framework are adjusted as systems are built and as the enterprise evolves.

Information engineering is made practical by the use of CASE (computer-aided systems engineering) tools. It is important to choose a toolkit in which the planning, analysis, design, and construction tools are integrated and share the same encyclopedia. The code generator is particularly important; it generates code directly from the encyclopedia and hence greatly speeds up implementation.

Information engineering can drastically reduce the systems maintenance costs and difficulties in an enterprise. The tools enforce fully structured design and make designs easy to modify in most cases. New program code is *generated* from the changed design. The tools eliminate the difficult task of investigating how unstructured, ill-documented programs work and how they can be patched or modified.

Part I of this book is about the top layer of the information engineering pyramid—information strategy planning. A primary concern here is how to use technology to make the corporation more profitable, to attack its competition more successfully, or to make it grow faster. Computers should not be regarded as a necessary overhead cost item; they should be regarded as a competitive weapon. Part II of this book is concerned with the data models and process models that constitute the detailed framework within which many separate systems are built.

As described in Book III of this trilogy, system building does not wait until the framework (Fig. 1.2) is completely finished. Systems that directly affect the profit of a business must be built quickly but should be built with CASE tools, which allow quick retrofitting of the information engineering framework as it evolves.

FAST DEVELOPMENT

An objective of I.E. is that systems should be built and modified quickly using a code generator driven from the same I.E. encyclopedia. To create systems that meet end-user needs as fully as possible requires a family of techniques which are described in Book III of this trilogy.

REPRESENTING METHODOLOGY PROCEDURES

These books are concerned with methodologies. To draw diagrams of methodology procedures, it is appropriate to use the CASE tools with which system procedures are drawn. A data flow diagram, for example, can show a sequence of tasks, some of which are done simultaneously; it can show the inputs to each task and the deliverables. A Gantt chart (with horizontal bars) can also show a sequence of tasks, some of which are done simultaneously, and can set these tasks on a time scale. An action diagram can provide text relating to a sequence of steps with conditions (IF. . .ELSE. . .), repetition (e.g., DO UNTIL. . .), and mutually exclusive alternatives, escapes, subroutines, inputs, and deliverables. Of these diagram types, the action diagram (with its EXPAND and CONTRACT capabilities) is the most appropriate for showing lists of actions and structured textual descriptions. Action diagrams are described in Appendix II.

None of the foregoing types of diagrams is completely satisfactory by itself; a combination of them is desirable. If a data flow diagram is used, its blocks should be expandable as action diagram windows. If a Gantt chart is used, its bars should be expandable as action diagram windows. Figure 1.4 shows the combination of a data flow diagram (or dependency diagram) and an action diagram. Figure 1.5 shows the combination of a GANTT chart and an action diagram. In a similar way, a combination of a PERT chart and an action diagram could be used.

In a book it is difficult to show windows that can be opened and closed as on a CASE tool screen. Therefore, to simplify the representation of methodology details, they are shown simply as action diagrams throughout the book. Boxes 4.1, 5.1, 6.1, and 7.4 show methodologies in action diagram format. The complexities of showing window navigation in print apply when printed procedures are given to end users or managers. It is often appropriate to give them a Gantt chart or action diagram rather than attempt to print a windowed set of diagrams that might be confusing in print.

Throughout this trilogy the methodology diagrams are likely to be adjusted in practice to meet the needs of a particular situation or the perspective of a particular team or particular consultant. An action diagram can quickly be tailored to the situation in question, and all the participants can be given printouts of the part of the procedure that involves them. An action diagram editor is a particularly convenient tool for building and editing representations of human procedures. The diagram can be contracted to show an overview or expanded repeatedly to show detailed text or checklists. A large library of procedure modules and tutorial guidance may be maintained. Box 1.1 lists the procedures in this book which are in action diagram format and fits them into the overall information engineering contcxt.

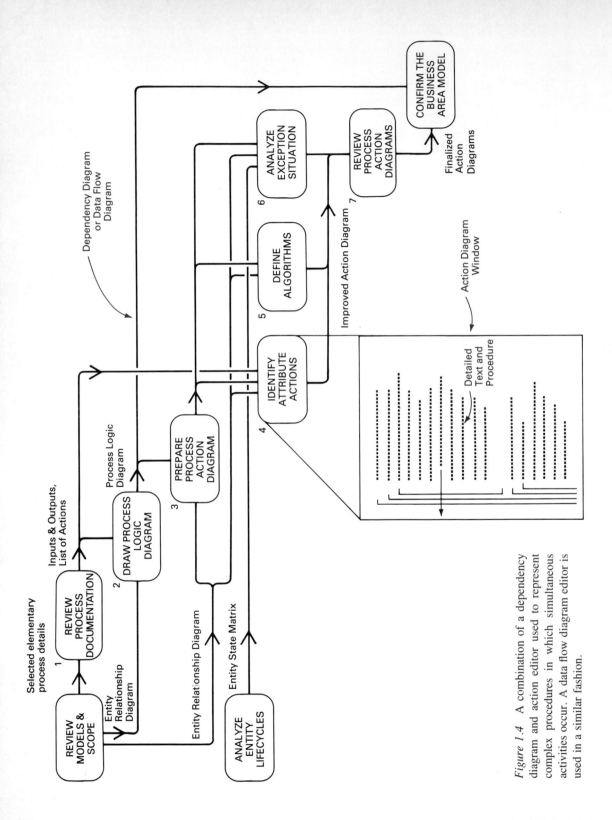

Figure 1.4 A combination of a dependency diagram and action editor used to represent complex procedures in which simultaneous activities occur. A data flow diagram editor is used in a similar fashion.

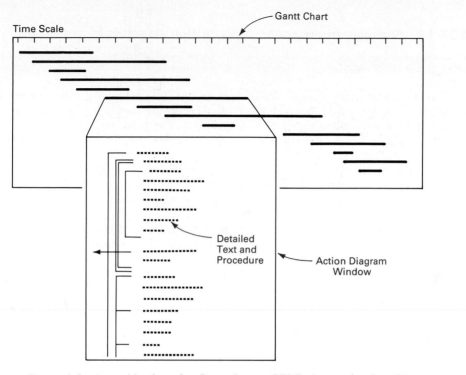

Figure 1.5 A combination of a Gantt chart or PERT chart and action diagram editor used to represent complex procedures in which simultaneous activities occur.

BOX 1.1 Summary of the methodology action diagrams in this book

The I.S. procedures manual should not be an unchanging paper document but, rather, a computerized representation of a family of procedures which can be adapted to the specific requirements of projects. The procedures need to encompass all planning and analysis techniques, and techniques for high-productivity development, such as the use of CASE tools, code generators, fourth-generation languages, prototyping, joint requirements planning, joint application design, timebox techniques, expert systems, design automation, the building of decision-support systems, executive information systems, and new forms of development lifecycles.

All such procedures need to be tailored to the circumstances in which they are used. The tool for representing the procedure should facilitate this tailoring.

It is useful to represent procedures for today's methodologies with action diagrams because much flexibility is needed in adjusting the procedures. An action diagram editor makes it easy to customize the procedures as required. The details represented in action diagrams can be fitted into other CASE diagrams, such as data flow diagrams of methodologies.

```
┌─ Information Engineering Procedure
│  ┌─ The overview model of the enterprise
│  │   o─────────────────────────────────────────────────────o
│  │   │ BOX 3.2. Creating an Overview Model of the Enterprise │
│  │   o─────────────────────────────────────────────────────o
│  │  ┌─ The organizational chart represented as an action diagram.
│  │  │   o─────────────────────────────────────o
│  │  │   │ Figure 3.2.  Organizational Chart   │
│  └──└   o─────────────────────────────────────o
│
│  ┌─ Create Information Strategy Plan for the enterprise.
│  │   o──────────────────────────────────────────────────o
│  │   │ BOX 2.1.  Procedure for Information Strategy Planning │
│  │   o──────────────────────────────────────────────────o
│  ┌─ Business-Oriented Strategic Planning
│  │  ┌─ Analysis of goals and problems
│  │  │   o──────────────────────────────────────────────────────o
│  │  │   │ BOX 4.1.  Procedure for Analysis of Goals and Problems │
│  │  │   o──────────────────────────────────────────────────────o
│  │  │   Illustration of goals:
│  │  │   o─────────────────────────────────────o
│  │  │   │ Figure 4.3.  A Hierarchy of Goals   │
│  │  └   o─────────────────────────────────────o
│  │  ┌─ Critical Success Factor Analysis
│  │  │   o──────────────────────────────────────────────────────o
│  │  │   │ BOX 5.1. Procedure for Critical-Success-Factor Analysis │
└──└──└   o──────────────────────────────────────────────────────o
```

BOX 1.1 *(Continued)*

Technology Impact Analysis

| BOX 6.1. A Detailed Representation of Technological Change |

| BOX 6.2. A Representation of Business Opportunities |

| BOX 6.3. Procedure for Technology Impact Analysis |

Strategic Information Systems Analysis

| BOX 7.1. Examples of Strategic Systems |

| BOX 7.2. A Categorization of Strategic Thrusts |

| BOX 7.3. Examples of Technology for Strategic Thrusts |

| BOX 7.4. Procedure for Identifying Strategic Systems |

Clustering the enterprise model into cohesive systems

| BOX 9.1. Entity Relationship Models and Clustering |

Preparation for Business Area Analysis

| BOX 10.1. Follow-on from Strategic Planning |

For each business area, do a Business Area Analysis

| BOX 11.2. Procedure for Business Area Analysis. |

| BOX 14.1. The Kernel of Business Area Analysis. |

Detailed data modeling

| BOX 12.3. Procedure for Data Modeling |

Detailed Process Modeling

| BOX 14.1. Procedure for Process Modeling |

| BOX 15.1. Preparing for System Design |

PART I

PHASE I: INFORMATION STRATEGY PLANNING

2 INFORMATION STRATEGY PLANNING

INTRODUCTION   The top part of the information technology pyramid is concerned with strategic planning. The simple four-level pyramid diagram shows strategy as a single level at the top of the pyramid. When looked at in detail, it is appropriate to divide this into two sublayers, as shown in Fig. 2.1. The top sublayer contains the types of planning of most direct interest to top management, including the corporate president. The second sublayer contains the modeling of the enterprise and its information, which is primarily of interest to the top-level I.S. planners.

The top sublayer is concerned with the future impact of technology on an enterprise, how technology can be used to make the enterprise more competitive or more profitable, the factors most critical for success in managing the enterprise, and the goals and problems of the enterprise. These are analyzed with methodologies that are the subjects of Chapters 4 through 7:

- Analysis of goals and problems (Chapter 4)
- Critical success factor analysis (Chapter 5)
- Technology impact analysis (Chapter 6)
- Strategic systems vision (Chapter 7)

The second sublayer is concerned with modeling of the enterprise. This is discussed in Chapters 3 and 12 through 14:

- The overview model of the enterprise (Chapter 3)
- Entity-relationship modeling (Chapter 9)
- Data modeling (Chapters 12 and 13 and Appendices III through VI)
- Process modeling (Chapter 14)

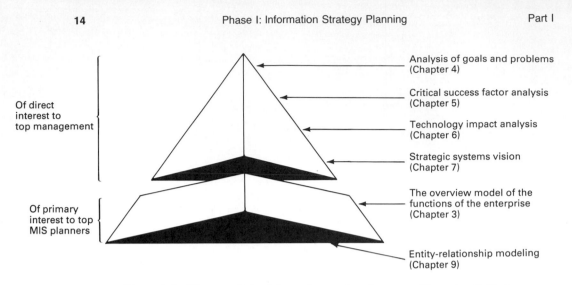

Of direct
interest to
top management

Of primary
interest to top
MIS planners

Analysis of goals and problems
(Chapter 4)

Critical success factor analysis
(Chapter 5)

Technology impact analysis
(Chapter 6)

Strategic systems vision
(Chapter 7)

The overview model of the
functions of the enterprise
(Chapter 3)

Entity-relationship modeling
(Chapter 9)

Figure 2.1   The top of the information engineering pyramid can be divided
into two parts, one of direct interest to top management, and one of primary
interest to MIS planners.

- **Analysis of Goals and Problems** creates a structured representation of the
  goals and problems of an enterprise and associates them with departments or
  organizational units and with the *management-by-objectives* motivation of individual managers. Goals and problems are associated with information needs
  and systems.

- **Critical Success Factor Analysis [1]** is concerned with identifying those areas
  where "things must go right" if the enterprise is to succeed fully. It is concerned with concentrating resources on the most critical areas. It has proven to
  be a powerful way of improving corporate success. It identifies critical assumptions that need checking, critical information needs, and critical decisions for
  which decision-support systems are needed.

- **Technology Impact Analysis** is concerned with the extremely rapid evolution
  of technology and the business opportunities and threats created by it. It maps
  a taxonomy of new technology against the opportunities for new products, services, changes in corporate structure, and so on. Top management is often not
  fully aware of all the implications of advancing technology. This can result in
  lost opportunities or dangerous competition. Technology impact analysis attempts to identify and prioritize the opportunities and threats and bring them to
  the attention of executives who can take appropriate action.

- **Strategic Systems Vision** is concerned with strategic opportunities for creating
  new systems to make a corporation more competitive. These "strategic" systems may require restructuring of the corporation or the way it does business
  rather than automation of what already exists.

- **The Overview Model of the Functions in the Enterprise** maps the business
  functions hierarchically. It associates these with the organizational units, loca-

tions, and the entities about which data is stored. The mapping is done by means of a set of computerized matrices.

- **Entity-Relationship Modeling** creates a chart of the entities and their relationships which is an overview of the data that must be stored in the enterprise databases. The entities are associated with business functions in a matrix, and the matrix is clustered to find naturally cohesive groups of entities and functions.

Information is a corporate resource and should be planned on a corporate-wide basis regardless of the fact that it is used in many different computers and departments. The information needs often remain the same when the corporation itself is reorganized. The information architecture should therefore be designed independently of the current corporate organization. *Implementation* of the architecture will reflect the current organization and its concerns. These will affect the choice of which modules of the architecture are implemented first.

SEQUENCE OF ANALYSIS　　In practice, the overview modeling of the enterprise and initial entity-relationship modeling is sometimes done before the top sublayer of Fig. 2.1. The reason for this is that a thorough understanding of the structure of the enterprise is desirable before dialogs are conducted with top management which may lead to possible restructuring. The dialog about goals, critical success factors, strategic computing, and the potential impact of technology is best carried out when the enterprise is understood in detail. After or during the analysis of goals, problems, critical success factors, technology impact, and strategic opportunities, the modeling of the enterprise and its information needs will be refined.

The bottom half of Fig. 2.1 creates an overall framework into which more detailed analysis will fit. The framework consists of an overview of the entities in an enterprise (anything about which data should be stored), a decomposition of the business functions, and a matrix showing which entities are used by which business functions. These entities and functions will be clustered into cohesive groupings (described in Chapter 9). The groupings become *business areas,* which are then analyzed in more detail in the business area analysis stage (Part II of this book).

Business area analysis provides more detail about the entities and functions, so the model of the enterprise that resides in the encyclopedia becomes more precise and detailed when this is done. This successive refining of the models of the enterprise is made more practical with computerized tools. The models stored in the encyclopedia are easily expandable and updatable. Figure 2.2 shows a suggested sequence for the types of analysis included in information strategy planning (ISP). The procedure is shown in more detail in Fig. 2.5.

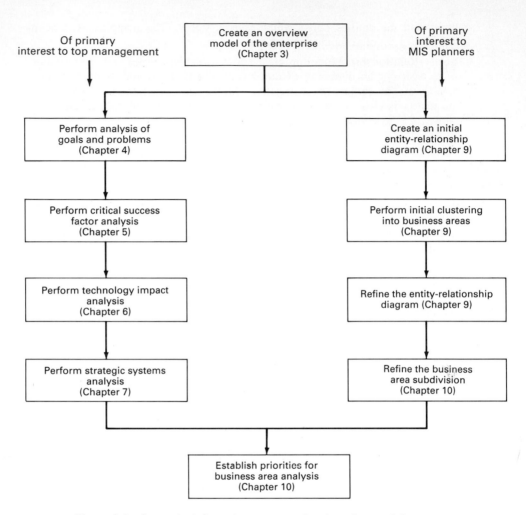

Figure 2.2 Stages in information strategy planning. Some of these stages may in practice be performed concurrently.

BUSINESS PLANNING AND MIS PLANNING

At least a third of large corporations in the United States (more than $1 billion in revenues) do long-range MIS planning; however, McLean and Soden [2] reported that in many of these corporations the planning is done with little involvement from end users and even less from top management. They comment about a conference of long-range data processing planners [2]:

Interestingly, only a very few of the participants reported any involvement whatsoever in their longer range MIS planning effort by members of the business planning staff of the corporation. One might conclude from this that the MIS planning activities were not closely tied to the strategy of the overall corporation—a hypothesis that is further supported by the observation that only one-third of the participants linked their MIS planning process to the overall business planning effort of the enterprise.

Today, most corporate presidents are well aware of the importance of information technology. They know that they are building a computerized corporation and need help. They need a chief information officer who talks the same language as they do. The methodologies at the top of Fig. 2.1 provide an excellent means for establishing rapport between top management and the top MIS executives and planners.

To do strategic planning of information systems in isolation from strategic business planning is to ask for trouble. It is likely to lead to expensive systems that do not fully serve the needs of the enterprise. Unless the long-range MIS plan reflects the long-range business plan, future organization changes may not be factored into the MIS plan. Conversely, if MIS executives and technology professionals are not involved in the *business* planning, the plans may miss major technological opportunities and threats. The top of the pyramid in Fig. 2.1 provides methodologies that should be used by the business planners, not merely by the computer system planners.

The business plans need control mechanisms to monitor progress and make adjustments so that the plans can be achieved as successfully as possible. As in all control mechanisms, feedback is essential. When the business plans are created, the MIS organization should be involved to ensure that the desirable information systems come into existence. Sometimes these systems are complex because they involve information from a number of functions in the enterprise. An overall data architecture is needed to ensure that the various types of data are compatible and are available.

OVERALL ARCHITECTURE

Strategic planning of information systems involves more than merely project development plans. It requires an architectural framework into which separate systems fit. Many separate systems are built in an enterprise by separate teams of people. It is desirable that these separate building blocks of a computerized enterprise fit together. This will not happen without a structured top-down approach to designing the overall corporate information architecture. The top layer of the pyramid creates the framework of this architecture, and later, business area analysis projects extend the architecture into more detail.

An ISP study, then, has two overall purposes, as shown in Fig. 2.3:

1. To link information technology and systems planning to the strategic business planning in order to help the strategic planning and help in the building of control mechanisms to implement the plans.

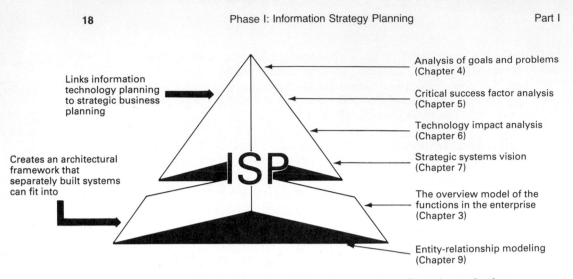

Figure 2.3 ISP has two overall purposes: to link information technology planning to strategic business planning, and to create an architectural framework into which further analysis and design will fit so that separately developed systems will work together.

2. To create an architectural framework into which further analysis and design will fit so that separately developed systems will work together.

THE RANGE OF THE STUDY

In most enterprises information engineering ought to be based on the entire enterprise. There are major exceptions to this. Some enterprises consist of separate corporations with little or no similarity or connection. In these a separate study would normally be done of each corporation.

Often the range of an information engineering study has been something less than the entire enterprise. This is usually due to the following concerns:

- The enterprise seems too big and complex.
- The enterprise is multinational and it is difficult to coordinate a study in many countries.
- Different subsidiaries relate to fundamentally different types of business or markets.
- Different subsidiaries have different management philosophies or missions.

In general, if one person manages an enterprise, an information engineering study ought to be done for that enterprise. *If it is too big to study, it is too big to manage.* The overview study of a vast corporation will quickly recommend fragmenting the study for practical reasons, but the fragments with separate encyclopedias should be coordinated with an overview study through its own encyclopedia.

One reason why separate or localized studies are done is that they fall under the jurisdiction of separate or localized I.S. organizations. The existence of separate I.S. organizations should not be a reason for limiting the definition of the enterprise and its business functions. At the peak of the pyramid the entire enterprise is the subject of study. The enterprise *needs* a strategy for enterprise-wide information systems. Sometimes a large enterprise has a top-level CIO reporting to the CEO, even though that enterprise has many separate I.S. organizations. The CIO should be the instigator and champion of the IE study.

Information strategy planning is a top-down definitional process that begins at the highest level and stops at the point where activities have an accurate generic definition. The enterprise is split into separate areas for study before detailed analysis of process and data is done. No attempt is made to combine fundamentally different organizations, business strategies, or markets into inappropriate common structures.

TOP MANAGEMENT INTEREST

It is often stated by I.S. planners that they cannot get top management or the corporate president to take any interest in information technology planning. This is usually because their approach is too technical. The types of analysis at the top of Fig. 2.1 go to the heart of what top management is interested in: how the corporation can be run better.

Technology impact analysis and strategic systems analysis survey future technology and technological trends and ask how they can be used to run the enterprise better, to provide new opportunities, and to make a preemptive strike against competition. They ask how technology may cause new competitive threats.

Critical success factor analysis [1] identifies the areas most critical for success in running the enterprise. It is designed to focus management's attention on the things most critical for them to accomplish. It identifies the critical decisions and critical information, and ought to lead to the building of information systems that help in these areas.

Both technology impact analysis and critical success factor analysis can be done relatively quickly with low resources; for example, each can be done with two skilled analysts interacting with top management for a month. They are not expensive to perform but can have a major effect on the management of the enterprise.

The analysis of goals and problems is also directly related to how the enterprise operates. It helps to provide a control mechanism throughout the enterprise, and relates directly to setting objectives for individual managers.

Most important of all, the creation of strategic systems vision is concerned with how computers can be used to change the way a corporation does business and as weapons to make a preemptive strike against the competition, or alternatively, to protect the corporation from strategic attacks by its competition. This goes to the heart of what top management is interested in.

The forms of analysis at the top of Fig. 2.1, then, have a direct effect on how an enterprise is managed. Even if subsequent stages of information engineering were never carried out, the top part of Fig. 2.1 would be likely to be very valuable in focusing the attention of executives on what can be improved in the enterprise.

RETHINKING THE ENTERPRISE STRUCTURE

While these forms of analysis are of *direct* interest to top management, who participate in them directly, top management should also be interested in the results of the second sublayer of Fig. 2.1. The analysis of corporate functions and data often results in rethinking the organization of the enterprise. The forms of strategic planning in Fig. 2.1 should therefore be presented together to the top-management team in a kickoff meeting at the initiation of an information strategy planning (ISP) session. The results should be reviewed together.

Databases, networks, and desktop computers provide the challenge of improving the procedures in an enterprise to such an extent that basic enterprise reorganizations are needed. The management structures of enterprises that use today's technology well are likely to be fundamentally different from the management structures of the 1970s.

The first motor cars were called "horseless carriages" and were the same shape as a carriage without a horse. Much later it became recognized that a car should have a different shape. Similarly, the first radio was called "wireless telegraphy" without the realization that broadcasting would bear no resemblance to telegraphy. Today we talk about the "paperless office" and "paperless corporation," but we build systems with screens and databases that duplicate the previously existing organization of work. It will be increasingly realized that we now have the technology to make *any* data available at *anybody's* desk, and to provide major computational aids to decision making at that desk. We must ask the question: Where would decisions *best* be made? Answers to this question are likely to change the structure of the enterprise.

Senior management should regard enterprise modeling (the bottom layer of Fig. 2.1) as a means not merely of studying the existing organization, but of asking how the organization should be changed. Analysts should be made to think creatively. It is easy for them to document today's paper flow, but the early stages of information engineering should not do that. They are concerned with distinguishing the *fundamental* activities that must occur and the *fundamental* information needs. Rather than being concerned with today's documents, analysts should ask: What data is important now? What data will be important in the future? This links directly to the conceptualization of strategic information systems, discussed in Chapter 7.

Done creatively, enterprise modeling and data modeling are likely to suggest structural changes, new procedures, or corporate reorganization. In most cases senior managers could not care less about being involved in computerizing the existing procedures. However, if there is a threat of organizational change, or a promise of better information sources, senior managers usually want to know what is going on and want to be able to influence it. Often what senior managers take an active interest in is the ability to make decisions about how the business *should* be run.

The modeling in the bottom half of Fig. 2.1 will be more fruitful *if it is accepted from the beginning that it is likely to change the corporate procedures or organization.* If this is understood, top managers are likely to take more interest in the study. The study will be staffed differently and its reporting procedures will be different.

AN EXTERNAL CONSULTANT

It is often difficult for managers inside an enterprise to take a detached viewpoint. They spend most of their mental energies on specific problems and most of their business emotions on internal politics. A major new opportunity for the application of technology is sometimes alien to the prevailing culture. The need to wind down or replace certain current procedures is usually far from apparent to people involved with those procedures. Intelligent external consultants can often see an organization's problems with clarity and may be highly inventive in pointing out new opportunities. Some consultants are highly skilled with regard to the methodologies in Fig. 2.1 and can move quickly in implementing them. However, internal staff have essential experience of the enterprise, its key players, and how it operates. The methodologies at the top of Fig. 2.1 are often best performed by a two-person team, one being an external consultant skilled and experienced with the methodology and the other being an internal person who knows the enterprise well and who has good rapport with top management.

Sometimes different external consultants may be used with different portions of the methodology. Some are experienced with critical success factor analysis, some with technology impact analysis, some with strategic system planning, and some with data modeling. The team members should get along well together, move fast and professionally, have the full support of top management, and elicit all the help they need from diverse managers and staff.

It is important that team members have the highest credibility and respect among the upper echelons of operating management. Such persons can be identified in most organizations. They are the managers or analysts who are already in highest demand for other pressing tasks. External consultants used should also have the highest credibility, which means a wide range of knowledge and experience in the subject area as well as an appropriate personality. Top management should ensure the acceptability of the team and contribute to its success by formally announcing the program and endorsing the team.

TOP-MANAGEMENT COMMITMENT The ISP methodology shown in Fig. 2.4 and Box 2.1 must begin with top management sponsoring it and commiting other senior executives to being involved in it. The ISP study is designed to reflect their view of the business and should not begin without their commitment. Most of the input will come directly or indirectly from these senior executives. Certain preliminaries, listed in Box 2.1, are necessary prior to obtaining top-management commitment.

The commitment ought to be to employ information engineering throughout the enterprise. In some organizations this commitment is made cautiously, in stages. Full commitment is often slow where (inadequate) second- or third-generation methodologies are entrenched. An ISP has major benefits for top

```
┌─ ISP procedure
│   ┌─ Initiate
│   │  ...Understand the benefits of an ISP study.
│   │  ...Determine the scope of the ISP.
│   │  ...Ensure that the prerequisites exist.
│   └     Select the senior management participants.
│
│   ...Obtain top-management commitment.
│   ┌─ Prepare
│   │     Determine which locations are involved.
│   │     Determine which ORGANIZATIONS locations are involved.
│   │  ...Establish the ISP team for this project.
│   │  ...Ensure that the appropriate tools are installed and working.
│   │  ...Ensure that the ISP team is adequately trained.
│   │  ...Collect and evaluate existing strategic plans.
│   │  ...Define a plan for successfully completing this ISP project.
│   └     Determine the target date for completing the study.
│
│   ...Hold kickoff meeting
│   ...Create an overview model of the enterprise.
│   ┌─ Conduct business-oriented strategic analyses.
│   │
│   │  ...Conduct Analysis of Goals and Problems.
│   │  ...Conduct Critical Success Factor Analysis.
│   │  ...Conduct Technology Impact Analysis.
│   └  ...Conduct Strategic Information Systems Study.
│
│   ...Create a top-level analysis of corporate data.
│   ...Refine the enterprise model.
│   ...Group the enterprise model into natural clusters.
│   ...Determine business area boundaries for BAA.
│   ...Analyze current systems to determine what changes are needed.
│   ...Prepare follow-on from Strategic Information Planning.
└   ...Make top-management presentation.
```

Figure 2.4 Procedure for performing the ISP project: an overview of information strategy planning, drawn with an action diagram. Box 2.1 shows the same action diagram with parts of it EXPANDed.

management independently of how systems are designed, so sometimes an ISP is done before a full commitment to information engineering has been made.

The results of portions of the ISP are likely to be presented to top management independently of the overall results. This is particularly true with technology impact analysis (Chapter 6), critical success factor analysis (Chapter 5), and the analysis of strategic information systems (Chapter 7). When the overall results are presented, a follow-on plan should be ready for approval.

FOLLOW-ON PLAN

The follow-on plan should list and prioritize areas of the enterprise for business area analysis. It is likely that one business area will be analyzed *first*. As experience is gained in doing this, other business area analyses will follow. The first business area should be one where the payoff is high and one without excessive technical or political complexities.

Top management always asks how long the ongoing process of information engineering will take. The team should have an answer to this question prepared, showing a buildup of business area analysis studies proceeding in parallel. The payoff in building certain critical systems should not be too far in the future. An estimate of the return on investment from I.E. should be made as described in Book I of this trilogy.

The ISP project almost always reveals certain system needs that should be filled *immediately* without waiting for a business area analysis to be completed. These are often critical decision-support systems and executive information systems. A quick-and-crude version of such systems may be implementable quickly using spreadsheet tools, decision-support software, or executive information system software. While there may be a business need to implement certain systems immediately, and this should be done, it should be stressed that the entire point of information engineering is to build a systems *architecture* for the enterprise. This architecture will enable systems to be created, changed, and interlinked more rapidly when it exists. There is always some compromise needed between long-range architectural planning and immediate results.

Implementing an entire information architecture will take years. It is necessary to decide what to do first, and in general to prioritize the stages of implementation. It is desirable that the components of the architecture that are implemented first should be those that solve immediate problems and have a rapid payoff. The implementations should proceed on a pay-as-you-go basis, usually with multiple implementations being done by different teams at the same time.

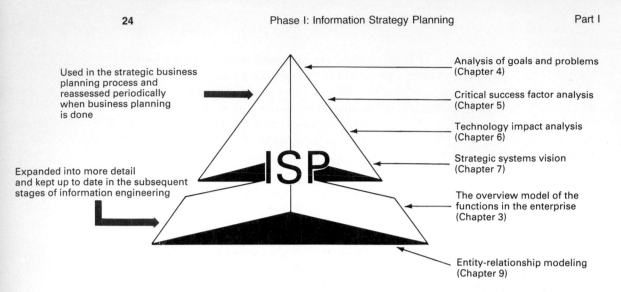

Figure 2.5 The management information in the encyclopedia that results from an ISP study is updated periodically and the enterprise model is extended into more detail and kept up to date in business area analysis and system design activities.

ONGOING REVIEWS

The information in the encyclopedia that results from the ISP study is a valuable asset and should be updated periodically. The study is not put on a shelf and forgotten. Information is extracted from it to guide the business planning process on an ongoing basis. In conjunction with this, a periodic review of goals, problems, critical success factors, and technology impact is made. Goals and problems may be reviewed when managers are counseled and appraised as part of a management-by-objectives procedure. Critical success factors and technology impact may be assessed annually as part of the business planning procedure. The technology impact diagrams may have an ''owner'' who is responsible (among other things) for adding to them as new technologies or opportunities become apparent. This is a task that some technology enthusiasts enjoy. The strategic systems vision should pervade the entire corporation and be an ongoing topic of discussion between the chief information officer and top management.

The models of the enterprise become more detailed as business area analysis studies are done. The ISP is thus used and kept up to date as indicated in Fig. 2.5. Box 2.2 lists the potential benefits of information strategy planning.

BOX 2.1   A suggested procedure for information strategy planning

This is represented in the form of a computerized action diagram because it will differ from one enterprise to another. The action diagram will be edited to fit the circumstances in question.

```
┌  The top layer of Information Engineering
│                                       /│\
│                                     /** │ **\
│      INFORMATION STRATEGY PLANNING /****│****\
│                                   /******│******\
│                                  /*******│*******\
│                                 /        │        \
│      BUSINESS AREA ANALYSIS  /           │          \
│                           /              │            \
│                        /_____ │              \
│      SYSTEM DESIGN  /                     │                \
│                  /                        │                  \
│               /_____                    \
│      CONSTRUCTION  /                      │                      \
│            /                              │                        \
│         /_____  \
│                          DATA             │         ACTIVITIES
└
```

```
┌  ISP procedure
│     ┌─────────────────────────────────────────────────────────┐
│     │  The procedure given below may be modified with Action   │
│     │  Diagrammer to meet the needs of the particular situation.│
│     └─────────────────────────────────────────────────────────┘
```

```
┌  Initiate
│   ┌  Understand the benefits of an ISP study
│   │     See BOX 2.2.
│   └
│   ┌  Determine the scope of the ISP
│   │     Will the whole enterprise be studied ?
│   │     If not, what parts of it are included ?
│   └
│   ┌  Ensure that the prerequisites exist
│   │       o    A champion for the project is committed to it.
│   │       o    Appropriately skilled individuals are available.
│   │       o    The scope of the plan is identified.
│   │       o    A charter for the plan has been established.
│   │       o    A strategic business plan exists.
│   │       o    A data administration function exists.
│   └
│        Select the senior management participants.
└
```

(Continued)

BOX 2.1 *(Continued)*

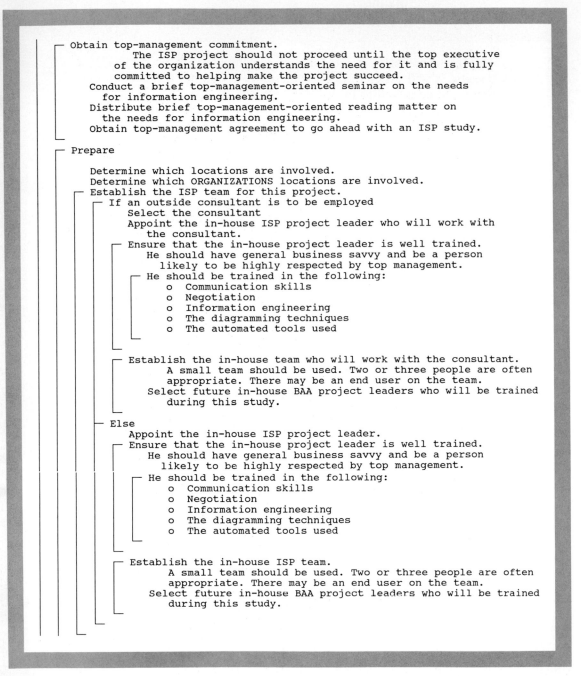

Obtain top-management commitment.
    The ISP project should not proceed until the top executive
    of the organization understands the need for it and is fully
    committed to helping make the project succeed.
Conduct a brief top-management-oriented seminar on the needs
    for information engineering.
Distribute brief top-management-oriented reading matter on
    the needs for information engineering.
Obtain top-management agreement to go ahead with an ISP study.

Prepare

    Determine which locations are involved.
    Determine which ORGANIZATIONS locations are involved.
    Establish the ISP team for this project.
        If an outside consultant is to be employed
            Select the consultant
            Appoint the in-house ISP project leader who will work with
                the consultant.
            Ensure that the in-house project leader is well trained.
                He should have general business savvy and be a person
                    likely to be highly respected by top management.
                He should be trained in the following:
                    o Communication skills
                    o Negotiation
                    o Information engineering
                    o The diagramming techniques
                    o The automated tools used

            Establish the in-house team who will work with the consultant.
                A small team should be used. Two or three people are often
                    appropriate. There may be an end user on the team.
                Select future in-house BAA project leaders who will be trained
                    during this study.
        Else
            Appoint the in-house ISP project leader.
            Ensure that the in-house project leader is well trained.
                He should have general business savvy and be a person
                    likely to be highly respected by top management.
                He should be trained in the following:
                    o Communication skills
                    o Negotiation
                    o Information engineering
                    o The diagramming techniques
                    o The automated tools used

            Establish the in-house ISP team.
                A small team should be used. Two or three people are often
                    appropriate. There may be an end user on the team.
                Select future in-house BAA project leaders who will be trained
                    during this study.

BOX 2.1 *(Continued)*

Ensure that the appropriate tools are installed and working
- o   An encyclopedia-based workbench appropriate for later extension into the follow-on phases of information engineering.

Ensure that the ISP team is adequately trained

They should be trained in the following:
- o   Communication skills
- o   Information engineering
- o   The diagramming techniques
- o   The automated tools used

Collect and evaluate existing strategic plans.
- o   The strategic business plan
- o   Existing ISP plans (if any)
- o   Strategic information technology plans (if any)
- o   Existing critical success factor studies (if any)
- o   Top management goals and objectives
- o   Existing data models (if any)
- o   Other relevant plans or system architecture documents.

Define a plan for successfully completing this ISP project
Modify this action diagram as required.

Determine the target date for completing the study.

Hold kickoff meeting
All the senior management participants should attend.
Have the chief executive of the enterprise make the opening speech.
Review with the participants the purpose and objectives.
Review the business assumptions that are to be made.
Review the agenda.
Give participants the preparatory material for them to study.

Create an overview model of the enterprise
Enter the following information into the encyclopedia:
An organizational chart showing all organizational units.
The persons who manage the organizational units.
Identify the major business functions.
Decompose into lower-level functions with a function decomposition diagram.
Add detailed comments to the above diagrams where necessary.
Create a matrix mapping executives against business functions
The involvement of the executive may be recorded with the following codes:
R: Direct management RESPONSIBILITY
A: Executive or policy-making AUTHORITY
I: INVOLVED in the function
E: Technical EXPERTISE
W: Actual execution of the WORK

Create a matrix mapping functions against organizational units.
Create a matrix mapping functions against executives.

Print relevant versions of the above diagrams from the encyclopedia for the participants to review.

(Continued)

BOX 2.1 *(Continued)*

```
┌─ Conduct business-oriented strategic analyses
│     The following four types of analyses may carried on in parallel
│     with, or independently of, the other ISP analyses.
│
│     ┌─ Conduct Analysis of Goals and Problems
│     │   o─────────────────────────────────────o
│     │   │ See action diagram in BOX 4.1       │
│     └   o─────────────────────────────────────o
│
│     ┌─ Conduct Critical Success Factor Analysis
│     │    o─────────────────────────────────o
│     │    │ See CSF action diagram: BOX 5.1 │
│     └    o─────────────────────────────────o
│
│     ┌─ Conduct Technology Impact Analysis
│     │    o─────────────────────────────────o
│     │    │ See TIA action diagram: BOX 6.1 │
│     └    o─────────────────────────────────o
│
│     ┌─ Conduct Strategic Information Systems Study
│     │    o─────────────────────────────────o
│     │    │ See SIS action diagram: BOX 7.1 │
│     └    o─────────────────────────────────o
│
┌─ Create a top-level analysis of corporate data.
│     Identify the data subjects.
│     Decompose into entity types.
│     Create an initial entity-relationship diagram.
│     Create a matrix mapping functions against entity types.
│     Create a matrix mapping organizational units against entity types.
│     Print relevant versions of the above diagrams from the
│        encyclopedia for the participants to review.
│
┌─ Refine the enterprise model and entity-relationship diagram.
│     Conduct meetings with end users and management to critique the
│        enterprise model.
│     Make any improvements to the enterprise model as a result of
│        the presentations to end users and management.
│     Refine the entity-relationship diagram.
│     Refine the matrix of entity types and business functions.
│     Refine the matrix of entity types and organizational units.
│     Obtain approval for the enterprise model.
│
┌─ Group the enterprise model into natural clusters
│     ┌─ Cluster the function/entity matrix to show natural systems.
│     │     Use the clustering algorithm of the strategic planning tool.
│     │     Cluster on the basis of what functions CREATE what entity types.
│     │     Assign all remaining functions and entity types to clusters.
│     │     Refine the groupings manually to identify natural systems.
│     │     Identify what data must flow from one system to another.
│     └     Refine the clusterings to minimize the interaction among systems.
```

BOX 2.1 *(Continued)*

Cluster the function/entity matrix to show natural business areas.
   Adjust the clustered function/entity matrix to form BAA boundaries.
   Assign all functions to a business area.
   Determine the locations of that business area.
   Build a matrix of business areas and locations.
   Build a matrix of business areas and departments.
   Refine the business areas as necessary.

Refine BAA project boundaries
   Consider:
   o Time to implement BAA.
   o Effort required to implement BAA.
   o How the proposed BAA fits with the current organization.
   o Risk Assessment
         User acceptance/participation
         User sophistication/readiness
         Technical complexity

Analyze current systems to determine what changes are needed
   Build a matrix mapping I.S. systems against organizational units.
   Build a matrix mapping I.S. systems against executives.
   Build a matrix mapping I.S. systems against business functions.
   Build a matrix mapping I.S. systems against entity types.
   Cluster the above matrices into business areas.
   Identify which systems are in need of replacement or redesign.
   Identify which systems are expensive in maintenance costs.

Prepare follow-on from Strategic Information Planning
   Comment
      When the ISP results are presented to top management a detailed
      action plan should accompany them saying what happens next. It
      is desirable that the ISP study is immediately followed by
      vigorous action which leads to implementing better systems.

Prioritize the business areas for Business Area Analysis
   There are multiple factors which affect the prioritization
   of which business area to work on first.
   Rank the factors below on a scale of 1 to 7
      Potential benefits
         Return on investment.
             (This may be difficult to calculate and requires
                value judgments.)
         o Tangibles.
         o Intangibles.

         o   Achievement of critical success factors.
         o   Achievement of goals.
         o   Solution to serious problems.

      Demand
         o Pressure of demand from senior end users for new or
             improved systems.
         o Assessed need.
         o Political overtones.

(Continued)

29

BOX 2.1 *(Continued)*

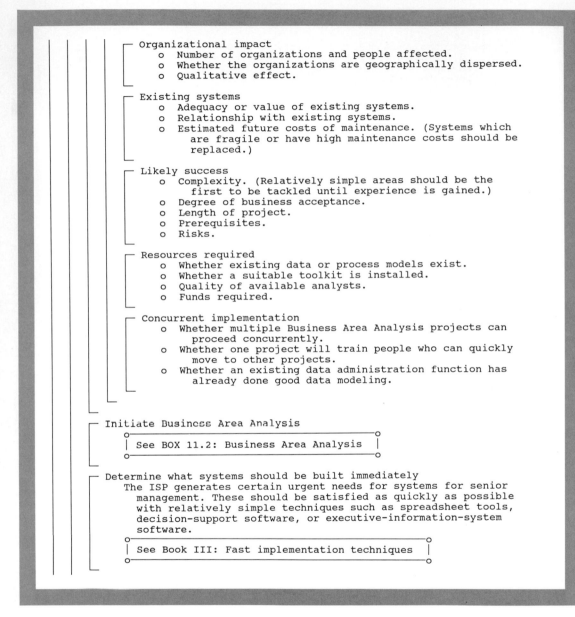

Organizational impact
- o   Number of organizations and people affected.
- o   Whether the organizations are geographically dispersed.
- o   Qualitative effect.

Existing systems
- o   Adequacy or value of existing systems.
- o   Relationship with existing systems.
- o   Estimated future costs of maintenance. (Systems which
       are fragile or have high maintenance costs should be
       replaced.)

Likely success
- o   Complexity. (Relatively simple areas should be the
       first to be tackled until experience is gained.)
- o   Degree of business acceptance.
- o   Length of project.
- o   Prerequisites.
- o   Risks.

Resources required
- o   Whether existing data or process models exist.
- o   Whether a suitable toolkit is installed.
- o   Quality of available analysts.
- o   Funds required.

Concurrent implementation
- o   Whether multiple Business Area Analysis projects can
       proceed concurrently.
- o   Whether one project will train people who can quickly
       move to other projects.
- o   Whether an existing data administration function has
       already done good data modeling.

Initiate Business Area Analysis

| See BOX 11.2: Business Area Analysis |

Determine what systems should be built immediately
The ISP generates certain urgent needs for systems for senior
management. These should be satisfied as quickly as possible
with relatively simple techniques such as spreadsheet tools,
decision-support software, or executive-information-system
software.

| See Book III: Fast implementation techniques |

BOX 2.1   *(Continued)*

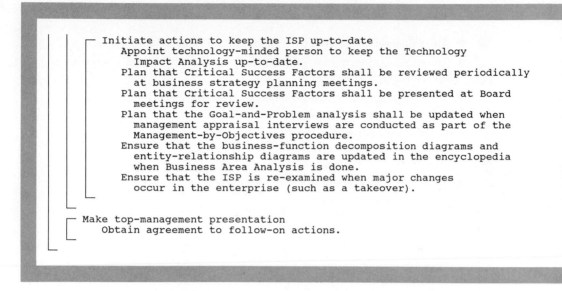

```
    ┌─ Initiate actions to keep the ISP up-to-date
    │     Appoint technology-minded person to keep the Technology
    │       Impact Analysis up-to-date.
    │     Plan that Critical Success Factors shall be reviewed periodically
    │       at business strategy planning meetings.
    │     Plan that Critical Success Factors shall be presented at Board
    │       meetings for review.
    │     Plan that the Goal-and-Problem analysis shall be updated when
    │       management appraisal interviews are conducted as part of the
    │       Management-by-Objectives procedure.
    │     Ensure that the business-function decomposition diagrams and
    │       entity-relationship diagrams are updated in the encyclopedia
    │       when Business Area Analysis is done.
    └─  Ensure that the ISP is re-examined when major changes
          occur in the enterprise (such as a takeover).

  ┌─ Make top-management presentation
  │     Obtain agreement to follow-on actions.
```

BOX 2.2   Potential benefits of information strategy planning

To executive management:

- An assessment of the opportunities from new technology

- An assessment of how the corporation should be changed strategically to attack competition better

- An assessment of the competitive threats from new technology

- Adaptation of the strategic business plan to accommodate five-year technology trends

- An assessment of the factors most critical for success

- Translation of the critical success factors into actions in building information systems, decision-support systems and manager motivations, and control mechanisms

- A defined logical approach to aid in solving management control problems from a business perspective

(Continued)

BOX 2.2 *(Continued)*

- An evaluation of the effectiveness of current information systems
- An assessment of future information system needs based on business-related impacts and priorities
- A planned approach that will allow an early return on the company's information systems investment
- Information systems that are relatively independent of organization structure

To functional and operational management:

- An assessment of goals and problems, and identification of computing facilities that can help with these
- An assessment of the factors most critical for success
- Translation of these factors into actions in building appropriate systems
- A defined logical approach to solving management control and operational control problems
- Top management involvement in establishing organizational goals and direction
- Increased probability of having the most valuable systems built
- Consistent data to be used and shared by all users
- Systems that are management and user oriented rather than data-processing oriented

To information systems management:

- Effective communication with top management
- Top-management support and interest in systems
- Better planning of systems that respond to business needs
- A long-range planning base for data processing resources and funding
- Agreed-upon system priorities
- Higher probability of delivering systems that are really useful

REFERENCES

1. J. F. Rockart and C. V. Bullen (eds.), *The Rise of Managerial Computing.* Homewood, Ill.: Dow Jones-Irwin, 1986.

2. E. R. McLean and J. V. Soden, *Strategic Planning for MIS.* New York: Wiley, 1977.

BIBLIOGRAPHY

Planning for MIS

Albrecht, Leon K., *Organization and Management of Information and Management of Information Processing Systems.* New York: Macmillan, 1973.

Anthony, Robert N., *Planning and Control Systems: A Framework for Analysis.* Boston: Graduate School of Business Administration, Harvard University, 1965.

Brooks, F. P., *The Mythical Man-Month.* Reading, Mass.: Addison-Wesley, 1975.

Curtice, Robert M., *Planning for Data Base Systems,* Data Base Management Monograph Series. Wellesley, Mass.: QED Information Sciences, 1976, 44 pp.

IBM, *Business Systems Planning: Information Systems Planning Guide,* Application Manual GE20-0527-l. White Plains, N.Y.: IBM Corporation, August 1975, 92 pp.

Keen, Peter T. W., and Michael Scott Morton, *Decision Support Systems.* Reading, Mass.: Addison-Wesley, 1978.

McLean, Ephraim R., and John V. Soden, *Strategic Planning for MIS.* New York: Wiley, 1977.

Rockart, J. F., and C. V. Bullen (eds.), *The Rise of Managerial Computing.* Homewood, Ill.: Dow Jones-Irwin, 1986.

Siegal, Paul, *Strategic Planning of Management Information Systems.* Princeton, N.J.: Petrocelli Books, 1975.

Sprague, R. H., and E. D. Carlson, *Building Effective Decision Support Systems.* Englewood Cliffs, N.J.: Prentice-Hall, 1982.

Steiner, George A., *Comprehensive Managerial Planning.* Oxford, Ohio: Planning Executives Institute, 1972, 36 pp.

Warren, McFarlan F., Richard L. Nolan, and David P. Norton, *Information Systems Administration.* New York: Holt, Rinehart and Winston, 1973.

Wiseman, Charles, *Strategy and Computers: Information Systems as Competitive Weapons*. Homewood, Ill.: Dow Jones–Irwin, 1985.

Comprehensive Managerial Planning

Abell, D. F., and J. S. Hammond, *Strategic Market Planning, Problems and Analytical Approaches*. Englewood Cliffs, N.J.: Prentice-Hall, 1979.

Andrews, K. R., *The Concept of Corporate Strategy*. New York: Dow Jones-Irwin, 1971.

Ansoff, Igor H., *Corporate Strategy*. New York: McGraw-Hill, 1965.

Anthony, Robert N., *Planning and Control Systems: A Framework for Analysis*. Boston: Graduate School of Business Administration, Harvard University, 1952.

Chandler, A. D., Jr., *The Visible Hand: The Managerial Revolution in American Business*. Cambridge, Mass.: Harvard University Press, 1977.

Drucker, Peter F., *Management*. London: Heinemann, 1974.

Kotter, J. P., *The General Managers*. New York: Free Press, 1982.

Porter, M. E., *Competitive Strategy*. New York: Free Press, 1980.

Managerial Skills and Managerial Tools

Anthony, R. N., *Planning and Control Systems*. Boston, Harvard Business School, Harvard University, 1965.

Beer, Stafford, *Decision and Control*. New York: Wiley, 1966.

Drucker, Peter F., *Management*. London: Heinemann, 1974.

Hayes, Robert H. and Steven C. Wheelright, *Restoring Our Competitive Edge: Competition through Manufacturing*. New York: Wiley, 1984.

Kotler, Philip, *Marketing Management: Analysis, Planning, and Control*, 5th ed. Englewood Cliffs, N.J.: Prentice-Hall, 1984.

Mintzberg, H., *The Nature of Managerial Work*. New York: Harper & Row, 1973.

Organization Design and Structure

March, James G., and Herbert A. Simon, *Organizations*. New York: Wiley, 1958.

Sayles, Leonard R., and Margaret K. Chandler, *Managing Large Systems: Organizations for the Future*. London: Harper & Row, 1971.

Sloan, Alfred P., Jr. *My Years with General Motors*. London: Pan Books, 1969.

Webb, James E., *Space Age Management*. New York: McGraw-Hill, 1969.

The Top-Management Job

Chandler, Alfred D., Jr., and Stephen Salisbury, *Pierre S. DuPont and the Making of the Modern Corporation*. New York: Harper & Row, 1971.

Mason, Philip, *The Men Who Ruled India*. London: Jonathan Cape, 1985.

Sloan, Alfred P., Jr., *My Years with General Motors*. London: Pan Books, 1969.

Strategies and Structures

Abell, Derek, *Defining the Business*. Englewood Cliffs, N.J.: Prentice-Hall, 1980.

Chandler, Alfred D., Jr., and Stephen Salisbury, *Pierre S. DuPont and the Making of the Modern Corporation*. New York: Harper & Row, 1971.

Dale, Ernest, *The Great Organizers*. New York: McGraw-Hill, 1960.

Guth, William, *Organizational Strategy: Analysis, Commitment Implementation*. Homewood, Ill.: Richard D. Irwin, 1974.

Hax, Arnaldo C., and Nicolas S. Majluf, *Strategic Management: An Integrated Perspective*. Englewood Cliffs, N.J.: Prentice-Hall, 1984.

Sayles, Leonard R., and Margaret K. Chandler, *Managing Large Systems: Organizations for the Future*. London: Harper & Row, 1971.

Wittgenstein, L., *Culture and Value,* translated by Peter Winch. Chicago: University of Chicago, 1980.

Yip, George S., *Barriers to Entry: A Corporate Strategy Perspective*. Lexington, Mass.: D.C. Heath, 1982.

The Multinational Corporation

Brooke, M. Z., *The Strategy of Multinational Enterprise*. London: Longman, 1970.

Dunning, John H., *The Multinational Enterprise*. London: Allen & Unwin, 1971.

Rolfe, Sidney E., and Walter Damon (eds.) *The Multinational Corporation in the World Economy*. New York: Praeger, 1970.

Vernon, Raymond, *Sovereignty at Bay: The Multinational Spread of Private Enterprise*. London: Longman, 1971.

Wells, Richard, *Global Corporations*. New York: Interbook, 1973.

The Innovative Organization

Argyris, Chris, *Organization and Innovation*. New Haven, Conn.: Yale University Press, 1963.

Bennis, W. G., *Changing Organizations*. New York: McGraw-Hill, 1966.

Drucker, Peter F., *The Age of Discontinuity*. London: Heinemann, 1969.

Drucker, Peter F. (ed.), *Preparing Tomorrow's Business Leaders Today*. Englewood Cliffs, N.J.: Prentice-Hall, 1969.

Peters, Tom, *Thriving on Chaos. A Handbook for the Managerial Revolution*. New York: Alfred A. Knopf, 1987.

Peters, Tom, and R. H. Waterman. *In Search of Excellence*. New York: Alfred A. Knopf, 1985.

Townsend, Pat, *Commit to Quality*. New York: Wiley, 1986.

Twiss, Brian, *Managing Technological Innovation*, 2nd ed. London: Longman Group, 1980.

3 THE OVERVIEW MODEL OF THE ENTERPRISE

INTRODUCTION   At the top of the pyramid an overview model of the corporation is created. We describe the creation of this model in two stages. The first stage identifies the organizational units, locations, functions, and entity types. It identifies where functions are carried out, what entity types they use, how they relate to the organization chart, what organizational units are in what locations, and so on.

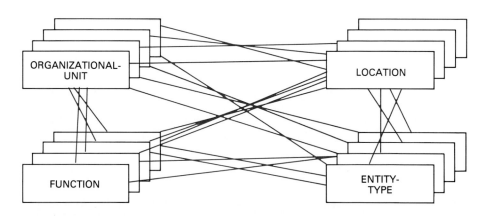

The second stage creates an overview entity-relationship diagram, creates a detailed matrix of entity types and functions, and clusters this into natural groupings. This stage is described in Chapter 9.

Thus on the left side of the pyramid an overview of the data is created. On the right side of the pyramid an overview of the business functions is created. These are mapped together with matrices. The matrices may be clustered to help define business areas that become a focus point for business area analysis.

This overview model should not be too detailed. It is desirable to establish a broad overview in a fairly short time. Detail will be added when the second level of the pyramid is tackled. The top level might be thought of as being like an author planning a book and creating its table of contents. He surveys the overall contents of the book and divides it into parts and chapters. He decides which chapters he should write first. Similarly, at the overview modeling stage he scopes out the overall structure and information needs of the enterprise, divides it into areas, and decides which area should first be analyzed in detail.

The overview model is stored in the encyclopedia. It will be updated over time. More detail will be added as the data and activities are analyzed further at the next level of the pyramid.

Many strategic planning studies for computing have in the past sat on shelves in binders and fallen out of use. An objective of information engineering is to make the strategic planning representation alive, have it reviewed as part of the business planning cycle, and kept updated so that it grows, as a valuable corporate resource.

THE ORGANIZATION CHART

The first step of enterprise modeling is to create a computerized version of the organization chart. The chart that exists in all major enterprises showing the divisions and departments is entered into the encyclopedia. Figure 3.1 shows a typical organization chart.

For a large enterprise the organization chart has many boxes. To be handled conveniently, it needs to be subdivided in some way (as do many of the other large diagrams we will use). Two of the upper boxes in Fig. 3.1 have three dots before their text. The three dots mean that more of the chart is available to be displayed. To display it, the user points to the boxes in question and uses an EXPAND command. Similarly, a section of a hierarchical chart can be shrunk to one box by using a CONTRACT command. Figures II.16 and II.17 in Appendix II show EXPAND and CONTRACT commands being used in a similar way on an action diagram.

Figure 3.2 shows an organization chart represented by an action diagram. An action diagram is more compact than the type of chart shown in Fig. 3.1, but managers are more familiar with organization charts drawn as in Fig. 3.1.

OBJECTS

The boxes of the organization chart are *objects* in the encyclopedia. We will use many other types of objects. An object is an entity about which data are stored in the encyclopedia.

The user of an information engineering tool should be able to display a window for each object. The window is designed to collect or display information about that particular type of object. For example, where the object is ORGANIZATIONAL UNIT, as in Fig. 3.1, the associated window may display

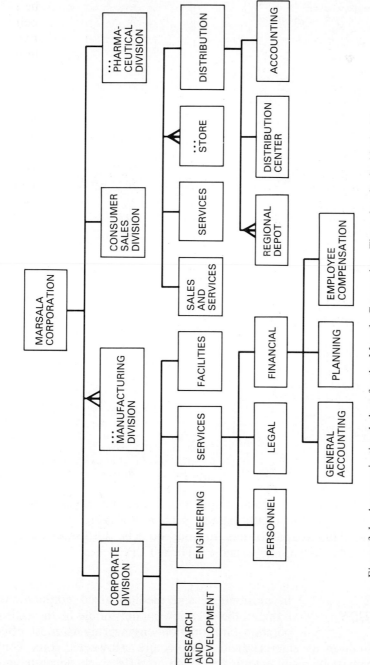

Figure 3.1 An organizational chart for the Marsala Corporation. Three dots in the blocks Man-ufacturing Division and Pharmaceutical Division indicate that these blocks can be expanded to show more of the chart.

```
┌─ Marsala Corporation
 │   ┌─ Corporate Division
 │   │    Research and Development
 │   │    Engineering
 │   │   ┌─ Services
 │   │   │    Personnel
 │   │   │    Legal
 │   │   │   ┌─ Financial
 │   │   │   │    General Accounting
 │   │   │   │    Planning
 │   │   │   │    Employee Compensation
 │   │   │   └─
 │   │   │
 │   │   └─  Facilities
 │   │
 │   ▐  Manufacturing Division
 │   ▐    Sales Department
 │   ▐    Marketing
 │   ▐    Field Service
 │   ▐    Manufacturing Plant
 │   ▐    Maintenance
 │   ┌─ Consumer Sales Division
 │   │    Sales and Marketing
 │   │    Services
 │   ▐  Store
 │   │   ┌─ Distribution
 │   │   │
 │   │   ▐  Regional Depot
 │   │   │
 │   │   │    Distribution Center
 │   │   └─   Accounting
 │   │
 │   ┌─ Pharmaceutical Division
 │   │    Research Laboratory
 │   │   ▐  Distribution Depot
 │   │   ▐    Order Processing
 │   │   ▐    Delivery
 │   │   │
 │   └─   Accounting
 │
 └─
```

Figure 3.2 An action diagram which is an alternative way to display the organization chart shown in Fig. 3.1.

details of who manages that organizational unit. The window may give the user the ability to display related information, such as location, goals, or critical success factors. This chapter refers to four objects: ORGANIZATIONAL-UNIT, LOCATION, FUNCTION, and ENTITY-TYPE.

THE SCOPE OF THE STUDY

In most small and medium-sized corporations the scope of the overview model should be the entire corporation. Information engineering is most effective when it is based on an enterprisewide architecture. However, some complex corporations consist of many enterprises which are effectively separate and different. A pragmatic decision is needed about what the span of information engineering encyclopedia can be. The information strategy plan should encompass the entire organization where possible. As noted earlier, if an organization is too complex to study, it is too complex to manage. As the study is driven down below the top level of the pyramid, separate business areas will be analyzed. In some cases separate ISP studies are linked with a common overview and require a coordinating encyclopedia.

Often, a valuable result of information engineering is that reusable designs and code can be employed in multiple factories or subsidiaries within a widespread corporation. A corporatewide span for the top-level study is desirable to achieve this. The existence of separate information systems organizations in an enterprise should not be allowed to be a deterrent to enterprisewide planning. Their existence, charter, or responsibilities are not jeopardized by enterprisewide planning.

GEOGRAPHIC LOCATIONS

An enterprise may have offices, factories, warehouses, and so on, at many locations. An organizational unit can exist at a number of locations. We can represent this on a diagram showing a many-to-many relationship between the objects ORGANIZATIONAL-UNIT and LOCATION:

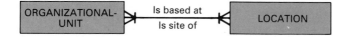

This says:

> ORGANIZATIONAL-UNIT *is based at* one or many LOCATIONS.
>
> and
>
> LOCATION *is the site of* one or many ORGANIZATIONAL-UNITS.

Whenever a many-to-many relationship exists between two entity types, as here, we can draw a matrix showing which entities are associated with which. Thus:

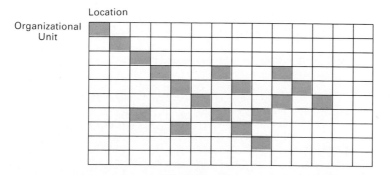

ORGANIZATIONAL UNITS	LOCATIONS	Head Office	Manufacturing Plant	Sales Headquarters	Santa Clara Sales Office	Chicago Sales Office	New York Sales Office
	1	2	3	4	5	6	7
1 President		*					
2 Finance & Administration		*					
3 Production			*				
4 Sales				*	*	*	*
5 Marketing			*				
6 Research & Development		*					
7 Planning		*					
8 Accounting		*					
9 Cash Management		*					
10 Investments		*					
11 Purchasing			*				
12 Facilities		*					
13 Human Resource Development		*					
14 MIS		*					
15 Legal		*					
16 Manufacturing			*				
17 Quality Assurance			*				
18 Packaging			*				
19 Materials Management			*				
20 Sales Regions				*			
21 Customer Services				*	*	*	*
22 Customer Education				*			
23 Order Processing				*			
24 Product Management				*			
25 Public Relations				*			
26 Market Research				*			
27 Distribution			*				
28 Engineering			*				
29 Research			*				
30 Prototype Manufacture			*				
31 Testing Laboratory			*				

Figure 3.3 A matrix mapping organizational units against locations.

Figure 3.3 shows a matrix in which organizational units are mapped against locations.

ENTERPRISE FUNCTIONS

After establishing the organization chart, the next step in modeling an enterprise is to create a chart decomposing the business functions. A *business function* is a group of activities which together support one aspect of furthering the mission of the enterprise. They have names that are nouns or gerunds (words ending in ''ing''): for example, *purchasing, receiving, financial planning*.

Business functions are sometimes grouped into *functional areas* as in Fig. 3.4. Functional areas refer to the major areas of activity; in a corporation they might be engineering, marketing, production, research, and distribution. One medium-sized manufacturing company listed its functional areas as follows:

- Business planning
- Finance
- Product planning
- Materials
- Production planning
- Production
- Sales
- Distribution
- Accounting
- Personnel

Business management books contain much discussion of the functional areas in a corporation. Each functional area may be subdivided into a number of functions. This is illustrated in Fig. 3.4. Box 3.1 shows examples of typical functional decomposition in various industries.

PROCESSES

The enterprise functions can be subdivided into *processes* (see Fig. 3.5). Whereas a function is ongoing and continuous, a process relates to a specific act that have definable beginning

Functional Area	Functions
Business Planning	Market analysis
	Product range review
	Sales forecasting
Finance	Financial planning
	Capital acquisition
	Funds management
Product planning	Product design
	Product pricing
	Product specification maintenance
Materials	Materials requirements
	Purchasing
	Receiving
	Inventory control
	Quality control
Production Planning	Capacity planning
	Plant scheduling
	Workflow layout
Production	Materials control
	Sizing and cutting
	Machine operations
Sales	Territory management
	Selling
	Sales administration
	Customer relations
Distribution	Finished stock control
	Order serving
	Packing
	Shipping
Accounting	Creditors and debtors
	Cash flow
	Payroll
	Cost accounting
	Budget planning
	Profitability analysis
Personnel	Personnel planning
	Recruiting
	Compensation policy

Figure 3.4 Typical corporate functional areas and functions.

BOX 3.1 Examples of function decomposition by industry

Insurance

Management Planning

Corporate direction planning
Long-range planning
Business planning
Acquisition/ventures planning

Product Management

Managing the book of business
Product service monitoring
Product reevaluation

Control and Measurement

Financial planning
Operational planning
Performance evaluation

*Product Development
and Maintenance*

Product design
Pricing
Product goals and measurement
Product implementation

*Facilities, Equipment, and
Supplies*

Facility planning
Facility services management
Equipment and supplies manage-
ment
Warehousing and distribution

Merchandising

Lead development
Selling
Customer qualification
Risk engineering
Establishing and maintaining cus-
tomer record
Billing and collections
Customer servicing

Product Service

Insurance
Insurance claim evaluation and
disposition
Noninsurance processing service
Noninsurance professional service

Finance

Cash management
Asset accounting
Expense allocation
Claim reserves
Tax processing
Corporate books and ledgers ad-
ministration
Investment management

Administration

Legal services
External relations
Advertising
Auditing
Information development
Operational support
Manpower management
External services management
Systems planning
System development/maintenance
and operations

(Continued)

BOX 3.1 *(Continued)*

Finance

Management Planning and Control

Objectives planning
Forecasting alternatives
Measurement and control
Organization
Policy setting
Resource allocation
External relations

Product Development

Review and approval
Resource evaluation
Strategy development
Education development
Pricing

Marketing

Market definition
Market research
Advertising and promotion
Public relations
Product implementation
Competitive analysis

Money Management

Investment management
Money market instruments

Customer

Investigation and acceptance
Account establishment
Account control
Account maintenance
Account termination

Funds Transfer Services

Letter of credit
Money transfer
Bond transfer
Stock transfer
Loan
Deposit/withdrawal checking
Collections
Lockbox
Automatic dividend reinvestment
Foreign exchange
Cash management

Trust

Accounting services
Asset management

Operations

Communications
Data processing
Transaction servicing
Inquiry servicing
Corrections
Mail

Finance

Budget planning and control
Financial analysis
Asset management
Liability management
Capital management
Financial reporting

Personnel

Planning
Recruiting and hiring
Training
Wage and salary administration
Employee relations
Benefits management
Career development
Retirement or separation
Government compliance

Legal

Litigation
Tax consequence advising
Contracts review
Legislation impact analysis
Legal compliance review

Administration

Accounting
Audit
Facilities
Regulatory compliance
Taxes
Payroll
Security

BOX 3.1 *(Continued)*

Process (Chemical)

Planning

Strategic planning
Market research
Technical feasibility
Economic analysis
Forecasting
Resource requirements

Product Development

Exploration
Engineering development
Licensing
Engineering design
Construction

Marketing

Sales forecasting
Advertising/promotion
Pricing
Selling/contracting
Order entry
Customer service
Sales analysis

Manufacturing

Production forecasting
Scheduling
Inventory
Plant operations
Packaging
Warehousing
Shipping
Maintenance

Quality control
Product cost control

Distribution

Carrier and rate negotiations
Supply/demand planning
Order processing
Rating and routing
Terminal operations
Warehouse planning/operations
Fleet planning
Fleet operations
Inventory control

Finance

Financial planning
Financial analysis
Capital transaction and control
Budgeting
General accounting
Cost accounting
Taxes
Government report
Payroll

Administration

Personnel development
Salary and benefits administration
Labor and personnel relations
External affairs
Legal
Insurance
Information services
Facilities services

(Continued)

BOX 3.1 *(Continued)*

Process (Paper)

Product Development

Product design
Raw material requirements
Facility planning
Market forecast
Financial requirements
Market planning

Marketing

Sales planning
Product plan
Sales analysis
Order entry
Customer services
Pricing

Production

Requirement planning
Production scheduling
Raw material planning
Receiving
Production reporting
Quality control
Inventory
Shipping
Maintenance

Engineering Support

Project engineering
Environment

Energy requirements
Standards
Material handling

Finance

Cash management
Budgeting
Capital expenditures
Cost analysis
Financial reporting
Payroll
Customer billing
Accounts receivable and payable
Audit

Administration

Purchasing
Personnel services
Traffic
Salary administration
Information services
Legal
Stockholder relations
Public affairs

Industry Relations

Labor relations
Personnel development
Safety

BOX 3.1 *(Continued)*

Manufacturing

Product Development and Application

Technology development
Product application
New product
Old product
Application engineering
Specifications

Product Planning

Determination of business case
Evaluation of business case

Marketing

Marketing planning
Market research, market development
Pricing
Publications, advertising, promotions
Sales analysis and forecasting
Warranty policy and other software
Market operations
Distribution network
Field sales and service
OEM sales and service
Order entry

Finance

Funds management
Cash
Short-term financing
Long-term financing
Financial control
Budget/expense
Managerial accounting
General accounting
Bookkeeping
Internal control

Administration

Legal
Public relations
Security
Governmental reporting
Office management

Planning, Control, and Measurement

Fiscal year business plan
Annual operating plan
Quarterly operating plan
Reporting and control

Personnel

Planning
Acquiring
Development and administration
Reporting
Termination

Operations Control

Master production plan
Transportation planning
Performance reporting
Inventory control

Capacity Management

Determination of optimum capacity
Capacity allocation
Acquisition of capacity

Material Acquisition

Vendor evaluation
Order control
Receiving and inspection

Plant Operations

Planning, schedule and control
Performance reporting
Expediting
Planning of material, manpower
Order processing–plant order boards
Product and process specifications
Execution
Order release
Dispatching
Storage/warehousing
Quality
Preventive maintenance
Material transfer: to/from supplier/customer

(Continued)

BOX 3.1 *(Continued)*

Distribution

Buying

Vendor selection
Requirements
When to buy
Allocation
Sales planning
Inventory control
Pricing
Markdowns

Selling

Presentation
Display
Manpower planning
New item introduction
Advertising
Customer service

General Operations

Purchasing
Facilities maintenance
Security

Public relations
Audit
Inventory control
Physical inventory control
Internal communications

Management and Financial Control

Budgets
Cash management
Profit planning
Measurement and control
Capital expenditure planning
Credit granting
Financial negotiation
New business

Administration

Accounts payable
Accounts receivable
Payroll
Statistical and financial reporting
Audit
Merchandise processing
Personnel/training

BOX 3.1 *(Continued)*

Government

Judicial

Prosecution
Defense
Court procedures
Control
Civil

Public Facilities

Definition
Construction
Maintenance
Property management

Public Protection Process

Enforcement
Confinement
Rehabilitation
Prevention
Inspection

Finance

Taxing
Licensing
Accounting
Collections
Funds management
Payroll
Purchasing

Personnel

Recruiting/hiring/terminating
Career development

Job classification
Labor relations
Compensation and benefits
Employee/position management

Management

Conflict
Measurement and control
Policy determination
Budgeting
Security/privacy
External relations
Record keeping

Community Service

Library
Public records
Election administration
Cultural and recreational support
Environmental control

Public Aid Process

Eligibility determination
Financial assistance
Manpower
Social services
Residential care

Health Services

Admissions
Inpatient care
Outpatient care
Education and research
Emergency care
Community health services

(Continued)

BOX 3.1 *(Continued)*

Education (University)

Student

Promotion/recruiting
Evaluation and admissions
Class registration
Academic and career advising
Financial aid
Student activities/life
Student services
Student status/archives

Credit Instruction

Curriculum development
Scheduling instructional resources
Teaching and learning
Evaluation and measurement

Research and Artistic Creativity

Project identification and definition
Procurement of resources
Project execution
Evaluation
Dissemination of results

Public Services and Extension

Activity development
Administrative and logistical services for clientele
Resource procurement and organization
Activity delivery
Activity evaluation

Finance

Income acquisition
Stewardship of funds
Receipting and disbursement of funds
Cash management
Protection against financial liabilities
Financial services
Financial record keeping

Personnel

Recruiting
Hiring/termination
Career development and evaluation
Salary and benefit administration
Employee relations
Assignment of responsibilities
Job classification
Record keeping

Institutional Planning and Management

Goals development
Strategic planning (long-term)
Tactical planning (short-term)
Allocation of resources
Monitor and control
Internal communications

Physical Plant Management

Program statement
Design
Construction and procurement
Maintenance/operation
Disposition
Protection
Rental property management

Goods and Services

Assessment of needs
Acquisition
Inventory of expendables
Inventory of nonexpendables
Distribution

Alumni Affairs

Tracking
Programs and services
Institutional evaluation

External Communication and Relations

Publicity
Negotiation
Public service
Extra-university affiliation

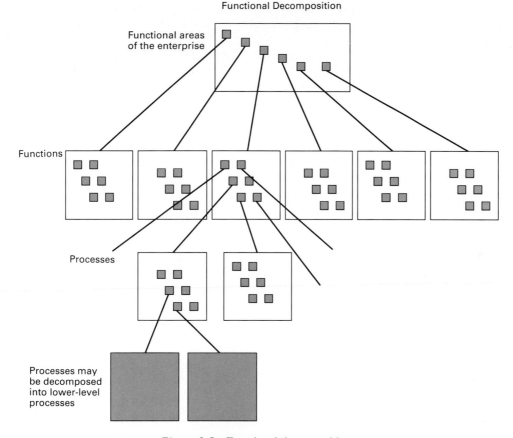

Figure 3.5   Functional decomposition.

and ending points. A process has identifiable inputs and outputs. The name of a process should be a verb clause, such as:

- Create purchase requisition
- Select supplier
- Follow up order
- Prepare information for accounts payable
- Analyze supplier performance

Decomposition of business functions and processes should be done independently of how the enterprise is split into departments. The organization may change its reporting structure periodically, but it still has to carry out the same functions and processes. Some corporations reorganize traumatically every two years or so. The identification of functions and processes should represent fundamental concern for how the corporation operates, independently of its current organization chart (which is often misleading).

Both functions are concerned with *what* has to be done to operate an enterprise, not with *how* it is done. *Procedures* are concerned with *how* it is done. Procedures change as technology changes. There are several types of procedures that *could* be used to accomplish given processes. Whereas the procedures may be scrapped or changed, the functions and processes still have to be carried out in order to run the enterprise. Functions and processes are basic statements

BOX 3.2   Characteristics of functions and processes

Functions are determined at the top level of the pyramid (information strategy planning). *Processes* are analyzed at the second level of the pyramid (business area analysis). *Procedures* relate to specifically *how* a process is carried out. These are designed at the third level of the pyramid (system design).

Enterprise Functions

- An enterprise *function* is a group of activities that together support one aspect of furthering the mission of the enterprise.
- A function is ongoing and continuous.
- A function is *not* based on organizational structures.
- A function categorizes *what* is done, not *how*.
- A function name should be a noun or a gerund (a word ending in ''ing''): for example, *advertising, account control, shipping, labor relations.*

Processes

- A *process* is a specified activity in an enterprise that is executed repeatedly.
- A *process* can be described in terms of inputs and outputs.
- A process has definable beginning and ending points.
- A process is not based on organizational structures.
- A process identifies *what* is done, not *how*.
- The name of a process should start with an action verb: for example, *create requisition, reorder parts, assemble orders.*

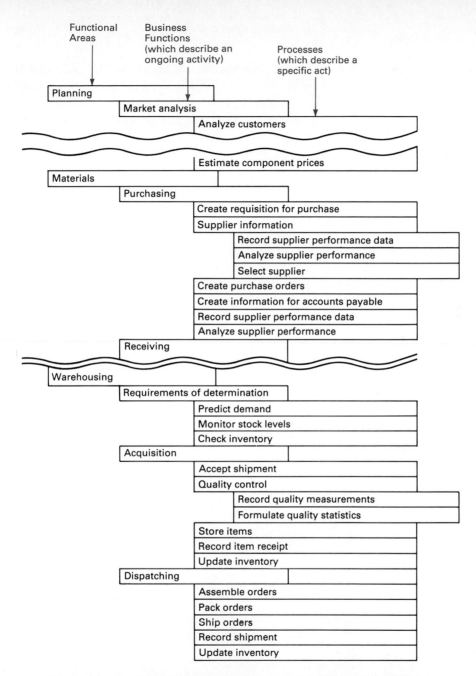

Figure 3.6   An enterprise chart: functional areas, functions, and processes. The name of a function should be a noun or gerund. The name of a process should normally begin with a verb. Procedures (not necessarily computerized) are designed to implement the processes. Processes are analyzed at the second level of the pyramid; procedures are designed at the third level.

about *what* must be done. Box 3.2 summarizes the characteristics of functions and processes.

> Functions are determined at level 1 of the pyramid (information strategy planning).
>
> Processes are analyzed at level 2 of the pyramid (business area analysis).
>
> Procedures are designed at level 3 of the pyramid (system design).

Figure 3.6 shows functions decomposed into processes and some processes decomposed into lower-level processes. The analysis of processes is not done in detail until the business area analysis stage of information engineering.

An analyst may write a definition of a function, putting the definition in the detail window that a workbench associates with that function. For example, INVENTORY MANAGEMENT may be defined as "the function of controlling the receipts and withdrawals of raw materials, parts, and subassemblies from the stores, and accounting for the stock." There may or may not be a separate department to accomplish this function; it is a function that may apply to several departments. The stores may be split or combined, but the function remains the same.

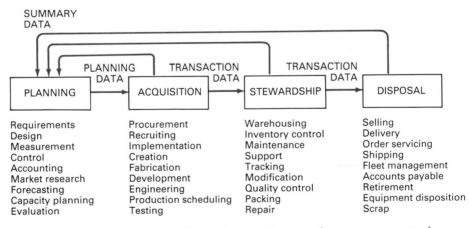

SUMMARY DATA			
PLANNING	ACQUISITION	STEWARDSHIP	DISPOSAL
Requirements	Procurement	Warehousing	Selling
Design	Recruiting	Inventory control	Delivery
Measurement	Implementation	Maintenance	Order servicing
Control	Creation	Support	Shipping
Accounting	Fabrication	Tracking	Fleet management
Market research	Development	Modification	Accounts payable
Forecasting	Engineering	Quality control	Retirement
Capacity planning	Production scheduling	Packing	Equipment disposition
Evaluation	Testing	Repair	Scrap

Figure 3.7 The functions that apply to products, services, or resources tend to be in the sequence of a four-stage lifecycle: *planning, acquisition, stewardship,* and *disposal,* as shown here.

LIFECYCLE OF FUNCTIONS

The products and services created by an organization, and the services needed to support them, tend to have a four-stage lifecycle: planning, acquisition, stewardship, and disposal. Figure 3.7 illustrates some of the types of functions at each stage in the cycle. It sometimes helps to identify the functions to think through all of the stages in the lifecycle of each type of product, service, or resource. This can be done with money, personnel, raw materials, parts, finished goods, capital equipment, buildings, machinery, fixtures, and so on.

MAPPING FUNCTIONS TO ORGANIZATIONAL UNITS

An organizational unit carries out several functions. A function may be performed by more than one organizational unit. We thus have a many-to-many association between functions and organizational units:

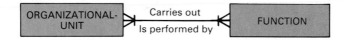

This says:

> ORGANIZATIONAL-UNIT *carries out* one or many FUNCTIONS.
>
> and
>
> FUNCTION *is performed by* one or many ORGANIZATIONAL-UNITS.

Like all such many-to-many associations, a matrix can be drawn (automatically by computer) and filled in to show which organizational units perform which functions:

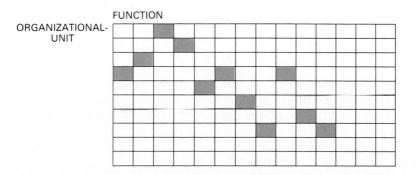

Similarly, functions may be mapped against geographical locations:

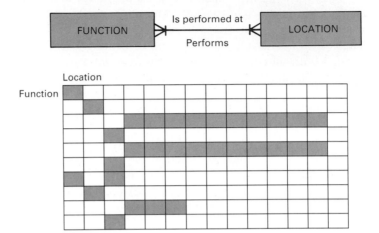

MAPPING EXECUTIVES TO FUNCTIONS

On an organization chart managers have a one-to-one association with organizational units. In principle, then, the matrix of organizational units and functions could be directly converted into a matrix mapping managers against functions. In practice, managers carry out informal activities not made clear on the organization chart. Indeed, in some enterprises the organization chart hides the true power structure of the enterprise. A separate matrix is often created in ISP projects mapping executives against business functions. Figure 3.8 is an example.

Recording the involvement of the executive is done with the following codes:

R   Direct management *responsibility*

A   Executive or policymaking *authority*

I   *Involved* in the function

E   Technical *expertise*

W   Actual execution of the *work*

These codes are entered into the matrix. I (Involved) may only be used when R (Responsible) or A (Authority) are not present. Some executives have the four codes R, A, E, and W; some have two or three codes; some have only one. The codes used vary somewhat from one enterprise to another. In some studies two versions of the chart are drawn: one to document the current situation and another to describe an ideal or target situation.

Figure 3.8 The business functions mapped against the executives in an enterprise.

EXECUTIVE	Marketing			Sales Operations				Engineering			Production				Materials Management				Facilities Management			Administration			Finance			Human Resources			Management			
	Planning	Research	Forecasting	Territory Management	Selling	Administration	Order Servicing	Design and Development	Prod. Spec. Main.	Information Control	Scheduling	Capacity Planning	Material Requirements	Operations	Purchasing	Receiving	Inventory Control	Shipping	Workflow Layout	Maintenance	Equipment Performance	General Accounting	Cost Planning	Budget Accounting	Financial Planning	Capital Acquisition	Funds Management	Personnel Planning	Recruiting/Development	Compensation	Business Planning	Organization Analysis	Review and Control	Risk Management
Vice President of Finance	RA/EW																					A/E	A/E	A/E	A/E	A/E	A/E				I	I	I	RA
Controller															I							RA/E	RA/E	RA/E	RA/E	RA/E	RA/E				I	I	I	RA
Personnel Director																									A/E	A/E	A/E	RA/EW	RA/E	RA/E				
Vice President of Sales	RA/EW	RA/E	RA/E	RA/E	RA/E	RA/E	RA/E																											I
Order Control Manager				I	I	I	I																											
Electronic Sales Manager			E	I	RA	RA	RA																											
Electrical Sales Manager			E	I	RA	RA	RA																											
Vice President of Engineering	I							RA	RA	RA									RA		RA	I	I	I							I			
Vice President of Production										I	RA	RA	RA	RA	RA	RA	RA	RA				I	I	I							I			
Plant Operations Director										I	RA	RA	RA	RA	RA	RA	RA	RA	I	I	I	I	I	I							I			
Production Planning Director												I	RA	RA	I		RA					I	I	I				I						
Facilities Manager	I																		RA	RA	RA	I	I	I				I			I			
Materials Control Manager															RA	RA	RA	RA	RA	RA	RA	I	I	I										
Purchasing Manager															RA	RA	RA	RA				I	I	I										
Division Lawyer	RA																								RA	RA	RA				I	I	RA	RA
Planning Director	RA																								RA	RA	RA				I	I	RA	I

R: Responsibility
A: Executive or policy making authority
I: Involved
E: Technical expertise
W: Actual execution of the work

A HIGH-LEVEL ENTITY CHART

While on the right-hand side of the pyramid a high-level decomposition of functions is being created, on the left-hand side an overview of the entities is created. Both sides will be expanded into more detail at the second layer of the pyramid:

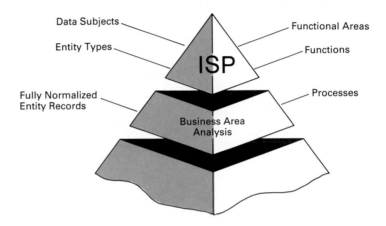

At the highest-level overview of data, broad data subjects are identified, such as:

SALES REGIONS

CUSTOMERS

ORDERS

PRODUCTS

PARTS

MATERIALS

VENDORS

EMPLOYEES

CAPITAL EQUIPMENT

For each data subject, entity types are identified. An entity is any person or thing, real or abstract, about which information is stored. For example:

SALES REGIONS
    SALES REGION
    BRANCH OFFICE
    SALESPERSON
    ANNUAL QUOTA

CUSTOMERS
    CUSTOMER
    ADDRESS
    CONTACT
ORDERS
    CUSTOMER ORDER
    ORDER ITEM
    INVOICE
    PAYMENT
    RECEIVABLE
    LEDGER ENTRY

Entity types can be associated with functions:

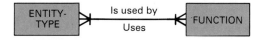

This says:

ENTITY TYPE *is used by* one or many FUNCTIONS.

and

FUNCTION *uses* one or many ENTITY TYPES.

Similarly, ENTITY-TYPE is associated with ORGANIZATIONAL-UNIT and LOCATION:

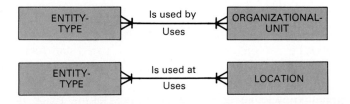

As before, a matrix can be drawn (automatically by a computer) and filled in to show which entities are associated with which organizational units and locations.

RELATIONSHIPS BETWEEN ENTITIES   Organizational units and functions are arranged hierarchically. One organizational unit manages zero or many other organizational units; and is managed by zero or one organizational unit:

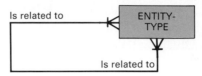

One function is composed of zero or many other functions, and is part of zero or one function:

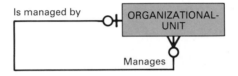

The associations among entity types are not necessarily hierarchical. An entity type has a many-to-many association with an entity type:

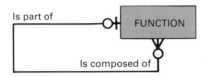

To model the associations among entities, entity-relationship diagrams are drawn (discussed in Chapter 9).

THINKING ABOUT THE CORPORATE STRUCTURE

In most corporations, activities have never been charted. When they are listed and related to the data they use, it is usually clear that much duplication exists. Each area of a corporation tends to expand its activities without knowledge of similar activities taking place in other areas. Each department tends to create its own paperwork. This does not matter much if the paperwork is processed manually. However, if it is processed by computer, the proliferation of separately designed paperwork is harmful because it greatly increases the cost of programming and maintenance. A computerized corporation ought to have different procedures from a corporation with manual paperwork. A corporation with workstations on all knowledge workers' desks, connected by a corporatewide network to databases, ought to have different procedures from a corporation with batch processing. The entry of data into a workstation replaces the need to create multiple carbon copies of forms that flow among locations. Information becomes instantly available and procedures should be changed to take advantage of this.

When strategic planning lists the activities and the data they use, it should minimize the duplication. Charts mapping data against activities that use those data reveal the duplication in activities and often suggest desirable ways of re-organizing the activities. In some enterprises the overview modeling began as a technique for examining *existing* procedures, and evolved into a technique for examining what procedures *ought* to be. The following quotation from an interview about the process are typical of what is discovered.

First, we found that the existing procedures were horrifyingly redundant. Every O & M guy in the business had invented his own bits of paper. You had many different forms where one computerized form would suffice. But unfortunately, each different department had its own different structured analyst who had cast the redundant methods into different COBOL programs. These, collectively, had become a maintenance nightmare.

Second, we found that it was more than just redundant paperwork. The procedures and the flow of work had anomalies, sometimes weird, expensive anomalies. For the last 20 years new procedures have kept springing up like mushrooms in the night. In some cases management had a vague sense that the anomalies were there, but they could only comprehend trees, not the forest.

Third—and it took months before we dared to express this heresy—the management structure itself was wrong. It needed a thorough reorganization of the departments and even divisions in order to get tight control and high administrative productivity. This perception could only come through a functional analysis of the entire organization.

Senior functional management said they could not afford the time to participate in the entity analysis, so they gave me their senior clerks. A very senior, senior clerk, who gloried in the title "provider," learned to map data and normalize it.

One day he asked me to talk with him and the planning manager because he had something important to say. He went in and said to the planning manager: "Our OPAS meeting is wrong!"

Now, OPAS is the *holy of holies* in this company. In the head office every Monday morning the priesthood gathers: the senior functional managers who decide *what* should be *where* in the three plants, in *what proportion,* with *what priorities,* and in *what yield.*

This senior clerk could now see that the output of the cold reduction mill becomes feed to the slitting mill, the output of that went into the next process, and so on, and the OPAS decisions near the head of this were screwing up export orders about 13 stages down the track.

He grabbed the planning manager and the planning manager wasn't even prepared to listen. But he wove the argument and the net and caught the manager within it. There was a draft of cold air of "Why's?" which blew all the way up to the OPAS meeting. They are questioning head office moves on the one hand and incentives on the other, and how export orders affect the planning.

All of this happened because a senior clerk saw that he had a funny thing in his relational map. When he traced it through, it shouldn't have been there.

They are making sure *that* senior clerk doesn't annoy that particular functional manager any more. They've promoted him for the first time in 20 years. He's not a ''provider'' any more; he's a senior production planner, which effectively removes him from harm's way.

In many enterprises there needs to be basic questioning about whether the current organization chart enables the essential processes to be carried out in the most efficient way. *Overview modeling can therefore move out of the realm of I.S. and into the realm of business management thinking about corporate reorganization.* In some cases *major* reorganization has resulted from an ISP study.

SUMMARY

In this chapter we have discussed relationships among organizational units, locations, functions, and entity types:

Figure 3.9 puts all these relationships on one diagram. There are six many-to-many relationships among these four objects:

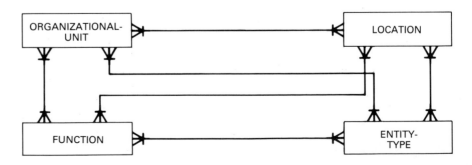

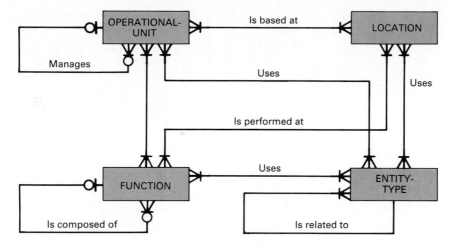

Figure 3.9 A model of the planning data described in this chapter. A matrix can be generated (by a computerized tool) for each of the six many-to-many associations on this chart.

BOX 3.3

```
┌─ Create an overview model of the enterprise
│  ┌─ Enter the following information into the encyclopedia:
│  │     An organizational chart showing all organizational units.
│  │     The persons who manage the organizational units.
│  │     Identify the major business functions.
│  │     Decompose into lower-level functions with a function decomposition
│  │        diagram.
│  │     Identify the data subjects.
│  │     Decompose into entity types.
│  │     Add detailed comments to the above diagrams where necessary.
│  │     Create an initial entity-relationship diagram (Chapter 9).
│  ┌─ Create a matrix mapping executives against business functions
│  │     The involvement of the executive may be recorded with the
│  │        following codes:
│  │           R: Direct management RESPONSIBILITY
│  │           A: Executive or policy-making AUTHORITY
│  │           I: INVOLVED in the function
│  │           E: Technical EXPERTISE
│  │           W: Actual execution of the WORK
│  │
│  │     Create a matrix mapping functions against organizational units.
│  │     Create a matrix mapping functions against entity types.
│  │     Create a matrix mapping organizational units against entity types.
│  │
│     Print relevant versions of the above diagrams from the
│        encyclopedia for the participants to review.
└─
```

Key:
C: Create
R: Read
U: Update
D: Delete

DATA SUBJECT	Plan Finances	Perform Accounting	Control Finances	Staff Organizations	Develop Individual Capabilities	Administer HR Programs	Plan Production	Research/Develop Project	Procure Materials	Produce Product	Plan Product	Market Product	Process Customer Orders	Manage Business	Manage Vendors	Manage Information
FUNCTION	1	2	3	4	5	6	7	8	9	10	11	12	13	14	15	16
1 Employees	R	R		CRUD	RU	R							R			
2 HR plans, procedures, regs.				CRUD	R	CRUD	R				R			R		R
3 Other people of interest			CRUD	CRUD										CRUD	R	
4 Financial plans, procedures, regs.	CRUD	RU	CRUD	R			R				R			R		R
5 Financial income	R	CRUD	R								R			R		
6 Financial outflow	R	CRUD	R											R		
7 Financial investments	R	CRUD	CRUD											R		
8 Product plans, procedures, regs.	R			R	R		R	R			CRUD	R		R		R
9 Product materials		R					R	CRUD	RU	RU		R				
10 Finished products		R					R	CRUD		RU	R	R	RU	R		
11 Facility plans, procedures, regs.	R			R			R	R		R	R			CRUD		
12 Company locations		R		R	R				R	R				CRUD	R	
13 Equipment		R					RU	CRUD		R	R			R		
14 Org. plans, procedures, regs.	R	R	R	CRUD	R						R			CRUD		R
15 Vendors		R							R				R		CRUD	
16 Customers	R	R									R	R	CRUD	R		
17 Other organizations of interest	R	R	CRUD		R	RU		R			R	R		CRUD		R
18 Info, plans, procedures, regs.	R			R										R		CRUD
19 Information models																CRUD
20 Information implementation																CRUD
21 Information operations																CRUD

Figure 3.10 Data subjects mapped against functions.

Any of these six many-to-many relationships can be represented as matrices. The analyst creating an enterprise model should fill in all six matrices. A computerized tool should cross-check the information to help ensure that a consistent model has been created before the analyst proceeds to add more interesting information to the model. Figures 3.3, 3.10, and 3.11 show examples of some of the matrices corresponding to Fig. 3.9.

Box 3.3 summarizes the steps taken in creating an overview model of the enterprise.

REFERENCE

1. IBM, *Business Systems Planning: Information Systems Planning Guide*. White Plains, N.Y.: IBM Corporation, 1980.

ENTITY	Paloma Displays, Inc. Locations	Home Office	Manufacturing Plant	Sales Headquarters	Santa Clara Sales Office	Chicago Sales Office	New York Sales Office
LOCATION	1	2	3	4	5	6	7
1 Employee		*	*	*			
2 Contract Employee		*	*	*			
3 Applicant		*					
4 HR Compensation Regs, Plans, etc.		*					
5 HR Benefits Regs, & Plans		*					
6 HR Staffing Requirements & Plans		*					
7 Job Requisition		*	*	*			
8 Stockholder		*					
9 Boardmember		*					
10 Misc. Contacts/VIPS		*					
11 Financial Plans		*	*	*			
12 Accounting Regs, Practices		*	*	*			
13 Ledger Accounts		*	*	*			
14 Customer Purchase Order/Invoice				*			
15 Customer Payments				*			
16 Other Income		*					
17 Company Purchase Orders		*	*	*			
18 Company Bills		*					
19 Company Checks/Payments		*					
20 Stocks & Bonds		*					
21 Loans		*					
22 Bank Accounts		*					
23 Product Plans		*	*	*			
24 Production Procedures			*				
25 Principles of Technology			*				
26 Raw Materials			*				
27 Utilities		*	*	*			
28 Supplies		*	*	*			
29 Products		*	*	*			
30 By-Products			*				
31 Bill of Materials			*				
32 Work in Progress			*				
33 Facility Plans		*	*	*			
34 Facility Procedures		*	*	*			
35 Facility Standards		*	*	*			
36 Land			*				
37 Sites		*	*	*			
38 Buildings		*	*				
39 Vehicles			*				
40 Equipment			*				
41 Tools			*				
42 Furniture & Fixtures		*	*	*			
43 Business Plans, Proposals		*	*	*			
44 Organization Units		*	*	*			

Figure 3.11   Entities mapped against locations.

4 ANALYSIS OF GOALS AND PROBLEMS

GOALS

An enterprise has certain goals. It is desirable to analyze its goals and put them in writing. If everybody understands the goals clearly, the enterprise is more likely to achieve them. One of the most common forms of human folly is to lose sight of goals.

Goals are used in a control mechanism for an enterprise. They set targets, and the success in progressing toward those targets is measured. If part of the enterprise falters in its achievement of goals, this needs to be detected and corrective action taken as quickly as possible.

Goals should be worded so as to express a precise course of action. "Be a market leader" is a vague goal. "Increase sales by 30 percent per year" is a precise goal. Goals should be precise where possible. Goals should focus on results. They should be decomposable into work that has to be done.

Goals should be *measurable*. In some cases the measure is binary: Either the goal has been achieved or not, for example "Hire new chief engineer." Where possible, a hard measure should be applicable. In some cases a soft measure has to be used, for example "Improve market image of the enterprise." The extent to which such a goal has been met may be established through market research interviewing techniques.

When high-level goals are identified, they should be broken down into lower-level goals that apply to lower-level departments (see Fig. 4.1). Goals are thus associated with the organizational units of an enterprise:

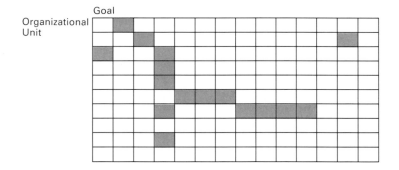

Figure 4.1   Related goals are established throughout the organization chart.

As with other many-to-many associations, this can be represented as a matrix:

Classical management literature describes *objectives* and *goals*. They have been defined as follows:

Objectives. Objectives are general statements about the directions in which a firm intends to go, without stating specific targets to be reached by particular times.

Goals. Goals are specific targets that are intended to be reached by a given time. A goal is thus an operational transform of one or more objectives.

Mission. The *mission* of an enterprise is the highest-level statement of objectives. It gives a broad description of the purpose and policy of the enterprise.

Strategy. A *strategy* in an enterprise is a pattern of goals, policies, and plans that specify how an organization should function over a given period. A strategy may define areas for product development, techniques for responding to competition, means of financing, size of the organization, image the enterprise will project, and so on.

Part of the *strategy* of an airline might be to improve the route structure over which it flies. An *objective* may be *"Develop more profitable route structure."* A *goal* should have specific targets for a specific time period, such as *"By year end, eliminate all routes with an average seat occupancy of less than 40 percent."*

PLANNING HORIZON

Different goals can have different planning horizons. It is useful to categorize them as being tactical, or long-term. *Tactical* goals relate to short-term tactics and have a planning horizon of about a year, occasionally two years. *Long-term* goals relate to a planning horizon of five years or so, occasionally longer.

Strategic planning in business is (or should be) done separately for the tactical and long-term horizons. Tactical planning focuses on such questions as: What is the target revenue and profit for the next fiscal year? What are sales quotas for the next fiscal year? What products will be introduced by the end of the next fiscal year? How many new salespersons should be recruited? Tactical planning creates budgets and quotas and builds these into a financial model for the next fiscal year. It tracks sales and expenses and compares them to the targets, and makes whatever adjustments are needed to achieve the target revenue and profit.

Long-term planning focuses on such questions as: What is the target revenue five years from now? How will that growth be achieved? How should the product line evolve over the next five years? What will make us a market leader (or survivor) five years from now, and what actions must we take to ensure that? In general, long-term planning creates a scenario for a time five years or so in the future and asks: How do we get from here to there? *"How do we get from here to there?"* is the crucial question in strategic planning.

The military asks what battlefield information systems will be needed eight years from now (there will be many), and what networks, data models, and standards will be needed in order that they can intercommunicate.

Most corporations build a long-term financial model, forecasting revenues, and expenses over a period of five years or more, and ask how the products and customer base must evolve to achieve the desired long-term growth.

It is useful to represent goals hierarchically. A high-level goal can be broken down into low-level goals of greater detail. Sometimes a *long-term* goal is regarded as a high-level goal and *tactical* goals are lower-level short-term goals needed to achieve this long-term goal. The enterprise *mission* statement can be regarded as the highest-level objective.

Figure 4.2 lists the goals of an electronics manufacturer. There are four long-term and 18 tactical goals. At the top of the list is the corporate mission statement. The goals in Fig. 4.2 can be represented hierarchically. An action diagram editor is a useful tool for doing this. Figure 4.3 shows the goals defined in Fig. 4.2 represented by an action diagram.

Figure 4.4 is a matrix mapping the tactical goals of Figs. 4.2 and 4.3 against the organizational units of an enterprise. The goals of a high-level organizational unit need to relate to the goals of its subordinate organizational units. Figure 4.5 shows a top-level goal of a government department of education being broken into lower-level goals for its organizational units.

Level	Goals
Corporate	Purpose and mission corporate objectives
Division	Division goals
Department	Department goals
Work center	Work center goals
Individual	Individual goals

Goal: Be Market Leader

Definition: Attain and achieve market leadership position in all phases of the business.
Planning Horizon: PE—PERMANENT

Goal: Increase Sales

Definition: Increase sales by 30 percent per year.
Planning Horizon: ST—STRATEGIC

Goal: Increase Productivity

Definition: Increase manufacture of video display units to meet increased sales without sacrificing product quality or increasing costs.
Planning Horizon: ST—STRATEGIC

Goal: Become Number 2 Workstation Vendor

Definition: Grow to become the second-largest workstation vendor.
Planning Horizon: ST—STRATEGIC

Goal: Finance Product Development

Definition: Generate sufficient funding for complete product development from both internal and external sources.
Planning Horizon: ST—STRATEGIC

Goal: Improve Sales Effectiveness

Definition: Shorten sales cycle to an average of 90 days. Provide better support so that personal sales contacts are more productive.
Planning Horizon: TA—TACTICAL

Goal: Identify New Target Markets

Definition: Locate new uses for video displays. Find customers who can be served by expanding or modifying current plant and equipment.
Planning Horizon: TA—TACTICAL

Goal: Improve Market Penetration

Definition: Increase market share to 35 percent by making workstations the dominant force in the marketplace.
Planning Horizon: TA—TACTICAL

Figure 4.2   A list of the goals of an enterprise.

(Continued)

Goal: Add Distribution Channels

Definition: Augment internal sales force with external distribution channels. Identify foreign distributors for market expansion in Europe and South America.
Planning Horizon: TA—TACTICAL

Goal: Address Absenteeism Problem

Definition: Improve working conditions and morale to reduce absenteeism in the plant to 1.5 percent of working days.
Planning Horizon: TA—TACTICAL

Goal: Exploit New Technology

Definition: Take advantage of advances in new technology to improve product quality and reduce manufacturing costs by 16 percent.
Planning Horizon: TA—TACTICAL

Goal: Improve Information Systems

Definition: Reduce database redundancy by data modeling. Standardize choice of DSS software. Increase fourth-generation language penetration to 45 percent of systems.
Planning Horizon: TA—TACTICAL

Goal: Streamline Shop Floor Operations

Definition: Simulate alternative layouts of equipment and manufacturing operations. Modify so as to maximize efficiency.
Planning Horizon: TA—TACTICAL

Goal: Enhance Employee Training

Definition: Develop new employee training programs and set up ongoing monitoring to assure that prescribed procedures are being followed.
Planning Horizon: TA—TACTICAL

Goal: Enhance Customer Support

Definition: Maximize repeat purchases by ensuring that customers are making the best use of our products. Establish "hot line" for emergency problems that require immediate response.
Planning Horizon: TA—TACTICAL

Goal: Improve Product Quality

Definition: Design and build products with less than 0.05 percent defect rate and with extended durability. Products should also be visually attractive.
Planning Horizon: TA—TACTICAL

Figure 4.2   (Continued)

Goal: Expand Product Line

Definition: Produce a wider variety of goods using video display to support market expansion strategy.
Planning Horizon: TA—TACTICAL

Goal: Upgrade Product Warranty

Definition: Extend warranty to two full years.
Planning Horizon: TA—TACTICAL

Goal: Reduce Inventory Investment

Definition: Plan manufacturing and raw material delivery schedules so that less than two weeks' inventory is on hand at any time.
Planning Horizon: TA—TACTICAL

Goal: Reduce Receivables to 45 Days

Definition: Improve collection procedures so that receivables are reduced to an average age of 45 days.
Planning Horizon: TA—TACTICAL

Goal: Improve Cash Flow Management

Definition: Plan investment strategy of cash-on-hand so that a maximum return is earned, yet ensuring that adequate supplies of cash are available to meet expenses.
Planning Horizon: TA—TACTICAL

Goal: Locate Venture Capital

Definition: Prepare prospectus to attract investment from venture capitalists to expand research and manufacturing facilities. Contact all known investors in high-tech manufacturing and design.
Planning Horizon: TA—TACTICAL

Goal: Enhance Corporate Image

Definition: Raise level of general awareness of our products in the marketplace. Ensure that the company receives all possible favorable publicity.
Planning Horizon: TA—TACTICAL

Figure 4.2   (Continued)

```
┌─ * Be Market Leader
│
│     ┌─── Increase Sales
│     │    . . . Improve sales effectiveness
│     │    . . . Identify new target markets
│     │    . . . Improve market penetration
│     │    . . . Add distribution channels
│     │
│     ┌─── Increase Productivity
│     │    . . . Address absenteeism problem
│     │    . . . Exploit new technology
│     │    . . . Improve information systems
│     │    . . . Streamline shop floor operations
│     │    . . . Enhance employee training
│     │
│     ┌─── Become Number 2 Workstation Vendor
│     │    . . . Enhance customer support
│     │    . . . Improve product quality
│     │    . . . Expand product line
│     │    . . . Upgrade product warranty
│     │
│     ┌─── Finance Product Development
│     │    . . . Reduce inventory investment
│     │    . . . Reduce receivables to 45 days
│     │    . . . Improve cash flow management
│     │    . . . Enhance corporate image
└─────┘
```

Figure 4.3   A hierarchy of goals represented as an action diagram. The definitions of the goal (shown in Fig. 4.2) may be included in the action diagram and displayed by executing an EXPAND, where three dots are shown.

The highest-level objectives must address the following questions (stressed by Drucker in his book *Management* [1]:

What is our business?

What will our business be?

What should our business be?

These are questions that top managers should ask continuously, so as to understand the business better and to manage it more effectively. Continual top-management questioning about what the business should be is vital.

Of primary importance in defining business objectives are questions about customers and their needs:

Who are the customers?

Where are they?

What are their needs?

What will they buy, and why?

At what price?

How do we reach them?

An organization's customers are its reasons for existence. A government department's customers may be taxpayers or welfare recipients. An organization that does not translate its customers' needs directly into a hierarchy of goals can develop forms of internal politics that serve no real external purpose.

To meet the needs of customers, various resources are needed: human resources, production resources, capital, equipment, materials, and others.

GOAL / FUNCTION	1 Improve Sales Effectiveness	2 Identify New Target Markets	3 Improve Market Penetration	4 Add Distribution Channels	5 Address Absenteeism Problem	6 Exploit New Technology	7 Improve Information Systems	8 Streamline Shop Floor Operations	9 Enhance Employee Training	10 Enhance Customer Support	11 Improve Product Quality	12 Expand Product Line	13 Upgrade Product Warranty	14 Reduce Inventory Investment	15 Reduce Receivables to 45 Days	16 Improve Cashflow Management	17 Locate Venture Capital	18 Enhance Corporate Image
	1	2	3	4	5	6	7	8	9	10	11	12	13	14	15	16	17	18
1 Planning																		
2 Accounting															*	*		
3 Cash Management																*		
4 Investments																*		
5 Purchasing														*				
6 Facilities								*										
7 Human Resource Development	*				*				*									
8 MIS																		
9 Legal													*				*	
10 Manufacturing					*						*	*		*				
11 Quality Assurance										*		*						
12 Packaging											*							
13 Materials Management							*						*					
14 Sales Regions	*											*			*			
15 Customer Services																		
16 Customer Education										*								
17 Order Processing	*			*								*						
18 Product Management				*		*						*						
19 Public Relations																	*	*
20 Market Research		*		*		*					*	*						
21 Distribution												*						
22 Engineering						*		*			*	*	*					
23 Research		*				*					*	*						
24 Prototype Manufacture						*		*			*	*						
25 Testing Laboratory						*					*	*	*					

Figure 4.4   Tactical goals of an enterprise mapped against its organizational units.

Level	Goals	Strategies
Department	To achieve government and public confidence	Achieve increasingly efficient use of human resources • •
Directorate (research and planning)	To increase the efficiency in the use of human resources	Progressively reduce the effort/time needed to collect data from schools • •
Branch (R&P statistics)	To reduce the time and effort required in collecting from schools	Coordinate and integrate data collections from schools • •
Officer (statistics)	To coordinate and integrate all data collections from all schools	Monitor and document all data collections; identify common data

Figure 4.5   Example of goal definition and refinement for a department of education.

Goals must be set that relate to the supply, utilization, and development of resources in an optimal manner.

SOURCES OF GOALS

Goals can be found written in a variety of documents in an organization, for example:

- Business plans
- Information technology plans
- Information plans
- Annual reports
- Executive reports/memos
- Management-by-objectives documentation

The ISP team should seek out these written sources of goals and enter them into the planning tool before conducting interviews with management to elicit their statements of goals. If the enterprise uses management-by-objectives and performs appraisal interviews with managers, these are a particularly fertile source of goals. It is often desirable that each manager set his own goals and that these relate to the hierarchy of goals in the enterprise. The goals of the enterprise need to be reassessed periodically.

PROBLEMS   Every enterprise has *problems* that make it more difficult to achieve the required *goals*. Sometimes a goal relates to the solution of a particular problem. Problems should be recorded along with goals. When attention is focused on a problem, the problem is more likely to be solved.

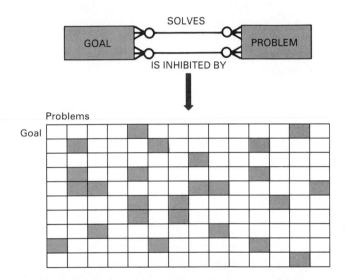

Like goals, problems can be mapped against organizational units:

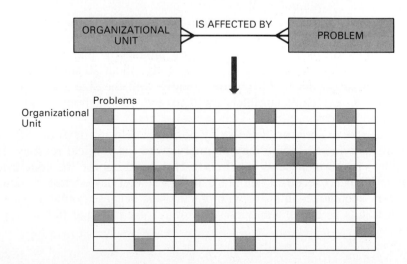

When executives are interviewed during the ISP study, they should be asked about problems as well as goals. What problems prevent them meeting the goals that are important? What possible solutions are there to the problem? What I.S. facilities would help them to meet a particular goal, and what would help them deal with a particular problem?

Figure 4.6 gives a list of problems quoted by a production executive. It lists the possible solutions to the problem, the criticality of solving the problem, the processes involved, and the system or information requirements.

CRITICALITY RANKING

Both goals and problems should be given a criticality ranking. A scale of 1 through 5 is appropriate for this:

5   Critical to operation of business (e.g., legal compliance); must be performed with rigid timetable

4   Critical to undisrupted operation of business (e.g., payroll)

3   Required to support business (e.g., management and financial reports)

2   Required to support business; however, the importance and timetable for the activity are lower than 3 (e.g., regular scheduled reports)

1   Desirable, but not absolutely required to support business

EXECUTIVE INTERVIEWS

The heart of goal and problem analysis is interviews with key executives, to understand their perspectives about the business, their information needs, and the problems they have. The interviews should validate the goals of the enterprise and the matrices modeling the enterprise. After each interview the information collected should be entered into the encyclopedia and coordinated and analyzed with the help of the planning software.

The executives interviewed will normally be no more than two levels below the company president. They will be responsible for major functions of the enterprise: director of finance, manager of production planning, purchasing manager, director of marketing. In a typical study, about 20 such interviews are conducted, although the number varies greatly with the size and requirements of the business. Typically, an interview takes two to four hours, and only two are scheduled per day.

The executive sponsor of the study normally helps to determine the list of executives interviewed. Some may be interviewed for political reasons. Executives omitted in the interviews could be resentful and oppose the conclusions of the study. Higher executives should usually be interviewed last, because the interviewers' techniques improve with practice and because doubts or suspicions about the results of earlier interviews can be resolved by questioning top management.

PROBLEM	SOLUTION	CRITICALITY RATING	INHIBITS GOAL:	CAUSED BY PROCESS:	IMPACTS PROCESS	REQUIRES ENTITY/SYSTEM
Lack of effective production planning impairs efficiency	Better production planning system	5	• Reduce manufacturing cost per item • Reduce inventory investment	• Plan production • Shop floor control		Better production planning system
Smaller, more frequent orders; higher costs of handling; smaller batches	Order trend analysis; Better preciction; Better system for batching small orders; longer lead times	4	• Reduce inventory investment • Reduce manufacturing cost per item		• Plan production • Customer relations	• ORDERS • ORDER FORECASTS
Inability to look at enough alternatives for shop floor layout	Shop floor simulation	4	• Reduce manufacturing costs per item • Reduce inventory investment	• Plan production		System for simulating shop floor operation
Lack of ability to identify promote and retain top-quality people	• Better information on personnel resources • Better incentive schemes • Improve morale	3	• High-efficiency production	• Personnel compensation		• Measurement of morale • Rating of production personnel
Lack of "what-if" capability on cost sheets	Online cost-sheet analysis	3	• Reduce manufacturing cost per item			Spreadsheet for "what-if" cost estimates

Figure 4.6 A form used in an executive interview.

An introductory meeting with all interviewees should be held before interviewing begins. At this meeting the executives are introduced to the concepts of the matrices and diagrams used, and given relevant lists of processes, definitions of goals, and matrices which they can examine and validate. They are asked to think about their goals and problems in preparation for the interview. They are asked to think about systems or information that could help to solve their problems.

The interviews for validating the overview model of the enterprise (discussed in Chapter 9) may also validate the goals and problems. Combining these interviews lessens the executive time involved and helps to integrate the overall results. When such interviews are done for the first time, the executives are told that the results will be stored in an updatable encyclopedia and will be reexamined periodically.

The purposes of the interviews are the following:

1. To validate the models in the encyclopedia

2. To agree on the goals of a department

3. To determine current problems

4. To discuss solutions to these problems

5. To determine information needed by the executive and to place a value on it

6. To determine and prioritize the need for future systems

7. To gain executive rapport and involvement

Typical questions in the interviews are as follows:

1. What are your responsibilities? Are they different from those indicated on the organization chart?

2. What are the basic goals of your area?

3. What are the three greatest problems you have had in meeting these goals? (Include not only current problems but also problems of the recent past.)

4. What has prevented you from solving them?

5. What is needed to solve them?

6. What value would better information have in these areas (in person-hours saved, dollars saved, better opportunities, etc.)?

7. In what other areas could the greatest improvements be realized, given better information support?

8. What would be the values of these improvements?

9. What costs may be incurred by inaccurate or untimely information?

10. What is the most useful information you receive? (The best aspects of current systems must be retained.)

11. What would you most like to receive?

12. How would you rate your current information support with respect to each of the following?
    Types of information
    Timeliness
    Accuracy
    Adequacy
    Cost
    Consistency
    Ease of use or clarity of presentation

13. How are you measured?

14. How do you measure your subordinates?

15. What other types of measurement are you expected to make?

16. What types of decisions are you expected to make? What computer aids might help in your decision making?

17. What major changes are expected in your area in the next year? In the next two, four, or six years?

18. What do you expect, and what would you like, to result from this study?

19. Any additional views or comments? (This is often a good way to terminate an interview.)

Wherever appropriate, the answers to the questions should be quantified, expressed in value ranges, or broken down into items that can be quantified. The interviewer may use a form for recording the information from the interview. Figure 4.6 shows one example of such a form. The information collected from the interview will be digested, structured, and entered into the encyclopedia.

In some cases the problems expressed in the interviews are *perceived* problems, which may or may not be *real* problems. Perceived problems are traced back to root causes and forward to quantifiable effects, if possible. As far as possible, *real* problems are recorded in the encyclopedia. Each executive is given a copy of what is recorded in the encyclopedia related to his interview or area, and is asked to confirm it.

CATEGORIZATION OF PROBLEMS

Recorded problems can be categorized as follows:

A   Problems unrelated to information systems (these are given to the executive who sponsored the study)

B   Problems related to *current* information systems

C   Problems related to *planned* information systems

D   Problems which could be aided by information systems that are *neither in existence nor, at present, planned*

A code for this categorization may be recorded with the problem description.

LINK TO SYSTEMS AND ENTITIES

Goals and problems should be associated in the encyclopedia with systems and entities, where relevant.

Matrices can show the relationships of goals and problems to relevant systems and entities. Figure 4.7 is a matrix mapping the tactical goals listed in Fig. 4.2 with the entities of an enterprise.

It is often the case that the information needed to help achieve a goal or solve a problem *already exists* in the databases of the enterprise but is not being put to use. Matrix analysis often shows that it is desirable to extract the relevant information and make it available to managers in spreadsheets, decision-support systems, or executive information systems.

PROCEDURE

Box 4.1 gives an action diagram of the procedure that may be followed in the analysis of goals and problems.

PERIODIC REEXAMINATION

The goals and problems need to be reexamined periodically. An overall review once a year will help ensure that information systems are evolving in an appropriate fashion. Counsel-and-appraisal interviews should be conducted with all managers periodically as part of the *management-by-objectives* process. One purpose of these interviews is to reestablish the goals of the manager and to track his progress in meeting these goals. The compensation and other incentives of the manager relate to his success in meeting the goals that are agreed upon by him. Some corporations conduct *management-by-objectives* interviews once a year, some once every six months, and some once every three months. At this time the goals and problems in the encyclopedia should be examined and updated. The portion of the encyclopedia that relates to the department in question should be printed for inspection, and any anomalies should be noted.

Similarly, at business planning meetings the information in the encyclopedia should be reviewed. Such reviews should encompass critical success factors and the technology impact analysis. These are discussed in the following two chapters.

REFERENCE

1. Peter F. Drucker, *Management*. London: Heinemann, 1974.

GOAL

1 Improve Sales Effectiveness
2 Identify New Target Markets
3 Improve Market Penetration
4 Add Distribution Channels
5 Address Absenteeism Problem
6 Exploit New Technology
7 Improve Information Systems
8 Streamline Shop Floor Operations
9 Enhance Employee Training
10 Enhance Customer Support
11 Improve Product Quality
12 Expand Product Line
13 Upgrade Product Warranty
14 Reduce Inventory Investments
15 Reduce Receivables to 45 Days
16 Improve Cashflow Management
17 Locate Venture Capital
18 Enhance Corporate Image

ENTITY	1	2	3	4	5	6	7	8	9	10	11	12	13	14	15	16	17	18
1 Employee	*				*			*	*	*								*
2 Contract Employee																		*
3 Applicant																		
4 HR Compensation Regs, Plans, etc.																*		*
5 HR Benefits Regs & Plans					*				*									
6 HR Staffing Requirements & Plans					*			*										*
7 Job Requisition																		
8 Stockholder																		
9 Boardmember																		
10 Misc. Contacts/VIPs																		
11 Financial Plans																	*	
12 Accounting Regs, Practices																*	*	
13 Ledger Accounts																*	*	
14 Customer Purchase Orders/ Invoice	*		*					*		*		*		*	*	*		
15 Customer Payments															*	*		
16 Other Income															*	*		
17 Company Purchase Orders														*		*		
19 Company Bills																*		
19 Company Checks/ Payments																*		
20 Stocks & Bonds																*		
21 Loans																*		
22 Bond Accounts																*		
23 Product Plans		*			*												*	
24 Production Procedures		*	*		*			*	*		*		*					
35 Principles of Terminology		*			*			*	*		*	*						
26 Raw Materials														*				
27 Utilities																		
28 Supplies														*				
29 Products	*	*	*	*		*		*	*	*	*	*	*	*			*	*
30 By-Products																		
31 Bill of Materials						*		*	*	*	*	*	*	*				
32 Work in Progress								*	*		*			*	*			
33 Facility Plans	*		*															*
34 Facility Procedures								*	*		*							
35 Facility Standards									*		*							
36 Land																		
37 Sites								*	*									
38 Buildings								*	*									
39 Vehicles								*	*					*				
40 Equipment						*		*	*					*				
41 Tools								*	*		*							
42 Furniture & Fixtures																		
43 Business Plans, Proposals	*	*	*			*											*	
44 Organizational Units	*			*				*	*	*						*	*	*
45 Committees & ????????																		
46 Vendor		*		*						*		*	*			*	*	
47 Vendor Contracts				*						*		*	*			*		
48 Customer	*	*	*							*		*				*	*	*
49 Customer Contracts	*	*	*							*					*			
50 Market Profiles	*	*	*	*		*						*	*					*
51 Competitors	*	*	*	*		*						*	*					*
52 Unions					*													
53 Governments																		
54 Technical & Educational Groups						*												
55 Financial Institutions														*	*	*		

Figure 4.7 The tactical goals of Fig. 4.2 mapped against entities used in monitoring those goals.

BOX 4.1 An action diagram of the procedure for analysis of goals and problems

```
┌─ Conduct Goal-and-Problem analysis
│   ┌─ Obtain any existing documentation which relates to goals
│   │     or objectives:
│   │         o   Business plans
│   │         o   Information system plans
│   │         o   Technology plans
│   │         o   Annual reports
│   │         o   Executive reports and memos
│   │         o   Reports on Management-by-Objectives interviews with
│   │               executives.
│   │   ┌─ Comment
│   │   │     o   Goals should focus on results.
│   │   │     o   Should be as precise as possible.
│   │   │     o   Goals should be measurable.
│   │   │     o   Goals should be decomposable into work which has to be done.
│   │   └─
│   └─
│
│   ┌─ Create an initial inventory of goals
│   │     Use an action diagram editor to represent the goal hierarchically.
│   │     o─────────o
│   │     │ See Figure 4.2 │
│   │     o─────────o
│   └─
│
│     Determine which executives will be interviewed.
│     Establish the format of the interview.
│     For each executive
│       ┌─ Conduct goal-and-problem interview
│       │     Review the portion of the business model which relates to
│       │       this executive.
│       │     Note any changes that are needed.
│       │     Establish the goals of the executive.
│       │     Identify the problems he perceives in achieving those goals.
│       │     Identify possible solutions to those problems.
│       │     Identify how information systems could help.
│       │     Rank the goals and problems.
│       └─
│
│       ┌─ Organize and record the interview information
│       │     Clean up the interview information and enter it into the
│       │       encyclopedia.
│       │     Refine the inventory of goals.
│       │     Rank the goals and problems.
│       │     Associate goals with organizational unit.
│       │     Associate problems with organizational unit.
│       │     Associate goals with problems.
│       │     Associate goals with information needs.
│       │     Associate problems with information needs.
│       │     Use the planning tool to analyze the goal and problem data.
│       │     Record any especially urgent information-system actions
│       │       that are needed.
│       └─
│
│         Submit the record of the interview to the executive for validation.
│         Record any changes that are requested.
└─
```

5 CRITICAL SUCCESS FACTOR ANALYSIS

INTRODUCTION The computer systems of the past have inundated executives with reports. The typical executive is overwhelmed by information. He asks: "Why do I have to wade through all these reports, yet I can't find most of the information I need to manage the business well?"

Many functional managers have an interest in feeding information to a higher-level manager. The higher-level manager is flooded with this information, yet cannot find the most critical pieces of information he needs to detect and solve problems. If not planned well, computers can have the negative effect of causing an overload of not-very-useful information. This problem is felt by high-level executives in all industries, and often their frustration level is high.

Despite this, if you ask an executive what information he needs, he tends to ask for everything. If you ask what decisions he makes, he can provide a daunting list. In practice, there are a small number of pieces of information that are particularly critical to an executive's job and a relatively small number of decisions that are especially important. A technique used with great success in a growing number of corporations analyzes the *critical success factors* of the enterprise and its executives.

John F. Rockart [1,2] originally developed the critical success factor (CSF) approach as a means to understand the information requirements of a chief executive officer. It has subsequently been applied to the enterprise as a whole and extended into a broader planning methodology [3]. It has been made the basis of several consulting practices* and has achieved major results where used well. Some large consulting firms have made CSF analysis an integral part of

*Consulting practices include Index Systems, Ernst and Young, McKinsey & Company, and James Martin Associates.

their information engineering methodology,† and this is clearly where it belongs.

Rockart defined CSFs as "those few critical areas where things must go right for the business to flourish" [2]. A corporate president can be asked to identify a handful of factors of paramount importance for the corporation to succeed fully—aspects of running the business that must be done well if overall success is to be achieved. He is asked to describe the factors *most* critical for success. Most corporate presidents find this question interesting and relevant, and, after thinking about it, produce a good answer.

Once the CSFs for the corporation as a whole are determined, a lower level of CSFs can be established for each of the top-management team. What are the CSFs for the vice-president of marketing, the vice-president of production, the vice-president of information systems, and so on? When these CSFs are determined, those for the next level can be established. In this way CSFs can be found for all the executives, and the motivations of the executives can be related to the achievement of the success described in the CSFs.

Consultants with much experience in critical success factor analysis have developed interviewing techniques for establishing the most appropriate CSFs for an enterprise. When a CSF is established, measurements must be determined so that executives can monitor continually whether the success in question is being achieved. Regular reports or screen graphics are needed. A monitoring process should alert managers to slippage below the desirable levels.

An appealing feature of CSF analysis is that it can be done quickly with little manpower. Two skilled interviewers working for three weeks or so have done a good job of CSF analysis in some corporations. It requires three hours or so of time of the executives interviewed. For this relatively low investment, results have been achieved which fundamentally improve the management processes and lead to far more effective information systems.

EFFECTS OF CSF ANALYSIS

Critical success factor analysis tends to have two effects on individual executives. First, it helps them focus on those activities that are most important. Baron von Clausewitz, writing his classic work *On War* for the German general staff, stated that the most effective general concentrates his forces on the few significant battles. A less effective general scatters his forces throughout the entire battle area. Similarly, an effective executive concentrates his efforts on the critical success factors.

Second, it helps them think through their information needs. It helps information system planners to identify critical information and get it to execu-

---

†Ernst and Young employs an integrated information engineering methodology which includes CSF analysis, with software built by KnowledgeWare Inc.

tives who need it, along with appropriate decision-support tools and resources. It helps in the planning and prioritizing of decision-support system building.

A good manager, like a good general, has *implicit* CSFs that he employs, often subconsciously. CSF analysis makes implicit CSFs *explicit*. The interviewing technique turns a spotlight on them, refines them, possibly adds to them, and enables managerial priorities to be set more knowledgeably. CSF analysis, then, is a valuable managerial technique independent of computers. Using computers turns it from a technique used by individuals into a control mechanism that pervades the entire enterprise and enables *business strategy planning* to be translated into *information strategy planning*.

Results from the CSF interviews are immediately useful. They are employed long before the requisite information systems can be built. They make human control mechanisms better and cause an enterprise to focus on what is most critical. With them, allocation of resources can be improved, particularly executives' time. It is important to stress, then, that CSF is extremely valuable in enabling a corporation to be managed better, independent of the use of the method for building better computer systems.

DEFINITIONS

Critical success factors are different from objectives or goals. The following definitions are used in the Center for Information Systems Research (CISR) at M.I.T. [2].

Objectives. Objectives are general statements about the directions in which a firm intends to go, without stating specific targets to be reached at particular points in time.

Goals. Goals are specific targets that are intended to be reached at a given point in time. A goal is thus an operational transformation of one or more objectives.

Critical Success Factors (CSFs). CSFs are the limited number of areas in which satisfactory results will ensure competitive performance for the individual, department, or organization. CSFs are the few key areas where "things must go right" for the business to flourish and the manager's goals to be attained.

A manager's goals are the targets he will shoot for. The CSFs are the factors that most affect his success or failure in the pursuit of these goals. A goal is an overall objective; a CSF is what has to be done to achieve that goal. Goals are *ends;* CSFs are *means* to those ends.

The mission and purpose statements of an enterprise are often quite different from the critical success factors. The former represent long-range vision or an endpoint that the corporation wishes to achieve, whereas goals include statements such as "growth of 30 percent per year," "increase market share to 40 percent," and so on; critical success factors relate to the conduct of current operations and the key areas in which high performance is necessary. They give the measures that are necessary in a control system for top management. They need careful and continuous measurement and management attention if the organization is to be successful.

A CSF at one level may become a *goal* at a lower level. For example, a CSF at the top level may be "Retain top-quality managers." For the personnel department this becomes a goal and the CSFs needed to achieve this goal are established: for example, "Establish appraisal scheme to recognize executive talent," "Establish scheme to develop executive loyalty," "measure effectiveness of bonus/incentive plan."

In a business the critical success factors relate to those aspects of the business that will ensure competitive performance. They differ greatly from one type of business to another. They differ from one *time* to another. The external environment can change the critical success factors. For example, the petroleum crisis in the late 1970s changed them for the automobile industry. As a small corporation grows, it needs to shift gears and change its critical success factors.

EXAMPLES OF CSFs

Figure 5.1 gives examples of top-level CSFs for different industries. Some CSFs are common to the industry as a whole. Others are unique to particular corporations in the industry. Figure 5.2 shows CSFs for the medical clinic industry and shows CSFs for three particular clinics with different characteristics [1].

Critical success factors vary with the situation of a corporation within an industry. It might be a new corporation trying to carve a foothold in an established industry. In this case a critical success factor is the creation of products that are perceived by the customers as being better value, in some way, than those of the existing corporations. It may depend on searching for a gap in existing product lines or creating something that adds value to existing product lines.

New critical success factors may emerge into importance at certain times. For example, two corporations may merge, and for a period a critical success factor is the integration of their product lines and sales forces. A problem may arise, such as a major product line being made obsolete by competition, or software gaining a bad reputation. Recovery from these situations may be a critical success factor. Sometimes new critical success factors arise from external causes, such as the petroleum crisis, a local war removing strategic mineral sources, a new union contract, or the effect of new legislation.

CSFs may be established first for the enterprise as a whole, or for a chief executive officer. They may then be developed for the level below that—the major divisions of an enterprise. Figure 5.3 shows CSFs for a chain store corporation at the top level and at the level of six vice-presidents. CSFs may be developed for the level below this.

Automobile Industry

- Fuel economy
- Image
- Efficient dealer organization
- Tight control of manufacturing costs

Software House

- Product innovation
- Quality of sales and user literature
- Worldwide marketing and service
- Ease of use of products

Prepackaged Food Corporation

- Advertising effectiveness
- Good distribution
- Product innovation

Seminar Company

- Obtaining the best speakers
- Identification of topics
- Mailing list size and quality

Microelectronics Company

- Ability to attract and keep the best design staff
- Government R&D support
- Support of field sales force
- Identification of new market needs

Life Insurance Company

- Development of agency management personnel
- Advertising effectiveness
- Productivity of clerical operations

Figure 5.1 Some examples of business critical success factor lists.

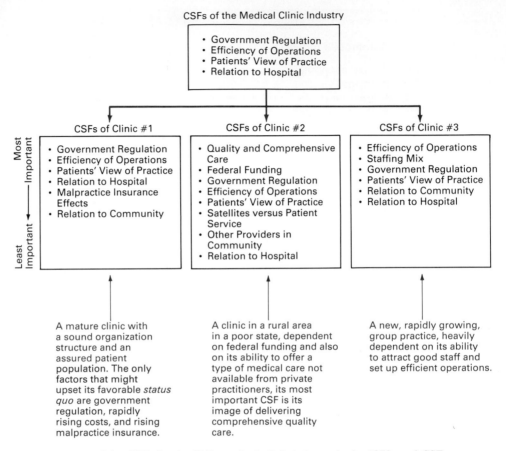

Figure 5.2   CSFs for the U.S. medical clinic industry in the 1970s and CSFs for three specific clinics studied by Gladys G. Mooradian [5]. Ten years later malpractice insurance effects had become a major CSF, along with controlling costs, which had risen to a much higher level.

NOT WHAT THE I.S. DESIGNER EXPECTED

Often, a chief executive's choice of critical success factors is not what an information system designer would have anticipated. For example, the following is a list from the president of a major oil company [1]:

1. Effecting organizational decentralization so that diversification can better take place to provide a broader earning base for future decades when petroleum supplies diminish

2. Liquidity (to facilitate acquisitions)

3. Relations with government

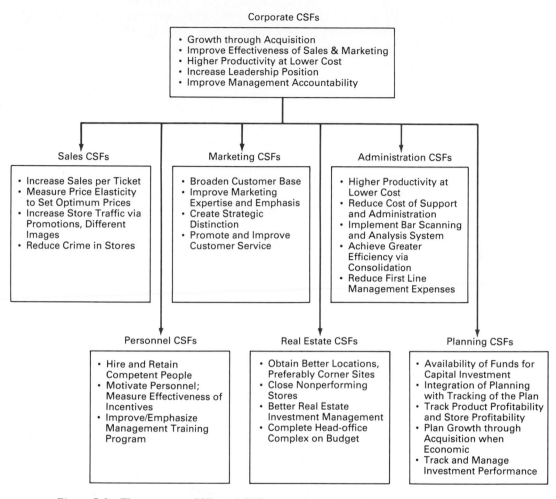

Figure 5.3 The corporate CSFs and CSFs at one level down for a chain store operation. CSFs may be established for managers a level below these.

4. Societal image

5. Success in new ventures

An information system designer often has a different view of what information is needed. It is essential therefore to develop the CSFs with the top management team using a methodology such as that described in this chapter.

CHARACTERISTICS OF CSFs   CSFs are quite different from "key indicators," which have been used by some earlier information system planners. They are not a standard set of measures that can be applied to all corporations. They are specific to a *particular* situation at a *particular* time. They have diverse measures. Some are evaluated with *soft* subjective measures. Some are evaluated through information *not currently gathered in an explicit way*.

Most CSFs are *internal;* some are *external*. Internal CSFs relate to actions that can be taken within the corporation, such as improving product quality or lowering inventory costs. External CSFs relate to factors in the outside world, such as company acquisitions or acquiring financing.

CSFs can be categorized as *monitoring* and *building*. *Monitoring* CSFs involve the scrutiny of existing situations, for example, tracking employee morale, or monitoring the quantity of defect reports. *Building* CSFs relate to changing the enterprise or future planning: for example, improving the product mix or setting up franchise operations. Managers who spend most of their time firefighting have mostly *monitoring* CSFs. Managers who are concerned primarily with planning have *building* CSFs. Most managers have a mix of building and monitoring CSFs.

Some top-level CSFs, as we said, are characteristics of an industry. Rockart quotes four CSFs of the supermarket industry [1]:

Product mix

Inventory

Sales promotion

Pricing

Every supermarket firm must be concerned about these four. Some firms may have CSFs unique to their particular needs: for example, ''Create marketing distinction'' or ''Growth through acquisition.''

CSFs can be thought of in a hierarchy. Some relate to an industry as a whole; some to the corporation; some to organizational units; and some to individual managers (Fig. 5.4). Rockart lists five sources of CSFs [2]:

- **The Industry.**
- **Competitive Strategy or Industry Position.** A corporation may have a particular niche or role within an industry. It may have unique strategies to grow faster than its competition in the industry.
- **Environmental Factors.** Environmental changes occur, such as rises in interest rates and changes in regulation. The corporation must take advantage of these if possible.
- **Temporal Factors.** These relate to short-term situations, often crises, such as a major accident, bad publicity, cash shortage, executive loss, or loss of a market segment because of sudden competitive products. Critical success factors relating to such crises may be important but short-lived.

Figure 5.4   The hierarchical nature of CSFs.

● **Managerial Position.** Some CSFs relate to a particular manager or his role. Certain jobs have certain CSFs associated with them.

MEASURES

It is necessary to measure critical success factors so that progress in achieving them can be tracked. Only very rarely do traditional financial accounting systems provide the required data. Sometimes, cost accounting systems provide useful data, but often the need for improved cost accounting is revealed in the critical success factor analysis.

A substantial proportion of the data needed cannot be provided as a *by-product* of conventional data processing. It must be specifically collected from other sources. It may then be stored in specially structured databases. Some of the required data comes from external sources.

Many critical success factors require data from a number of logical files that may be widely dispersed: for example, comparative profitability of all products, bid profit margin as a ratio of profit on similar jobs, and risk assessment in contracts by examination of experience with similar customer situations. These types of measures require database systems and high-level database languages that can assemble and manipulate the requisite data.

A small proportion of the critical success factors require subjective assessment rather than being easily quantifiable. Some factors can have only *soft* measures; however, usually there is some means of creating numeric measures. Top executives are used to this and spend much time with subjective judgments and measurements. Objective measures can often be found, but it takes considerable thought.

Sometimes considerable discussion is needed of how the factors will be measured. At other times there is too much data, and discussion relates to how the data can be appropriately summarized.

In some cases the discussion of how to measure a critical success factor results in several different measurements. For example, one organization needed to measure its *technological reputation with customers*. They developed seven possible measures of this. A simple numeric measure was the ratio of bids made to orders received. This had other factors affecting it, such as sales aggressiveness. Most soft measures consisted of person-to-person interviews. Several measures were used for the one factor. It was decided to initiate a process of top executives interviewing the customers because this was a highly critical success factor.

In the same organization the *morale of key scientists and engineers* was considered a critical success factor because of the importance to the company of these persons. Measures of this ranged from numeric data such as turnover, absenteeism, and lateness, to feedback from informal management discussions with employees. More formal employee assessment interviews could also be used, with the manager rating the employee on a morale scale.

Some critical success factors have revealed the need to build new, often small information systems. Today, these can usually be created with nonprocedural database languages. This makes them quick to create and easy to modify.

STRATEGIC PLANNING TOOL

A tool for strategic planning should store the critical success factors. The data model of the tool should store CSFs along with goals and problems described in Chapter 6. Figure 5.5 shows the data model for this tool.

Each manager (who manages one organizational unit) has typically from three to seven critical success factors. Whereas a goal may relate to multiple organizational units (and hence to multiple managers), a critical success factor

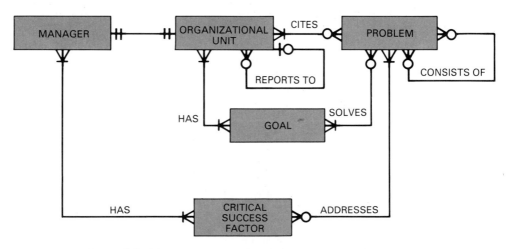

Figure 5.5 Metadata structure for goals and critical success factors.

is determined for a specific manager, and his performance in achieving it should be measured.

REPORTING

To track the achievement of critical success factors, a reporting system needs to be designed. This involves the design of appropriate databases. Executive information systems for monitoring CSFs should be developed.

Today, excellent software exists for building executive information systems. Executives can be provided with a color touch screen (or mouse-navigation screen) with excellent graphics, linked to an executive information system database. Building an executive information system with such software is relatively easy. The difficulty is identifying what information is really valuable to the executive. Executive information systems are discussed in Book III.

CRITICAL INFORMATION

To track the critical success factors, certain information must be available. This information should be modeled as part of the overall entity-relationship modeling described in Chapter 10. A list of critical information is created during the CSF analysis. Some of this information is internal. Some can be extracted from existing data processing systems. Some has to be specially developed. Some is information that exists externally and can be purchased. Some is external information that may be hard to obtain.

CRITICAL ASSUMPTION SET

Underlying the goals and CSFs of an enterprise are certain assumptions. The validity of these assumptions often changes with time. It is desirable to record the assumptions so that their validity can be discussed. Sometimes, to check the validity of the critical assumptions, certain information is needed. This becomes part of the critical information set.

Critical assumptions include such items as assumptions about competitive activities, the future price of oil, inflation, the effectiveness of incentive schemes, customer reaction to a new product, political factors, and social trends. These change with time. Experience indicates that a key to adapting the CSFs with time lies in understanding the assumption set that underlies the CSFs [3]. The critical assumptions need to be analyzed and monitored. A change in the business strategy may cause a change in the critical assumption set, which in turn changes the CSFs.

Executive information systems are sometimes designed to help track the

- Acquisition is the primary path to growth for convenience stores.
- Technology will improve productivity by 50 percent over the next three years.
- It will be two years before IBM markets a competing product.
- Characteristics of high-quality store managers are:
    Detail-oriented
    Works well with others
    High energy
    Able to develop people
    Good communications skills
    Meets budgets
- A 10 percent increase in price will reduce unit sales by 5 percent (this type of assumption should be represented with a price elasticity curve).
- We should grow through acquisition where economically feasible.
- The price of crude oil will rise by $5 in the next year.
- Expansion programs will be funded by cash flow.
- Technology dissemination will cause increased competition from small companies.
- Cash flow is the most significant restriction to growth
- The defined risk posture is appropriate to the objectives for growth.

Fig. 5.6   Typical examples of critical assumptions that underlie the CSFs.

critical assumptions. This ability is often *implicit* in the design; it should be made explicit. Figure 5.6 illustrates some typical examples of critical assumptions.

CRITICAL DECISIONS   Certain decisions are particularly critical in the running of an enterprise. When critical success factors are developed it is desirable to determine the particularly critical decisions. This leads to the building of decision support systems. In many cases actions can be taken quickly in information centers to provide aids for decision making; in some cases major decision-support system projects are necessary. Figure 5.7 lists typical examples of critical decisions.

Associated with the development of critical success factors, three lists should be produced: the critical information set, the critical assumption set, and the critical decision set:

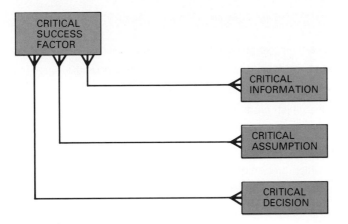

These lists are important input to the building of strategic data models, as shown in Fig. 5.8.

In some cases top executives take more interest in the critical assumption set than in the critical decision set. Much decision making, and the use of decision-support systems, is delegated to lower-level managers or staff. High executives may use executive information systems but less commonly use decision-support systems. Decision-support systems are used in great detail lower in the organization. High executives sometimes obtain critical information at the touch of a button, but do not often manipulate the information in a decision-support fashion. The critical *assumptions,* however, are regarded as part of the *judgment* that high executives are paid for.

ONGOING UPDATING　　　　Critical success factors change with time. New factors become important when competition changes or external factors change. For example, the rise of crude oil prices in the 1970s caused major changes in what was critical in various corporations. The decline in oil prices in 1986 dramatically changed the CSFs of oil companies. For some oil companies "corporate survival" became a CSF in 1986. CSFs may also change somewhat when the management team changes, because different executives have different views of what is critical and take different thrusts against competition.

In the following pages we describe a methodology for developing CSFs. A key part of that methodology is a *top-management focusing workshop* (Fig. 5.9). This workshop generates what is often a heated discussion of the enterprise and what is critical. The focusing workshop may be held, not once, but periodically to review the CSFs and update them as appropriate. Apart from modifications that result from changes in the enterprise and its world, modifications may be made as a result of experience with the CSFs and their consequent

- Determine the most profitable new product features.
- Determine priorities between development and acquisition.
- Determine appropriate debt/equity ratio.
- Determine which products should be dropped/replaced.
- Determine allocation between expenditures and debt retirement.
- Determine optimal advertising and promotion expenditure.
- Decide which properties to sell, acquire, or retain.
- Determine balance of entrepreneurial activity and controlled activity.
- Determine areas of maximum competitive advantage.
- Restructure worldwide maintenance activity taking advantage of computer network.
- Restructure MIS activities on the basis of fourth-generation methodologies.
- Determine whether new head-office complex should be built.
- Determine lease/purchase ratio for products.
- Should one objective be to have earning parallel to cash flow?
- Adjust rewards/incentives for key personnel.
- Determine maximum acceptable level of project risk.

Figure 5.7   Typical examples of critical decisions that are associated with CSFs.

building of executive information systems and decision-support systems. Reviewing the *critical assumption set* regularly can provide early warning that a change has occurred and the CSFs need modifying.

CSF ANALYSIS TEAM
Analysis and recording of the CSFs in an enterprise is sometimes done by the team that prepares the overall information strategy plan. Sometimes it is done by a specialized team. Some consultants have considerable expertise and experience in interviewing exccutives to establish CSFs. Often, the best arrangement is a two-person team one member of which is an external consultant skilled at this process, and the other an internal analyst who will maintain the CSF model when the external consultant has gone. The skill of the interviewers is critical. They should have as deep as possible an understanding of the industry, the enterprise, and the jobs of the executives they interview.

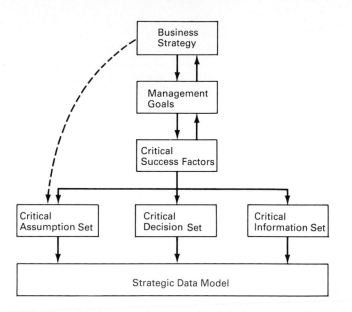

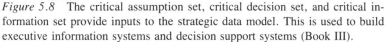

Figure 5.8 The critical assumption set, critical decision set, and critical information set provide inputs to the strategic data model. This is used to build executive information systems and decision support systems (Book III).

The CSF team has a unique opportunity to communicate with top management to achieve a better understanding of the corporation and its critical information needs. It must be well prepared for this opportunity. It often pays to use a top-level consultant who has performed CSF studies elsewhere, especially in other corporations in the same industry. The team should know the industry problems, issues, newsmakers, and its competitive drives. It should understand the corporation well, its industry positioning, its product thrust, its structure, and its politics.

Box 5.1 is an action diagram of a procedure for CSF analysis. Like all the action diagrams of procedures in this book, it may be adjusted to fit specific circumstances. The main stages in the procedure are shown in Fig. 5.9. When the CSFs, critical assumptions, critical information, and critical decisions are agreed upon, prototyping may be done of executive information systems and decision-support systems, as described in Book III.

PREPARATION
FOR THE STUDY
The second bracket in Box 5.1 is "Preparation by the CSF team." The team needs to study the CSF methodology and interviewing techniques (described below). The team members should make themselves as familiar with the industry as possible, reading appropriate articles in *Forbes, Business Week, Fortune, The*

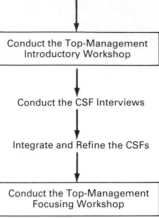

Prepare the CSF Team

Conduct the Top-Management
Introductory Workshop

Conduct the CSF Interviews

Integrate and Refine the CSFs

Conduct the Top-Management
Focusing Workshop

Figure 5.9 A methodology for developing CSFs. This is shown in detail in
the action diagram of Box 5.1.

Wall Street Journal, and so on, and perhaps reading market studies on the industry. One or more team members should be selected because of their knowledge of the industry.

The team members should study the corporation. They can study its annual
reports, internal documents, organization charts, and job descriptions. A computerized tool may facilitate the drawing of an organization chart and associate
windows of information with the organizational units. At least one member of
the team should be familiar with the enterprise as a whole, its politics, and its
top personalities. The strategy, opportunities, environment, and current problems should be discussed in detail. As part of its own preparation, the team
should record what it perceives to be the goals, problems, CSFs, and CSF measures for the enterprise. This is done as an exercise prior to the first top-management workshop and should not be allowed to bias the collection of goals,
problems, CSFs, and so on, as stated by management. The team members
should spend time with top management making themselves as familiar as possible with the current strategies, viewpoints, politics, and opportunities.

INTRODUCTORY   Before the management interviews begin, an intro-
WORKSHOP   ductory workshop should be conducted with a small
                         top-management group. This explains the CSF pro-
cedure and why it is valuable. It indicates that a rethinking of the enterprise is
likely to ensue, not merely the planning of information systems.

In the introductory workshop the goals and major problems of the enterprise are discussed and recorded. A list is established of the managers who
should be interviewed in the following weeks. Top management agrees to give

BOX 5.1 An action diagram of the procedure for establishing critical success factors, critical information, critical decisions, and critical assumptions

Initial Determination of Critical Success Factors

    Establish the CSF team

    (This may be comprised of one external CSF consultant and at least one internal analyst.)

    Preparation by the CSF team

        Study CSF methodology

        Study CSF interviewing techniques

        Be fully familiar with the industry

        Study the corporation (annual reports, history, organization chart, policies, products, competitive products, literature)

        Spend time with the company management and people who have views on its competitive position, problems and opportunities

        Probe and try to understand the internal company politics

        List the mission of the enterprise, along with its perceived goals and problems

        List possible CSFs and measures for the enterprise (this is done as preparation for the introductory workshop and should not be allowed to bias the collecting of goals, problems, and CSFs from top management)

    Conduct an introductory workshop with a small key top management group

        Explain the CSF procedure

        Establish the goals of the enterprise

        Establish the major problems

        Determine which managers should be interviewed

        Solicit the active involvement of a key member of top management

        Set a date of the focusing workshop in which the results will be examined and discussed

(Continued)

BOX 5.1 *(Continued)*

Set up the interviews

  Send letters to the interviewees

    Explain the purpose of the interview

    Show top management support

    Send them a copy of this chapter or book

    Send them an outline of the interview

  Arrange dates and times, interviewing the lowest level managers first

For each manager interviewed (with the lowest level managers first)

  Prepare for the interview

    Assume the role of the interviewee

    List his probable goals, problems

    List possible CSFs and CSF measures

    List possible critical decisions, critical assumptions, and critical information (this is done as an aid to preparation and should not be allowed to bias the interviewee's statements of CSFs, etc.)

  Conduct the interview

    Discuss the interviewee's views of the enterprise (possibly gathering information that will help in subsequent interviews)

    Clarify the interviewee's understanding about the CSF procedure

    Obtain the interviewee's description of his mission and role

    Discuss the interviewee's goals (the goals for his organizational unit)

    Determine the problems the interviewee perceives in meeting his goals

    Develop critical success factors

    Establish priorities for the CSFs

    Discuss ways to measure the CSFs

    Record all of the above with a computerized planning

BOX 5.1   *(Continued)*

```
L  L     tool

   ┌ Aggregate the results

        Produce a coordinated listing of critical success factors

        Establish a critical information set

        Establish a critical assumption set

        Establish a critical decision set

   ┌ Review results

        Distribute the statements of goals and CSFs to the top
        management team

        ┌ Conduct a top management focusing workshop

             Discuss the goals and CSFs with the top management
             team (this is a key meeting which usually provokes
             much argument about the enterprise, its goals,
             problems, and CSFs)

             Modify the goals and CSFs as appropriate

             Achieve consensus

             Revise critical information

             Revise critical assumptions

             Revise critical decisions

        Refine and distribute the goals and CSFs
```

full support to the interviewers. Active involvement of a key member of top management is solicited. A date is set for the focusing workshop, when the results of the CSF interviews will be reviewed and debated. This second workshop is very critical.

SETTING UP
THE INTERVIEWS

A letter is sent to each of the interviewees explaining the nature and purpose of the interviews and indicating top-management support. A date is set for the interview. The interviews should progress from the lowest-level managers to the highest level. Much information and experience will be gathered in the lowest-level interviews that will help in the higher-level ones. The interviewee is provided with an outline of the interview and some information about the CSF technique. He may be provided with a copy of this chapter or this book.

PREPARATION FOR THE INTERVIEW

Before a CSF interview the interviewer needs to be as thoroughly prepared as possible. He should assume the role of the interviewee. He should list his probable goals, problems, CSFs and CSF measures, critical assumptions, critical decisions, and critical information. There may be much discussion of these. This is done as an aid to preparing for the interview and should not be allowed to bias the real interview when it occurs.

Some corporations have elicited individual managers' CSFs with *one* interview; some have used *two* interviews: the first a preliminary interview which sets the manager thinking about his CSFs, and the second, a few days later, an interview to record his thoughts and discuss them. We describe the *one-interview* approach here, which is faster. Detailed discussion of the CSFs gathered follows in the top-management review workshop. Other interviews are needed when the activity moves to the later stage of defining and prototyping systems for CSF reporting.

The interview may begin with a general discussion of the interviewee's views of the enterprise. Information may be gathered in this discussion that will help in the other CSF interviews. The interviewer should then establish that the manager understands the CSF procedure and the purpose of the interviews. He should explain that earlier ''management information systems'' failed to meet the needs of management, and that the CSF procedure is intended to establish the most important information needs of management and help in identifying the most useful decision-support systems and executive support systems.

When the manager has had his questions about the purpose of the interview satisfied, the interviewer should ask the manager to describe his mission and role. The interviewer will sense to what extent the manager ''adds value'' to the information he handles. Does he perceive his role as being to change the enterprise or to carry out procedures developed by past managers?

The manager should be asked to identify his goals (or the goals of his organizational unit). The time span of the goals should be noted. Very long term goals have little effect on current CSFs. Goals that should be accomplished within a year or so are the ones that are important to the interviewer.

Many managers have written goals that were established in a counsel-and-appraisal interview or in a formal MBO (management-by-objectives) procedure. Managers are often measured on the accomplishment of these goals. The list is recorded by the interviewer and the interviewer asks the manager what goals he has that are not on the list—goals that are less formally stated. The informal goals can be important input to the CSF planning process. Occasionally, they are more important than the formally written goals.

Next, the manager may be asked what problems the enterprise, or his organization unit, has. Sometimes the goals relate to the *solution* of these problems; sometimes the problems *inhibit* the achievement of the goals.

Now the interview focuses on the most important subject—developing the critical success factors. Sometimes the manager has done his homework and produces a written list of CSFs; sometimes the interviewer has to elicit them through discussion.

Rockart recommends three questions for zeroing in on critical success factors [2]:

1. What are those things you see as critical success factors for your job at this time?
2. In what one, two, or three areas would failure to perform hurt you the most? Where would you hate to see something go wrong?
3. If you were isolated from the business for two weeks, with no communication at all, what would you most want to know about the business?

In practice, a good interviewer employs a variety of cross-checking questions as the interview proceeds. He needs to be helpful but not to put words into the manager's mouth. He should *draw out* CSFs, not tell the manager what the CSFs should be. The interviewer must avoid "leading the witness." This is more difficult if the manager has not thought about the concept and hence needs illustrations, anecdotes, and prompting. For this reason managers must be encouraged to do their homework prior to the interview.

The interviewer should check the list in the following ways to ensure that the interview has not had a limited focus:

- Have *external* CSFs been considered as well as *internal* CSFs: for example, CSFs relating to interest rates, the price of oil, competitive thrusts, new technology, regulatory issues, and so on?
- Have *building* CSFs been considered as well as *monitoring* CSFs: for example, new product designs, uses of new technology, restructuring the procedures or the organization?
- Have *short-term* factors been considered: for example, current crises, accidents, cash shortages, competitive announcements?
- Have CSFs been considered that relate to:
  the position or viewpoint of the manager in the enterprise?
  activities of competition?
  the industry in general?
- Make sure that the list is not restricted to CSFs that have *hard* measures. Some important CSFs have *soft* measures.

- Make sure that the list is not limited to CSFs that are appropriate for computerization. The objective is to elicit *all* information needs.

- Often, the same CSF is stated in multiple ways. Aggregate the CSF list to help prevent this redundancy.

- Often, a manager gets stuck discussing in many ways a current area of concern. Ensure that past and future concerns are also examined.

SETTING PRIORITIES FOR CSFs

Sometimes additional insight can be obtained by asking which of the CSFs are most important, and prioritizing them. Absolute priorities are not essential and would often be difficult to establish. Prioritization does help to focus on the most important concerns.

DETERMINING MEASURES FOR CSFs

It is essential to be able to measure a CSF. The appropriate measures, and sources of data to establish the measures should be discussed in the interview. Often, multiple measures are used for one CSF. The interviewee may indicate measures that he uses now, but which are unusual. It is useful to establish measures at this point, because these may be important in the establishment of data models. The final determination of measures may wait until a later stage when prototypes of information systems or decision-support systems are created.

Often, the establishment of measures leads to the need for a specific database. For example, in a large chain of convenience stores a critical success factor was the optimal pricing of the goods. A difference in price of 10 cents could make a large difference in sales and profit. Optimal pricing required the measurement of price elasticity. This could be done by installing bar-scanning equipment in the stores and experimenting with price changes to establish how sales of different goods responded to price changes, and so establishing points on a price elasticity curve. This price elasticity data was not measured prior to establishment of the critical success factor.

COORDINATING THE RESULTS

When the interviews are complete, the team should coordinate and refine the results. The CSFs lower in the hierarchy should relate to the CSFs higher in the hierarchy. A coordinated listing should be produced and distributed to the managers involved. Further dialog with them may produce more refinements before the top-management review workshop.

From the coordinated CSFs a critical information set, critical decision set, and critical assumption set should be established. Different managers and different organizational units have *some* critical information needs and critical decision sets in common. Decision-support systems will be built that serve the needs of more than one organizational unit. For example, several organizational units may list as critical the hiring and retention of competent high-quality people. A central personnel system concerned with finding, measuring, motivating and compensating good people may serve many organizational units. The list of CSFs, critical information, critical decisions, and critical assumptions should be circulated prior to holding the top-management focusing workshop.

TOP-MANAGEMENT FOCUSING WORKSHOP The workshop to review the CSFs is a particularly important meeting. One vice-president of finance commented about it: "This is the key meeting. The interviews are merely a preliminary, a "softening-up" process in which managers get an initial opportunity to think deeply about the corporation, as well as to develop relationships with the consultants" [4]. It is vital that the participants study the CSFs, think about them, and make notes

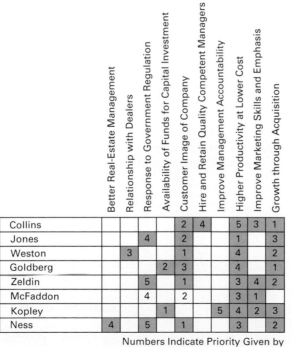

	Better Real-Estate Management	Relationship with Dealers	Response to Government Regulation	Availability of Funds for Capital Investment	Customer Image of Company	Hire and Retain Quality Competent Managers	Improve Management Accountability	Higher Productivity at Lower Cost	Improve Marketing Skills and Emphasis	Growth through Acquisition
Collins					2	4		5	3	1
Jones			4		2			1		3
Weston		3			1			4		2
Goldberg				2	3			4		1
Zeldin			5		1			3	4	2
McFaddon			4		2			3	1	
Kopley				1			5	4	2	3
Ness	4		5		1			3		2

Numbers Indicate Priority Given by Executive to CSF

Figure 5.10 CSFs of the top executives obtained in separate interviews are combined to obtain corporate CSFs in the top-management focusing workshops.

prior to this meeting. In this focusing meeting management should be ready for a vigorous discussion of what can make the company succeed. The debate is often heated. Differing perspectives and desires emerge. Untangling the differences and focusing on the basic needs of the business is an exciting process to most top managers.

A matrix such as that in Fig. 5.10 may be presented to the workshop, showing the CSFs listed by various executives and the priorities they placed on them. A matrix displayed with a computerized tool may be adjusted during the workshop with the objective of reaching consensus about the corporate CSFs. Seeing the CSFs in black and white is very different from an intuitively felt set of notions about the business. Sometimes it is a revelation. Some CSFs are a surprise to some executives.

The objective of this meeting is to achieve top-management consensus on identification of the CSFs. Rockart and Crescenzi [4] quote one executive as saying: "During the meeting our concept of the organization structure went from an organization chart that looked like that on the left [of Fig. 5.11] to one that looked like that on the right. This is important. It affected our system's design enormously. More important, it has *affected the way we manage the business.*"

IMMEDIATE SYSTEM PROTOTYPING

In general, *information engineering* advocates a progression through the stages of information strategy planning, business area analysis, design, and construction. However, when top management CSFs are developed it is desirable that these should be employed *immediately*. Extraction of the required data for tracking the CSF may be done quickly and this data summarized appropriately and made available in executive information systems.

When *critical decisions* are identified it is desirable to build a decision-

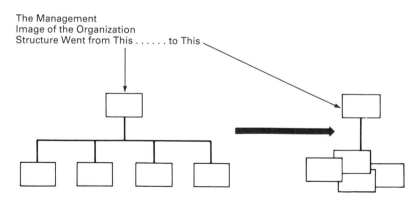

Figure 5.11 The focusing session enabled top management to see the interconnectedness of the critical success factors and critical decisions.

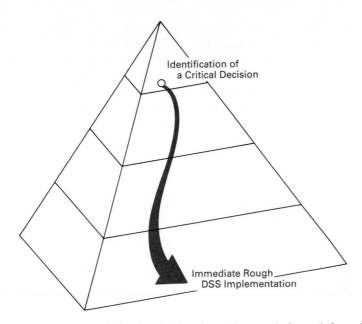

Identification of
a Critical Decision

Immediate Rough
DSS Implementation

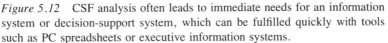

Figure 5.12   CSF analysis often leads to immediate needs for an information
system or decision-support system, which can be fulfilled quickly with tools
such as PC spreadsheets or executive information systems.

support decision as quickly as possible. Much decision making can be supported
with relatively simple tools such as LOTUS 1-2-3, Javelin, or multidimensional
spreadsheet tools. Some decisions need highly sophisticated systems that take
much longer to develop. In many cases a simple tool is a valuable stopgap until
a sophisticated system can be built.

     When executive information systems or decision-support systems are
planned, a prototype should be created quickly. Often, the prototype is highly
modified. Iteration through multiple prototypes is common.

     Prototyping of such systems related to critical success factors should be
done quickly, before the ISP or relevant BAAs are completed (Fig. 5.12). It is
clearly urgent to get CSF information to executives who need it. Later, as the
more comprehensive analysis and design is done, the early quick-and-dirty systems will evolve into more elegant integrated systems.

**INPUT TO THE
STRATEGIC
PLANNING
PROCESS**

Once an enterprise is being managed with the help of
critical success factors, these should be an ongoing
input to the top-management planning process. They
should be reviewed at strategic business planning sessions. In some corporations the top CSFs are used at

board meetings. Board members review them before the meeting and discuss whether they are still appropriate or whether a new one is necessary.

As we commented earlier, the focusing workshop, which is a key part of the procedure in Fig. 5.9, should be conducted periodically—once a year is often appropriate. CSFs, and their associated information systems and decision-support systems, then become a vital part of the ongoing process of management.

REFERENCES

1. John F. Rockart, Chief executives define their own data needs, *Harvard Business Review,* March–April 1979.

2. Christine V. Bullen and John F. Rockart, *A Primer on Critical Success Factors,* Center for Information Systems Research, Working Paper 69. Cambridge, Mass.: Sloan School of Management, M.I.T., June 1981.

3. John C. Henderson, John F. Rockart, and John G. Sifonis, *A Planning Methodology for Integrating Management Support Systems,* Center for Information Systems Research, Working Paper 116. Cambridge, Mass.: Sloan School of Management, M.I.T., September 1984.

4. John F. Rockart and Adam D. Crescenzi, Engaging top management in information technology, *Sloan Management Review 25* (4), 3–16, 1984.

5. Gladys G. Mooradian, The key variables in planning and control in medical group practices. Master's thesis, Sloan School of Management, M.I.T., Cambridge, Mass., 1976.

6 TECHNOLOGY IMPACT ANALYSIS

INTRODUCTION   It is the job of top management to perceive the enterprise not as it is today but as what it can become in the future. The view of what the enterprise can become is often reflected in a financial model that projects the revenues and expenses five or more years into the future and breaks them into detail. There are many assumptions inherent in such a model and they need to be documented and as far as possible validated. Over a five-year span a corporation may introduce many new products or services, and change or drop existing ones. The view of the future affects many of the current plans and expenditures. A major data processing system or corporate network takes two or more years to build, so it needs to be built with a view of future needs. Much of the planning of information systems needs to be long-range planning.

During the next five years great changes in technology will occur. We can expect to see new technology coming into use at a furious rate for the next two decades. New technology offers new business and management opportunities, and poses new competitive threats. At a time of great technological change there are many bankruptcies and takeovers among corporations whose managers did not have enough foresight or did not act on their foresight. Top management is often unaware of all the critical changes in technology and the business opportunities that they present, and often opportunities are missed or corporations find that competition is overtaking them.

Technology impact analysis employs a structured representation of technological changes and relates these to business and management opportunities and competitive threats. These become three objects in the encyclopedia:

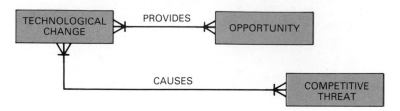

They relate to organizational units, goals, and problems:

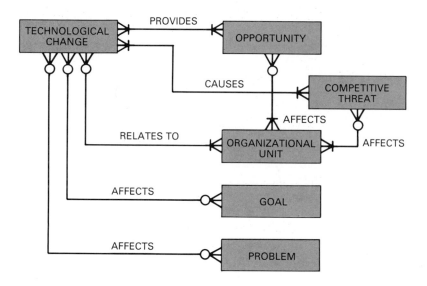

A TECHNOLOGY ACTION DIAGRAM   A taxonomy of technological changes can be hierarchical in nature and can conveniently be represented on an action diagram, as in Fig. 6.1. Box 6.1 shows a more detailed version of this action diagram. Saying "EXPAND" on any line preceded by three dots will reveal more detail. The version in Box 6.1 has had *Telecommunications* EXPANDED. This represents a view of what was happening in telecommunications in the late 1980s. The same model of technology also contained estimates for future periods of how the technology would evolve. This was valuable for assessing the possible business thrusts that the technology would make possible. James Martin Associates used a far more detailed model of future technology and its impact, represented in the form of an intelligent hyperdocument [1, 2].

The group responsible for strategic planning should maintain such a model of future technology. The diagram in Box 6.1 relates only to information technology. Others may be maintained relating to molecular biology, medicine, materials, and so on, as appropriate to the enterprise in question. The list of tech-

```
 ┌ Technological Changes

   ...COMPUTERS
   ...WORKSTATIONS
   ...NETWORKS
 ┌ TELECOMMUNICATIONS
   ┌ Technology
     ...Speeds
     ...Network digitization
     ...Switching
     ...ISDN
     ...Satellites and space
     ...Cellular radio
   └ ...Telecommunications standards

   ┌ Devices
     ...PBXs
     ...Facsimile machines
   └ ...Teleconferencing
 └

   ...STORAGE MEDIA
   ...DATABASE
   ...CHIPS, etc.
   ...SOFTWARE
   ...SECURITY TECHNOLOGY
   ...PRINT TECHNOLOGY, etc.
   ...VIDEO TECHNOLOGY
   ...INSTRUMENTS
   ...ARTIFICIAL INTELLIGENCE
   ...ROBOTS
   ...TOOLS AND TECHNIQUES
   ...NEW APPLICATIONS
 └ ...MISCELLANEOUS
```

Figure 6.1 An action diagram of technological changes.

BOX 6.1 A detailed representation of Fig. 6.1, technological change

```
 ┌ Technological Changes

   ┌ COMPUTERS
     ...Micros
     ...Personal computers
     ...Minis
     ...Mainframes
     ...Supercomputers
   └ ...Parallel processors
   ┌ WORKSTATIONS
     ...Low-cost terminals
     ...Personal computers
     ...Diskless PCs
     ...High-cost workstations
     ...Intelligent non-PCs
   └ ...Laser printers
```

(Continued)

BOX 6.1 *(Continued)*

```
NETWORKS
...Standards
  Within enterprise
  ...LANs
  Inter-enterprise
  ...EDI


TELECOMMUNICATIONS
  L80.Speeds
        Speed of fast single-strand optical fibers:   565 Mbps
        Capacity of major multi-fiber optical trunks: 50 Bbps

        Optical fibers increase in speed at a rapid rate.
        Bit rate X transmission distance (without repeaters) doubles
         every year, and will continue to double every year.

      L80.Bit rates of monomode single-strand optical fibers


                   1980      1990
         35 Bbps ..+....+....LLL
                  +     + LLL+
         8.8 Bbps .+....LLL..+
                  +  LL+    +
         2.2 Bbps .+.LL.+....FFF
                  +LL  +    +          ┌─────────────────────────┐
         565 Mbps .L....+.FFFF         │ LLLL = Bit rate in       │
                  L+   +    +          │         the laboratory.  │
         140 Mbps .+..FFFF...+         │ FFFF = Bit rate in       │
                  +    +   +           │         the field.       │
         35 Mbps FFFFF.+....+          └─────────────────────────┘
                   1980      1990


  L80.Network digitization
        A high proportion of PTT networks are now digital. By comparison
        with speech or television, text is inexpensive to transmit in
        that it requires a relatively small number of bits. One hour of
        video transmission is equivalent to about ten million Western
        Union telegrams.

  L80.Switching
        The first prototype optical switches are demonstrated.
        NEC had an 8x8 optical switch at Telecom '87, which they claimed
        was a commercial product used for in-house switched video.

  L80.ISDN

        First ISDN systems come into operation.
        First ISDN chip sets are produced, but some problems with ISDN
         standards have yet to be resolved.
        A few corporations adopt ISDN as a standard, using ISDN PBXs
         leased lines in most locations because ISDN public switching
         is not yet available.
        Most PBXs offer some form of ISDN interface, not all entirely
         comply with the CCITT standards; this causes some confusion.
        First attempts at ISDN tariffing are not favorable. ISDN is
         still seen as an expensive option when compared to 19.2 Kbps
         voice grade lines.
```

BOX 6.1 *(Continued)*

The concept and capabilities of ISDN are still not well
understood by many corporate DP and telecommunications managers.
Most PTTs and BOCs begin a major customer education program to
move customers to ISDN services. In the U.S., some customers
are experimenting with ISDN Centrex. In Europe, Centrex usage
is limited but is expected to expand as PTTs facing deregulation
see Centrex as a means of competing with PBX suppliers.

A lack of agreed inter-PBX common channel signaling standards
makes establishing multi-vendor ISDN PBX networks difficult.
In Europe the DPNSS standard is widely supported but lacks
support in the US.

CCITT standards for inter-PBX signaling are not expected until
1990/91.

L80. Satellites and space

After the disaster with the US space shuttle, and subsequent
problems with other launch vehicles, many telecommunications
satellites are not launched as planned.

The Soviets launch their large-capacity Energia booster.

There is growing corporate use of satellite communications in
the USA.

Fast growth of television seminars via satellite broadcasting
in the USA with dial-up telephone responses, for training,
sales presentations and company meetings. The increased
availability of satellite time in Europe causes the
introduction of US-style satellite seminars.

L80. Satellites in Europe

Europe launches the first Ka-band satellite, and demonstrates
very-small-aperture receive-only earth stations in use well
before they will be available in the USA.

Satellite television expands in Europe using existing Ku-band
and new Ka-band satellites.

Some of the consequences of pan-European satellite television
are arguments about standards for decency on TV, regulatory
problems, and pan-European advertising campaigns which help
stimulate intra-EEC trade.

There is a growth of black-market receive-only earth stations
in eastern Europe. The eastern-block countries complain of
their air-waves being polluted by capitalist propaganda and
decadent values, which fosters moral decay.

L80. Cellular radio

Cellular radio telephone systems spread.

Cellular phones in cars become popular and will require smaller
cell sizes, which in turn will lead to smaller, cheaper sets,
which in turn will lead to higher sales, which will lead to
smaller cell sizes...

L80. Telecommunications standards

The CCITT continues to develop standards for 64 Kbps ISDN,
particularly in the areas of #7 signaling, numbering schemes,
etc.

The CCITT agree on a 2.048 Mpbs transmission standard for videoconferencing.

ISDN rate standards for videoconferencing are not expected until
the end of 1990/91.

OSI standards mature to layer 6.

X.400, FTAM, and virtual terminal application layer standards
are in use. A major problem with ISO higher layer standards
is internationally agreed conformance testing.

OSI standards for network management are still not available;
this restricts some users' implementation of OSI networks.

(Continued)

BOX 6.1 *(Continued)*

There is continued government support in both Europe and the US
for OSI, most government computer network contracts specify
OSI conformance.
OSI is expected to get a major boost as more corporations
implement networks for EDI (electronic data interchange
between corporations).

Devices
...PBXs
...Facsimile machines
...Teleconferencing

STORAGE MEDIA
...Dropping storage costs
...Magnetic disks
Optical disks

Large optical disks

Compact disks
CD (music)
CD ROM
CDI
Players

Video disks

...Multi-disk units

...Tape and cartridge
...Microfiche, etc.
...Plastic cards
...Archival media

DATABASE
Database software
...Relational databases
...DSS databases

Database machines
Large DB machines
Small DB machines

CHIPS, etc
Memory chips

256K Rams (available 1984)
1 Mbit Rams (available 1987)
4 Mbit Rams (available 1989)
16 Mbit Rams (available 1992)

Processor chips
Intel
Intel 80286 (available 1983)
Intel 80386 (available 1986)
Intel 80486 (available 1990)

BOX 6.1 *(Continued)*

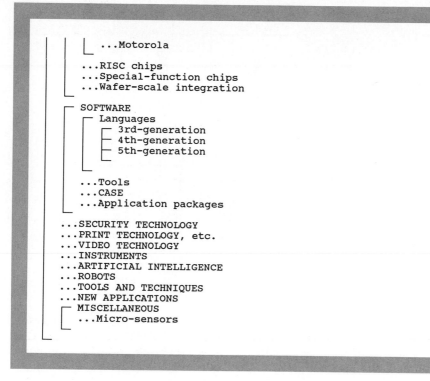

```
          └─ ...Motorola
       ...RISC chips
       ...Special-function chips
       └─ ...Wafer-scale integration
    ┌─ SOFTWARE
    │  ┌─ Languages
    │  │   ┌─ 3rd-generation
    │  │   ├─ 4th-generation
    │  │   ├─ 5th-generation
    │  └─
    │  ...Tools
    │  ...CASE
    └─ ...Application packages
    ...SECURITY TECHNOLOGY
    ...PRINT TECHNOLOGY, etc.
    ...VIDEO TECHNOLOGY
    ...INSTRUMENTS
    ...ARTIFICIAL INTELLIGENCE
    ...ROBOTS
    ...TOOLS AND TECHNIQUES
    ...NEW APPLICATIONS
 ┌─ MISCELLANEOUS
 │   ...Micro-sensors
 └─
```

nological changes needs modifying frequently, so it should be maintained on a medium which makes the updating of a taxonomy easy.

BUSINESS AND MANAGEMENT OPPORTUNITIES

An enterprise should develop its own list of business and management opportunities that result from technological changes. The list of competitive threats is related directly to the list of opportunities. Most of them result from competition using the technology in the same way, but perhaps with better marketing, greater capital, or different corporate alliances.

Box 6.2 shows a list of typical opportunities relating to information technology. An action diagram editor is used to show a hierarchical taxonomy.

Again hyperdocument software can be used as may link the opportunity model to the future-technology model. The technological changes can be mapped against business opportunities:

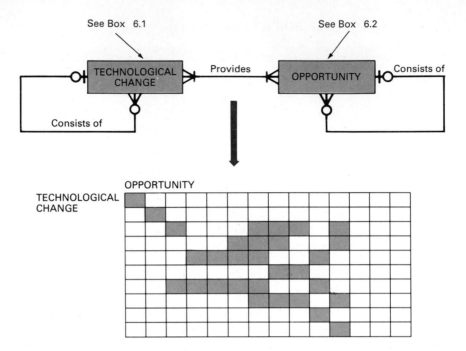

Because both the list of technologies and opportunities are large, it is desirable that the list and the corresponding matrix be CONTRACTable and EXPANDable, using the three-dots notation (seen in Boxes 6.1 and 6.2) to indicate where something can be expanded. The opportunities and competitive threats can be related to the organizational units affected by them.

EFFORT REQUIRED

Like critical success factor analysis, technology impact analysis can be done fairly quickly and inexpensively, if existing technology models are used. Two analysts who are alert to new technology can complete such a study in three months or so. Sometimes one of the two is from a consulting firm that has done such studies before. The return on this investment is often very high. It is a form of analysis that every major corporation should do.

The work may start by using existing models of technology trends and business/management opportunities, such as those in Boxes 6.1 and 6.2. The action diagrams can be added to and edited to meet the needs of the enterprise in question.

The identification of trends, opportunities, and threats may be done in initial brainstorming sessions. These often have five or so participants and a neutral moderator who organizes the session. A typical session lasts for two hours or so. It attempts to produce ideas in an uninhibited fashion. A principle

BOX 6.2 An action diagram of business and management opportunities

```
┌─* Business and Management Opportunities
│   ┌─ Production
│   │  ...Robots
│   │  ...Computer Integrated Manufacturing
│   │  ...Cellular Factory Organization
│   └─ ...Expert Systems for Production Scheduling
│
│   ┌─ Supplies and Inventory
│   │
│   │  ...Just-in-time Inventory Control
│   │  ...Online Terminals in Suppliers
│   │  ...Terminals on Line to Suppliers' Scheduling System
│   │  ...Integrated Control of Suppliers
│   └─ ...Suppliers Make in Factory Complex
│
│   ┌─ Engineering
│   │
│   │  ...Computer-Aided Design
│   │  ...C.A.D. Center
│   │  ...Simultaneous Engineering of Product and Production Facility
│   │  ...Expert Systems for Design
│   │  ...Computerized Training
│   └─ ...Online Parts Database
│
│   ┌─ Marketing
│   │
│   │  ...Telemarketing
│   │  ...Online Catalog
│   │  ...Expert System for Setting Discounts
│   │  ...Computerized Mailing
│   │  ...Customers on Line to Marketing Database
│   │  ...Terminals in Agents
│   │  ...Terminals in Retailers
│   │  ...Customer Corporations on Line
│   │  ...Dealers:  Smaller, Larger number, Online
│   └─ ...Worldwide Sales/Marketing Network
│
│   ┌─ Sales
│   │
│   │  ...Salesmen with Portable Terminals
│   │  ...Expert Systems for Salesmen
│   │  ...Expert System for Order Configuration
│   │  ...CDI for Training
│   │  ...Video Tapes for Training
│   └─ ...Screen Order Entry
│
│   ┌─ Products
│   │
│   │  ...Product Redesign for Robot Fabrication
│   │  ...Intelligence in Products
│   │  ...New Products
└───└─ ...Product Versions for International Sales
```

(Continued)

BOX 6.2 *(Continued)*

Services

...Toll-Free Number for Customer Service
...Online Services
...Service Using Expert Systems
...Strategic Alliances
...New Service Areas

Internal Systems

Office Automation

...Electronic Conferences/Meetings
...Electronic Mail Network
...Facsimile Machines
...In-House Electronic Publishing

Paperless Accounting Systems

...Interactive Screen Entry of Accounting Data
...Financial Support Software
...Accounting on Line to Financial Models
...Budget System on Line
...Link to Executive Information System

...Information System Network
...Electronic Training
...Selling Excess Processing Power

Decision Making

...Worldwide Information Network
...Increase Decision-Making Responsibility and Power

Decision-Support Systems

...Financial DSS
...Production DSS

Marketing DSS

...Online Bar Scanners
...Online Market Research
...Instant Modeling of Advertising Effectiveness
...Price-Elasticity Measurements
...Detailed ROI for all Products

...Miscellaneous DSS
...Easy-to-use Mouse-Driven DSS
...Integrated DSS Database

...Expert Systems for Decision Making

BOX 6.2 *(Continued)*

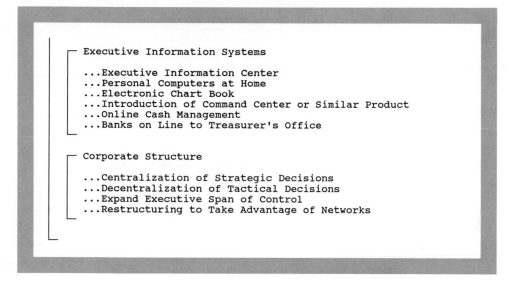

```
    ┌ Executive Information Systems

      ...Executive Information Center
      ...Personal Computers at Home
      ...Electronic Chart Book
      ...Introduction of Command Center or Similar Product
      ...Online Cash Management
    └ ...Banks on Line to Treasurer's Office


    ┌ Corporate Structure

      ...Centralization of Strategic Decisions
      ...Decentralization of Tactical Decisions
      ...Expand Executive Span of Control
    └ ...Restructuring to Take Advantage of Networks
```

of such a session is that in order to encourage the accumulation of ideas nobody can be criticized for suggesting an ill-thought-out or impractical idea. The maximum stimulation of inventive discussion about the future is required. The technology impact analysts will digest the ideas after the session, select those that seem appropriate, and add them to their action diagrams. The analysts then generate the matrices' mapping technology against opportunities and threats.

TIME SCALE   Some of the technologies and opportunities are immediate, some short term, and some longer term. The intersections of the matrices may be marked with a time-scale code:

0   Immediate

1   1 year away

2   2 years away

3   3 years away

etc.

PRIORITIES   The opportunities and threats may be ranked on a priority scale:

A   Very critical; immediate implementation is needed

B   Critical; should be implemented with some urgency

C   Should be implemented with medium priority

D   Required but with no urgency

E   Desirable but not absolutely required

The matrix intersection may thus have both a time-scale indicator and a priority indicator.

MANAGEMENT INTERVIEWS

When a rich set of technology trends, opportunities, and threats has been recorded, the analysts interview appropriate managers, sometimes adding to their lists, and determining which of the opportunities and threats are potentially important. The matrices are adjusted and appropriate segments of them printed.

When the analysts are satisfied with their conclusions so far, the results should be presented in senior-management meetings. There is usually heated discussion at this stage about the opportunities and threats. The priority codes may be adjusted. Action should be demanded on any items that remain in the top three priority categories. Memos should be created detailing the actions to be taken.

PERIODIC REVIEW

The action diagrams and matrices remain valuable on an ongoing basis. They should reside in the information engineering encyclopedia and be reviewed periodically. When this is done, they usually grow as more technology trends unfold and become better understood, and more ideas occur about corporate opportunities. This piece of the encyclopedia is of great value to any corporation wanting to control its destiny in an era of powerful, rapidly changing technology.

PROCEDURE

Box 6.3 summarizes the TIA procedure.

BOX 6.3   The procedure for technology impact analysis

```
Technology Impact Analysis can be done by a team of two people
   in two months. It often results in changes in an organization
   which strongly affect profits. It therefore has an exceptionally
   high return on investment. Every enterprise should conduct a TIA.
```

```
The procedure given below may be modified with Action
Diagrammer to meet the needs of the particular situation.
```

BOX 6.3 *(Continued)*

Procedure for TECHNOLOGY IMPACT ANALYSIS

Establish the TIA team
    The team may consist of two highly experienced people, one
        external consultant who specializes in conducting TIAs,
        and one technology-minded staff person whom top management will
        respect.
    The consultant should have a broad knowledge of the industry.
    The in-house person should have a broad knowledge of the enterprise
        and technology.

Prepare the TIA team
    Become fully familiar with the TIA methodology.
    Become fully familiar with current trends in technology.
    Be fully familiar with the industry.
    Study the organization (annual reports, history, organizational chart,
     policies, products, competitive products, literature).
    Spend time with the company management and people who have views
     on its competitive position, problems, and opportunities.
    List the mission of the enterprise, along with its perceived
     goals and problems.

Conduct an introductory workshop for a small key top-management group
    Explain the TIA procedure.
    Give them literature on the technique. (This Chapter).
    Determine which managers should participate.
    Solicit the active sponsorship of a key member of top management.
    Set a date for a focusing workshop in which the results will be
        examined and discussed.

Establish an action diagram showing a taxonomy of new technology
    Start with an existing action diagram.
    ```
    o───────────o
    │ See BOX 6.1  │
    o───────────o
    ```
    Brainstorm what other technology changes might be relevant.
    Description
        Brainstorming means that a creative group of individuals
        attempt to produce a stream of ideas without inhibition.
        A rule of a brainstorming session is that there can be
        no implied criticism for making an impractical or stupid
        suggestion. The session is intended to generate as many
        ideas as possible. At the end of the session only certain
        of the ideas will be recorded for possible use.

Establish an action diagram showing potential business opportunities.
    Start with an existing action diagram.
    ```
    o───────────o
    │ See BOX 6.2  │
    o───────────o
    ```
    Brainstorm what other opportunities might be relevant.
    Description
        Brainstorming means that a creative group of individuals
        attempt to produce a stream of ideas without inhibition.
        A rule of a brainstorming session is that there can be
        no implied criticism for making an impractical or stupid
        suggestion. The session is intended to generate as many
        ideas as possible. At the end of the session only certain
        of the ideas will be recorded for possible use.

(Continued)

BOX 6.3 *(Continued)*

```
┌─ Establish a matrix mapping technology against business opportunities.
│   ┌─ Mark the matrix with time scale codes
│   │        0:   Immediate.
│   │        1:   1 year away.
│   │        2:   2 years away.
│   │        3:   3 years away.
│   └        Etc.
│
│   ┌─ Mark the matrix with priority codes
│   │        A:   VERY CRITICAL. Immediate implementation is needed.
│   │        B:   CRITICAL. Should be implemented with some urgency.
│   │        C:   Should be implemented with medium priority.
│   │        D:   Required, but with no urgency.
│   └        E:   Desirable, but not absolutely required.
│
│      Eliminate unimportant items.
│      Print the matrix.
└
┌─ Review results
│      Distribute statements about potential technology impact to
│        the top-management team.
│   ┌─ Conduct a top-management focusing workshop
│   │      Discuss the matrix with the top-management team.
│   │          This is a key meeting which usually provokes much argument
│   │              about the enterprise, its competition, and the potential
│   │              impact of technology.
│   │      Modify the matrix as appropriate.
│   └      Determine what actions to take.
│
│      Refine and distribute the results.
└
┌─ Determine any needs for immediate action
│      Determine any business actions which should be taken immediately.
│      Determine any needs for immediate action in creating executive
└          information systems or decision-support systems.
```

REFERENCES

1. James Martin Associates 2020 study, Reston, VA; London; Amsterdam.

2. James Martin, *Hyperdocuments and How to Create Them*, Prentice Hall, Englewood Cliffs, NJ, 1990.

7 STRATEGIC SYSTEMS VISION

STRATEGIC SYSTEMS
In recent years there have been many examples of a corporation pulling vigorously ahead of its competition by using information technology better than its competition. There have been other examples of corporations with earnings declining, sometimes to the edge of bankruptcy, because their competition used computers, microelectronics, networks, or information in new competitive thrusts. One of the most important questions in corporate computing is: How can we use information technology to gain competitive advantage?

Systems that enable a corporation to achieve a direct advantage over its competition are referred to as *strategic systems*. Some of these are online systems which directly enable the corporation to accomplish a mission and are referred to as *mission-critical* systems [1]. Examples of mission-critical systems are an airline operating a network of terminals in travel agents' offices or a manufacturer using online computers in customer locations. A mission-critical system is at the heart of the business, enabling it to function in certain ways. If the system stops, that aspect of the business stops. It is thus critical to the functioning of the business rather than being a backroom, paperwork processing system—as were most commercial computers in the recent past.

A corporate president is strongly concerned with how his organization can do better than its competition or how to prevent the competition from taking business away from his organization. He needs to regard the computer and information system as critical weapons in his battle with competition. Some corporate presidents do not have this vision yet. They still regard computers as an overhead cost that should be minimized whenever possible. One president of a large corporation in Manhattan commented to the author: "I am the enemy of computers in this place. All I want to know about them is how much they cost—and it's too much." At the same time, his competition was devising inventive ways of using information technology to capture a major part of his business.

The term *strategic systems vision* has been used to describe the ability to see ways in which systems can enhance the competitive position of a corporation. It is desirable that general executives and I.S. professionals should develop such vision and become used to exploring how information technology can help achieve new competitive thrusts.

The methodologies of the previous three chapters—the analysis of goals and problems, technology impact analysis, and critical success factor analysis—should all be used, but perhaps the most important of the techniques for top-level planning is the development of strategic systems vision. The habit of thinking about how technology can change the enterprise to make it more competitive needs to start at the top and pervade the entire enterprise. End users with information center tools need to be encouraged to explore how they can use computing strategically.

EXAMPLES OF STRATEGIC SYSTEMS

Box 7.1 gives examples of corporations that have used new technology to create a major innovative business thrust. Some of these were established corporations that changed their method of operating. Some were new corporations that used technology in an innovative way to grow rapidly. Some fundamentally changed a basic link in the industry chain, as when American Airlines put travel agents online to its computer center, or American Hospital Supply put order-entry terminals into clinics. Some were David and Goliath situations, where a small company challenged the giants by using technology better than they did. Federal Express was once a small upstart confronted with numerous competing airfreight companies. Benetton in Italy in the early 1970s was a small family business in a no-growth industry with tough established large corporations.

Reuters in the 1850s used the technology of carrier pigeons to distribute news and details of transactions on the Brussels stock exchange faster than its competition. In the 1970s it again outdid its competition by providing financial information on terminal screens with its worldwide news network and then enabling its customers to make trades over that network.

The term *preemptive strike* is used to describe a corporation making a thrust which establishes an advantage that cannot be dislodged by its competition. When American and United Airlines established terminals (and later, online PCs) in travel agents' offices, other airlines were left out in the cold. It would have been equally expensive for other airlines to build such a system, and most travel agents would not have replaced their established terminals. American and United acquired a long-lasting advantage. American Hospital Supply similarly preempted their competition. Their terminals were attractive to clinics and hospitals and usually were not dislodged by competition once they

American Airlines' SABER system

American Airlines placed terminals in travel agents' offices, online to its computer center in Dallas, before most other airlines. This increascd the number of seats sold on American's flights, at the expense of their competition. American Airlines also collected revenue from other airlines when bookings for their flights were made with the SABER system. Once the terminals were in place in travel agents' offices, other airlines generally could not displace them.

This system was a very expensive and risky strategic thrust which had a massive payoff for American Airlines when it succeeded.

American Hospital Supply (now Baxter), the ASAP system

American Hospital Supply placed terminals (and later PCs) in its customers' offices. These enabled customers to search a catalog of over 100,000 health-care products, place orders easily, and reorder automatically. The system allows customers to simplify their administration and reduce inventory costs.

The American Hospital Supply system transformed a basic link in the industry chain. It was a new attractive service to customers and it tended to lock in customers because it raised the cost for a customer to switch to a different vendor.

Benetton

Benetton grew from a small operation in Italy to a billion-dollar worldwide business with thousands of franchised stores, by building a network with online point-of-sale terminals in its stores. Many small and flexible manufacturers were also online. Benetton's system allowed it to respond ahead of its competition to changes in demand for colors or fashions, and to avoid the costs associated with demand misjudgements.

Benetton rethought how a manufacturer and retailer of fashion goods ought to operate if they take full advantage of a worldwide network, databases and decision-support computing.

(Continued)

BOX 7.1 *(Continued)*

United Stationers

United Stationers grew from a small start-up company to a billion-dollar operation by putting terminals, and later online PCs, into stationary stores, with a highly reliable network, so that the delivery of supplies in 24 hours could be guaranteed. This enabled their customers, including start-up stores, to operate with low-cost inventories and hence do business with United Stationers rather than their long-established competition.

American Express

American Express built an expert system which help the authorizers of credit card purchases to detect possible frauds. This lessened the loss from fraud and enabled American Express to remove the cash limit for a large class of customers.

Equitable Life

Equitable created a computer assisted underwriting system for use at client sites permitting annual renewal analysis for policies based on historical data. The system recommended changes in premium rates based on underwriting objectives and experience. The objective was to provide underwriters with the skills of a top actuary.

Fidelity Brokerage Services

This discount brokerage house grew much faster than its competition, passing several larger rivals, by providing brokers with terminals and allowing them to negotiate a discount with their customers because online trades could be executed less expensively (and more quickly). Later customers with a personal computer were given the capability to enter trades online, at a lower fee.

Dun and Bradstreet

D&B stated their strategic vision as including the ability to collect timely and relevant information for their customers' decision making, and use technology to maximize information delivery and utility [3]. To help achieve this mission they acquired:

BOX 7.1 *(Continued)*

- NCSS, a computer time-sharing business with a national network,
- McCormack and Dodge, a leading software company,
- A.C. Nielsen, the nation's leading consumer research company.

They formed an agreement with IBM to market the PC with D&B products. The combination of these thrusts enabled them to emerge as a powerful information services provider.

Pacific Intermountain Express

PIE, a large trucking company, differentiated itself from its many rivals by building a computer application for tracking the status of a shipment at any point on its route. The system produces various types of valuable information for PIE customers.

Merrill Lynch

Merrill Lynch used computers to create a new product, a Cash Management Account, which combined three services: credit through a standard margin account, cash withdrawal by check or debit card, and automatic investment of cash and dividends in a money market fund. This was attractive to customers. Merrill Lynch sold over a million CMA accounts and had this market to itself for four years. Six years after its introduction many banks and financial service organizations started to erode Merrill's position.

Federal Express

Federal Express based its business on a new use of information systems. It used a hub-and-spoke organization for the rapid airfreight of packages. Planes flew packages into the hub at Memphis, Tennessee, where they were sorted, and then the planes flew back carrying packages for their destination. The ground and air facilities were linked by a computer network. Customer requests from anywhere in the country were processed by that system so that customers could be guaranteed fast pickup and delivery. Federal Express grew much faster than the many other airfreight companies, and became a billion dollar company after 10 years.

(Continued)

BOX 7.1   *(Continued)*

Reuters

Reuters, unlike its competitors AP and UPI, implemented a strategic thrust to develop computerized information systems using a world-wide network of databases, display terminals and teleprinters, to provide prices of stocks, bonds, currencies, oil, commodities, etc. and, later, link its customers directly to dealers for trading. It provided a large client base for other products. Reuters pretax profit climbed from $2.7 million in 1980 to $43.5 million in 1983.

First Boston

First Boston, a New York investment banking house, created a computer-based network for providing mortgages to house buyers through real-estate brokers, bypassing the banks and saving-and-loan organizations. The buyer could receive a conditional commitment for a loan in less than an hour, and the final clearance in a much shorter time than the banks. After nine months the system generated $14 billion worth of mortgages.

First Boston created other innovative financial vehicles faster than its competition. It was able to do this because it used a code generator linked to information engineering techniques for developing the necessary programs quickly.

The Wall Street Journal

Dow Jones and Company, which publishes the Wall Street Journal, was the first private non-common-carrier company to operate its own satellite earth stations. These are used to transmit pages of the Journal to a dozen printing plants across the USA. Later Journal pages were transmitted internationally. This enabled the Journal to substantially increase its circulation.

were in place. Charles Wiseman [2] quotes industry executives as saying that the American Hospital Supply ASAP system was ''largely responsible for driving competitors like A.S. Aloe Company and Will Ross, Inc. from the hospital supply distribution business. Once a hospital got an ASAP terminal, American couldn't be budged.''

The examples in Box 7.1 relate to large corporations (although some were small when the strategic decisions were initiated). Strategic systems vision is highly relevant to small corporations and there are numerous examples of small-scale strategic thrusts. Some small accounting firms, for example, with less than a hundred customers, realized in the 1980s that they could introduce personal computer packages to their customers and grow their client base rapidly. Those competitors that did not move in this direction *lost* clients.

An analysis of strategic opportunities may make it clear that a corporation requires technology that it does not possess. It may need to buy a corporation which *does* have that technology. Some strategic thrusts have been to make acquisitions. A strategic vision may be spelled out by corporate planners and then a search made for potential acquisitions. A dramatic example of that is Dun & Bradstreet. In the late 1970s Dun & Bradstreet determined that two critical success factors were the collection of timely and relevant information for decision-making use by its customer groups, and the application of technology to maximize information delivery and utility [3]. Dun & Bradstreet searched for appropriate takeover candidates to acquire both information and technology that would further their strategic vision. Dun & Bradstreet purchased National CSS (NCSS), a leading time-sharing company with an innovative fourth-generation language (NOMAD) and a nationwide time-sharing network. They purchased McCormick and Dodge, one of the largest software companies, with strong financial packages. They merged with A.C. Nielsen, America's leading consumer research organization. Dun & Bradstreet also purchased several television stations and cable television systems. Later it refined the facilities it needed to help meet its mission by selling its television stations and systems and selling the NOMAD language (which by then looked somewhat old-fashioned). This process of acquiring and selling facilities can adjust a corporation's resources to help it meet its strategic vision.

In 1986 the CASE segment of the software industry was evolving. KnowledgeWare developed a strategic vision which indicated that to succeed fully it needed an integrated toolset that could tackle all the layers of the information engineering pyramid. This required a code generator, which KnowledgeWare did not possess; therefore, KnowledgeWare examined all the companies with code generators and merged with Tarkington Software. The Tarkington code generator become integrated into the KnowledgeWare product line.

To succeed fully in an era of rapidly changing technology, a corporation needs to understand that technology and to develop a strategic vision of how it can use technology to achieve something better than its competition. It may plan a preemptive strike against its competition. The strategic vision should be bold and clear. To implement it, systems may be created in-house, acquired externally, or acquisitions or mergers may be planned.

BUSINESS RISKS

Strategic systems often require a corporation to do business in a different way. They are innovative in the sense that an entrepreneur is innovative. Not all business innovations succeed, just as not all entrepreneurial startups succeed. There are examples of strategic systems that have failed. Federal Express reaped great benefits from the innovations that led to its basic business, but it failed when it attempted to innovate ZAPMAIL. ZAPMAIL was a system for using electronic transmission combined with the Federal Express computer-controlled delivery fleet for delivering documents in an hour or so. ZAPMAIL was a very expensive strategic thrust that failed.

If the American Airlines SABER system for travel agents had failed, that would have been disastrous for American Airlines. American spent $350 million on building the system. It was taking a major business risk in the way a startup company takes a business risk. The payoff from succeeding justified the risk handsomely.

Because a strategic information system is a business risk, the decision to build it cannot be taken by an I.S. executive alone. The decision must come from top management. The strategic vision may be initiated by a computer executive or chief information officer, but that vision must be passed to top management, who will refine it and take action.

CATEGORIES OF STRATEGIC THRUSTS

Some of the examples in Box 7.1 were sweeping changes that resulted in a new mode of operations for their industry. Most examples of strategic systems are less dramatic but of major importance to the corporation in question. Charles Wiseman classifies strategic thrusts into five categories [2]:

- Differentiation
- Cost
- Innovation
- Growth
- Alliance

For each of these, the thrusts can be either *offensive* or *defensive*. There is thus a matrix of possibilities:

	Differentiation	Cost	Innovation	Growth	Alliance
Offensive					
Defensive					

Differentiation. A corporation can move to differentiate its product or services from those of its competition. The move to make a product stand out from its competition is an offensive strategy. A defensive strategy is to improve the product to reduce the differentiation that competing products have.

Cost. There are many types of thrusts to reduce the cost of a product. A company may also manipulate a variety of factors that would raise the costs of competition.

Innovation. There should be a constant search for innovative ideas, to improve products, improve services, improve production techniques, and so on. Innovation may be used offensively to preempt competition, or it may be used defensively to lessen an advantage that competition has.

Growth. Growth may be geographical expansion, expansion within an existing territory, vertical expansion of a product line or diversification by adding new types of products. Growth may be done offensively, or it may be done to protect the sales from competing thrusts.

Alliance. A corporation may buy or merge with another corporation or form a strategic partnership in order to expand its market or make its product line more complete or more useful. This, again, may be an offensive strategy to preempt competition, or it may be defensive to lessen an advantage that competition has.

Box 7.2 gives examples of strategic thrusts in these five categories. Although the five categories are useful, not all strategic systems can be fitted into these categories. The list in Box 7.2 is not intended to be comprehensive. Much business inventiveness is needed in identifying opportunities for strategic use of computers.

The technology that makes new strategic thrusts possible is very different now from when Baron de Reuter or Baron de Rothschild used carrier pigeons.

BOX 7.2 Five categories of strategic thrusts

```
 ┌ DIFFERENTIATION
 │  ┌ Increase the attractiveness of the product
 │  │   Use microelectronics to improve the functionality of the product.
 │  │   Work out in what ways the product can be made "intelligent."
 │  │   Increase the reliability of the product.
 │  │   Use CAD/CAM techniques to improve product quality.
 │  │   Package automated guidance or training with the product.
 │  └   Package an expert system with the product.
 │
 │  ┌ Create a more integrated product line than the competition
 │  │   Extend the product vertically to meet all the customers' needs.
 │  │   Extend the range of products to create one-stop shopping.
 │  └   Create a complete family of services for the customer.
 │
 │  ┌ Strengthen the affiliation with the customer
```

(Continued)

BOX 7.2 *(Continued)*

Take actions which help the customer to be profitable.
Provide a consulting service to help the customer maximize the
    benefits from the product.
Provide an excellent customer training service.
Build online links to the customer.
Give the customer PC software for reordering.
Provide the customer with a PC expert system to aid in using the
    product and solving problems.
Tailor the services to the customer's needs.
Find ways to lock in the customer.
Increase the customer cost of switching to a different product.

Increase the barrier to new competitive entrants
    Achieve vertical integration of the product line.
    Achieve horizontal integration of the product line.
    Create a complete family of services for the customer.

COST
Lower the manufacturing costs
    Automate the manufacturing process.
    Use CAD/CAM techniques.
    Redesign the product for robot fabrication.
    Use cheap foreign labor, possibly with satellite transmission.

Lower the inventory holding costs
    Just-in-time inventory control.
        Build online links to suppliers.
        Build online links to transportation companies.
        Produce only for the orders on hand, by having manufacturing
            planning on line to a worldwide order-processing system.

    Consolidate multiple inventories with centralized inventory control.
    Eliminate low-turnover items.

Lower the cost of supplies
    Find lower-cost suppliers.
    Improve the bargaining power with suppliers
        Buy bulk lots.
        Use supplies with alternate sources.

INNOVATION
Product innovation
    Analyze the ways in which new technology could impact the product.
    Conduct a TIA study concerned with possible product
        innovations.
    Examine the product features to determine what could be improved.
    Ask customers what improvements they would like.
    Determine whether the product could be put to new uses.
    Use microelectronics to improve the functionality of the product.
    Work out in what ways the product can be made "intelligent."
    Examine the possible impact of artificial intelligence and

BOX 7.2 *(Continued)*

neurocomputers.
Package automated guidance or training with the product.
Package an expert system with the product.

Process innovation
Examine the entire industry chain from purchasing to sales and service.
Brainstorm what innovations could be made.
Determine whether parts of the industry chain could be bypassed.
Brainstorm how computers could improve services.

Production innovation
Use online links to suppliers.
Redesign the products for more automated fabrication.
Use CAD/CAM techniques to increase the speed of making product innovations
Use high-capital facilities 24-hours-per-day, 7-days-per-week.
Create expert systems for diagnostics and maintenance.

Innovation in sales, marketing, distribution, retailing.
Brainstorm opportunities to change normal procedures.
Use online links to customers.
Use online links to agents or distributors.
Use online links to retailers.
Use online links to the public.
Design software to place in customer locations.
Use expert systems.

GROWTH
Increase the sales of existing products
Maximize international marketing.
Find new marketing channels.
Use expert systems to improve the productivity of salesmen.
Use automated proposal generators.

Extend the product line
Extend the products vertically, integrating the product line.
Extend the products horizontally, diversifying the product line.

ALLIANCES
Consider strategic acquisitions and mergers
In order to:
o Achieve vertical integration of the product line.
o Achieve horizontal integration of the product line.
o Create a complete family of services for the customer.
o Achieve economies of scale.
o Improve international marketing.
o Broaden the customer base.

Consider strategic partnerships
In order to:
o Acquire the talent for a new type of innovation.
o Acquire the finance for development.

(Continued)

BOX 7.2   *(Continued)*

```
o  Broaden the customer base.
o  Achieve international marketing.
o  Achieve faster growth.
o  Achieve vertical linkage of product lines.
o  Achieve horizontal integration of products.
o  Create a complete family of services for the customer.
```

Today the technology keeps changing, constantly opening up new possibilities. Box 7.3 lists three types of relatively new technology and the possibilities they offer: intercorporate networks, expert systems, and CASE tools. Many others could be added to those in Box 7.3.

METHODOLOGIES THAT LIMIT VISION

One of the dangers of most methodologies used for strategic planning is that they tend to *prevent* their users from seeing the strategic systems opportunities.

The reason is that they are concerned with automating *today's* corporate functions. Strategic systems vision is concerned with changing the corporate functions or building new activities in the corporation.

Many strategic planning methodologies are derived from IBM's BSP (Business Systems Planning). Methodologies with different names used by large consulting or accounting firms are often variants on BSP. The ideas of BSP have been taught in various forms in thousands of IBM training classes and are the basis of various IBM guides on systems planning [4]. IBM's BSP manual states that its objective is "to provide an information systems plan that supports the business's short- and long-term information needs and is integral with the business plan."

BSP defines "environment" as being those things that lie outside the scope of the planning study, and it lists them as the economy, government regulations, labor, consumerism, competition, industry position, industry trends, suppliers, and technology. The BSP manuals instruct planners to ignore these "environmental" factors when conducting the BSP study. Strategic systems vision is very concerned with competition, technology, suppliers, customers, industry trends, and in general, factors that facilitate new competitive thrusts. Rather than use a planning method that excludes these, it is desirable to focus on them specifically. In general, it is desirable strategically to focus on how the enterprise might be changed rather than solely to examine and model what exists today.

Charles Wiseman [2] comments that the use of computers in corporations

BOX 7.3 Some of the types of new technology that offer opportunities for strategic thrusts

Intercorporate networks
- Online links to suppliers
  - In order to:
    - o Achieve just-in-time inventory control
    - o Reduce inventories
    - o Support continuous-flow manufacturing
    - o Shorten manufacturing cycle
    - o Locate buying opportunities
    - o Exchange quality control information

- Online links to customers
  - To enable the customer to:
    - o Place orders easily
    - o Obtain quick delivery
    - o Look for items in online catalogs
    - o Check the status of orders
    - o Reorder automatically
    - o Reduce inventory
    - o Solve product problems
    - o Obtain expert advice
    - o Control quality
    - o Analyze costs

  The system should help to lock in the customer and lock out the competition.

- Online links to retailers
  - To provide retailer with:
    - o Help in marketing
    - o Product information
    - o Automatic reordering
    - o Guaranteed quick delivery
    - o Help in minimizing inventory
    - o Expert advice
    - o Customer profile analysis
    - o Financial help
    - o Bookkeeping
    - o Office services
    - o Improved communications

- Online links to agents
  - To provide the agent with:
    - o Product information
    - o Expert advice
    - o Help in marketing
    - o Aid in contract design
    - o Financial help
    - o Bookkeeping
    - o Office services
    - o Improved communications

- Online links to transportation companies
  - To help achieve:
    - o Quick pickup and delivery
    - o Just-in-time inventory control
    - o Discounts where possible

(Continued)

BOX 7.3 *(Continued)*

Online links to distributors or middlemen
    To help achieve:
      o Bulk rates
      o Discounts where possible
      o Low inventories
      o Quick pickup and delivery
      o Improved communications
      o Customer profile analysis

Online links to the public
    via home PCs, home videotext, ATM machines, other public machines.
    To help achieve:
      o Online shopping or reservations
      o Direct factory ordering
      o Large sales volume
      o On-line ordering to avoid paperwork
      o Avoidance of middleman costs and charges
      o Services of interest to the public
      o Direct market-research information

Uses of artificial intelligence
  Expert system for diagnostics
    Expert system for diagnosing and correcting problems with products.
    Expert system for preventive maintenance.
    Expert system for maintenance enabling complex factory equipment to
      be used 24 hours per day, 7 days per week, without having skilled
      diagnostic experts present.

  Expert system for sales proposals
    Expert system for designing complex technical configurations.
    Expert system for complex pricing.
    Steady accumulation of sales expertise coupled to automatic assembly
      of proposal information.
    Expert system coupled to electronic publishing to generate elegant
      proposals quickly.
    Expert system to make new salesmen productive quickly.
    System to increase the number of proposals a salesman can make.

  Expert system for risk assessment
    Expert system for assessing insurance risks.
    Expert system for assessing customer risks, for example, American
      Express detecting suspicious credit card usage.

  Expert system for customer service
    A phone-in customer service center with staff using an expert
      system to guide customers on how to deal with problems.

  Expert system for customers
    Expert system installed to help customers make profitable decisions
      which involve product purchases. For example, ICI (UK) system for
      providing guidance to wheat farmers.
    Product manuals with an intelligent front end.
    Expert system to guide customers in using a product effectively. For
      example, L. M. Baroid providing an expert system with their drilling
      fluids to guide users in obtaining the best mix of lubricants.

BOX 7.3 *(Continued)*

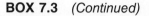

```
    ┌─ Expert system to aid in corporate acquisitions
    │      For example, an expert system used by a large software company to
    │      provide guidance in considering purchases of small software
    │      companies.



  ┌─ Use of CASE and 4GL tools
  │    ┌─ Spread of end-user computing.
  │    │     Encouraging strategic systems thinking among all knowledge workers.
  │    │     Enabling end users to build strategic systems.
  │    │     Building better decision-support systems.
  │
  │    ┌─ Use of information engineering
  │    │     Getting the right information to the right people at the right time.
  │    │     Development of software which can continuously evolve and grow.
  │    │     Achieving corporate transparency so that data from multiple areas can
  │    │     be used to help better control.
  │
  │    ┌─ Automation of application building
  │    │     Ability to create new business procedures quickly.
  │    │     Ability to change business procedures quickly.
  │
  │    ┌─ Use of planning tools
  │    │     Use of tools and methodologies to help identify strategic systems
  │    │     opportunities.
  │    │     Analysis of decision making so that decisions are made in the best
  │    │     location, by the most appropriate person, with the best information,
  │    │     and the best decision support computing.
```

evolved from traditional data processing (MIS) systems to management support systems (MSS) and now needs to evolve to strategic information systems (SIS). Traditional data processing systems processed predefined transactions to produce predefined results. They included payroll, invoicing, purchasing, inventory control, accounts payable, accounts receivable, and so on. MSS were designed to satisfy the information needs of managers and assist in the decision-making process. They provided query facilities, ''what-if'' capability, spreadsheets, and decision-support tools. Wiseman comments that many traditional data processing veterans resisted the emergence of MSS, refusing to admit their existence. Others argued that they were merely extensions of existing MIS systems. Similarly, many of today's systems planners are ignoring strategic information systems and concentrating solely on the functions of today's enterprise.

MSS systems were often built by different people from those who built traditional MIS systems. MSS developers differed culturally from MIS developers. MIS developers learned to *observe* what was happening, draw charts of it, and design systems to replace existing procedures. MSS developers, on the other hand, had to satisfy unmet information needs of managers and professionals, which were not observable and not expressed with precision. Some MSS systems were built by end users or planning staff in an information center environment.

Wiseman suggests that strategic information systems should be conceived and designed by a different group in a corporation from those that design MIS or MSS. SIS are not designed by observing existing functions but by inventing new functions. They require a different type of creativity and business acumen. People good at conceiving SIS differ culturally from most people who design traditional MIS or MSS. Once specified, SIS might be constructed by the professionals who construct other systems.

PERSONAL COMPUTING

The habit of thinking in terms of strategic uses of computers ought to pervade the entire enterprise. It can have a major effect on the return on investment from personal computers. A study by Nolan, Norton & Co. [5] concluded that the return on investment of most personal computer use is quite low—about 10 to 20 percent—because they are used for automating individual tasks. When there is higher-level planning and personal computers are used for automating business processes, a three-fold return on investment may be obtained. However, when a strategic vision is implemented by means of personal computers, a ten-fold return on investment is sometimes obtained.

This study emphasizes what has been found elsewhere when computer benefits have been measured: it pays to identify the most important uses of systems and concentrate on those. This requires management leadership and strategic business-oriented planning. I.S. professional computing should not be left to end users. Both require strategic business-oriented planning. As illustrated in Figure 7.1, it is desirable to refocus personal computing so that it is used systematically to achieve a strategic business vision.

METHODOLOGY FOR IDENTIFYING STRATEGIC SYSTEMS OPPORTUNITIES

The methodology for identifying strategic systems may be similar to technology impact analysis, described in Chapter 6. A detailed taxonomy is used of new technology and directions. A taxonomy is created of possible strategic opportunities, like that in Box 7.2. Links are built between these. Brainstorming sessions should be held about new technology and about possible strategic thrusts.

The taxonomy of new technology and the taxonomy of strategic thrusts have many cross-linkages. It is desirable to represent these taxonomies with

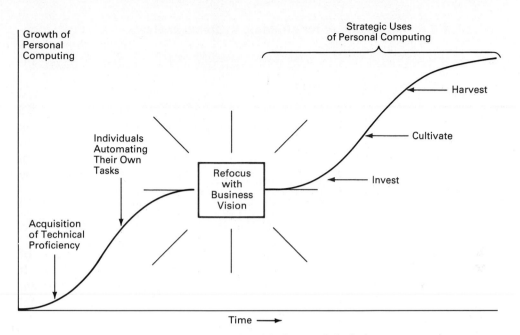

Figure 7.1 Personal computing is achieving a relatively low return on investment in many organizations because it is individuals automating their own tasks. Where it has been refocused with strategic business vision, a very much higher return on investment has been achieved. (Based on a survey by Nolan, Norton, and Co. [5].)

software that enables the cross-linkages to be built and followed easily by using the stack and button techniques employed in hypercard and hypertext software.

The model of possible strategic uses of technology is refined, and the most likely examples are discussed in top management workshops. When a strategic systems opportunity is found that appears to be a candidate for implementation, it needs to be examined in detail. A business proposal should be created that spells out the advantages and risks of the systems. There should be a detailed discussion of how to maximize the advantages and minimize the risks. A detailed calculation should be made of the costs over time and the increased revenues that would result, tangible and intangible. A discounted cash flow should be created for the system and its likely return on investment computed.

Making a proposal for a strategic system is rather like going to venture capitalists and asking for money for a startup corporation. There are risks involved. The venture capitalists have to be convinced that the risks are not too great and that the eventual payoff justifies the risks. The risks need to be spelled out in detail and spreadsheets generated showing the net return on investment for different scenarios. Box 7.4 suggests a methodology for strategic systems analysis.

BOX 7.4 Methodology for strategic systems analysis

```
Procedure for Strategic Systems Analysis

  Determine who is responsible for strategic systems analysis
       The Chief Information Officer normally has the overall responsibility.
       He should appoint one or more people to carry out the details listed
       below.

  Initiate a dialogue with top management
       Conduct an introductory workshop with a small key top management group.
       Explain the concepts of strategic information systems.
       Give examples of competitive preemptive strikes.
       Give examples of strategic systems relevant to the enterprise.
       Illustrate the dangers of competition using strategic systems first.
       Explain the action that will be taken to evaluate strategic systems
        opportunities.

  Establish a detailed taxonomy of possible strategic thrusts
       Start with an existing action diagram.
       o────────────────o
       | See BOX 7.2 |
       o────────────────o
       Brainstorm what other strategic thrusts might be possible.

  Establish a detailed model of new technology and technology trends
       Start with an existing action diagram.
       o──────────────────────────────o
       | See Technology Action Diagram |
       o──────────────────────────────o
       Brainstorm what other technology changes might be relevant.

  Evaluate the possible strategic significance of each technology
       Build cross links between the taxonomy of technology and the taxonomy
        of possible strategic thrusts. (It is desirable to represent these
        taxonomies with software which enables the cross linkages to be built
        and followed easily by using the stack and button techniques used
        in hypercard and hypertext software.)

  Relate the technologies to the opportunities for strategic thrusts
       Create a taxonomy showing this relationship.
       o────────────────o
       | See BOX 7.3 |
       o────────────────o
       Discuss this list with appropriate end-user executives.
       Refine and add to the list.
         Mark the taxonomy with priority codes
            A: Very critical. Immediate management attention is needed.
            B: Critical. Some urgency for management attention.
            C: Medium priority for management attention.
            D: Interesting but no urgency.
            E: Low level of interest.

       Eliminate unimportant items.
       Print the taxonomy.
```

BOX 7.4   *(Continued)*

```
  ┌─ Conduct a top-management workshop
  │     Discuss the strategic opportunities with the top management team.
  │       (This is a key meeting which usually provokes much argument about
  │       the enterprise, its competition, opportunities, and dangers.)
  │     Refine the computerized taxonomy based on management's reaction.
  │     Identify which strategic thrusts should have top priority.
  │
  │   ┌─ Determine any needs for immediate action
  │   │    Determine any business actions which should be taken immediately.
  │   │    Determine any needs for immediate action in creating information
  │   │      systems.
  │   └─
  │
┌─ Conduct seminars for end-user management and professionals
│     Explain the concept of strategic information systems to end users.
│     Give examples relevant to the business.
│     Introduce the taxonomy of strategic technology opportunities.
│     Discuss strategic opportunities which have been given high priority.
│     Brainstorm other possibilities.
│     Refine the computerized taxonomy based on the end-user reaction.
│     Discuss actions that end users can take, for example, in end-user
│       computing.
└─
```

THE CHIEF INFORMATION OFFICER

The CIO is often the primary initiator of strategic systems. This person should combine an excellent feel for business and competition with a gut feel for technology and what can be made to work. The CIO should initiate the analysis of strategic systems opportunities and, in general, develop the strategic systems vision. He should help other planners and user executives to think in strategic systems terms.

The model of future technology and strategic opportunities should be maintained by the staff of the CIO and added to when new ideas arise. The model will grow more comprehensive as it is successively updated, and periodic planning sessions should use it to examine the opportunities for strategic thrusts. The four types of strategic studies described in this and the preceding three chapters all relate to one another, and one planning person should probably be responsible for them.

Sometimes, critical success factor analysis is done without considering how new strategic thrusts might change the enterprise. In practice, succeeding in a preemptive strategic thrust might be one of the most important of the CSFs. Strategic systems analysis might be done before CSF analysis (or before the latest update of the CSFs). On the other hand, CSF analysis might focus attention on strategic system analysis for one aspect of the business.

REFERENCES

1. James Martin, *Mission Critical Systems*. Naperville, Ill.: ALI, 1987 (video-tape).

2. Charles Wiseman, *Strategy and Computers*. Homewood, Ill.: Dow Jones-Irwin, 1985 (an interesting book with many examples of strategic information systems).

3. Dun & Bradstreet, *Annual Report,* 1979.

4. IBM, *Business Systems Planning: Information Systems Planning Guide,* 3rd ed. White Plains, N.Y.: IBM Corporation, 1981.

5. *Managing Personal Computers in Large Organizations*. Lexington, Mass.: Nolan, Norton & Co., 1987.

8 TOOLS FOR INFORMATION STRATEGY PLANNING

INTRODUCTION   Different corporations use different variations on the theme of strategic information planning. The process generates much data that needs to be recorded and analyzed. The results of the planning need to be made visible by all those who are affected by it.

Strategic planning, and the enterprise modeling that accompanies it, should not be something that is done once and never repeated. That has been the fate of many BSP (business systems planning) studies [1]. Instead, the planning process should build a knowledge base that is updated continually.

Most organizations change. A top-down planning methodology is needed which keeps pace with the changes. The enterprise model should be computerized and easily updatable. Often, strategic information planning reveals anomalies that need changing in an organization. The computerized representation of the planning should be flexible so that it can be examined from multiple viewpoints.

This book was written with the assumption that a strategic planning tool is used. If one is not used, similar methodologies *could* be done by hand, but that entails much more work, and usually the large hand-drawn charts are not kept up to date.

METADATA   To store strategic planning information (and also the information for the subsequent stages of information engineering), we need an encyclopedia, as discussed in Book I of this trilogy. Part of the encyclopedia is a database. The entity types in this database are those that represent the planning information. They include the following:

Entity types concerned with the enterprise:

ORGANIZATIONAL UNIT
EXECUTIVE
LOCATION
GOAL
CRITICAL SUCCESS FACTOR
STRATEGIC SYSTEM OPPORTUNITY
PROBLEM

Entity types concerned with activities or applications:

FUNCTION
PROCESS
PROCEDURE
PROGRAM
MECHANISM

Entity types concerned with data architecture:

SUBJECT AREA
ENTITY TYPE
RELATIONSHIP
ATTRIBUTE
DATA COLLECTION

Entity types concerned with planning:

PROJECT
SYSTEM
TECHNOLOGY FORECAST
REASON FOR DISTRIBUTION

The term *metadata* means data about data. A person, for example, is an entity. Information about a person is stored in his passport. The passport contains his name, age, and sex. *Metadata* would give data about these data, for example:

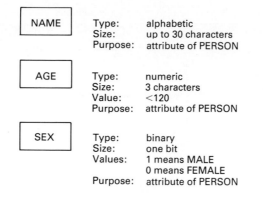

The entity types stored in the encyclopedia are sometimes referred to as metadata. These entity types are not physical things such as CUSTOMER, PRODUCT, and MACHINE TOOL, but abstract things used in planning, such as GOAL, PROCEDURE, and ATTRIBUTE.

Relationships among these entity types give information that is used in the strategic planning process:

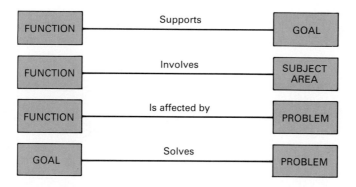

Using such relationships an entity-relationship diagram can be built of the database needed for strategic information planning. Figures 8.1 through 8.3 show portions of such an entity-relationship diagram. The following chapters contain illustrations of various pieces of such a diagram and use them in discussing the strategic planning techniques.

The database of metadata for strategic information planning has certain characteristics that are different from a typical production database. The number of instances of each entity type are tens or hundreds, rather than thousands or hundreds of thousands. There are a relatively small number of goals, organiza-

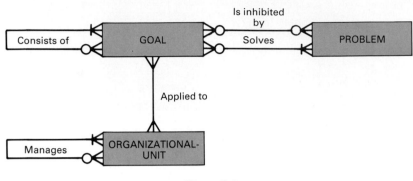

Figure 8.1

tional units, problems, procedures, critical success factors, and so on. Most of the relationships are many-to-many, for example:

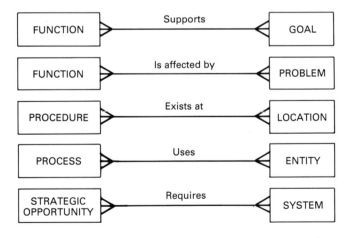

MATRICES   Because of these many-to-many relationships it is usually helpful to display the relationship in the form of a matrix, as shown in Figures 8.4 through 8.6. The screen is normally not big enough to show the entire matrix at one time, so a windowing mechanism is needed which enables the viewer to scroll vertically or horizontally so that he can see any given items mapped against one another.

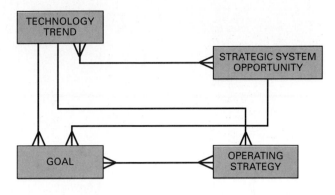

Figure 8.2

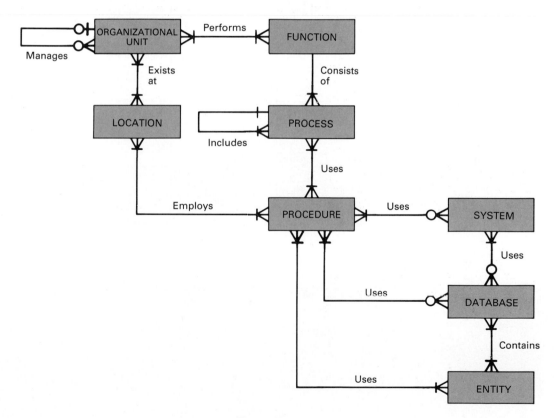

Figure 8.3

PROCESSES	Employee	Contract Employee	Applicant	HR Compensation Regs, Plans, etc.	HR Benefits Regs & Plans	HR Staffing Requirements & Plans	Job Requisition	Stockholder	Boardmember	Misc. Contacts/VIPs	Financial Plans	Accounting Regs, Practices	Ledger Accounts	Customer Purchase Order/Invoice	Customer Payments	Other Income
ENTITIES	1	2	3	4	5	6	7	8	9	10	11	12	13	14	15	16
1 Evaluate Financial Proposals																
2 Estimate Near-Term Earnings														R		
3 Budget Finances	R	R		R	R						CRUD	R	CRUD			
4 Receive Funds												R		R	CRUD	CRUD
5 Pay Funds	R											R				
6 Report Finances	R											R	RU	R	R	R
7 Administer Taxes												R	R		R	R
8 Maintain Financial Reg, Policies											R	CRUD				
9 Audit Finances												R	R		R	R
10 Manage Financial Investments								CRUD				R				
11 Plan Human Resources	R	R				CRUD	CRUD		R		R					
12 Acquire Personnel	CRU	CRU	CRUD			R	R		CRU							
13 Position People in Jobs			R			R	RU		R							
14 Terminate/Retire People	RUD	RUD							RUD							
15 Plan Career Paths	RU			R	R	R										
16 Develop Skills/Motivation	RU	RU			R	R										
17 Manage Individual Emp Relations	RU	RU			R											
18 Manage Benefits Programs					CRUD											
19 Comply with Govt HR Regulations	R			R												
20 Maintain HR Regs, Policies					CRUD		CRUD									
21 Determine Production Requirement														R		
22 Schedule Production	R	R														

Figure 8.4 A matrix mapping processes (vertical) against entities (horizontal).

ORGANIZATIONAL UNITS	TACTICAL GOALS																	
	Improve sales effectiveness	Identify new target markets	Improve market penetration	Add distribution channels	Address absenteeism problem	Exploit new technology	Improve information systems	Streamline shop floor operations	Enhance employee training	Enhance customer support	Improve product quality	Expand product line	Upgrade product warrantee	Reduce inventory investment	Reduce receivables to 45 days	Improve cashflow management	Locate venture capital	Enhance corporate image
	1	2	3	4	5	6	7	8	9	10	11	12	13	14	15	16	17	18
1 Planning																		
2 Accounting															*	*		
3 Cash Management																*		
4 Investments																*		
5 Purchasing														*				
6 Facilities								*										
7 Human Resource Development	*				*				*									
8 MIS																		
9 Legal													*				*	
10 Manufacturing					*						*	*		*				
11 Quality Assurance											*			*				
12 Packaging											*							
13 Materials Management								*						*				
14 Sales Regions	*											*			*			
15 Customer Services																		
16 Customer Education										*								
17 Order Processing	*			*								*						
18 Product Management			*		*							*						
19 Public Relations																	*	*
20 Market Research		*		*		*					*	*						
21 Distribution												*						
22 Engineering						*		*			*	*	*					
23 Research		*				*					*	*						
24 Prototype Manufacture						*		*			*	*						
25 Testing Laboratory						*					*	*	*					

ORGANIZATIONAL UNIT — Has — TACTICAL GOAL

Figure 8.5 A matrix mapping organizational units (vertical) against tactical goals (horizontal).

PROCESS / SYSTEM

SYSTEM \\ PROCESS	Marketing — Planning	Research	Forecasting	Sales Operations — Territory Management	Selling	Administration	Order Servicing	Engineering — Design and Development	Product Specification Maintenance	Information Control	Production — Scheduling	Capacity Planning	Material Requirements	Operations	Materials Management — Purchasing	Receiving	Inventory Control	Shipping	Facilities Management — Work-Flow Layout	Maintenance	Equipment Performance	Administration — General Accounting and Control	Cost Planning	Budget Accounting/Tax Accounting	Finance — Financial Planning	Capital Acquisition	Funds Management	Human Resources — Personnel Planning	Recruiting/Development	Compensation	Management — Business Planning	Organization Analysis	Review and Control	Risk Management
Customer Order Entry				c/p			c/p				c/p	c/p	c/p																		c/p			
Customer Order Control							C			C	C	C	C																					
Invoicing															C							C			C									
Engineering Control										P																								
Finished Goods Inventory									C	C					C	C	C					C	C											
Bills of Material									C						C	C	C					C	C											
Parts Inventory							C				C				C	C	C																	
Purchase Order Control													c/p		c/p																			
Routings										C	c/p	C	c/p	C																				
Shop Floor Control										C		C		C			C																	
Capacity Planning												P		P													P							
General Ledger																						P												
Expense																						C												
Product Costing										c/p				c/p			c/p					C	c/p											
Operating Statements																						C									C	C		C
Accounts Receivable																						C		C								C		C
Accounts Payable																						C		C		C					C			C
Asset Accounting																								C		C								C
Marketing Analysis				C			C															C		C									C	
Payroll																						C								C			C	

C Current   P Planned   c/p Current and Planned

Figure 8.6 The business processes mapped against current and existing systems.

The intersection data is often small enough to show on the matrix, as on the following example, which shows the entities (left) used by processes (top):

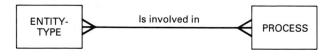

		Contact providers	Prepare coverage categories	Compare costs & benefits	Prepare purchase order
8 Budget			R U	R	R
9 Payables				R	U
10 Loans				R	
11 Vendor		C R U D		R	R

Intersection Property: Action
C = create entity
R = read entity
U = update entity
D = delete entity

Where the intersection data is not small enough to show on the matrix, the user may point to the intersection and display a separate window containing the intersection data.

Often it is useful to show the intersection data on the matrix because the user can see an overview of clustering or distribution. He may rearrange the sequence of items to display clusters, or may use computerized algorithms for clustering.

HIERARCHIES

Some of the entity types in Figures 8.1 through 8.4 have a relationship with themselves. For example:

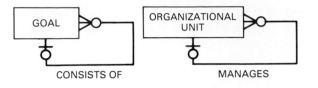

These recursive entity relationships can be drawn as tree structures, for example, a hierarchy of goals or a hierarchy of organizational units (the conventional organization chart). A tool for analyzing and displaying strategic planning information therefore needs to be able to display matrices and hierarchies. It needs to display windows for entering or displaying intersection data on matrices and for entering displaying information about objects such as goals, critical success factors, processes, organizational units, competitive threats, or whatever other entities form the metadata of strategic planning.

ENTITY-RELATIONSHIP DIAGRAM

An entity-relationship diagram is created of the entities in an enterprise (Chapter 9). The planning tool needs to be able to represent such a diagram. The entities in this diagram are mapped in matrices with *processes, organizational units, locations,* and so on.

As information engineering progresses from *strategic planning* to *analysis, design,* and *construction,* more detailed diagrams are used. The representation of this more detailed information needs to be a natural extension of what is stored in the encyclopedia for strategic planning.

ANALYSIS

Various types of analysis can be applied to the planning data. Some forms of analysis provide validation techniques to help ensure that the business model provides an accurate, consistent, and complete foundation for decision making. Other forms of analysis provide decision-support tools to assist in such matters as setting priorities for projects based on which have the most effect on meeting the corporate goals, clustering entity types into subject databases, or clustering entity types and processes into systems, and examining the distribution of data or processing. Some types of analysis are as follows:

> **Exception Analysis.** Exception analysis uses rules to ensure the integrity of information in the encyclopedia, and to list any occurrences that do not meet the criteria. A check may be made that the required properties of the data are entered, for example that all goals have a performance-ranking measurement, and that all important associations have been entered. The lack of an association may be de-

tected: for example, a goal that does not relate to an organizational unit. Redundancies may be detected: for example, two organizational units perform the same function. Interesting facts or inconsistencies about the organization may be highlighted, such as entities that are required by critical processes but are not implemented.

Level Consistency Analysis. This analysis verifies that associations between two hierarchies are logically consistent. It may locate at a high level associations that lack supporting links at detailed levels. It may detect parts of the organizational-unit hierarchy that do not have corresponding goals in the goal hierarchy.

Affinity Analysis. If affinity numbers can be established between the objects in a set of objects, the objects may be clustered into groups to achieve greater efficiency. This is done with entity types to study the grouping of entities into subject databases or distributed databases. Clusters of entities or processes are sometimes a starting point for *business area analysis* or data modeling projects. When priorities conflict, comparing clusters from several affinity analyses provides insight into alternatives—highlighting problems that need compromises or technical solutions if one approach is chosen over others. Goals are often used as a clustering determinant.

Project Action Analysis. Project definitions may be defined with the help of affinity analysis. A project employs certain entity types and processes. The data must be created by certain processes. A project may relate to certain goals. It may be associated with multiple locations. Matrices showing these relationships are examined and adjusted as necessary.

Project Ranking Analysis. The planning process may estimate how much various data projects contribute to the accomplishment of specified goals. Planning tools may be used to rank alternate projects in terms of their value in meeting goals, and hence in terms of their effect on potential profit. Groups of projects may require shared databases. The combined value of implementing such databases may be assessed. New applications may be assessed in terms of the business problems they solve. Migration from old systems to new systems with better technology, better structuring, a greater level of automation, and lower maintenance cost may be desirable. The implications of such migration may be examined with matrix manipulation, and the resources assessed. The value of migration in terms of solving business problems may be examined.

AFFINITY ANALYSIS AND CLUSTERING   When affinities among objects in the planning process can be calculated, a computer can group them into clusters of high affinity. A human planner at a workstation may want to operate this clustering, adjusting parameters that affect the cluster sizes, and applying manual overrides to take heuristic factors into account.

Let us suppose that we have two entities, E_1 and E_2. If the two entities are never used for the same activity, their affinity will be zero. If two entities are always used together for every activity, their affinity will be 1. Many entities are used together for some activities only. A computer can examine every activity and calculate:

1. $a(E_1)$ = number of activities using entity E_1
2. $a(E_1,E_2)$ = number of activities using both entities E_1 and E_2

Using these figures, an affinity factor for the two entities can be calculated. One way of defining the affinity factor is:

$$\text{affinity of } E_1 \text{ to } E_2 = \frac{a(E_1,E_2)}{a(E_1)}$$

The affinity factor can be printed in a matrix such as that in Fig. 8.7.
If two entities have a high affinity, they should be in the same subject

	E_1	E_2	E_3	E_4	E_6	E_6	E_7	E_8	E_9	E_{10}	E_{11}	E_{12}
E_1	■	0	0	0.92	0	0.09	0.07	0	0	0	0	0
E_2	0	■	0	0	0	0	0	0.85	0	0	0.34	0.09
E_3	0.01	0	■	0	0	0.12	0	0	0.07	0	0.18	0
E_4	0.64	0	0	■	0.09	0	0.56	0.15	0.09	0	0	0.03
E_5	0	0.02	0	0.08	■	0	0.09	0	0	0.01	0.02	0.07
E_6	0.21	0	0.05	0	0	■	0.88	0	0	0.01	0	0.02
E_7	0.17	0	0	0.76	0.08	0.54	■	0.18	0.06	0	0.17	0.01
E_8	0	0.48	0	0.12	0	0	0.21	■	0	0.74	0.49	0.03
E_9	0	0	0.02	0.11	0	0	0.07	0	■	0	0	0.03
E_{10}	0	0	0	0	0.01	0	0	0.38	0	■	0.02	0.87
E_{11}	0.01	0.18	0.09	0	0.02	0.01	0.16	0.90	0	0.01	■	0.02
E_{12}	0	0.01	0	0.02	0.06	0.02	0.01	0.02	0.04	0.39	0.02	■

Figure 8.7 A matrix showing the computed affinity between different entities. This can be employed when clustering the entities into subject databases.

database. If they have an affinity of zero, they should definitely not be. Where is the dividing line?

A computer can group the entities into clusters based on their affinity factors. If it puts entities with affinity factor = 0 in the same cluster, there will be only one cluster. If it puts entities with affinity factor = 1 in the same cluster, there may be as many clusters as entities. It could be instructed to set the affinity factor so as to produce 20 clusters, 30 clusters, or whatever the designer decides. These clusters are then used as subject databases.

The affinity factor does not take into account the volumes of use of each activity. A different way of calculating affinity may take usage volumes into consideration. The method has given good results, in practice, when automatically clustering the entities into subject databases.

CLUSTERING ALGORITHM   Suppose that we want to cluster the entities in Fig. 8.7 into databases. The entity pairs are sorted by affinity number and we begin with the highest affinity numbers. Entity pairs with the highest affinity form the nuclei of the clusters, thus:

E_1, E_4 (affinity = 0.92)
E_{11}, E_8 (affinity = 0.90)
E_6, E_7 (affinity = 0.88)
E_{10}, E_{12} (affinity = 0.87)

Eventually, we arrive at an entity pair in which one of the entities is already in one of the clusters. The next entity pair we encounter is such:

E_2, E_8 (affinity = 0.85)

E_8 is already assigned to a cluster nucleus E_{11}, E_8. Should we now link E_2 to that cluster? To determine that, we need to calculate the weighted affinity of E_2 to the cluster E_{11}, E_8.

$$\frac{(\text{affinity of } E_2 \text{ to } E_{11}) \times a(E_{11}) + (\text{affinity of } E_2 \text{ to } E_8) \times a(E_8)}{a(E_{11}) + a(E_8)}$$

Suppose that entity E_{11} is used by three activities and entity E_8 is used by 48 activities. Then the composite affinity of E_2 to the cluster E_{11}, E_8 is

$$\frac{0.34 \times 3 + 0.85 \times 48}{3 + 48} = 0.82$$

This is higher than any remaining affinity number in Fig. 8.7, so the cluster E_2, E_{11}, E_8 is formed.

After forming a proposed cluster of entity types or subject database, a matrix may then be displayed, mapping this against the activities that use those entities. This matrix may cause the planner to make other manual adjustments.

SUMMARY

The strategic planning information collected at the top level of the pyramid may be analyzed and examined in a variety of ways in order to understand better how to deploy the information system resources. The analysis and decision making are best done with the graphics capability of a personal computer extracting information from a mainframe encyclopedia.

The knowledge in the encyclopedia is added to and refined as information engineering progresses to the lower levels of the encyclopedia. Affinity analysis, clustering, and other forms of analysis are valuable in the more detailed stages, for example, in the planning of distribution and migration.

9 ENTITY-RELATIONSHIP MODELS AND CLUSTERING

INTRODUCTION   In Chapter 3 we referred to entity types. The entity types are grouped into data subjects. As described earlier, there are relationships among entities. During the ISP procedure an entity-relationship diagram is created showing the relationships among entities. As the analysts identify entities as described in Chapter 3, they should put these into an entity-relationship diagram built on a computer screen so that it can be quickly added to and reorganized.

The relationship between two entities is given a name (as in previous chapters), often a name in both directions.

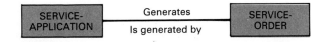

This says:

SERVICE-APPLICATION *generates* SERVICE-ORDER.

and

SERVICE-ORDER *is generated by* SERVICE-APPLICATION.

The relationship line shows the cardinalities in both directions:

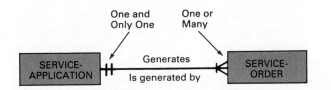

When a tool is used to build an entity-relationship diagram, the tool should give the analyst a panel asking for information about the relationship. It asks for the *minimum* and *maximum* cardinality in each direction. It may also ask for *average* cardinality because this can be used later for physical design calculations.

There are sometimes two or more relationships between two entities. Such relationships have different names. Sometimes an entity has a relationship with *either* one entity *or* another:

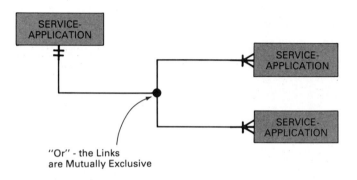

The following is an example of a simple entity-relationship diagram:

A CUSTOMER *places* one or more ORDERS.

An ORDER *has* one or more ORDER-LINES.

An ORDER-LINE *relates* to one and only one PRODUCT.

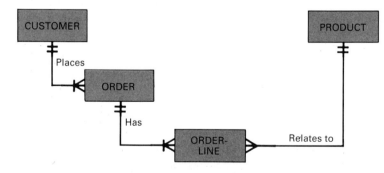

Such a representation is a statement about the fundamental nature of the data. It is independent of current procedures, systems, or departmental structures. The systems and procedures may be drastically redesigned and the departments that use them reorganized, but the statement above about CUSTOMERS, ORDERS, ORDER-LINES, and PRODUCT will remain valid. Figure 9.1 shows a portion of an entity-relationship diagram for a telephone company.

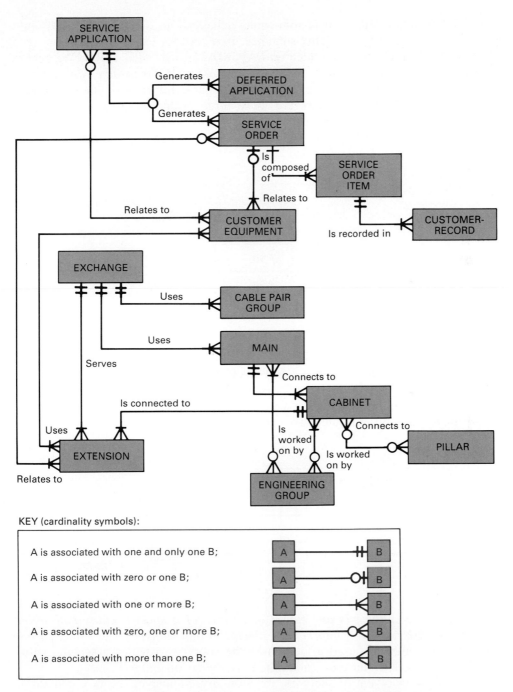

Figure 9.1   A portion of an entity-relationship diagram for a telephone company.

ENTITY SUBTYPES   It is sometimes necessary to divide entity types into entity subtypes. In a zoo, for example, the entity type CREATURE might be subdivided into ANIMAL, FISH, and BIRD. We regard these as entity subtypes *if they have different associations to other entity types*. If, on the other hand, we store essentially the same information about animals, fishes, and birds, we would regard these three categories as merely attribute values of the entity type CREATURE.

We can draw entity subtypes as divisions of the entity-type box, thus:

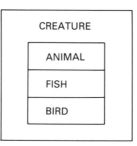

The entity type SATELLITE might be subdivided into LOW-ORBIT and GEOSYNCHRONOUS. LOW-ORBIT SATELLITE has a one-with-many association to the ORBIT DETAIL entity type. GEOSYNCHRONOUS SATELLITE has a one-with-many association with POSITION DETAIL. These two entity types have different attributes. This is drawn as follows:

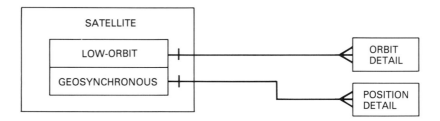

An entity subtype is any subset of entities of a specific entity type about which we wish to record information special to that subtype. The values of one or more attributes are used to determine the subtype to which a specific entity belongs. These attributes are called the *classifying attributes*.

If a group of entity subtypes are mutually exclusive, the box containing them is subdivided by solid lines (like an action diagram case structure) thus:

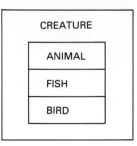

The entity is one and only one of these subtypes

If they are alternative choices, but there can be other subtypes not shown, there is a blank portion in the subtype box:

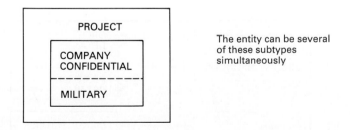

The entity can be one or none of these subtypes

If the entity could be several of the subtypes at the same time, the subtypes are separated by a dashed line.

The entity can be several of these subtypes simultaneously

An entity may be subdivided into more than one subtype grouping:

An entity subtype may itself be subdivided into sub-subtypes:

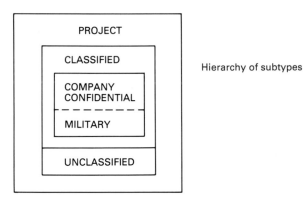

Hierarchy of subtypes

Associations to other entity types may be drawn from the subtypes:

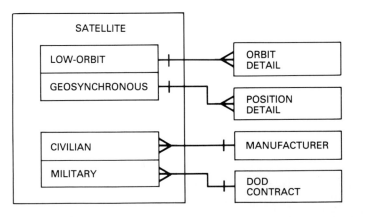

Entity subtypes behave in every way as though they were entity types. They have attributes and relationships with other entities. Palmer stresses that in his experience of data analysis the newcomer confuses the concepts of entity subtypes, and relationships among entity types [1]. He emphasizes the importance of recognizing these to be completely different concepts despite the fact that most database management systems ignore the concept of entity subtypes.

A simple test can help avoid confusion. We ask "Is *A* a *B*?" and "Is *B* an *A*?" The permissible answers are ALWAYS, SOMETIMES, and NEVER. If both answers are NEVER, we are not concerned with subtyping. If both answers are ALWAYS, then *A* and *B* are synonyms. If the answers are:

"Is *A* a *B*?"   ALWAYS

"Is *B* an *A*?"   SOMETIMES

Then *A* is a subtype of *B*.

Let us look at a case that might be confusing. A somewhat bureaucratic organization has people with the following titles: OFFICIAL, ADVISOR, SUBAGENT, and REPRESENTATIVE. Should each of these be a separate entity type, or are they subtypes, or merely attributes?

The cells in the following table answer the question "Is *A* a *B*?"

Is A a B?		B: OFFICIAL	ADVISOR	SUBAGENT	REPRESENTATIVE
A:	OFFICIAL		Sometimes	Never	Always
	ADVISOR	Never		Never	Never
	SUBAGENT	Never	Never		Always
	REPRESENTATIVE	Sometimes	Never	Sometimes	

The word "always" appears twice. An OFFICIAL and a SUBAGENT are *always* a REPRESENTATIVE. These can be subtypes of the entity type REPRESENTATIVE. An OFFICIAL is *never* a SUBAGENT, and vice versa, so they are mutually exclusive subtypes. Can there be representatives other than OFFICIALS and SUBAGENTS? *No.* Therefore, we draw:

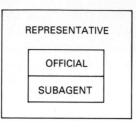

An ADVISOR is *never* any of the others, so that is a separate entity type.

Do we *really* want to regard an OFFICIAL and a SUBAGENT as an entity subtype, or should they be attributes of REPRESENTATIVE? To answer this, we ask: Do they have associations which are different from those of REPRESENTATIVE that we need to include in the data model? *Yes,* they do. An OFFICIAL supervises a SUBAGENT. A SUBAGENT is an external employee working for a CORPORATION about which separate records are kept. An association from OFFICIAL to SUBAGENT is needed. This can be drawn inside the entity-type box:

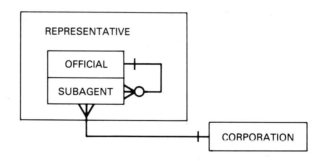

This conveys more information than an attempt at entity analysis without subtyping, which might show the following:

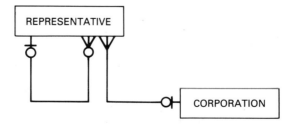

ENTITY-TYPE DECOMPOSITION DIAGRAM

Where the subtyping of an entity is nontrivial, a decomposition diagram may be used to represent it, as here:

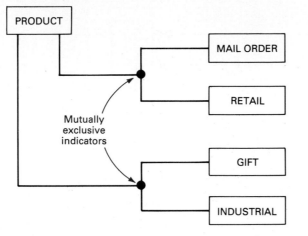

Figure 9.2 shows a two-level decomposition of the entity type EM-PLOYEE.

DECOMPOSITION SHOWN ON AN ENTITY-RELATIONSHIP DIAGRAM

Figure 9.3 shows an entity-relationship diagram which includes decomposition of entity types.

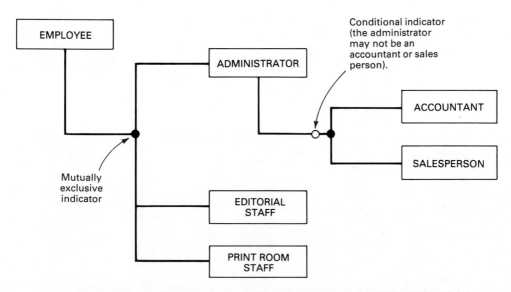

Figure 9.2   A two-level decomposition of the entity type EMPLOYEE.

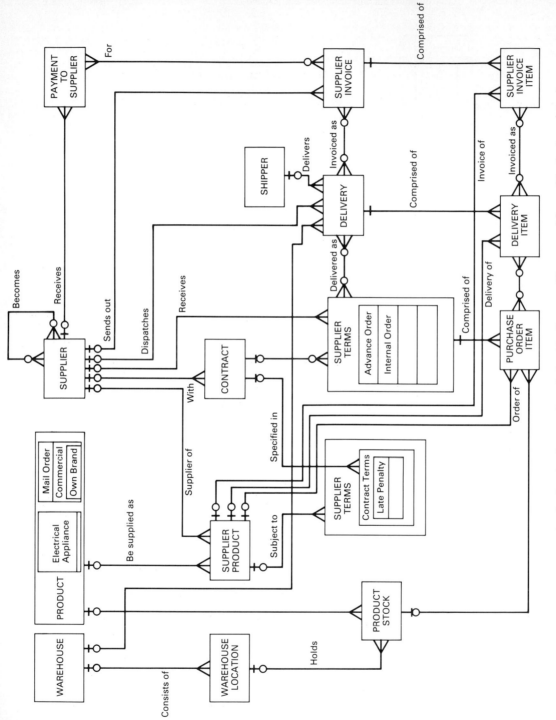

Figure 9.3 Example of subtyping in an entity relationship diagram. (Courtesy of James Martin Associates.)

AVOIDANCE OF TOO MUCH DETAIL

An ISP creates an overview of the enterprise which acts as a logical framework into which further analysis and procedure design can fit. An objective is to do this fairly quickly, maintaining the interest of senior management. Some strategic planning efforts have attempted to identify data *attributes* as well as *entity types* and to normalize the data. To create a normalized data model takes *much* longer than merely identifying the entity types and relationships. It is important to complete the ISP study quickly (the goal should be no more than six months) and not bog down in too much detail. Detail such as normalization of data does not interest senior management. This detail follows in business area analysis studies, which each analyze a coherent portion of the enterprise rather than the entire enterprise.

Normalization of data leads to the identification of concatenated keys, discussed in Chapter 12. At the ISP level there is no need to identify concatenated keys. This occurs when a normalized data model is built.

While the methodology avoids technical detail at the ISP stage, the analysts *can* enter attributes and concatenated keys into a computerized data model *if this can be done without slowing down the overall effort*. It will help when full normalization is done later.

In the attempt to move quickly, some ISP studies have avoided building an entity-relationship diagram. They have merely identified the entities. The entity-relationship diagram has been left until the later detailed data modeling. It helps to build an entity-relationship diagram at this stage *if an appropriate computerized tool is used*. The entering of relationships takes little time and helps to validate the identification of entity types. It sometimes provokes the discovery of other entities. It helps in the splitting of entities and business functions into separate groups for business area analysis.

THE ENTITY/FUNCTION MATRIX

The entities and functions from the previous steps can be transferred automatically to a matrix diagram which maps functions against entities, as shown in Fig. 9.4. The analyst fills in the intersections of this diagram to indicate which functions create, read, update, and delete each entity. The codes C, R, U, and D are entered at the intersections:

C Create

R Read

U Update

D Delete

Both the number of functions and the number of entity types are too large for one screen display, so the tool must be able to scroll the matrix horizontally and vertically. The analyst should be asking at this stage what entity types are

FUNCTION

DATA SUBJECT	Financial Planning	Accounting	Financial Control	Staff Organizations	Training	HR Programs	Production Planning	Research and Development	Purchasing	Production	Product Planning	Marketing	Order Processing	Business Management	Vendor Relations
Employees	R	R		CRUD	RU	R							R		
HR Plans, Procedures, Regs				CRUD	R	CRUD	R				R			R	
Financial Plans, Procedures, Reg	CRUD	RU	CRUD	R			R				R			R	
Financial Income	R	CRUD	R								R			R	
Financial Outflow	R	CRUD	R											R	
Financial Investments	R	CRUD	CRUD											R	
Product Plans, Procedures, Regs	R			R	R		R	R			CRUD	R		R	
Product Materials		R					R	CRUD	RU	RU		R			
Finished Products		R					R	CRUD		RU	R	R	RU		
Facility Plans, Procedures, Regs	R			R			R	R		R	R			CRUD	
Company Locations		R		R	R				R	R				CRUD	R
Equipment		R					RU	CRUD		R	R			R	
Org. Plans, Procedures, Regs	R	R	R	CRUD	R						R			CRUD	
Vendors		R							R				R		CRUD
Customers	R	R									R	R	CRUD	R	

Figure 9.4   A matrix mapping functions against data subjects.

used in conjunction with each function. In the early stages of the analysis he usually discovers entity types not yet on his list. He adds these to the entity-relationship diagram and function decomposition diagrams, and they are then automatically added to the matrix.

The matrix diagram can automatically highlight problems: for example, an entity type that is not *created* by any function, or a function that does not use any entity type. It can highlight situations that should be examined *in case* they are a problem, for example, an entity type that is not updated by any function, or an entity type that is created by more than one function.

VALIDATING THE MATRIX

The items on the matrix can be grouped together in a variety of ways. The analyst uses the matrix to validate his design and check its completeness. He can resequence the rows and columns in a variety of ways to help in the validation.

Originally, the computer may sequence the functions in accordance with the functional decomposition chart, grouping together functions that have the same parent. The analyst may highlight a function or a group of functions and ask that the associated entity types be displayed together. He then checks the group for completeness. Similarly, he may highlight an entity type or related group of entity types and ask that the associated functions be displayed together. He may be able to highlight a related group of entity types on the entity-relationship diagram and see this grouping on the matrix with their associated functions.

The entity-relationship diagram, function decomposition diagram, and entity/function matrix form an interlinked set of diagrams which when used together enable a person to check the completeness and validity of the analysis. They enable the analysis to be discussed with management.

OTHER MATRICES

Two other matrices may be created and manipulated with similar software. The organization chart (e.g., the items on Fig. 3.2) may be mapped against the functions or the entity types.

The analyst may map functions against the departments on the organization chart, again checking for completeness and validity. He may map entity types against departments. The *create, read, update,* and *delete* codes may be automatically transferred from the function/entity type matrix to the department/entity type matrix. The analyst may gain an understanding of the extent to which departments share the use of data or are in conflict in ownership of data or the right to update it. When top managers examine the mapping of the organization chart against the functions or entity types, they sometimes become persuaded that the organization chart needs modifying.

In some strategic planning studies the executives who are interviewed are themselves listed on a matrix like that of Fig. 3.8. This is done in BSP (Business Systems Planning) studies as recommended by IBM, for example. Figure 3.8 shows a matrix mapping key employees against functions and indicating their degree of involvement with that function. If a function/entity type matrix exists, the information of Fig. 3.8 can be converted into a matrix mapping the executives against the data they are involved with. The executives in question may assist in validating the analysis.

CLUSTERING
THE MATRIX

A function/entity type matrix should be clustered to show what functions and data fit naturally together. These groupings form the basis for establishing *business areas,* which will be examined in more detail during *business area analysis.* The groupings may form the basis of systems and help determine what functions a specific system should perform and what data it will use.

Two types of computer algorithm can be used to cluster a function/entity matrix. The first uses a list of functions arranged in the sequence of a natural lifecycle and clusters the entity types which are created by each function. This method is described in this chapter. The second uses affinities among entity types as a basis for clustering the entity types. The affinities may be provided by an analyst who may mark them on an entity-relationship diagram, or may be computed based on how many activities use both of the entity types in question. Chapter 8 discussed the latter clustering algorithm.

Figure 9.5 shows a function/entity type matrix. High-level groupings of entities are shown, sometimes referred to as *data subjects* or simply *subjects*. The functions in Fig. 9.5 are the same as those in Fig. 3.4. They are listed *in the sequence of the lifecycle of the product:* first planning the business, then obtaining the finance, then market study, and so on, until finally the product is delivered; then the accounting is completed. The function that does not directly relate to the product lifecycle is the personnel function, so that is listed last.

To cluster the items in Fig. 9.5, the sequence of the entity types is changed. A "C" on Fig. 9.5 indicates that a given function *creates* or *updates* a given entity type. An "R" indicates that it *reads* but does not modify that entity type.

The entity type that is created or updated by the first function is moved to the left. Then the entity type (if any) created or updated by the second function is moved to the left. This continues for all entity types. The resulting matrix, shown in Fig. 9.6, has its "C's" arranged on a top-left-to-bottom-right diagonal.

The functions and data can now be grouped into major system areas by boxing the groupings as shown in Fig. 9.7. The analyst may examine the groupings that result, again endeavoring to validate the functions and entity types. The boxes represent logical information subsystem groupings with responsibility for creating and maintaining the various classes of data. A variety of subjective considerations may cause the analyst to adjust the groupings. Groupings such as those in Fig. 9.7 may be used to form *business areas,* which become the basis for business area analysis—the building of more detailed models of data and processes (level 2 of the pyramid).

In Fig. 9.8 names are given to the clusters of functions. When a use of data (U) falls outside any box on Fig. 9.8, the functions in the box must access a database elsewhere, or else data must flow from one subsystem to another. The dashed line on Fig. 9.8 illustrates this. The *materials control* function uses *bill of materials* data. This data may be passed from the product design subsystem to the manufacturing subsystem. Many such data flows could be drawn among the subsystems of Fig. 9.8, as shown on Fig. 9.9.

DEPENDENCIES AMONG FUNCTIONS

The functions in an enterprise are highly interdependent. One function uses data that are generated by other functions. Dependencies among functions are drawn on a *dependency diagram*. A dependency diagram draws functions (or processes) as round-cornered boxes. A dependency between two functions is drawn as a line with an arrow connecting the two boxes. The following diagram means that function *B* is dependent on function *A*:

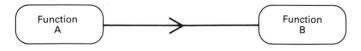

FUNCTION	Customer	Budget	Financial	Vendor	Procurements	Materials Inventory	Fin. Goods Inventory	Orders	Costs	Sales	Sales Territory	Payments	Planning	Employee	Salaries	Facilities	Work in Progress	Machine Load	Open Requirements	Shop Floor Routings	Product	Product Design	Parts Master	Bill of Materials
Market Analysis	R									R	R		R								R			
Product Range Review									R				R											
Sales Forecasting	R	C								R	R		C								R			
Financial Planning		R							R				C											
Capital Acquisition		R	C										R											
Funds Management		R	R																					
Product Design													R								C	C	C	
Product Pricing	R								R												C	R		
Product Spec. Maint.																					R		C	C
Materials Requirements					R														C		R		R	R
Purchasing				C	C																R		R	
Receiving				R	R	R															R		R	
Inventory Control						C											R							
Quality Control					C																			
Capacity Planning					R												R	C	R	R				
Plant Scheduling																	R	C	R	R	R			
Workflow Layout																	C		C	R				
Materials Control					R												R		C	R				R
Sizing and Cutting																	R		C	R				R
Machine Operations																	R		C					
Territory Management	C							R			R													
Selling										C	C													
Sales Administration								R			R													
Customer Relations	R								R	R														
Finished Stock Control							C										R				R			
Order Servicing	R						C														R			
Packing							R														R			
Shipping																					R			
Creditors & Debtors	R			R								R												
Cash Flow	R		R	R				R	R			R			R	R								
Payroll												C		R	R									
Cost Accounting					R			C	C															R
Budget Planning		C	R						R	R			R			R								
Profitability Analysis									R	R														
Personnel Planning			R											C	C									
Recruiting														R	R									
Compensation Policy			R											R	R									

Figure 9.5

175

DATA SUBJECT

FUNCTION	Planning	Budget	Financial	Product	Product Design	Parts Master	Bill of Materials	Open Requirements	Vendor	Procurements	Materials Inventory	Machine Load	Work in Progress	Facilities	Shop Floor Routines	Customer	Sales	Sales Territory	Fin. Goods Inventory	Orders	Payments	Cost	Employee	Salaries
Market Analysis	R			R												R	R	R						
Product Range Review	R																					R		
Sales Forecasting	C	C		R												R	R	R						
Financial Planning	C	R																				R		
Capital Acquisition	R	R	C																					
Funds Management		R	R																					
Product Design	R				C	C	C																	
Product Pricing		R			C																	R		
Product Spec. Maint.					R	C	C																	
Materials Requirements					R	R	R	C	R															
Purchasing					R		R		C	C														
Receiving					R		R	R	R	R														
Inventory Control											C		R											
Quality Control											C													
Capacity Planning								R	R			C		R	R									
Plant Scheduling				R								R	C	R	R									
Workflow Layout				R										C	C									
Materials Control				R			R	R				R												
Sizing and Cutting				R			R					R		C										
Machine Operations												R		C										
Territory Management																C		R		R				
Selling																C	C							
Sales Administration																	R		R					
Customer Relations																R	R			R				
Finished Stock Control				R									R						C					
Order Servicing				R												R			C					
Packing				R															R					
Shipping				R															R					
Creditors & Debtors										R						R					R			
Cash Flow								R	R	R						R				R	R	R		R
Payroll																						C	R	R
Cost Accounting							R			R											C	C		
Budget Planning	R	C	R									R							R			R		
Profitability Analysis				R															R			R		
Personnel Planning				R																			C	C
Recruiting				R																			R	R
Compensation Policy				R																			R	R

Figure 9.6

FUNCTION	Planning	Budget	Financial	Product	Product Design	Parts Master	Bill of Materials	Open Requirements	Vendor	Procurements	Materials Inventory	Machine Load	Work in Progress	Facilities	Shop Floor Routines	Customer	Sales	Sales Territory	Fin. Goods Inventory	Orders	Payments	Cost	Employee	Salaries
Market Analysis	R		R	R												R	R	R			R			
Product Range Review	R																				R			
Sales Forecasting	C	C		R												R	R	R			R			
Financial Planning	C	R																			R			
Capital Acquisition	R	R	C																					
Funds Management		R	R																					
Product Design	R				C	C	C														R			
Product Pricing		R			C																R			
Product Spec. Maint.	R					C	C																	
Materials Requirements					R			R	R	C	R													
Purchasing					R			R	C	C														
Receiving					R		R	R	R	R	C													
Inventory Control											C			R										
Quality Control											C													
Capacity Planning							R	R				C		R	R									
Plant Scheduling					R							R	C	R	R									
Workflow Layout					R								C	C										
Materials Control					R		R		R			R												
Sizing and Cutting					R		R					R		C										
Machine Operations												R		C										
Territory Management																C		R	R					
Selling																	C	C						
Sales Administration																	C	R		R				
Customer Relations																R	R			R				
Finished Stock Control					R											R			C					
Order Servicing					R											R				C				
Packing					R															R				
Shipping					R														R					
Creditors & Debtors							R									R					R	R		R
Cash Flow								R	R							R			R		R	C	R	R
Payroll																					C		R	R
Cost Accounting							R			R											C	C		
Budget Planning	R	C	R													R					R	R		
Profitability Analysis					R																R	R		
Personnel Planning	R																						C	C
Recruiting																							R	R
Compensation Policy	R																						R	R

Figure 9.7

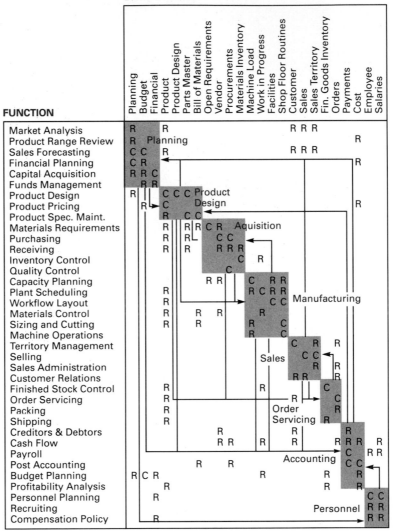

Figure 9.8

DATA SUBJECT

FUNCTION	Planning	Budget	Financial	Product	Product Design	Parts Master	Bill of Materials	Open Requirements	Vendor	Procurements	Materials Inventory	Machine Load	Work in Progress	Facilities	Shop Floor Routines	Customer	Sales	Sales Territory	Fin. Goods Inventory	Orders	Payments	Cost	Employee	Salaries
Market Analysis	R			R												R	R	R						
Product Range Review	R																				R			
Sales Forecasting	C	C		R												R	R	R						
Financial Planning	C	R																			R			
Capital Acquisition	R	R	C																					
Funds Management		R	R																					
Product Design	R				C	C	C																	
Product Pricing				R	C																R			
Product Spec. Maint.					R	C	C																	
Materials Requirements					R		R	R	C	R														
Purchasing					R		R		C	C														
Receiving					R		R		R	R	R													
Inventory Control										C			R											
Quality Control										C														
Capacity Planning								R	R			C		R	R									
Plant Scheduling					R							R	C	R	R									
Workflow Layout					R								C	C										
Materials Control					R		R		R			R												
Sizing and Cutting					R		R					R		C										
Machine Operations												R		C										
Territory Management																C	R			R				
Selling																	C	C						
Sales Administration																		R		R				
Customer Relations																R	R			R				
Finished Stock Control					R											R			C					
Order Servicing					R													R	C					
Packing					R														C					
Shipping					R														R					
Creditors & Debtors								R								R				R				
Cash Flow								R	R				R			R				R	R	R	R	R
Payroll																				R	C		R	R
Post Accounting							R		R											R	C	C		
Budget Planning	R	C	R										R							R		R		
Profitability Analysis					R															R		R		
Personnel Planning					R																		C	C
Recruiting																							R	R
Compensation Policy					R																		R	R

Cluster labels shown within the matrix: Planning, Product Design, Aquisition, Manufacturing, Sales, Order Servicing, Accounting, Personnel.

Figure 9.9

BOX 9.1   A procedure for clustering a matrix of entities and functions

```
Create a top-level analysis of corporate data.
    Identify the data subjects.
    Decompose into entity types.
    Create an initial entity-relationship diagram.
    Create a matrix mapping functions against entity types.
    Create a matrix mapping organizational units against entity types.
    Print relevant versions of the above diagrams from the
        encyclopedia for the participants to review.

Refine the enterprise model and entity-relationship diagram.
    Conduct meetings with end users and management to critique the
        enterprise model.
    Make any improvements to the enterprise model as a result of
        the presentations to end users and management.
    Refine the entity-relationship diagram.
    Refine the matrix of entity types and business functions.
    Refine the matrix of entity types and organizational units.
    Obtain approval for the enterprise model.

Cluster the function/entity matrix to show natural systems.
    Use the clustering algorithm of the strategic planning tool.
    Cluster on the basis of what functions CREATE what entity types.
    Assign all remaining functions and entity types to clusters.
    Refine the groupings manually to identify natural systems.
    Identify what data must flow from one system to another.
    Create a dependency diagram showing the dependencies among the groupings.
    Refine the clusterings to minimize the interaction among systems.

Cluster the function/entity matrix to show natural business areas.
    Adjust the clustered function/entity matrix to form BAA boundaries.
    Assign all functions to a business area.
    Determine the geographical locations of each business area.
    Refine the business areas so that they are naturally cohesive.
```

If function *A* does not take place, function *B* cannot take place. The most common reason for the dependency is that *A* generates or updates data that are required by *B*. The data may pass directly from *A* to *B,* or *A* may update database records which are used by *B.*

Some corporations doing information strategy planning draw the dependencies among functions; others do not. Process dependency diagrams are an essential part of the second stage of information engineering (business area analysis). They may not be necessary to achieve the objectives of the first stage. The essential information needs of an enterprise can be determined without drawing dependency diagrams. The clustering of functions into business areas does not necessarily need dependency diagrams. However, function dependency diagrams can clarify the overview model of the enterprise.

An entity/function matrix such as Fig. 9.8 could be *automatically* converted into a dependency diagram showing the dependencies among the eight subsystems on the diagram. Figure 9.9 shows the dependencies. Box 9.1 shows a procedure for clustering the entities and functions into cohesive systems.

TOO MUCH DETAIL   There is often a tendency when doing overview modeling to drop down into greater depth. Some analysts have drawn dependency diagrams or data flow diagrams; some have attempted to normalize the data. We have stressed that the objective at the top level of the pyramid is to create a high-level overview and to do this quickly so as not to lose the interest of senior management. Dropping into too much detail slows down the overview modeling. Detail such as drawing dependency diagrams should be saved for the second level of the pyramid—business area analysis.

10 FOLLOW-ON FROM STRATEGIC PLANNING

INTRODUCTION It is desirable that the ISP study is followed immediately by vigorous action that leads to implementing better systems. Some strategic planning studies are not followed by action, and this makes them of little value. When the ISP results are presented to top management, a detailed action plan should accompany them saying what happens next.

If the enterprise has no experience with data modeling, the ISP may be followed by *one business area analysis (BAA)*. The area selected should be one where the results will be especially valuable and the complexities are not too great. A function of this project should be to build a nucleus of experienced analysts who can move on to perform other BAAs quickly.

If the enterprise has a well-established data administration function, it can act more quickly in business area analysis. There may be a project needed to enter existing data models and process models into the encyclopedia. There may be some areas where data modeling is yet to be done. It may be possible to move quickly into the *system design* and *construction* phases for areas already modeled.

The ISP project identifies certain critical and urgent needs for systems. These are often decision-support systems or executive information systems. Sometimes, management wants these quickly and they can indeed be built quickly with information center techniques, decision-support systems, spreadsheets, and so on. Sometimes an executive information center (Book III) can provide senior management with critical information quickly. As we commented, these urgent needs may short-circuit middle layers of the pyramid so that senior management can see that important business needs can be addressed expediently.

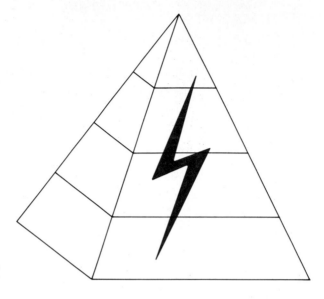

IDENTIFYING BUSINESS AREAS

A "business area" is a naturally cohesive grouping of business functions and data that forms the basis for business area analysis. A matrix of business functions and entity types is clustered to form business areas. This clustering may be done with the aid of clustering algorithms as discussed in Chapter 8. The clusters may be adjusted by hand to meet a variety of constraints. A business area should be:

- Clear-cut with definable boundaries
- Small enough that business area analysis can proceed quickly
- Large enough to take advantage of shared databases in a natural coherent way
- Nonoverlapping with other business areas (i.e., not sharing business functions)
- Generally not updated by other business areas, although some data will be passed among business areas

The clustering into business areas should be done as part of the overview enterprise modeling. It can lead to a rethinking of the basic structure of the enterprise.

A business area contains several business systems. A business system also consists of a cluster of naturally cohesive entity types and processes. Natural business systems may be identified at the same time that business areas are determined. The boundaries of a natural business system will be determined with more precision when business area analysis is done. A natural business system should not span two business areas. We thus have two clusterings of the business-function/entity-type matrix, one into natural business systems, and one into business areas ready for business area analysis.

CHOICE OF BUSINESS AREA(S) TO ANALYZE
When an enterprise has been split into areas for business area analysis, it is necessary to decide which area or areas to tackle first. It would be nice to have a simple return-on-investment computation for determining priorities, but in practice multiple considerations are likely to affect the choice. It is recommended that the criteria be grouped for consideration as follows:

Potential benefit
- Return on investment (This may be difficult to calculate and requires value judgments.)
     Tangibles
     Intangibles
- Achievement of critical success factors
- Achievement of goals
- Solution to serious problems

Demand
- Pressure of demand from senior end users for new or improved systems
- Assessed need
- Political overtones

Organizational impact
- Number of organizations and people affected
- Whether the organizations are geographically dispersed
- Qualitative effect

Existing systems
- Adequacy or value of existing systems
- Relationship with existing systems
- Estimated future costs of maintenance (Systems that are fragile or have high maintenance costs should be replaced.)

Likely success
- Complexity (Relatively simple areas should be the first to be tackled until experience is gained.)
- Degree of business acceptance
- Length of project
- Prerequisites
- Risks

Resources required
- Whether existing data or process models exist
- Whether a suitable toolkit is installed
- Quality of available analysts
- Funds required

Concurrent implementation
- Whether multiple business area analysis projects can proceed concurrently
- Whether one project will train people who can quickly move onto other projects
- Whether an existing data administration function has already done good data modeling

It is suggested that the areas for possible BAA analysis be ranked on a scale of 1 to 7 for each of the categories in the foregoing list. An informed decision can then be made about which area(s) to tackle first. Since information should be treated as a business resource, information system projects should be evaluated by management in much the same way as business projects are evaluated. The return on investment, requisite manpower, and possible risks should be evaluated like any new business venture. This can be done if the corporation as a whole is being examined with the involvement of suitably high executives.

ANALYSIS OF CURRENT SYSTEMS

An enterprise usually has many data processing systems which were established before information engineering came into use. They do not use the data models of information engineering and do not link into the encyclopedia with its knowledge coordination. It is desirable to chart the existing systems and clarify how they currently support the business. Three matrices may be used for this, as shown in Fig. 10.1. These matrices are shown in more detail in Figs. 10.2 through 10.4. They help to clarify system voids and redundancies. There are often major redundancies in systems developed without information engineering.

There is often a major need to rebuild old systems. They have often been maintained by multiple programmers with different styles and are often lacking in integrated design. They become fragile and difficult to change. When they are rebuilt this should be done with the data models and automated design techniques of information engineering. Migration from old systems to cleanly engineered systems is discussed in Book III.

Matrices such as those in Figs. 10.2 through 10.4 may include both the information-engineered systems and the old incompatible ones. Priorities need to be established for the rebuilding of the old systems.

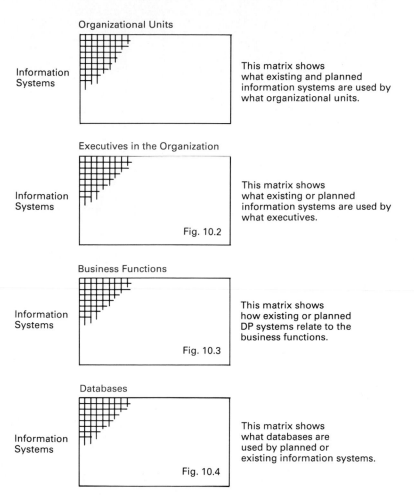

Figure 10.1 Matrices showing existing systems. These are shown in more detail in Figs. 10.2 through 10.4.

TOP-LEVEL TECHNOLOGY PLANNING

Certain types of technology planning need to be done at the highest level in an enterprise. For example, it is desirable to have a data network that links all parts of the enterprise and goes to every knowledge worker's desk like a nervous system. Achieving full compatibility, so that any computer can be connected to this network, raises many complex issues and needs substantial planning and design. This planning can only be done at the top level in an enterprise because the network needs to serve all the divisions and locations. The network design relates to the permissible choice of computers and workstations.

INFORMATION SYSTEMS	President	Vice President of Finance	Controller	Personnel Director	Vice President of Sales	Order Control Manager	Electronic Sales Manager	Electrical Sales Manager	Vice President of Engineering	Vice President of Production	Plant Operations Director	Production Planning Director	Facilities Manager	Materials Control Manager	Purchasing Manager	Division Lawyer	Planning Director
Customer Order Entry	✓				✓	✓	✓	✓		✓	✓	✓					
Customer Order Control	✓				✓	✓	✓	✓		✓	✓	✓		✓	✓		
Invoicing		✓	✓														
Engineering Control									✓								
Finished Goods Inventory	✓	✓	✓		✓		✓	✓		✓		✓	✓				
Bills of Material									✓	✓	✓	✓	✓				
Parts Inventory		✓	✓		✓	✓	✓	✓				✓					
Purchase Order Control					✓	✓	✓	✓		✓	✓	✓					
Routings										✓	✓	✓	✓				
Shop Floor Control										✓	✓	✓	✓				
Capacity Planning	✓								✓	✓	✓	✓	✓				✓
General Ledger		✓	✓														
Expense			✓		✓												
Product Costing	✓	✓	✓		✓		✓	✓				✓		✓	✓		
Operating Statements	✓	✓	✓														
Accounts Receivable																✓	
Accounts Payable	✓	✓	✓														✓
Asset Accounting	✓	✓	✓													✓	
Market Analysis	✓				✓		✓	✓									✓
Payroll				✓													

Figure 10.2   The existing (or planned) systems are mapped against the organization structure. The top of this matrix lists executive positions. This matrix hence forms a basis (in part) for executive interviews.

Also complex is the choice of software in the enterprise. In an earlier era, software ran in a largely stand-alone fashion on one computer. Increasingly today, integration of software is needed. In IBM installations it is usually important to standardize on IBM's SAA (Systems Application Architecture). Software on personal computers needs to link to software on departmental computers and mainframe computers. Application software needs to link to database software and data is increasingly distributed. Different knowledge workers with their own decision-support capabilities need to be able to exchange information via the enterprise network and need to be able to discuss by telephone complex representations of information which both have on their screens. Knowledge

INFORMATION SYSTEMS \ BUSINESS FUNCTIONS	Planning	Research	Forecasting	Territory Management	Selling	Administration	Order Servicing	Design and Development	Product Specification Maint	Information Control	Scheduling	Capacity Planning	Material Requirements	Operations	Purchasing	Receiving	Inventory Control	Shipping	Work Flow Layout	Maintenance	Equipment Performance	General Accounting & Control	Cost Planning	Budget Accounting/Tax Accounting	Financial Planning	Capital Acquisition	Funds Management	Personnel Planning	Recruiting/Development	Compensation	Business Planning	Organization Analysis	Review and Control	Risk Management
Customer Order Entry			✓				✓				✓	✓	✓																		✓			
Customer Order Control							✓				✓	✓		✓		✓																		
Invoicing																						✓		✓										
Engineering Control								✓																										
Finished Goods Inventory															✓	✓	✓					✓	✓											
Bills of Material								✓	✓	✓			✓										✓											
Parts Inventory					✓								✓		✓																			
Purchase Order Control											✓	✓	✓		✓																			
Routings											✓		✓	✓																				
Shop Floor Control											✓		✓	✓			✓																	
Capacity Planning													✓	✓																				
General Ledger																						✓					✓							
Expense			✓																			✓												
Product Costing											✓		✓		✓								✓											
Operating Statements																						✓									✓	✓		✓
Accounts Receivable																						✓												✓
Accounts Payable																						✓										✓		✓
Asset Accounting																									✓		✓							✓
Market Analysis			✓	✓		✓																										✓		
Payroll																						✓			✓					✓				

Figure 10.3 The business processes are mapped against current and existing systems.

workers need to be able to exchange computerized business models or other computations.

Top-level technology planning involves a variety of issues which are beyond the scope of this book, such as production technology, network technology, standards for personal computers, and so on. In general, information engineering requires *open* networks (i.e., networks that facilitate full interconnectability of facilities on machines of different vendors). Open networks require *standards*. The choice and implementation of standards for interconnectability is critical.

It is important that top-level plans and standards not impede creativity. In

INFORMATION SYSTEMS \ DATABASES	Customer	Order	Vendor	Product	Routings	Bills of Material	Cost	Parts Master	Raw Material Inventory	Finished Goods Inventory	Employee	Sales Territory	Financial	Planning	Work in Progress	Facilities	Open Requirements	Machine Load
Customer Order Entry	√	√	√	√			√			√			√					
Customer Order Control	√	√	√	√	√	√	√			√			√		√			
Invoicing	√	√	√				√						√					
Engineering Control				√	√	√	√	√	√	√							√	
Finished Goods Inventory		√		√					√	√			√		√			
Bills of Material		√	√	√	√	√	√	√	√	√			√		√		√	
Parts Inventory			√	√				√	√	√			√		√			
Purchase Order Control		√	√	√			√						√		√			
Routings		√	√	√	√				√	√			√					√
Shop Floor Control		√	√	√	√	√				√					√			√
Capacity Planning		√	√	√	√	√	√	√	√	√			√		√	√		√
General Ledger		√		√			√		√	√	√		√		√			
Expense														√	√			
Product Costing		√		√			√	√					√		√	√	√	
Operating Statements												√	√	√		√		
Accounts Receivable	√	√	√									√	√					
Accounts Payable											√		√				√	
Asset Accounting													√	√			√	
Marketing Analysis	√	√		√									√	√				
Payroll											√							

Figure 10.4   The planning team needs to understand what data currently exists, and which systems use which data. A matrix such as this will refer to existing *databases* as well as *files*.

practice, creativity in application building is enhanced if interconnectability is made easy. To achieve interconnectability, we need networking standards and data standards. Machines must be easy to interconnect technically, and different locations must employ the same data model. An encyclopedia with a knowledge coordinator can ensure that different applications or parts of applications can intercommunicate.

In this book we do not discuss technology planning such as network standards and design. The corporate network and other technology affect the implementation of business plans and offers opportunities for improving the functioning of the enterprise: for example, better connections with customers, agents, buyers, and suppliers; better decision making; lower inventory; new types of business; and so on. Business strategy planning therefore needs to link to top-level technology planning as well as strategic information planning:

WHO KEEPS THE ISP UP TO DATE?

Some person must have an ongoing responsibility for keeping the ISP information in the encyclopedia up to date. The technical information about entity types and business functions becomes more precise as business area analysis studies are done. The charts of new technology and business opportunities should be kept up to date by a person who is enthusiastic about technology and keeps himself up to date.

Goals and problems should be reviewed whenever management-by-objectives interviews are done for guiding executives and department heads. Periodically (not less than once a year), strategic business planning meetings take place. At these meetings the *technology impact analysis, critical success factor analysis* and *strategic systems studies* should be revisited and should help to guide the business planning. In some corporations critical success factors are part of the documentation for board meetings, and modifications to them may be recommended by the board. This is useful and should be done for the board meetings of most corporations. Some corporations have a technical advisory board. This board should review the technical impact analysis, strategic systems study, and possibly also, critical success factor analysis. These aids to top-management planning should be a live and vigorous part of the ongoing planning process.

PROCEDURE

Box 10.1 summarizes the steps in the transition from ISP to business area analysis.

BOX 10.1 Steps in the transition for ISP to BAA

Group the enterprise model into natural clusters.

- Cluster the function/entity matrix to show natural systems.
  - Use the clustering algorithm of the strategic planning tool.
  - Cluster on the basis of what functions CREATE what entity types.
  - Assign remaining functions and entity types to clusters.
  - Refine the groupings manually.

- Cluster the function/entity matrix to show natural business areas.
  - Adjust the clustered function/entity matrix to form BAA boundaries.
  - Assign all functions to a business area.
  - Determine the locations of that business area.
  - Build a matrix of business areas and locations.
  - Build a matrix of business areas and departments.
  - Refine the business areas as necessary.

- Refine BAA project boundaries
  - Consider:
    - o Time to implement BAA.
    - o Effort required to implement BAA.
    - o How the proposed BAA fits with the current organization.
    - o Risk Assessment
      - User acceptance/participation
      - User sophistication/readiness
      - Technical complexity

Analyze current systems to determine what changes are needed
- Build a matrix mapping I.S. systems against organizational units.
- Build a matrix mapping I.S. systems against executives.
- Build a matrix mapping I.S. systems against business functions.
- Build a matrix mapping I.S. systems against entity types.
- Cluster the above matrices into business areas.
- Identify which systems are in need of replacement or redesign.
- Identify which systems are expensive in maintenance costs.

Prepare follow-on from Strategic Information Planning
- Comment
  - When the ISP results are presented to top management a detailed action plan should accompany them saying what happens next. It is desirable that the ISP study is immediately followed by vigorous action which leads to implementing better systems.

- Prioritize the business areas for Business Area Analysis
  - There are multiple factors which affect the prioritization of which business area to work on first.
  - Rank the factors below on a scale of 1 to 7
    - Potential benefits
      - Return on investment.
        - (This may be difficult to calculate and requires

BOX 10.1 *(Continued)*

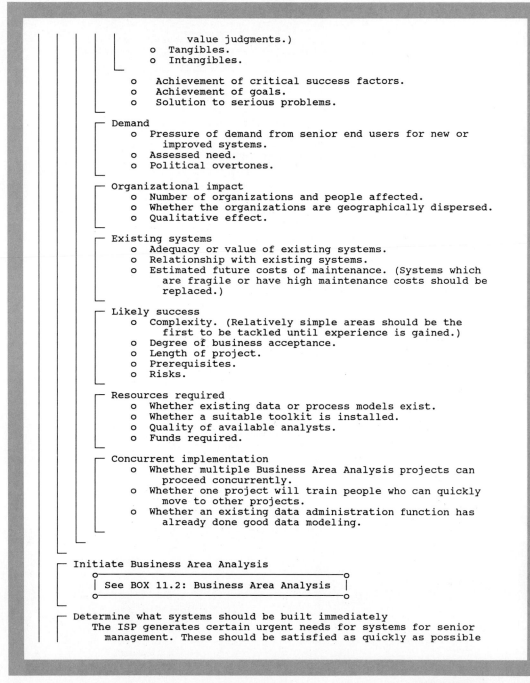

```
                          value judgments.)
                   o  Tangibles.
                   o  Intangibles.

            o   Achievement of critical success factors.
            o   Achievement of goals.
            o   Solution to serious problems.

    Demand
            o   Pressure of demand from senior end users for new or
                   improved systems.
            o   Assessed need.
            o   Political overtones.

    Organizational impact
            o   Number of organizations and people affected.
            o   Whether the organizations are geographically dispersed.
            o   Qualitative effect.

    Existing systems
            o   Adequacy or value of existing systems.
            o   Relationship with existing systems.
            o   Estimated future costs of maintenance. (Systems which
                   are fragile or have high maintenance costs should be
                   replaced.)

    Likely success
            o   Complexity. (Relatively simple areas should be the
                   first to be tackled until experience is gained.)
            o   Degree of business acceptance.
            o   Length of project.
            o   Prerequisites.
            o   Risks.

    Resources required
            o   Whether existing data or process models exist.
            o   Whether a suitable toolkit is installed.
            o   Quality of available analysts.
            o   Funds required.

    Concurrent implementation
            o   Whether multiple Business Area Analysis projects can
                   proceed concurrently.
            o   Whether one project will train people who can quickly
                   move to other projects.
            o   Whether an existing data administration function has
                   already done good data modeling.


Initiate Business Area Analysis

    |   See BOX 11.2: Business Area Analysis   |


Determine what systems should be built immediately
    The ISP generates certain urgent needs for systems for senior
       management. These should be satisfied as quickly as possible
```

(Continued)

BOX 10.1 *(Continued)*

with relatively simple techniques such as spreadsheet tools,
decision-support software, or executive-information-system
software.

See Book III: Fast implementation techniques

Initiate actions to keep the ISP up-to-date
   Appoint technology-minded person to keep the Technology
      Impact Analysis up-to-date.
   Plan that Critical Success Factors shall be reviewed periodically
      at business strategy planning meetings.
   Plan that Critical Success Factors shall be presented at Board
      meetings for review.
   Plan that the Goal-and-Problem analysis shall be updated when
      management appraisal interviews are conducted as part of the
      Management-by-Objectives procedure.
   Ensure that the business-function decomposition diagrams and
      entity-relationship diagrams are updated in the encyclopedia
      when Business Area Analysis is done.
   Ensure that the ISP is reexamined when major changes
      occur in the enterprise (such as a takeover).

Make top-management presentation
   Obtain agreement to follow-on actions.

PART II PHASE II: BUSINESS AREA ANALYSIS

11 BUSINESS AREA ANALYSIS

INTRODUCTION   Business area analysis establishes a detailed framework for building an information-based enterprise. It takes one business area at a time and analyzes it in detail. It uses diagrams and matrices to model and record the data and activities in the enterprise and to give a clear understanding of the elaborate and subtle ways in which the information aspects of the enterprise interrelate. The diagrams and matrices are designed to be understood by management, end users, and data processing professionals, and to increase greatly communication among these groups.

Business area analysis uses the knowledge recorded in the encyclopedia at the top level of the pyramid and extends it into more detail. The results are recorded in the encyclopedia and are used in subsequent system design. This detailed model of the enterprise is kept up to date as the enterprise changes and as systems are built. It provides the architectural framework for the information-based enterprise.

Business area analysis is not an end in itself. Its purpose is to facilitate the design of systems and ensure that they work together appropriately. There is often pressure to finish the analysis stage or avoid it completely and spend the effort on building much-needed systems. However, business area analysis is an essential stage in getting the right information to the right people at the right time.

Box 11.1 gives the objectives of business area analysis. Figure 11.1 illustrates the interactions that occur among processes in a business area. The red lines represent the interchange of information. Figure 11.2 shows the business area being analyzed by building a *data model* and a *process decomposition diagram*. Within one business area there are complex interactions among the processes. Figure 11.3 shows the interactions among processes and data being analyzed with a *process dependency diagram* and a *process/entity matrix*.

BOX 11.1   Objectives of business area analysis

- Provide a clear understanding of the business and how its activities interrelate.

- Provide an architectural framework for the building of systems in an information-based enterprise.

- Provide a framework such that separately built systems will work together. This framework consists of:
  A fully normalized data model which becomes the foundation stone of application design and construction.
  A model of the business activities and their interdependencies.
  A linkage of the foregoing models to show what processes use what data.

- Trigger the rethinking of procedures in the enterprise so that they are as efficient as possible for the era of desktop computers, information networks, and flexible databases.

- Identify requirements of highest priority for information center activities and system design.

- Create an overview so that joint application design sessions (Book III) can proceed rapidly and coherently.

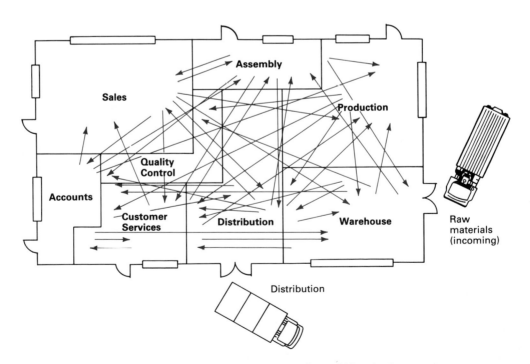

Figure 11.1   There are complex interactions within a business area.

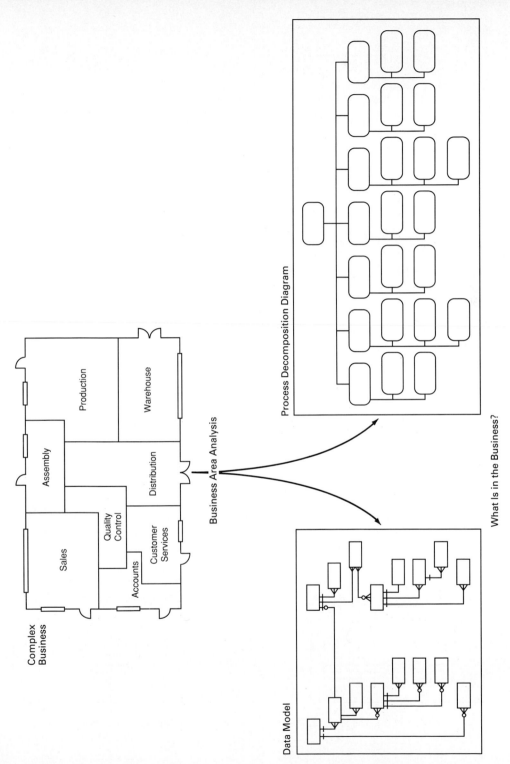

Complex
Business

Sales

Quality
Control

Assembly

Production

Accounts

Distribution

Warehouse

Customer
Services

Business Area Analysis

Data Model

Process Decomposition Diagram

What Is in the Business?

Figure 11.2 Business area analysis creates a data model and its process model of the business
area.

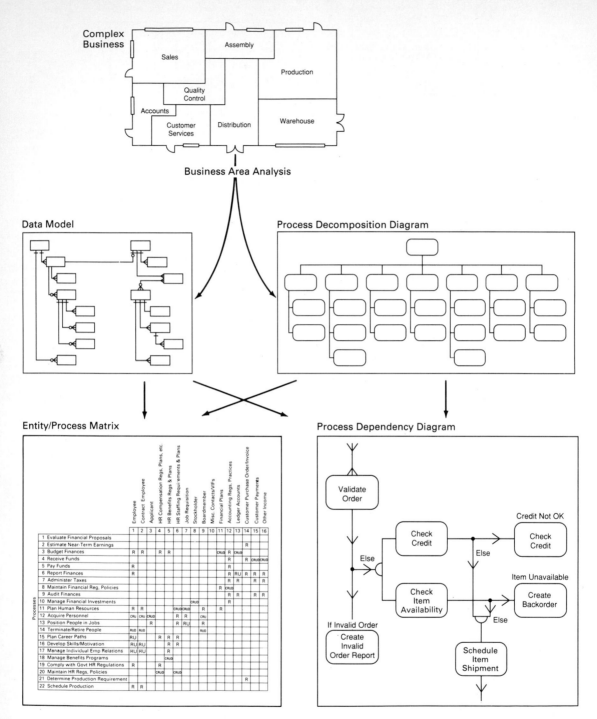

Figure 11.3   The four main types of diagrams used in business area analysis.

KEEP IT SIMPLE   Business area analysis should not be allowed to become too complex. In the author's view the steps described in the following chapters are the appropriate level of complexity. There is sometimes a tendency to make it more detailed or more bureaucratic. Finer detail than that described should be left for the system design stage. *The objective of business area analysis is not to design systems but.to establish a framework which will ensure that separately designed systems will fit together.*

It establishes *what* data and *what* processes are required to operate the enterprise. It does not establish *how* procedures operate. Determining how procedures should operate is done in the following stage, for example in an IE-JAD session (Book III).

Business area analysis should not be confused with requirements planning for a specific system. It will speed up subsequent system requirements planning, but the BAA itself is concerned with the fundamental data and processes, not with *how* a specific system should function.

SHORT PROJECT   The analysis of a business area should not take too long. The tools and procedures should be such that it can be completed in three to six months. The enterprise should be subdivided into areas small enough to make this practical.

Fully automated diagramming tools with an encyclopedia are needed for efficient business area analysis. The tools should be an extension of those used for information strategy planning. They should, in turn, become the tools used in system design. Computerized tools can provide analyses and coordination of the enterprise knowledge to an extent that far surpasses that of human analysts.

The knowledge of the enterprise is represented not by text that a computer cannot understand, but by diagrams and data. Text is used only where brief paragraphs are needed for human-oriented definitions. An objective should be to avoid the burdensome paperwork and bureaucracy of earlier methodologies, and replace it with diagrams and data designed for computerized analysis and coordination.

INDEPENDENT OF TECHNOLOGY AND ORGANIZATIONAL STRUCTURE   Business area analysis creates models of the fundamental data and processes which are necessary for the business. It does this in a manner that is *independent of technology*. This is important because technology is changing rapidly, but the fundamental processes, such as factory scheduling, warehousing, and so on, still have to be carried out.

The models are also *independent of the current systems*. The systems and procedures used are likely to change. Systems for an era of batch processing are different from online systems, and systems change fundamentally in an era of desktop computing, enterprisewide networks, and flexible databases. When the information needs of the enterprise are clearly understood, it is likely that different systems and procedures will be created.

The analysis should also be *independent of the current organizational structure*. It should not be tied to specific organizational units. The enterprise is likely to be reorganized periodically, but the fundamental data and processes remain. The model of its data and processes should be valid independently of how the organization is subdivided into departments. A specific organizational unit will frequently change its activities and composition to meet fluctuating business requirements.

ORGANIZATIONAL CHANGES

Important questions to ask in business area analysis are: What decisions must be made to run the business? What is the optimum place for each decision to be made? What individual should be responsible for the decision?

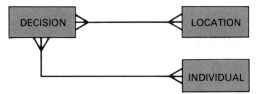

The answers to these questions often result in new systems, changed procedures, and organizational changes. An information-based enterprise needs to be organized differently from an older form of enterprise, as discussed in Chapter 8 in Book I.

BAA studies (along with their parent ISP study) make visible the need for organizational changes and have often, in practice, triggered major corporate reorganizations. One enterprise with 12 layers of management was restructured with only five layers as it became an information-based enterprise. The possibility of such upheavals can make the ISP and BAA projects highly political. Because of this, the support of top management is essential. A suitably high executive needs to be the sponsor of a BAA, committed to making it happen efficiently and to acting on the results. Top management commitment is needed to lessen the effects of middle-management politics.

IDENTIFICATION OF THE BUSINESS AREA

The division of the enterprise into business areas is done as part of the information strategy plan, with the aid of a tool for clustering the entity–

Business Functions

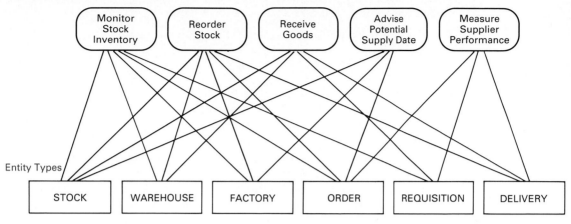

Figure 11.4   A business area is a collection of closely related business functions and entity types.

function matrix. There are no hard-and-fast boundaries to a business area, but experience shows that it is relatively easy to find pragmatic subdivision of the enterprise.

For example, Fig. 11.4 shows a collection of business functions and entity types which are closely interconnected. Such a closely interconnected grouping may be defined as a business area. Clustering algorithms help to find closely interwoven groupings from a large collection of entity types and business functions.

There may be multiple departments or organizational units involved with the cluster. For example, the purchasing, warehouse, and goods receipt departments are involved with the functions in Fig. 11.1, and there may be more than one factory and warehouse in different locations. Several organizational units employ the same data and interact in carrying out the business function.

A simple event such as a customer phoning and asking to place an order may trigger processing that involves multiple departments:

The ORDER OFFICE receives the call.

The ORDER OFFICE asks if the customer's credit is okay.

The CREDIT OFFICE replies.

The ORDER OFFICE asks when delivery can be scheduled.

The WAREHOUSE is low on stock and asks when it can have more stock.

PRODUCTION SCHEDULING asks when production will be available.

PLANT MAINTENANCE replies.

PRODUCTION SCHEDULING determines that additional raw materials are needed for the order and asks a supplier about these.

The SUPPLIER replies.

. . . And so on.

An information system, as automated as possible, should enable the order clerk to respond to the customer quickly and accurately.

It is this complex interaction between separate business organizational units that make providing good business information systems difficult. *The traditional approach of building separate systems for each organizational unit fails to meet the integrated needs of business.* Business area analysis needs to cross departmental boundaries to model how the business works and show what interdepartmental systems are needed. The departments may be reorganized but the information processing above still needs to be done to respond to a customer's request. Business area analysis charts the necessary processes and data.

SOLVING THE COMMUNICATION PROBLEM

The end user often has serious worries about computer systems:

- The current systems don't tackle my real problems.
- I'll have to wait years to get the new systems I need.
- Systems cost too much to develop and run.
- We have reorganized and my systems can't cope.
- I need to replace my existing procedures but my current systems can't be changed for a year or more.

On the other hand, the business system developer has corresponding worries:

- What does the user want now?
- What will the user want in six months' time? in six years' time?
- How can I respond quickly enough?
- How can I build a new application system when the user doesn't know what he wants?
- Who will be the users?
- What happens if they change their mind?
- How can I avoid expensive long-term maintenance?

By creating a model of the data, processes, and their interactions, business area analysis addresses the fundamental information needs. The diagrams used are easy to understand so as to facilitate communication between users and developers. The diagrams and their underlying details are maintained in a computer, readily available, and are updated as the business changes and its system needs are further clarified. The encyclopedia, with computerized coordination of its complex facts, spans the business and interlinks the systems knowledge of many departments. It builds bridges between users who may be far apart and makes possible the creation of systems that interlink diverse parts of the business. Often this results in drastic simplification of business systems because complexity arises from inadequate communication and lack of understanding. Lack of communication in the past has resulted in massive redundancy and incompatibility of data files and programs. It has resulted in systems that do not work together, and extensive human processing because of system inadequacies. The necessary coordination, however, is far too complex for humans to achieve without the help of a computerized encyclopedia which coordinates the knowledge of the business and its systems.

REUSABLE DESIGN

A major objective of business area analysis is to identify components which are used in multiple places. An entity type is used in many different applications. The attributes associated with the entity are correctly normalized, and this data does not have to be redesigned for each application. Different functions have common process modules. This commonality is identified in order to reduce the amount of process design and coding that will be needed. Similar user screens and dialogs are employed in multiple activities. Making the user dialogs as common as possible in appearance lessens the work of design, coding, building HELP screens, and documentation, and lessens training requirements. From the users' point of view it makes systems more familiar and hence easier to use.

Reusable data structures, reusable designs, and reusable code are major goals. They can greatly lessen the work of construction, training, documentation, and maintenance. They are achieved by identifying common entities, by nonredundant data modeling, and by identifying common processes and subroutines associated with those entities.

Sometimes the term *object-oriented* design is used. The entity is described as an *object,* and common processes are invoked whenever that object is used. An object has a certain behavior, no matter what application it is used in.

FOUR TYPES OF DIAGRAMS

Four main types of diagrams are needed for business area analysis (Fig. 11.3).

- **Data Model Diagram.** A fully normalized model is built of the data used in the business area. This is an extension of the entity-relationship diagram from the top level of the pyramid. The tool used will help coordinate the data with that for other business areas. In Chapter 13 and the appendices, we discuss data modeling.

- **Process Decomposition Diagram.** The functions of a business area, established during the ISP study, are decomposed into processes; high-level processes are decomposed into lower-level processes. A tree-structured decomposition is produced. This is discussed in Chapter 14.

- **Process Dependency Diagram.** Some processes are dependent on other processes; they can only be performed *after* the processes on which they are dependent. The dependency may be because data used by a dependent process is created by another process. A process dependency diagram maps the dependencies. It is illustrated in Chapter 14. Sometimes a *process dependency diagram* is called a *process flow diagram*. It shows the data flows from one process to another, but it does not show what this data is, as on a data flow diagram.

- **A Process/Data Matrix.** A process/data matrix maps the processes against normalized data, showing which processes create, read, update, or delete the records. Creating this matrix helps to ensure that the data and processes have been discovered and that the process dependencies have been assessed correctly. This is also discussed in Chapter 14.

In some cases other diagram types are used in a business area analysis to help clarify how a function operates. State transition diagrams and process action diagrams are sometimes used. These other types of diagrams should not be used routinely because that increases the amount of work needed. The objective is to establish a data model and process architecture as quickly as possible and then proceed with building the urgent systems.

THE INITIAL DIAGRAMS

The study proceeds by successive refinement of the four main diagram types. The initial versions of these will be extracted from the ISP knowledge in the encyclopedia. If time has elapsed since the ISP, these models should be reviewed to determine whether they are an accurate description of the current business environment.

In some corporations data administration has existed for years before the BAA. The existing data models and descriptions will be entered into the encyclopedia and may be subjected to further analysis. Sometimes a BAA is conducted when there has been no previous ISP. In this case the relevant ISP information for the business area needs to be obtained and entered into the encyclopedia.

LINKS WITH OTHER BAAs

The different business areas in an enterprise are interlinked. Some data subjects are used in more than one business area. Some processes in one business area are dependent on processes in a different business area.

The matrix developed during information strategy planning which maps business functions against data subjects is shown again in Fig. 11.5. This matrix has been clustered into business areas. The information on this matrix can be

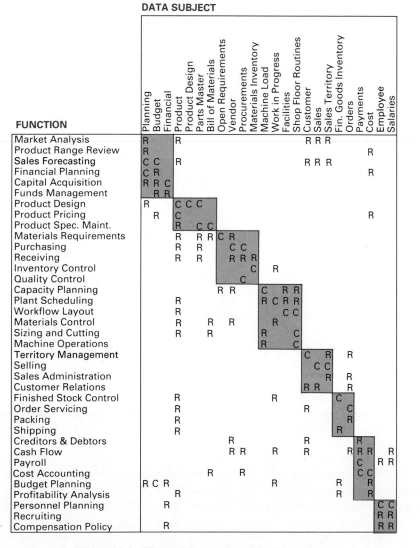

Figure 11.5 Figure 9.5 reproduced for convenience.

DATA SUBJECT

BUSINESS AREA	Planning	Budget	Financial	Product	Product design	Parts master	Bill of materials	Open requirements	Vendor	Procurements	Materials inventory	Machine load	Work in progress	Facilities	Shop floor routings	Customer	Sales	Sales territory	Fin. goods inventory	Orders	Payments	Costs	Employee	Salaries
Planning	P	P	P	S												S	S	S			S			
Product design	S	S		P	E	P	P															S		
Acquisition				S		S		P	P	P	E		S											
Manufacturing				S			S	S	S			E	P	E	E									
Sales																P	P	P	S					
Order servicing				S									S			S				E	P			
Accounting	S	S	S	S			S			S	S		S			S	S			S	E	P		S
Personnel			S																				E	P

Figure 11.6 Matrix showing responsibility for data subject definition by business area, derived from Fig. 11.5.

condensed automatically into a smaller matrix that maps business areas against data subjects, as shown in Fig. 11.6. This matrix marks which business areas use data subjects exclusively, which have primary responsibility, and which have secondary responsibility. The following notation is used:

E   *Exclusive,* meaning the definition can proceed independently of any other business area.

P   *Primary responsibility,* meaning that this business area defines the object in question and that others should use the definition (or negotiate to have it modified).

S   *Secondary responsibility,* meaning that a different business area defines the object in question. In practice this business area may define it if it is done first, but the business area with primary responsibility is ultimately responsible.

Much data passes across the boundaries between different business areas. Where this interchange exists, coordination is necessary of the separate business area perspectives. There is usually some incompatibility of representation of data or processes between business areas; it is difficult to achieve perfection. The IE software should be able to handle synonyms and be designed to allow inconsistencies because these always arise in practice. The ownership of objects and perspectives should be recorded in the encyclopedia.

SELECTING WHICH BUSINESS AREA TO ANALYZE

Setting priorities for which business area should be analyzed first is also done as part of the ISP. The selection of the business area may be done with the following considerations:

- The business urgency for automating that area, or rebuilding its current systems
- The potential impact on the goals of the enterprise as determined in the ISP study
- The strategy or competitive impact of new systems
- The current management priorities
- The potential for automation of the business area
- The cost, difficulty, or inadequacy of maintenance of current systems
- The project staff availability and expertise

In some cases new uses of automation can have a direct effect on a company's competitive position, as when American Airlines built its first system with terminals in travel agents' offices. Such opportunities should be tackled with urgency.

STAFFING A BAA PROJECT

Business area analysis, like all of information engineering, needs close cooperation between end users and I.S. professionals. An enterprise is likely to conduct many BAA studies. It may conduct one initial study to gain experience and then conduct several studies in parallel until models of all or most of the enterprise are complete. Certain people develop a high level of skill at handling the subtleties of data modeling and process modeling. These professionals should move from one study to another. They become very valuable in enabling the study to be done quickly and produce high-quality results. A professional BAA team emerges from the training and experience. The most skilled members of this team have a promotion path that may lead them to become the *data administrator* or *knowledge administrator* (encyclopedia administrator) or *chief information engineer*.

The first study is often done with the aid of consultants who specialize in such work. The consultants should train internal staff to become skilled in the modeling processes and the coordination of information engineering. Often the team that created the information strategy plan goes on to lead the BAA projects.

The BAA team members need skill in interviewing and human communication as well as in technical modeling. They need to have credibility and respect among operating management and end users.

End-user participation is essential in BAA studies. Sometimes one or two

```
┌*
│         BUSINESS AREA ANALYSIS.
│
│    ┌ Initiate.
│    │  ┌ Obtain commitment of executive sponsor.
│    │  │     The BAA project should not proceed unless a suitably high
│    │  │        level executive is fully committed to helping make the
│    │  └     project succeed.
│    │
│    │  ┌ Ensure that the appropriate tools are installed and working
│    │  │     o   A data modeling tool.
│    │  │     o   A encyclopedia-based workbench (which should have been
│    │  └            used for the Information Strategy Planning study).
│    │
│    │  ┌ Select the business area.
│    │  │     Dividing the enterprise into business areas and determining
│    │  │        which to analyze first was the final stage of Information
│    │  └        Strategy Planning.
│    │
│    │  ┌ Determine the scope of the business area.
│    │  │
│    │  │     Determine which entities are involved.
│    │  │     Determine which business functions are involved.
│    │  │     Determine which locations are involved.
│    │  │     Determine which departments are involved.
│    │  │     Examine relevant goals, problems, and critical success factors
│    │  └        (from the encyclopedia).
│    │
│    │  ┌ Develop BAA project plan.
│    │  │     Edit this action diagram as appropriate to form the
│    │  └        project procedure.
│    │
│    │  ┌ Establish the BAA team for this project.
│    │  │  ┌ If an outside consultant is to be employed
│    │  │  │     Select the consultant.
│    │  │  │     Appoint the in-house BAA project leader who will work with
│    │  │  │        the consultant.
│    │  │  │  ┌ Ensure that the in-house project leader is well trained.
│    │  │  │  │     A BAA project leader should have this as his job for a year
│    │  │  │  └        or more. BAA leaders become skilled with experience.
│    │  │  │
│    │  │  │  ┌ Establish the in-house team who will work with the consultant.
│    │  │  │  │     A small team should be used. Two or three people are often
│    │  │  │  │        appropriate. There may be an end user on the team.
│    │  │  │  │     Select future in-house BAA project leaders who will be trained
│    │  │  │  └        during this study.
│    │  │  ┌ Else
│    │  │  │     Appoint the in-house BAA project leader.
│    │  │  │  ┌ Ensure that the in-house project leader is well trained.
│    │  │  │  └
│    │  │  │  ┌ Establish the in-house BAA team.
│    │  │  │  │     A small team should be used. Two or three people are often
│    │  │  │  │        appropriate. There may be an end user on the team.
│    │  │  │  │     Select future in-house BAA project leaders who will be trained
│    │  │  └  └        during this study.
│    │
│    │  ┌ Ensure that the BAA team is adequately trained.
│    │  │
│    │  │     They should be trained in the following:
│    │  │     o   Information engineering
│    │  │     o   Analysis and design
```

Figure 11.7   The initial steps of business area analysis.

```
          o  Data modeling
          o  The diagramming techniques
          o  The automated tools used
          o  Communication skills


  Prepare.
     Create initial documentation.
        Extract the relevant functional decomposition diagram from
           the encyclopedia.
        Extract the relevant entity-relationship diagram from
           the encyclopedia.
        Add detailed comments to the above diagrams where necessary.
        Print relevant versions of the above diagrams from the
           encyclopedia for the participants to review.

     Select the user participants.

     Prepare the user participants.
        Give user participants literature on the BAA procedure.
        Give them the initial printouts from the encyclopedia.
        Conduct training class for the user participants.
           Introduce user participants to the BAA technique.
           Train user participants in the diagramming techniques.
           Review the initial printouts from the encyclopedia.


        Determine the target date for completing the study.

     Hold kickoff meeting.
        Have the executive sponsor make the opening speech.
        Review with participants the purpose and objectives.
        Review the agenda.
        Give participants the preparatory material for them to study.
           Inform them that they must understand it well before the first
           workshop.
        Review the initial data models and process models with the
           participants.
        Review relevant goals, problems, and critical success factors.
        Review the business assumptions that are to be made.
  ...Create a preliminary data model.
  ...Create a preliminary process model.
  ...Successively refine the information
  ...Prepare for system design.
     Present the results to the executive sponsor.
```

Figure 11.7   (Continued)

end users are allocated full time to the study. Such users should have thorough knowledge of the entire business area. Where full-time participation is not possible, users with an appropriate range of knowledge should be allocated on a part-time basis with, perhaps, a quarter of their time committed until the study of their area is complete. Other users will need to be interviewed but have less time committed.

A short seminar should be given to those users who will assist in the project, particularly those who will be asked to approve the decisions and plans.

This should cover the motivation and objectives of the project, its scope, and the techniques used. The participants should be taught how to read the diagram types. Prior to this seminar the relevant overview of the business area should be extracted from the encyclopedia. The relevant portion of the entity-relationship model and the function decomposition model should be explained to the participants. Goals and problems, critical success factors, and strategic opportunities for the organization units in question should be discussed.

Full-time team members should be given more complete education on information engineering as a whole. They should know how their analysis is likely to lead to the system design, joint application design sessions, prototyping, and information center operations. Some of these activities may follow directly from the BAA. An executive sponsor is needed for the study. This person should be committed to a successful completion of the study in the scheduled time.

Preparation for the BAA should thus include the steps shown in Fig. 11.7. Box 11.2 gives a complete action diagram for the BAA procedure. As with the other procedures of information engineering, it is useful to represent the procedure on an action diagram disk or hyperdocument because the procedure can be quickly edited and adjusted to the circumstances in question. BAA studies differ somewhat from one organization to another.

PROJECT PLAN   The plan for the BAA project should be represented by means of an action diagram. The planning starts with a standard BAA action diagram such as that shown in Box 11.2. This diagram (which should be part of the toolkit) is edited to represent the specific

BOX 11.2   **An action diagram showing the steps in business area analysis**

As with the other procedures of information engineering, it is useful to represent the procedure on an action diagram disk or hyperdocument because the procedure can quickly be edited and modified to suit the circumstances in question. These procedures differ somewhat from one organization to another.

BOX 11.2 *(Continued)*

```
*      BUSINESS AREA ANALYSIS.

    ┌ Initiate.
    │   ┌ Obtain commitment of executive sponsor.
    │   │    The BAA project should not proceed unless a suitably high
    │   │       level executive is fully committed to helping make the
    │   └       project succeed.
    │
    │   ┌ Ensure that the appropriate tools are installed and working:
    │   │    o   A data modeling tool.
    │   │    o   A encyclopedia-based workbench (which should have been
    │   └           used for the Information Strategy Planning study).
    │
    │   ┌ Select the business area.
    │   │    Dividing the enterprise into business areas and determining
    │   │       which to analyze first was the final stage of Information
    │   └       Strategy Planning.
    │
    │   ┌ Determine the scope of the business area.
    │   │
    │   │    Determine which entities are involved.
    │   │    Determine which business functions are involved.
    │   │    Determine which locations are involved.
    │   │    Determine which departments are involved.
    │   │    Examine relevant goals, problems, and critical success factors
    │   └       (from the encyclopedia).
    │
    │   ┌ Develop BAA project plan.
    │   │    Edit this action diagram as appropriate to form the
    │   └       project procedure.
    │
    │   ┌ Establish the BAA team for this project.
    │   │   ┌ If an outside consultant is to be employed
    │   │   │    Select the consultant.
    │   │   │    Appoint the in-house BAA project leader who will work with
    │   │   │       the consultant.
    │   │   │   ┌ Ensure that the in-house project leader is well trained.
    │   │   │   │    A BAA project leader should have this as his job for a year
    │   │   │   └       or more. BAA leaders become skilled with experience.
    │   │   │
    │   │   │   ┌ Establish the in-house team who will work with the consultant.
    │   │   │   │    A small team should be used. Two or three people are often
    │   │   │   │       appropriate. There may be an end user on the team.
    │   │   │   │    Select future in-house BAA project leaders who will be trained
    │   │   │   └       during this study.
    │   │   └ Else
    │   │        Appoint the in-house BAA project leader.
    │   │       ┌ Ensure that the in-house project leader is well trained.
    │   │       │
    │   │       ┌ Establish the in-house BAA team.
    │   │       │    A small team should be used. Two or three people are often
    │   │       │       appropriate. There may be an end user on the team.
    │   │       │    Select future in-house BAA project leaders who will be trained
```

(Continued)

BOX 11.2 *(Continued)*

during this study.

Ensure that the BAA team is adequately trained

They should be trained in the following:
o Information engineering
o Analysis and design
o Data modeling
o The diagramming techniques
o The automated tools used
o Communication skills

Prepare
Create initial documentation.
Extract the relevant functional decomposition diagram from the encyclopedia.
Extract the relevant entity-relationship diagram from the encyclopedia.
Add detailed comments to the above diagrams where necessary.
Print relevant versions of the above diagrams from the encyclopedia for the participants to review.

Select the user participants.

Prepare the user participants.
Give user participants literature on the BAA procedure.
Give them the initial printouts from the encyclopedia.
Conduct training class for the user participants.
Introduce user participants to the BAA technique.
Train user participants in the diagramming techniques.
Review the initial printouts from the encyclopedia.

Determine the target date for completing the study.

Hold kickoff meeting.
Have the executive sponsor make the opening speech.
Review with participants the purpose and objectives.
Review the agenda.
Give participants the preparatory material for them to study.
Inform them that they must understand it well before the first workshop.
Review the initial data models and process models with the participants.
Review relevant goals, problems, and critical success factors.
Review the business assumptions that are to be made.

Create a preliminary data model.
Extract the entity-relationship model for this business area from the encyclopedia.
Determine what events occur in this business area.
Associate the events with entity types (a behavior model)
Draw the lifecycle of each entity.
Enter initial attributes of each entity.

BOX 11.2   *(Continued)*

Create a preliminary process model.
   Extract the business-function decomposition model for this
      business area from the encyclopedia.
   Decompose the functions into processes.

Successively refine the information
   in the following stages until a complete representation of the
   data and processes is achieved.
   Create a detailed data model.

> | See BOX 12.3. |

   Create a detailed process model.

> | See BOX 14.2. |

      Create a process decomposition diagram.
         Decompose processes eventually into elementary processes.
            An elementary process is one which cannot be decomposed
               further without stating HOW a procedure is carried out.

      Create a process dependency diagram.
         Correlate this with the process decomposition diagram.
         Consider what information flows from one process to another.

   Build matrices.
      Generate an entity-type/process matrix.
         Build a matrix mapping elementary processes and entity types.
         Indicate what process CREATES each entity record.
         Indicate what processes UPDATE, READ, or DELETE each entity recor

      Associate entity types, processes, and events with organizational
         units and locations.
      Associate entity types, processes, and events with goals and
         problems.

   Analyze and correlate (automatically) the above information.
      Use a workbench tool which analyzes and correlates the above
         information with a knowledge coordinator.
      Use the knowledge coordinator of the design tool to ensure
         that the BAA is internally consistent and consistent with
         other knowledge in the encyclopedia.

Prepare for system design.
   Review the analysis of current systems created during the ISP study.
   Identify system design projects.
   Refine system design project boundaries.
   Prioritize the system-building projects
      There are multiple factors which affect the prioritization
         of system building.
      Rank each of the factors below on a scale of 1 to 7:
         o   Return on investment.
         o   Achievement of critical success factor.
         o   Achievement of goal.
         o   Solution to serious problem.

(Continued)

BOX 11.2 *(Continued)*

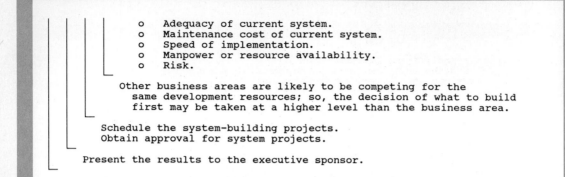

```
        o   Adequacy of current system.
        o   Maintenance cost of current system.
        o   Speed of implementation.
        o   Manpower or resource availability.
        o   Risk.

    Other business areas are likely to be competing for the
        same development resources; so, the decision of what to build
        first may be taken at a higher level than the business area.

    Schedule the system-building projects.
    Obtain approval for system projects.

  Present the results to the executive sponsor.
```

BOX 11.3   Characteristics of business area analysis

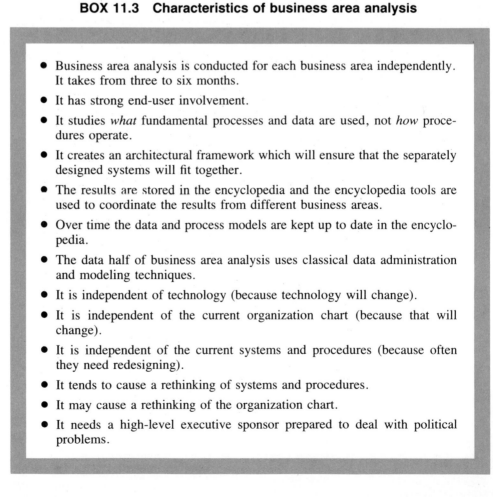

- Business area analysis is conducted for each business area independently. It takes from three to six months.

- It has strong end-user involvement.

- It studies *what* fundamental processes and data are used, not *how* procedures operate.

- It creates an architectural framework which will ensure that the separately designed systems will fit together.

- The results are stored in the encyclopedia and the encyclopedia tools are used to coordinate the results from different business areas.

- Over time the data and process models are kept up to date in the encyclopedia.

- The data half of business area analysis uses classical data administration and modeling techniques.

- It is independent of technology (because technology will change).

- It is independent of the current organization chart (because that will change).

- It is independent of the current systems and procedures (because often they need redesigning).

- It tends to cause a rethinking of systems and procedures.

- It may cause a rethinking of the organization chart.

- It needs a high-level executive sponsor prepared to deal with political problems.

details of the project in question. An interview schedule is developed. Key end users who are not assigned to the project are identified. The interview schedule should be added to the BAA action diagram.

SUMMARY

Box 11.3 lists some of the characteristics of business area analysis.

12 ENTITIES AND NORMALIZATION

ENTITIES
An entity, as we stated earlier, is something about which we store data. It may be a tangible object such as an employee, a part, a customer, a machine tool, or an office. It may be nontangible, such as a job title, a profit center, an association, a financial allowance, a purchase, an estimate, or an insurance claim.

In analyzing information we study the entities of the enterprise in question. A typical corporation has several hundred entity types. Its set of entity types does not change much as time goes by unless the corporation moves into a fundamentally different type of business. The entity types are charted on an entity-relationship diagram as discussed in Chapter 7.

An entity has various *attributes* which we wish to record, such as size, value, date, color, usage code, address, quality, performance code, and so on. Often in data processing we are concerned with a collection of similar entities, such as employees, and we wish to record information about the same attributes of each of them. A programmer commonly maintains a *record* about each entity, and a data item in each record relates to each attribute. Similar records are grouped into *files*. The result, shown in Fig. 12.1, is a two-dimensional array.

Inside the box in Fig. 12.1 is a set of data items. The value of each data item is shown. Each row of data items relates to a particular entity. Each column contains a particular type of data item, relating to a particular type of attribute. At the top of the diagram, outside the box, the names of the attributes are written. The leftmost column in the box contains the data items that *identify* the entity. The entity in this example is a person, an employee. The attribute referred to as the entity identifier in this case is EMPLOYEE-NUMBER.

Such a two-dimensional array is sometime referred to as a *flat file*. The use of flat files dates back to the earliest days of data processing when the file might have been on punched cards. Each card in a file or deck of cards such as that in Fig. 12.2 might contain one record, relating to one entity. Certain card

EMPLOYEE-NUMBER	NAME	SEX	GRADE	DATE-OF-BIRTH	DEPART-MENT	SKILLCODE	TITLE	SALARY
53730	JONES BILL W	1	03	100335	044	73	ACCOUNTANT	2000
28719	BLANAGAN JOE E	1	05	101019	172	43	PLUMBER	1800
53550	LAWRENCE MARIGOLD	0	07	090932	044	02	CLERK	1100
79632	ROCKEFELLER FRED	1	11	011132	090	11	CONSULTANT	5000
15971	ROPLEY ED S	1	13	021242	172	43	PLUMBER	1700
51883	SMITH TOM P W	1	03	091130	044	73	ACCOUNTANT	2000
36453	RALNER WILLIAM C	1	08	119041	044	02	CLERK	1200
41618	HORSERADISH FREDA	0	07	071235	172	07	ENGINEER	2500
61903	HALL ALBERT JR	1	11	011030	172	21	ARCHITECT	3700
72921	FAIR CAROLYN	0	03	020442	090	92	PROGRAMMER	2100

Record structure

Values of the attributes

Some attributes are themselves entity identifiers of another file

An occurrence of a record

A set of values of one data-item type

Entity identifier

An occurrence of a logical file or relation

Figure 12.1 Terminology of various components of records (see also Box 12.2).

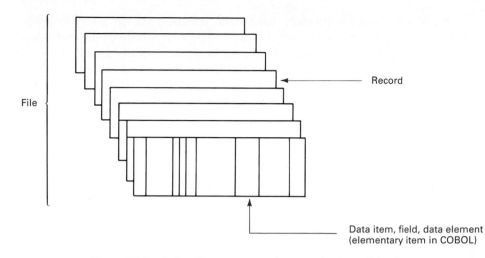

Figure 12.2   A flat file: programmer's or user's view of the data.

columns were allocated to each data-item type, or attribute, and were called a *field*. When magnetic tapes replaced decks of cards and disks replaced magnetic tapes, many programmers retained their view of data as being organized into flat files.

ENTITY RECORDS   In examining the data that needs to be stored in a corporation we will think of it initially as a collection of flat files such as Fig. 12.1 or 12.2. Each flat file contains information about one type of entity. A record in that file contains information about one occurrence of that entity. For example, a CUSTOMER record contains information about one CUSTOMER. We will refer to this as an *entity record*.

The entity record is a *logical* view of the data. The data may be stored in a different form *physically* in a database. The entity record contains data about *one and only one* type of entity. It contains *all* of the attributes of that entity that are stored. When we use the term *entity record*, then, we are not referring to any old collection of data items but to a rather special grouping of data. We refer to this as *normalized* data and use the term *fourth normal form*, which we explain in this chapter.

NORMALIZATION   The term *normalization* of data refers to the way data
OF DATA   items are grouped together into record structures.
                    Fourth (or third) *normal form* is a grouping of data designed to avoid the anomalies and problems that can occur with data. The concept originated with the mathematics of E. F. Codd, which is given in Appendix III.

With fourth-normal-form data, each data item in a record refers to a particular key which uniquely identifies that data. The key itself may be composed of more than one data item. Each data item in the record is identified by the whole key, not just part of the key. No data item in the record is identifiable by any other data item in the record which is not part of the key.

The basic simplicity of fourth normal form makes the data records easy to understand, and easier to change than when data is organized in less rigorous ways. It formally groups the data items that are associated with each entity type (and also those which are associated with more than one entity type), and separates the data items that belong to different entity types. Fourth normal form prevents anomalies that can otherwise occur. It permits rules to be established for controlling semantic disintegrity in query languages.

Data exists in real life as groups of data items. It exists on invoices, weighbills, tax forms, driving licences, and so on. These groupings are usually not in a normalized form. Not surprisingly, systems analysts have often implemented computer records that are also not normalized. However, data that is not normalized can lead to various subtle problems in the future.

Experience has shown that when computer data is organized in fourth normal form, the resulting data structures are more stable and able to accommodate change. Each attribute relates to its own entity and is not mixed up with attributes relating to different entities. The actions that create and update data can then be applied with simple structured design to one normalized record at a time.

At the time of writing only a small proportion of existing databases are normalized. Some corporations have several years of experience of operation of fourth (or third) -normal-form data structures. There is no question that they have greatly benefited from this type of design, especially when it is combined with other steps that are part of good data administration [1].

Reacting to the perceived benefits, some corporations have incorporated into their database standards manuals the requirement that all database structures be *designed* in fourth normal form. The physical implementation may occasionally deviate from fourth normal form if the trade-off is fully explored and documented. Usually, normalized data is better in terms of *machine* requirements as well as in logical structuring, but this is not always the case. Sometimes the physical designer finds it desirable to deviate from fourth normal form. A compromise is then needed. Which is preferable: somewhat better machine performance, or better protection from maintenance costs? Usually, the potential maintenance costs are much the more expensive.

To put data into fourth normal form, four steps may be used. It is put into *first normal form,* then *second, third,* and *fourth normal form.* Box 12.1 summarizes these. The basic ideas of this normalization of data are simple, but the ramifications are many and subtle, and vary from one type of database usage to another. It is important to note that normalization describes the *logical* represen-

BOX 12.1 The normalization of data

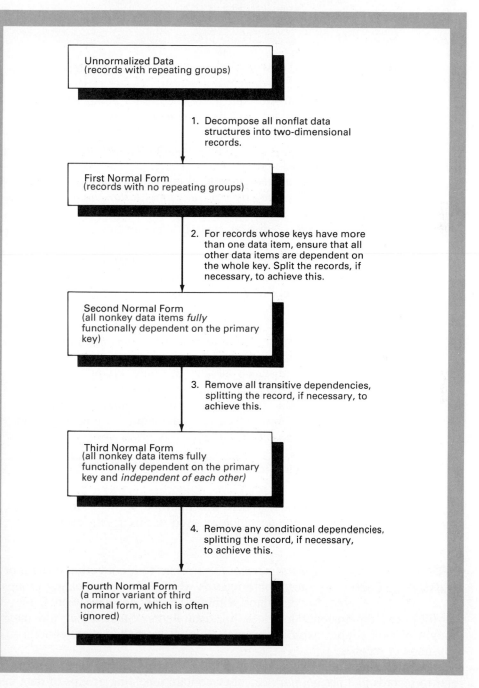

Unnormalized Data
(records with repeating groups)

1. Decompose all nonflat data
   structures into two-dimensional
   records.

First Normal Form
(records with no repeating groups)

2. For records whose keys have more
   than one data item, ensure that all
   other data items are dependent on
   the whole key. Split the records, if
   necessary, to achieve this.

Second Normal Form
(all nonkey data items *fully*
functionally dependent on the primary
key)

3. Remove all transitive dependencies,
   splitting the record, if necessary, to
   achieve this.

Third Normal Form
(all nonkey data items fully
functionally dependent on the primary
key and *independent of each other)*

4. Remove any conditional dependencies,
   splitting the record, if necessary,
   to achieve this.

Fourth Normal Form
(a minor variant of third
normal form, which is often
ignored)

**BOX 12.2   Vocabulary used in discussing data
(see also Fig. 12.1)**

The reader should distinguish clearly between the terms *data type* and *data-item type*.

Data type refers to the data itself (i.e., data about data). Examples of data types are *integer, rational number, boolean,* and *alphabetic string*.

Entity type refers to a given class of entities, such as *customer, part, account, employee,* and so on.

Attribute refers to a characteristic of an entity type: for example, *color, shape, shipment date, type of account, dollar value,* and so on.

When we say *data-item type*, we are referring to either an *entity type* or an *attribute*.

Data item expresses an attribute or entity identifier (a special type of attribute) in computable form, sometimes described as a *field*.

Data-item type refers to a given class of data items. Examples of data-item types are *customer number, account number, address, dollar-value,* and *color*.

Entities, and data items are *instances* of entity types and data-item types. For example, DUPONT is an instance of the entity type *customer*. RED is an instance of the attribute *color*. Data item 4789123 is an instance of the data-item type *employee number*.

In discussion of data we sometimes use shorthand. We say "entity" when we mean "entity type", "data item" when we mean "data-item type", and so on. "Data type" is never abbreviated.

tation of data, not the physical. There are multiple ways of implementing it physically. Box 12.2 gives the terminology used in discussing data.

FIRST NORMAL FORM

First normal form refers to a collection of data organized into records which have no repeating groups of data items within a record. In other words, they are flat files, two-dimensional matrices, of data items. Such a flat file may be thought of as a simple two-dimensional table. It may, however, contain many thousands of records.

Most programming languages give programmers the ability to create and refer to records that are not *flat* (i.e., they contain repeating groups of data items within a record). In COBOL these are called *data tables*. There can be data tables within data tables—repeating groups within repeating groups.

The following COBOL record contains two data groups, called BIRTH and SKILLS.

```
RECORD NAME IS PERSON
       01                      EMPLOYEE# PICTURE "9(5)"
       01                      EMPNAME TYPE CHARACTER 20
       01                      SEX PICTURE "A"
       01                      EMPJCODE PICTURE "9999"
       01                      SALARY PICTURE "9(5)V99"
       01                      BIRTH
              02                      MONTH PICTURE "99"
              02                      DAY
              02                      YEAR PICTURE "99"
       01                      NOSKILLS TYPE BINARY
       01                      SKILLS OCCURS NOSKILLS TIMES
              02                      SKILLCODE PICTURE "9999"
              02                      SKILLYEARS PICTURE "99"
```

PERSON

					BIRTH			SKILLS	
EMPLOYEE#	EMPNAME	SEX	EMPJCODE	SALARY	MONTH	DAY	YEAR	SKILLCODE	SKILLYEARS

BIRTH causes no problems because it occurs only once in each record. SKILLS can occur several times in one record, so it is a data table and record is not in first normal form. It is not a *flat,* two-dimensional record. To *normalize* it, the table SKILLS must be removed and put into a separate record, thus:

PERSON

					BIRTH		
EMPLOYEE#	EMPNAME	SEX	EMPJCODE	SALARY	MONTH	DAY	YEAR

SKILLS

EMPLOYEE# + SKILLCODE	SKILLYEARS

The lower record has a concatenated key EMPLOYEE# + SKILLCODE. We cannot know SKILLYEARS (the number of years of experience an employee has had with a given skill) unless we know EMPLOYEE# (the employee number to whom this refers) and SKILLCODE (the skill in question).

In general, a nonflat record is normalized by converting it into two or more flat records. If the normalized records above were implemented in a CODA-SYL, DL/1, or other nonrelational database management system, we would not repeat the data item EMPLOYEE# in the lower record. A linkage to the upper record would imply this key:

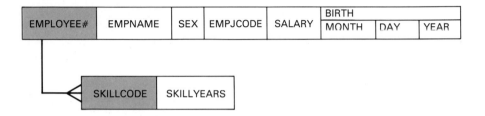

A relational database *would* employ a separate SKILLS record (relation) with a key EMPLOYEE + SKILLCODE; it thus avoids pointer mechanisms in the logical representation of data. Here we are concerned not with how the physical implementation is done, but with the overall *logical* representation of data. We need to analyze and chart an enterprise's information resources and how they are used. We draw the lower record with its complete concatenated key so that it can stand alone and the key uniquely identifies the data in the record.

FUNCTIONAL DEPENDENCE

In attempting to lay out the relationships between data items, the designer must concern himself with which data items are *dependent* on which other. The phrase *functionally dependent* is defined as follows [2]:

> Data item B of a record R is functionally dependent on data item A of R if, at every instant of time, each value in A has no more than one value in B associated with it in record R.

Saying that B is functionally dependent on A is equivalent to saying that A *identifies B*. In other words, if we know the value of A, we can find the value of B that is associated with it. For example, in an employee record, the SALARY data item is functionally dependent on EMPLOYEE#. For one EMPLOYEE# there is one SALARY. To find the value of SALARY in a database, you would normally go via EMPLOYEE#. The latter is a key that identifies the attribute SALARY.

We will draw a functional dependency with a line that has a small bar (like a "1") on it, thus:

EMPLOYEE# ─────────┼ SALARY

This indicates that one instance of SALARY is associated with each EMPLOYEE#. Consider the record for the entity EMPLOYEE:

EMPLOYEE#	EMPLOYEE-NAME	SALARY	PROJECT#	COMPLETION-DATE

The functional dependencies in this record are as follows:

EMPLOYEE#	is dependent on EMPLOYEE-NAME
EMPLOYEE-NAME	is dependent on EMPLOYEE#
SALARY	is dependent on either EMPLOYEE-NAME or EMPLOYEE#
PROJECT#	is dependent on either EMPLOYEE-NAME or EMPLOYEE#
COMPLETION-DATE	is dependent on EMPLOYEE-NAME, EMPLOYEE#, or PROJECT#

EMPLOYEE# is not functionally dependent on SALARY because more than one employee could have the same salary. Similarly, EMPLOYEE# is not functionally dependent on PROJECT#, but COMPLETION-DATE is. No other data item in the record is fully dependent on PROJECT#. We can draw these functional dependencies as follows:

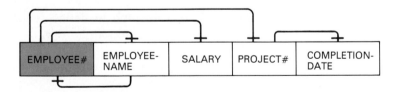

A data item can be functionally dependent on a *group* of data items rather than a single data item. Consider, for example, the following record, which shows how programmers spent their time:

PROGRAMMER-ACTIVITY

PROGRAMMER#	PACKAGE#	PROGRAMMER-NAME	PACKAGE-NAME	TOTAL-HOURS-WORKED

The fields that constitute the primary key (unique identifier) are shown in red. TOTAL-HOURS-WORKED is functionally dependent on the concatenated key (PROGRAMMER#, PACKAGE#). The functional dependencies in this record can be drawn as follows:

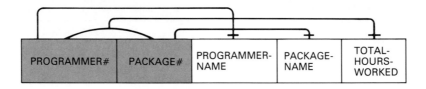

FULL FUNCTIONAL DEPENDENCY

A data item or a collection of data items, *B,* of a record *R* can be said to be *fully functionally dependent* on another collection of data items, *A,* of record *R* if *B* is functionally dependent on the whole of *A* but not on any subset of *A.* For example, in the record above, TOTAL-HOURS-WORKED is fully functionally dependent on the concatenated key (PROGRAMMER#, PACKAGE#) because it refers to how many hours a given programmer has worked on a given package. Neither PROGRAMMER# alone nor PACKAGE# alone identifies TOTAL-HOURS-WORKED.

TOTAL-HOURS-WORKED, however, is the *only* data item that is fully functionally dependent on the concatenated key. PROGRAMMER-NAME is fully functionally dependent on PROGRAMMER# alone, and PACKAGE-NAME is fully functionally dependent on PACKAGE# alone. The lines with bars above make these dependencies clear.

SECOND NORMAL FORM

We are now in a position to define second normal form. First a simple definition:

Each attribute in a record is functionally dependent on the entire key of that record.

Where the key consists of more than one data item, the record may not be in second normal form. The record above with the key PROGRAMMER# + PACKAGE# is not in second normal form because TOTAL-HOURS-WORKED depends on the whole key, whereas PROGRAMMER-NAME and PACKAGE-NAME each depend on only one data item in the key. Similarly, the following record is not in second normal form:

PART#	SUPPLIER#	SUPPLIER-NAME	SUPPLIER-DETAILS	PRICE

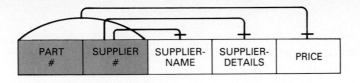

An instance of this record:

PART#	SUPPLIER#	SUPPLIER-NAME	SUPPLIER-DETAILS	PRICE
1	1000	JONES	x	20
1	1500	ABC	x	28
1	2050	XYZ	y	22
1	1900	P-H	z	30
2	3100	ALLEN	z	520
2	1000	JONES	x	500
2	2050	XYZ	y	590
3	2050	XYZ	y	1000
4	1000	JONES	x	80
4	3100	ALLEN	z	90
4	1900	P-H	z	95
5	1500	ABC	x	160
5	1000	JONES	x	140

To convert the records above into second normal form, we split it into two records, thus:

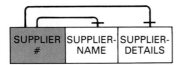 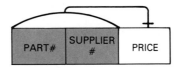

An instance of the pair of records above:

SUPPLIER#	SUPPLIER-NAME	SUPPLIER-DETAILS
1000	JONES	x
1500	ABC	x
2050	XYZ	y
1900	P-H	z
3100	ALLEN	z

PART#	SUPPLIER#	PRICE
1	1000	20
1	1500	28
1	2050	22
1	1900	30
2	3100	520
2	1000	500
2	2050	590
3	2050	1000
4	1000	80
4	3100	90
4	1900	95
5	1500	160
5	1000	140

Figure 12.3 Conversion to second normal form.

There are a few problems that can result from this record *not* being in second normal form:

1. We cannot enter details about a supplier until that supplier supplies a part. If the supplier does not supply a part, there is no key.

2. If a supplier should temporarily cease to supply any part, the deletion of the last record containing that SUPPLIER# will also delete the details of the supplier. It would normally be desirable that SUPPLIER-DETAILS be preserved.

3. We have problems when we attempt to update the supplier details. We must search for every record which contains that supplier as part of the key. If a supplier supplies many parts, much redundant updating of supplier details will be needed.

These types of irregularities can be removed by splitting the record into two records in second normal form, as shown in Fig. 12.3. Only PRICE is fully functionally dependent on the concatenated key, so all other attributes are removed to the separate record on the left, which has SUPPLIER-NUMBER only as its key.

Splitting to second normal form is the type of splitting that natural database growth tends to force, so it might as well be anticipated when the database is first set up. In general, every data item in a record should be dependent on the *entire* key; otherwise, it should be removed to a separate record. Figure 12.3 illustrates splitting the record above into second-normal-form records.

CANDIDATE KEYS

The *key* of a normalized record must have the following properties:

1. **Unique Identification.** For every record occurrence the key must uniquely identify the record.

2. **Nonredundancy.** No data item in the key can be discarded without destroying the property of unique identification.

It sometimes happens that more than one data item or set of data items *could* be the key of a record. Such alternative choices are referred to as *candidate keys*.

One candidate key must be designated the *primary key*. We will draw the functional dependencies for candidate keys which are not the primary key *underneath* the record, thus:

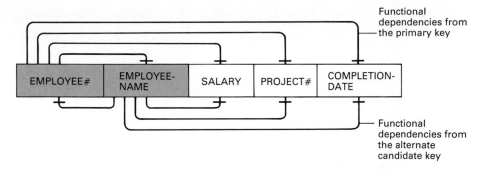

In this illustration EMPLOYEE-NAME is regarded as a candidate key—an alternative to EMPLOYEE#. This is not generally done in practice because two employees *might* have the same name. Only EMPLOYEE# is truly unique.

The possible existence of candidate keys complicates the definitions of second and third normal form. A more comprehensive definition of second normal form is [2]:

> A record *R* is in second normal form if it is in first normal form and every non-prime data item of *R* is fully functionally dependent on each candidate key of *R*.

In the EMPLOYEE record above, the candidate keys have only one data item, and hence the record is always in second normal form because the non-prime data items *must* be fully dependent on the candidate keys. When the candidate keys consist of more than one data item, a first-normal-form record may not be in second normal form.

THIRD NORMAL FORM

A record that *is* in second normal form can have another type of anomaly. It may have a data item which is not a key but which itself identifies other data items. This is referred to as a *transitive dependence*. Transitive dependencies can cause problems. The step of putting data into *third normal form* removes transitive dependencies.

Suppose that *A, B,* and *C* are three data items or distinct collections of data items of a record *R*. If *C* is functionally dependent on *B* and *B* is functionally dependent on *A,* then *C* is functionally dependent on *A.* If the inverse mapping is nonsimple (i.e., if *A* is not functionally dependent on *B or B* is not functionally dependent on *C*), *C* is said to be *transitively dependent* on *A.*

In a diagram *C* is transitively dependent on *A* if

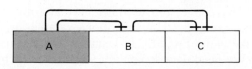

Conversion to third normal form removes this transitive dependence by splitting the record into two, thus:

The following record is not in third normal form because COMPLETION-DATE is dependent on PROJECT#.

EMPLOYEE

EMPLOYEE#	EMPLOYEE-NAME	SALARY	PROJECT#	COMPLETION-DATE

A few problems might result from this record not being in third normal form.

1. Before any employees are recruited for a project, the completion date of the project cannot be recorded because there is no EMPLOYEE record.

2. If all the employees should leave the project so that the project has no employees until others are recruited, all records containing the completion date would be deleted. This may be thought an unlikely occurrence, but on other types of files a similar danger of loss of information can be less improbable.

3. If the completion date is changed, it will be necessary to search for all records containing that completion date, and update them all.

A simple definition of third normal form is:

A record is in second normal form and each attribute is functionally dependent on the key and *nothing but the key*.

A more formal definition that incorporates candidate keys is as follows [2]:

A record R is in third normal form if it is in second normal form and every nonprime data item of R is nontransitively dependent on each candidate key of R.

Figure 12.4 shows the conversion of the EMPLOYEE record above to third normal form. The conversion to third normal form produces a separate record for each entity-normalized record. For example, Fig. 12.4 produced a separate record for the entity PROJECT. Usually, this normalized record would be needed anyway. We need data separately storing for each entity.

An instance of this record:

EMPLOYEE#	EMPLOYEE-NAME	SALARY	PROJECT#	COMPLETION-DATE
120	JONES	2000	x	17.7.84
121	HARPO	1700	x	17.7.84
270	GARFUNKAL	1800	y	12.1.87
273	SELSI	3600	x	17.7.84
274	ABRAHMS	3000	z	21.3.86
279	HIGGINS	2400	y	12.1.87
301	FLANNEL	1800	z	21.3.86
306	MCGRAW	2100	x	17.7.84
310	ENSON	3000	z	21.3.86
315	GOLDSTEIN	3100	x	17.7.84
317	PUORRO	2700	y	12.1.87
320	MANSINI	1700	y	12.1.87
321	SPOTO	2900	x	17.7.84
340	SCHAFT	3100	x	17.7.84
349	GOLD	1900	z	21.3.86

To convert the above record into third normal form we split it into two records, thus:

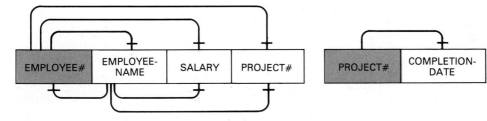

An instance of the above pair of records:

EMPLOYEE#	EMPLOYEE-NAME	SALARY	PROJECT#
120	JONES	2000	x
121	HARPO	1700	x
270	GARFUNKAL	1800	y
273	SELSI	3600	x
274	ABRAHMS	3000	z
279	HIGGINS	2400	y
301	FLANNEL	1800	z
306	MCGRAW	2100	x
310	ENSON	3000	z
315	GOLDSTEIN	3100	x
317	PUORRO	2700	y
320	MANSINI	1700	y
321	SPOTO	2900	x
340	SCHAFT	3100	x
349	GOLD	1900	z

PROJECT#	COMPLETION-DATE
x	17.7.84
y	12.1.87
z	21.3.86

Figure 12.4 Conversion to third normal form.

STORAGE AND PERFORMANCE
The concept of normalization applies to all databases. Experience has shown that the records of a CODA-SYL system, the segments of a DL/1 system, or the group of data items in other systems can benefit from being normalized.

Objections to normalization are occasionally heard on the grounds that it requires more storage or more machine time. A fourth-normal-form structure usually has more records after all the splitting described above. Isn't that worse from the hardware point of view? Not necessarily. In fact, although there are more records, they almost always take less storage. The reason is that non-fourth-normal-form records usually have much *value* redundancy.

Compare the records in Fig. 12.3. Here records not in second normal form are converted to second normal form by splitting. It will be seen that the lower *shaded* part of Fig. 12.4 has fewer *values* of data written down than the red part at the top. There are fewer values of SUPPLIER-NAME and SUPPLIER-DETAILS. This shrinkage does not look very dramatic on such a small illustration. If there had been thousands of suppliers and thousands of parts, and many attributes of both, the shrinkage would have been spectacular.

Again, compare the *shaded* parts of Fig. 12.4. Here a record is converted to third normal form by splitting. The number of *values* of data shrinks. There are fewer values of COMPLETION-DATE recorded after the split. Once more, if there had been many employees, many projects, and many attributes of those projects, the shrinkage would have been dramatic.

CONDITIONAL DEPENDENCIES
Usually, the normalization process stops at third normal form. There are two subtleties that could result in a further stage of normalization. First, if the primary key (unique identifier) has three or more fields with multivalued dependencies within the key, a further stage of cleaning up may be needed. This is described in my *Managing the Data-Base Environment,* Chapter 13 [1]. Second, a record in third normal form might have a conditional dependency in it, and this is removed by splitting the record again.

Consider the following record with the primary key CUSTOMER-NUMBER:

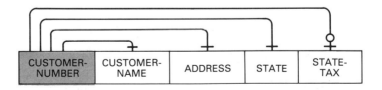

STATE-TAX exists only for customers in the state of the shipping company, Vermont, say. For most customers there is no state tax because they are out of state. The existence of the field is conditional. The record may therefore be split so that STATE-TAX is in a separate (relatively small) file:

CUSTOMERS

CUSTOMER-NUMBER	CUSTOMER-NAME	ADDRESS	STATE

VERMONT CUSTOMERS

CUSTOMER-NUMBER	STATE-TAX

The link from CUSTOMER-NUMBER to STATE-TAX is referred to as a *conditional dependency*. The removal of conditional dependencies is sometimes referred to as the fourth stage of normalization. It is shown as the bottom step in Fig. 12.1.

Conversion to third normal form almost always reduces the amount of storage used, often dramatically. What about machine time and accesses? Often this is less after normalization. Before normalization many aspects of the data are tangled together and must all be read at once. After normalization they are separated, so a small record is read.

Also, because there is less value redundancy in third normal form, there is less duplicated updating of the redundant values. Suppose that project *x* slips its completion date (which it does every week!). In the record at the top of Fig. 12.4 the completion date has to be changed seven times; in the third-normal-form version it has to be changed only once. A similar argument applies to SUPPLIER-NAME and SUPPLIER-DETAILS in Fig. 12.3. The argument would have more force if the examples had hundreds of employees, thousands of suppliers, and many attributes that have to be updated. There are, however, exceptions to this. On rare occasions a designer may consciously design non-third-normal-form records for performance reasons. Normalization relates to the logical structure of data, not necessarily the physical.

SEMANTIC DISINTEGRITY
A further reason for using normalized data is that certain database queries can run into problems when data is not cleanly structured. A query, perhaps entered with a database query language, can appear to be valid, but in fact has subtle illogical aspects sometimes referred to as *semantic disintegrity*. When the data is in third normal form, rules can be devised for preventing semantic disintegrity or warning the user about his query.

CLEAR THINKING ABOUT DATA

Normalization is an aid to clear thinking about data. It is a formal method of separating the data items that relate to different entities. A record in fourth normal form has the following clean, simple structure:

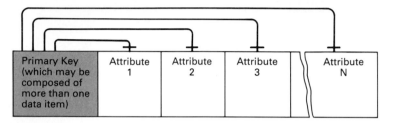

The functional dependency lines all come from the primary key. There are no hidden dependencies not relating to the key. If the key is concatenated, all data items are dependent on the entire key.

We can give a loose definition of fourth normal form, which has the advantage of being easy to remember:

Every data item in a record is dependent on the key, the whole key, and nothing but the key.

If a systems analyst remembers this definition (understanding that it is not rigorous like those earlier in the chapter), he can quickly spot and modify records that are not in fourth normal form. He should be familiar enough with this that alarm bells go off in his mind whenever he sees records that are not in third normal form. This clean, simple data grouping is easy to implement and to use. There will be complications in store in the future if more complex record structures are used.

For the database administrator, normalization is an aid to precision. A normalized database can grow and evolve naturally. The updating rules are straightforward. A fourth-normal-form record type can have records added to it or can have records deleted without the problems that could occur with nonnormalized record types. Fourth-normal-form structuring gives a simple view of data to the programmers and users, and makes them less likely to perform invalid operations.

Figure 12.5 gives a simplified illustration of the three main steps in achieving normalized data; Fig. 12.6 illustrates the progression to fourth normal form.

A SUGGESTED EXERCISE

Probably the best way for a data processing user to become convinced of the value (or otherwise) of normalization is to take a section of his files and write down what third-normal-form records would be used to represent them. A group

Conversion to First Normal Form

Conversion to Second Normal Form

Conversion to Third Normal Form

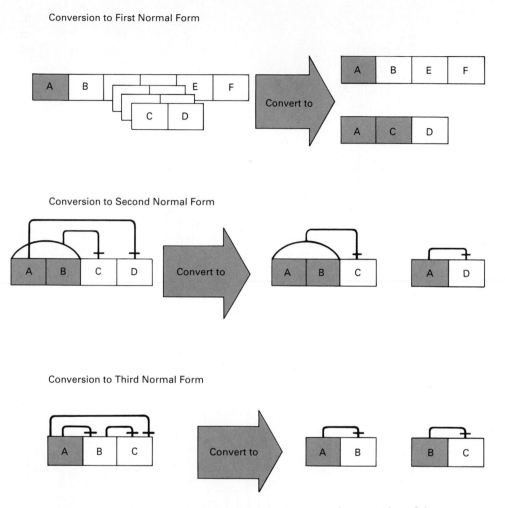

Figure 12.5 A simplified illustration of the three steps in conversion of data
to third normal form. Figure 12.6 gives an illustration with real data.

of systems analysts should then list all the plausible changes that might occur
to the files as data processing evolves in the years ahead, and see how many of
these changes would necessitate restructuring the records in such a way that
previously written application programs would have to be changed. Compare
this with what reprogramming would be needed if the same changes were applied to the existing records.

In examining existing databases it has been our experience that time and
time again they are not normalized. This spells trouble for the future. Unless it
was the conscious policy of management to create normalized data, the design
has been far from these principles.

Unnormalized record:

ORDER

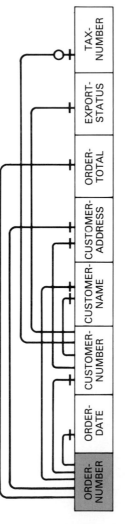

First normal form: Remove the repeating group.

ORDER

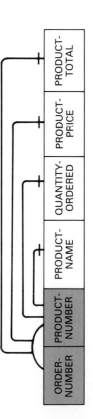

ORDER-PRODUCT

Figure 12.6   An illustration of the three stages of normalization.

AN EXAMPLE OF NORMALIZATION

Consider an ORDER record with the following unnormalized structure:

ORDER (*Order number,* order date, customer number, customer name, customer address, export status, tax number, ((product number, product name, quantity ordered, product price, product total)), order total.)

Applying the four normalization steps to this example is illustrated in Fig. 12.6. Application of the *first normal form* rule (remove repeating groups) creates two records: ORDER and ORDER-PRODUCT. The primary key is made up of *Order#* and *Product#*.

Second normal form removes the product name from the ORDER PRODUCT record into a new record: PRODUCT. Product name is wholly dependent on product number; it is only partially dependent on the primary (combined or compound) key of ORDER PRODUCT: *Order# + Product#*.

Third normal form removes the customer details from the ORDER record to a separate CUSTOMER record. Customer name and address are wholly dependent on customer number; they are not dependent at all on the primary key

Second normal form: Remove attributes not dependent on the whole of a (concatenated) primary key, as in the ORDER-PRODUCT record above.

ORDER

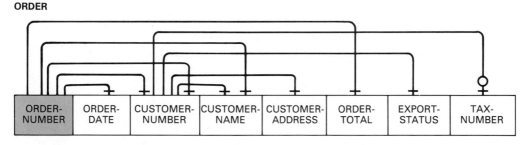

ORDER-NUMBER	ORDER-DATE	CUSTOMER-NUMBER	CUSTOMER-NAME	CUSTOMER-ADDRESS	ORDER-TOTAL	EXPORT-STATUS	TAX-NUMBER

ORDER-PRODUCT

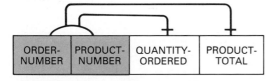

ORDER-NUMBER	PRODUCT-NUMBER	QUANTITY-ORDERED	PRODUCT-TOTAL

PRODUCT

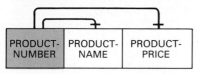

PRODUCT-NUMBER	PRODUCT-NAME	PRODUCT-PRICE

Figure 12.6   (Continued)

239

Third Normal Form:

Remove attributes dependent on data item(s)
other than the primary key, as in the ORDER record above.

ORDER

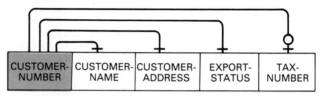

ORDER-NUMBER	ORDER-DATE	CUSTOMER-NUMBER	ORDER-TOTAL

CUSTOMER

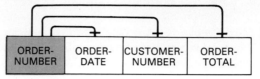

CUSTOMER-NUMBER	CUSTOMER-NAME	CUSTOMER-ADDRESS	EXPORT-STATUS	TAX-NUMBER

ORDER-PRODUCT

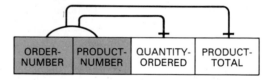

ORDER-NUMBER	PRODUCT-NUMBER	QUANTITY-ORDERED	PRODUCT-TOTAL

PRODUCT

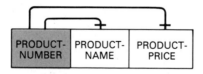

PRODUCT-NUMBER	PRODUCT-NAME	PRODUCT-PRICE

Fourth Normal Form:

Remove conditional dependencies.

TAX-NUMBER exists only if EXPORT-STATUS is "D," meaning
"DOMESTIC"; therefore, a separate record is created
for domestic customers:

CUSTOMER

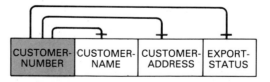

CUSTOMER-NUMBER	CUSTOMER-NAME	CUSTOMER-ADDRESS	EXPORT-STATUS

DOMESTIC CUSTOMER

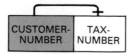

CUSTOMER-NUMBER	TAX-NUMBER

Figure 12.6   (Continued)

BOX 12.3   A description of the procedure for data modeling

```
CREATE A DETAILED DATA MODEL

    Detailed data modeling is tackled in one business area at a
time. Although described here as a self-contained activity it
needs to be an integral part of the Business Area Analysis
procedure.
o───────o
| See BOX 11.2  |
o───────o
    Comprehensive checks on the modeling process are described below
which are sometimes referred to as STABILITY ANALYSIS. The objective
is to make the data model as stable as possible so that it can
support major changes in corporate procedures. Stable data models
have had the effect of drastically reducing program maintenance costs.

    ┌─────────────────────────────────────────┐
    │ The procedure given below may be modified with Action
    │ Diagrammer to meet the needs of the particular situation.
    └─────────────────────────────────────────┘

Preparation
    Appoint a data-modeling professional to lead the activity
        If a skilled data-modeling professional exists in house
            Make him responsible for completion of the model on time.
        Else
            Employ a consultant skilled in data modeling.
            Make him responsible for completion of the model on time.
            Appoint one or more in-house professionals to become
                data-modeling experts.
            Appoint an in-house professional to take over the work
                from the consultant and be responsible for the model.

    Ensure that the necessary tools are installed and working
        Install a data modeling tool which synthesizes and normalizes
            multiple views of data.
        Use an encyclopedia-based tool (the one used in the earlier
            stages of information engineering) to form an enterprise-wide
            dictionary, repository, and coordination tool. The tool which
            does synthesis and normalization should preferably be part
            of the encyclopedia-based workbench.

    Form an end-user committee.
        Select end-user participants.
            End users selected should
                o  be intelligent,
                o  be creative,
                o  have good human communication skills,
                o  want to understand information-system techniques,
                o  be highly knowledgeable about their own business areas.
        Give the participants a one-day course in the basic principles
            of database techniques.
            Book: James Martin, An End-Users' Guide to Database,
                    Prentice-Hall, Englewood Cliffs, NJ.

    Document a naming convention for the data items.
```

(Continued)

BOX 12.3 *(Continued)*

Top-down data modeling
    Select the entity types for this business area from the ISP
      entity-relationship model.
    Enter the primary keys for these entity types.
    Add intersection entity types where appropriate (with automated
      assistance).
    Add whatever attributes can be identified.
    Ensure that the attribute groupings are in Fourth Normal Form.
    Enhance this data model with the synthesis and user-checking
      techniques described below.

Data synthesis

    THE FOLLOWING STEPS ARE DONE ITERATIVELY UNTIL THE MODEL IS COMPLETE

    Identify all possible user views of data
        Capture all documents that will be derived from the systems.
        Capture all documents that will be input to the systems.
        Examine all information requirements identified during the ISP.
        o————————o
        | See BOX 2.1 |
        o————————o
        Determine by discussion with the end users what types of data
          they want to obtain from the systems, now and in the future.
        Determine from the systems analysts whether any new record
          or document requirements are emerging.
        Examine existing files, databases, or dictionaries which
          relate to this data.
        Plan whether existing files or databases will coexist with
          new systems or be converted. If they will coexist, plan what
          data is needed in the new systems to form a bridge with the
          old systems.
        Will application package files or databases coexist with the
          new systems. If so, plan what data is needed in the new
          systems to form a bridge with the packages.

    Do the following for all the above user views
        Inspect each input
            Employ the naming convention.
            Inspect each input to see whether it can be simplified.
            Check whether any of the input data items already exist in
              the model under a different name or in a slightly different
              form. If so ensure that this redundancy is removed.
            For each data item check that no different data item in
              the model has the same name.
            Be sure that concatenated keys are correctly represented
              in the input to the synthesis process.
            Be sure that all attributes entered are dependent on the
              WHOLE of the key which identifies them.
            Be sure that all attributes entered as input contain no
              transitive dependencies (no hidden keys)
            Question the validity of all links which represent business
              rules, as opposed to the natural properties of the data.
              Could these rules be changed in the future ?
            Question any link with a "1" cardinality to ask whether it
              could become a "many" cardinality in the future.

BOX 12.3 *(Continued)*

```
Enter the view into the synthesis tool.
Create a dictionary entry to document the meaning of each
   data item.

Check the synthesized model.
    With the user committee, review the data dictionary listing
        to ensure that all end users agree about the definitions
        of the data items.
    With the user committee, review the data model to ensure that
        their data requirements can be derived from it.
    With the user committee, brainstorm the possible future uses
        of the data. For any uses which the model does not serve,
        create new input to the synthesis process.
    Description
        Brainstorming means that a creative group of individuals
        attempt to produce a stream of ideas without inhibition.
        A rule of a brainstorming session is that there can be
        no implied criticism for making an impractical or stupid
        suggestion. The session is intended to generate as many
        ideas as possible. At the end of the session only certain
        of the ideas will be recorded for possible use.

    Examine every attribute field in the model to see whether it
        could become a primary key in the future.
    Complete the reverse mapping of any links between keys to
        identify any possible MANY-TO-MANY links. Create an extra
        concatenated key to take care of any possible future
        intersection data.
    If candidate keys exist in the data model, ensure that they
        are in fact likely to remain candidate keys in the future.
    Use fast, computerized redesign after any changes are made to
        maintain the interest of the end users.

Ensure that the data modeling is integrated into the BAA procedure.
    See BOX 11.2
```

of ORDER (i.e., *Order#*). (A customer will not change his name and address with each new order—unless he doesn't intend to pay for it!)

The four resulting records in Fig. 12.6—ORDER, CUSTOMER, ORDER-PRODUCT, and PRODUCT—are in third normal form.

The final step in Fig. 12.6 removes the conditional dependency that causes there to be a tax number for domestic customers, but not for foreign customers.

PROCEDURE   A detailed description of the procedures for data modeling is given in Box 12.3.

REFERENCES

1. James Martin, *Managing the Data Base Environment*. Englewood Cliffs, N.J.: Prentice-Hall, 1983.

2. E. F. Codd, Further normalization of the data base relational model, in Courant Computer Science Symposia 6, *Data Base Systems,* R. Rustin, (ed.). Englewood Cliffs, N.J.: Prentice-Hall, 1972 (reproduced in Appendix IV).

3. James Martin, *System Design from Provably Correct Constructs*. Englewood Cliffs, N.J.: Prentice-Hall, 1985.

13 END-USER HELP IN DATA MODELING

INTRODUCTION   A vital part of business area analysis is the creation of a stable, fully normalized model of the data that is used in the business area. This data model is the foundation on which applications will be built.

A data model contains hundreds (and sometimes thousands) of types of data items. Thousands of data items are used in the running of a big corporation. To computerize the activities of a corporation, the data items it uses must be defined, cataloged, and organized. This is often difficult and time consuming because data has been treated rather sloppily in the past. What is essentially the same data item has been defined differently in different places, represented differently in computers, and given different names. Data items that were casually thought to be the same are found to be not quite the same.

The data administrator has the job of cleaning up this confusion. Definitions of data items must be agreed upon and documented. Much help from end users is often needed in this process. For years many enterprises have had a data administration function charged with modeling the data in the enterprise. Some have done an excellent job of data modeling and make the models available in computerized form for system building. In such enterprises information engineering is regarded as an extension of the data administration activity.

THE MESS IN   In the first decades of computing, the programs in a
DATA LIBRARIES   corporation became an unruly mess, far removed from the orderliness one would normally associate with an engineering discipline. We now have techniques that can create better programs: CASE tools, code generators, fourth-generation languages, prototyping tools, and computable specification languages.

These tools alone, however, are not enough because in data processing there is another mess—the data. Most large corporations' tape and disk libraries have vast numbers of volumes containing redundant, inconsistent collections of data, chaotically organized. What is, in effect, the same data is represented in numerous different incompatible ways on different tapes and disks. The grouping of data items into records is such that it leads to all manner of anomalies and maintenance problems. The use of fast and rigorous techniques for generating programs would not eliminate these problems without overall management and control of the *data* in an enterprise.

THE FAILURE OF DATA ADMINISTRATION

Many enterprises have disastrously failed in achieving overall coordination of data. This failure is extremely expensive in the long run, in inflated I.S. costs, failure to implement needed procedures, and in lost business. Box 3.1 in Book I listed the reasons for failure of corporate data administration. Top managers need to understand the financial importance of successful data administration. We have stressed that the foundation for building a computerized corporation is the data models that are used.

THE COSTS OF BAD DATA ADMINISTRATION

A large commercial volume library has tens of thousands of tapes and disks, most of them containing different types of data items. One commercial application receives data from, or passes data to, many other applications. If these applications are developed without integrated planning of the data, the result is a Tower of Babel. Higher management cannot extract data that needs to be drawn from multiple systems. Expensive conversion is needed, and often important business options are lost because the data is not available in the right form.

When a corporate president angrily protests that for years he has been asking for weekly cash balances and he is no nearer to receiving them in spite of millions spent on computers and networks, the cause of this problem is that the data needed for such computation is ill-defined and incompatible. The computer world is full of horror stories about information being urgently needed by management or customers but the computers being unable to provide that information even though the requisite data was in their volume library.

When the Franklin National Bank failed, one other bank in New York compiled a set of questions that top management urgently wanted answered. They related to conditions that might apply in the bank, and to answer them data from many differently written applications had to be assembled. After two days the computing executive had to admit defeat. *Yes,* the data was on disks, but *no,* the questions could not be answered.

Again in New York a bank tried to introduce an online cash management service. Competition had introduced this and it had great customer appeal. No new data was needed; it was all on the disks, but the urgent application could not be introduced without massive data conversion, which required very time-consuming reprogramming. The competition stayed ahead.

In many organizations the lack of good database design and integration results in huge maintenance costs and delays. Procedures cannot be changed quickly. New procedures which are urgently needed take years to introduce.

EXPERIENCE OF WHAT SUCCEEDS   In data modeling, there is much experience of what works well and what does not. To attempt to create a fully normalized model of all the data in an enterprise in one step is difficult because it takes too long. It is more practical to start with a rough overview model of the entities and their relationships, and expand this into detail in one business area at a time. The same is true with process modeling, so information engineering progresses from the top level of the pyramid, which creates a high-level overview, to the analysis in detail of separate business areas. It is like an architect creating an overall plan of a house and then drawing one room at a time in detail. Figure 13.1 (repeated from Book I) shows the overview being created during the information strategy planning study, the fully normalized data model being created during business area analysis, and the extracts from the model being used to design systems.

In this chapter and the next we discuss a technique for achieving a fully normalized data model. A database can be defined as *a collection of data from which many different end-user views are derived*. The top of Fig. 13.2 illustrates this. The task of designing the database is to capture the end-user views and synthesize them into a database structure, as in the bottom half of Fig. 13.2.

Data modeling is a *synthesis* procedure. The data for different applications, the data on documents, and the information needs of management are captured and synthesized into an overall data model. This is done with a formal technique using a formal set of rules, which produces a fully normalized data model. It is tedious and difficult to do by hand because there are many hundreds (sometimes thousands) of data items and different views of the data come from different analysts. The procedure needs a computerized tool that enables analysts to enter different views of data, and which synthesizes the views into a fully normalized data model. The tool produces reports and diagrams that facilitate checking of the data model. It should be linked to the encyclopedia so that the data model can evolve with time and be tightly coupled into the other procedures of information engineering.

The synthesis tool might be thought of as having a hopper into which we can feed all manner of views of data: entity-relationship diagrams and diagrams showing detailed structures of data items on documents or screens. The tool digests these into the overall data model. To do this correctly, it must be told the *functional dependencies* that exist in the data (which we will describe shortly). The analyst must ensure that the data items are named with appropriate

During the first stage of information engineering an overview
entity-relationship model is created:

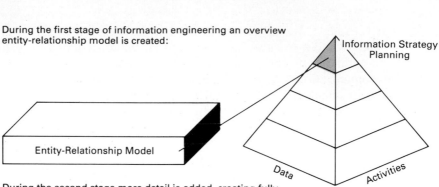

During the second stage more detail is added, creating fully
normalized data models for each business area:

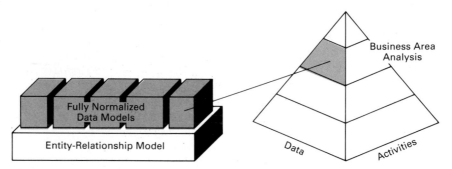

At the third stage, systems are designed using the fully
normalized data model.

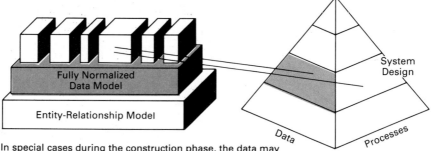

In special cases during the construction phase, the data may
be denormalized for machine performance reasons.

Figure 13.1

naming conventions and that when the same data item exists in different inputs,
it has the same name. The tool sorts the names in alphabetical order, and sorts
attributes by entity so that the analyst can look for unintended double naming.

The first step of detailed modeling, then, is to extract that portion of the
entity–relationship diagram which relates to the business area in question. Pri-

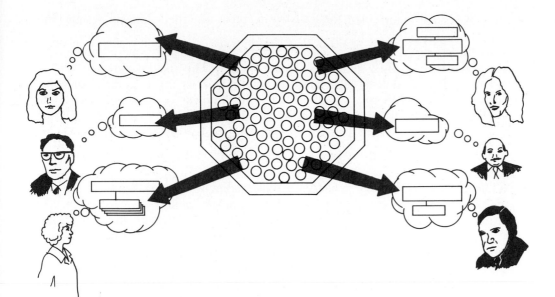

A database can be defined as a collection of data from which multiple different end-user views are derived.

The task of designing the data is then to capture the end-user views and synthesize them into a database structure:

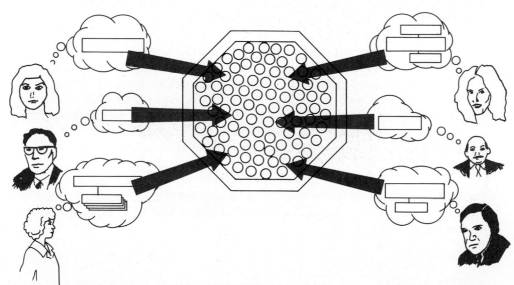

The resulting structure must be as stable as possible and must represent the inherent properties of the data.

Figure 13.2

mary keys are determined for each entity type. Detailed data modeling builds on this beginning.

Given any collection of data-item types, there is only one combination of them which is a fully normalized data model. This is the simplest minimal nonredundant model. It is sometimes referred to as the *canonical* model. A dictionary definition of "canonical" is "in simplest or standard form." The synthesis process follows a formal set of rules to achieve this model. The process is sometimes referred to as *canonical* synthesis.

TOP-DOWN AND BOTTOM-UP DESIGN

The distinction is sometimes made between *top-down* planning of data and *bottom-up* logical design. Top-down planning surveys the organization as a whole and determines what data resources it needs. Bottom-up design looks in detail at the documents, screens, and data needs that will be used in a given area and *synthesizes* their data into a third-normal-form model. The bottom-up process is sometimes described as *data analysis*.

Bottom-up data analysis is often perceived as looking at the *current* data in an organization and modeling it. This can be done by analysts from the data processing department and does not require a perception of future data needs, which is much more difficult to acquire. Top-down planning is often described as "strategic" planning and is intended to identify the data resources which the enterprise needs to support its future evolution.

Top-down design creates an *entity-relationship diagram* which gives an overview of the data entities that the organization should work with, but not fine detail of the data structures. It should look at the future evolution of the enterprise and its use of information. Detailed design then extends this overview and creates a normalized data model. Detailed design may be done in one business area at a time. As the detailed model emerges, a stage at a time, the detail is checked by management and users, who ask: How might this data be used in the future? Brainstorming the future uses of the data is part of the procedure called *stability analysis,* which is discussed in Appendix VI.

The detailed design is thus an extension of the overview design, and both should be cognisant of future uses of the data. Figure 13.3 shows the modeling process. The top-down analysis of the ISP is augmented by bottom-up synthesis of many user views of data.

MODELS AND SOFTWARE SCHEMAS

The term *data model* means *a representation of the structure of data showing data-item types and their relationships in a manner that is independent of technology.* It represents clear thinking about the nature of the data and is independent of computers, software, or procedures that use

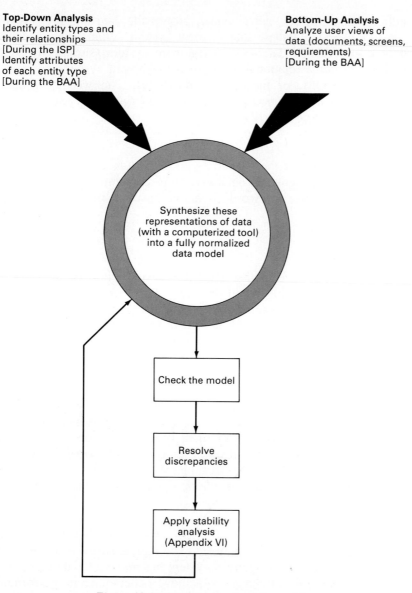

Figure 13.3   Synthesizing the data model.

the data. This is important because computers, software, and procedures change.

The word *schema* is also used to mean a logical representation of data. It is commonly used in a way that is *not* independent of the software used. We talk about a CODASYL schema, for example, meaning a structure of data which although it is logical, not physical, groups the data into the sets that are used by a CODASYL database management system. This structure would not be used in a hierarchical database management system (such as IMS, DL/1, TOTAL, IMAGE) or a relational database management system (such as DB2, ORACLE, DATACOM, or the AS/400 database). The word *schema,* then, means *a version of a data model that is oriented toward a particular DBMS approach to representing logical data.*

Sometimes the word "schema" is used to mean a software-independent representation of data. The term *conceptual schema,* for example, is used to refer to a representation of the properties and structure data which is independent of how we implement the database. It is conventional to use the word "model" for this because the word "schema" usually implies a type of software structure.

THREE REPRESENTATIONS OF DATA

Effective database design goes through the stages illustrated in Fig. 13.4. First, logical models are created of the data needed to run a corporation. They are designed to represent the inherent properties of the data in as stable a fashion as possible. They are *independent of the software or hardware* that is used. They are a statement about the data needed to run the corporation—documented, precise, clear thinking about these data.

When databases are implemented, the models are translated into the logical structures which a particular database management system is designed to handle. For CODASYL-based database management systems they are represented as set structures. For IBM's IMS they are represented as DL/1 structures. For relational databases they are represented as tuples.

The database designer designs *physical* representations of these logical structures (the right-hand octagon of Fig. 13.4). He designs the physical layout of the data and selects the access methods.

The physical database design will change when usage patterns of the data change, or when the hardware is upgraded. The logical software schemas should not change if the database management system has *thorough* data independence. In fact, it often *does* need to change to achieve better machine performance (a criticism of some of today's database management systems).

The model, however, is entirely independent of current software, implementations or usage volumes. The models of corporate data can, and should, be created long before databases employing those models are actually implemented. That is important because the data models will be a corporate resource that will remain valuable long after the software representations of data have changed.

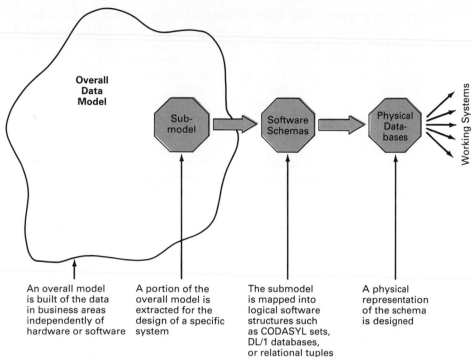

Figure 13.4   The overall corporate data model is much broader in scope than any specific database. Multiple submodels and schemas may be derived from it for individual database implementations. Because they are derived from a common model, data can be interchanged among them. The overall data model is held in the central I.E. encyclopedia, and submodels are extracted from it into the workbenches of individual analysts and designers.

THE END-USER COMMITTEE

A technique that has proved highly successful is to form a team of users who have expert knowledge of their own data. The team is composed of selected users who meet periodically with the data administrator, who will think about the data structures needed in their area. The data administrator, with the help of systems analysts, feeds the user views of data into a data modeling process and into the I.E. encyclopedia. Appropriate printouts of the models, from the encyclopedia, are then given to the user committee to check. Normally, there will be much argument about the definitions of data items and about which data items are standard. It is the task of the data administrator to resolve these arguments.

The following comments are from an end-user committee in a large insurance company trying to model the subject database for policyholder data.

We are a group representing many departments, with key people in each department. In order to analyze the data dealing with policyholder information, we are trying to make sure that this information is organized so that we can produce the various products that each department deals with—and to make sure that we're able to give management the information they need.

It was kind of amazing that we're all working for the same company but when a particular term was mentioned, that there were three or four different definitions of that term, and that each department was using the term to mean something else. So we started by coming up with some unique definitions of each term, and then we spent an awful lot of time trying to understand the relationship of each item to other items.

We've just gone through this over and over and over again to assure a good logical organization.

The task of designing databases involves cleaning up the data that are used in a corporation. This is usually a formidable task because for decades the data has evolved in an uncontrolled fashion. When computers were first used for inventory control, they revealed what a mess the stores were really in. The mess had to be cleaned up before computerized inventory control worked. Similarly, database design reveals what a mess the data in an organization is in. The I.E. encyclopedia and tools help to clean up that mess, and steadily evolve to cleanly engineered systems which are easy to maintain.

Over the 50 years that we have been writing group business, we wrote anything and everything. Standardization did not exist; it was a you-pick schedule for everyone, all a little different. I think when you have a highly automated system and you're coming from a very uncontrolled environment, the process of picking up data elements and converting them has got to be slow, painful, laborious; I don't think there's any alternative and that's got to be sold up front. It wasn't, I don't think, in this case.

It is a long and tedious job to clean up the discrepancies. But doing so is essential to building the foundation stone of future network database systems.

In this insurance company the data item CLAIM ADDRESS had different meanings:

For example, there's the physical address of the claims office itself, and then there are the addresses of the people that will receive the benefits directly. It seemed that somewhere along the line in our structure, that didn't come through very clearly, and we had to find out the hard way, by kind of locking horns to find out that that was a conflict.

Often the conflicts are much more complicated:

There is a conflict in the definition of a plan. What is a plan? Particularly for people that go back over five years, their definition of a plan will vary. If you took 20 people I think you would have 20 different ones. It's only been the people that have been exposed to a couple of the more recent systems that would have a relatively consistent definition, and even then, though, if you dig beneath the plan level and get into the benefit level, you'd find differences there.

Twenty different people with different definitions. That must take quite a bit of resolving in the user's group.

I think you'll find that the user's group will have to spend a great deal of time on definition.

END-USER ITERATIONS

When the users look at the resulting design, they often suggest changes. It is desirable that these changes be made quickly so that the users can see their effects on the overall design. If the modeling is done by computer, changes can be made quickly. The effects of these changes need not be inserted into the official data model until they have been examined by the systems analysts and users. This fast, automated response to suggested changes enables the database design process to be highly interactive, which is what it should be. The data administrator can experiment with various forms of user requirements quickly and easily. In particular, he should think about future needs to determine how data models serving future applications fit in with what is being done today. The impact of proposed changes on the existing database can be evaluated quickly.

When the data administrator has to do *manual* designs, the process is slow, tedious, and error-prone. The result is usually not an optimal structure. Because it is so tedious and time consuming, the data administrator repeatedly avoids redoing the design. But repeated redesign is often very important in clarifying the nature of the data. *The more thinking, iteration, and interaction with the users that goes on before a database is implemented, the better the final product will be*.

In many cases with *manual* data modeling, the data administrator hardly dare show his model to users because so much work has gone into it and he knows they will change it. A computerized data modeling tool and a CASE encyclopedia permit this iteration and enforce clarity of thinking about the data. We believe that they are *essential* tools for the data administrator. We have observed in installations beginning to use them a sharp change in the conceptual clarity and quality of the design process.

Many database designers have flip charts on sheets of paper, with arrows straggling wildly out of control from one block to another. Pointers to pointers to pointers. A bird's nest of linkages, frequently patched, often incomplete, almost impossible for a third party to check. This type of confused diagram leads to bad database design and prevents effective communication with users.

A good modeling tool should draw clear diagrams of database structures. Changes should be simple to make and when made, the tool should implement the redrawing of the diagrams. These diagrams can be given to analysts and users to check, think about, and provide feedback for redesigns. Together with the encyclopedia, they form the basis for that communication link with user departments without which database installations will not be truly successful.

Data integration across an organization has proven virtually impossible to accomplish by I.S. staff alone. It has been effectively accomplished where non-I.S. management and end users are strongly involved and motivated by top management, and the complexities of the synthesis process are handled by automated techniques.

PROCEDURE

The procedure for involving end users in data modeling is described in Box 12.3.

14 PROCESS MODELING

INTRODUCTION Data modeling is one half of the second layer of the pyramid. The other half is process modeling (Fig. 14.1). Data modeling and process modeling are done at the same time (unless a detailed data model already exists). A workbench tool is needed which integrates the data modeling and process modeling activities.

When a business process is examined, the paper documents or computer records associated with it are analyzed with the synthesis techniques described in the previous two chapters. The information that must pass between processes is examined similarly. When entities are described in data modeling, the question is asked: What processes use these entities?

PROCESS DECOMPOSITION The input to process modeling is the decomposition of business functions that resides in the encyclopedia after *information strategy planning (ISP)*. During *business area analysis* the business functions are decomposed into processes, which are further decomposed into lower-level processes. This is done with a tree-structure diagram, as in Fig. 14.2.

A *business function* may be defined as:

A group of business activities which together completely support one aspect of furthering the mission of the enterprise.

A *process* may be defined as:

A defined business activity, executions of which may be identified in terms of the input and/or output of specified types of data.

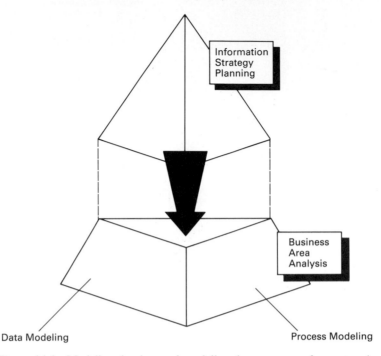

Figure 14.1   Modeling the data and modeling the processes of an enterprise go on hand in hand. A workbench tool is needed which integrates these activities.

Function decomposition is the breakdown of the activities of the enterprise into progressively greater detail. It starts at the top of the pyramid with the broad identification of business functions, and is continued during business area analysis until elementary processes are identified.

An *elementary process* may be defined as:

The smallest unit of activity of meaning to the end user, and which when complete leaves the information area in a self-consistent state.

The bottom nodes of the process decomposition tree are elementary processes.

"COMPOSED-OF" DIAGRAMS   In function and process decomposition diagrams a parent block *is composed of* its offspring blocks. It could be described as a *"composed-of"* diagram. The offspring together completely describe the parent. In some other tree structures this is not true. In *some* program structure diagrams a parent block *invokes* its child blocks but may itself contain functions which are not in the child blocks;

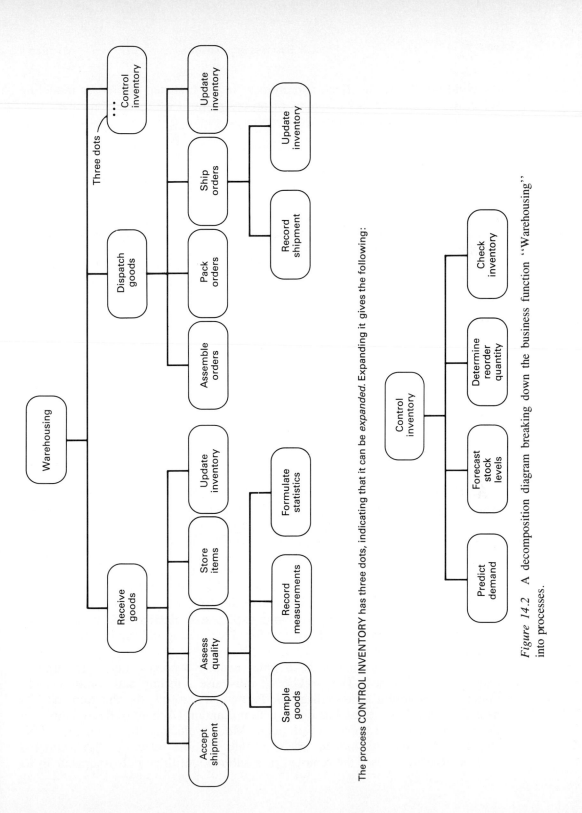

The process CONTROL INVENTORY has three dots, indicating that it can be *expanded*. Expanding it gives the following:

Figure 14.2 A decomposition diagram breaking down the business function "Warehousing" into processes.

the child blocks are, in effect, subroutines. In the first step of process modeling we draw ''composed-of'' diagrams of processes until we reach elementary processes that cannot be decomposed further.

NAMING CONVENTIONS

As commented earlier the names of business functions are usually nouns, such as ''marketing,'' ''inventory control,'' ''engineering,'' and ''financial planning.'' The names of processes should be constructed of an active verb and an object, for example:

> Allocate payment
>
> Accept order
>
> Determine gross receipts
>
> Calculate interest

Where possible, the object of an elementary process should be an entity type or an attribute that is in the data model, for example:

> Create invoice
>
> Check customer credit
>
> Issue material

The names of processes should not reflect *who, when,* or *where,* but only *what* the process does.

USE OF A DIAGRAMMING TOOL

The process decomposition diagram is built at the screen of a workbench. If the naming conventions discussed above are followed, it is usually unnecessary to enter explanatory details of a process. The workbench should provide a detail window for entering descriptive detail about a process if so desired.

The process decomposition diagram usually becomes much too large to display on one screen. The workbench must use scrolling and zooming techniques for exploring a large diagram. Particularly useful, the diagram may be nested. Three dots are used as on an action diagram (Appendix II) to show that the components of a process are hidden. Mouse-selecting the command ''EXPAND'' displays the hidden tree structure. Mouse-selecting the command ''CONTRACT'' causes the removal of a subtree and three dots to appear in its parent block. Figures 14.3 and 14.4 show illustrations of process decomposition diagrams printed from analysis workbench tools.

PROCESS DEPENDENCY DIAGRAMS   Processes do not exist in isolation; they are dependent on other processes. A process dependency diagram shows how processes relate to one another. The following diagram notation shows that process *B* happens after process *A*. Process *B* cannot take place until process *A* has completed, so we say that process *B* is *dependent* on process *A:*

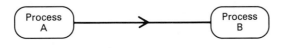

Sometimes there is a string of dependent processes:

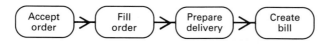

Sometimes one activity is dependent on many other activities. Lines from the preceding activity boxes join and enter the dependent activity box:

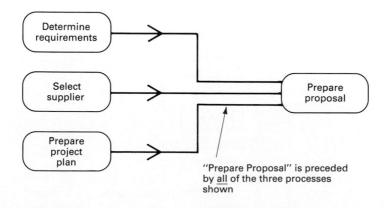

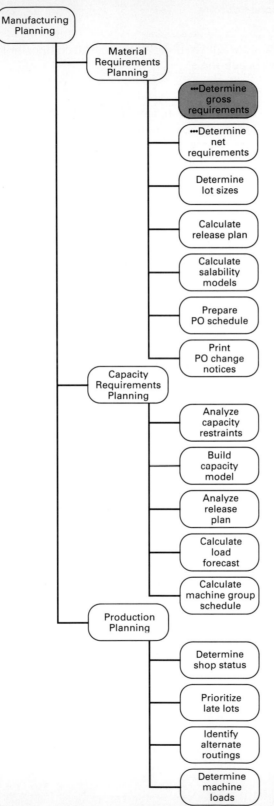

Figure 14.3(a) A decomposition of "Manufacturing Planning" into processes, using a vertical decomposition diagram format. Part (b) shows an expansion of the processes "Determine gross requirements." (Courtesy of Texas Instruments.)

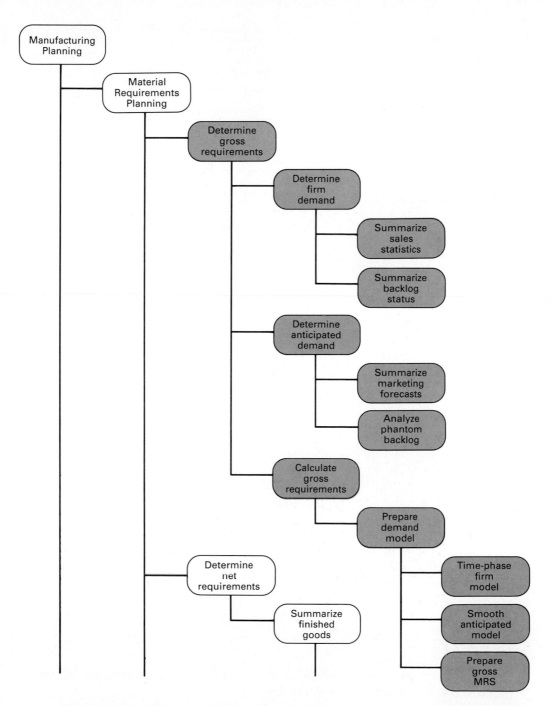

Figure 14.3(b)   The process decomposition diagram of part (a) with the "Determine gross requirements" process expanded.

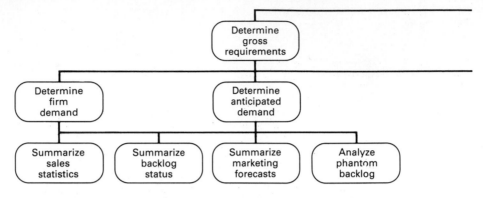

Figure 14.4(a)   A portion of a process decomposition diagram on a work-bench screen. The analyst can scroll around the diagram, shrink it to fit the screen, or point to individual blocks and display details of the block. (Courtesy of KnowledgeWare.)

Conversely, one activity may give rise to many others:

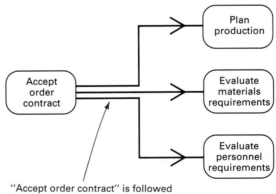

Figure 14.5 shows a dependency diagram. Complex diagrams should be broken into "layers" as shown in Fig. 14.5.

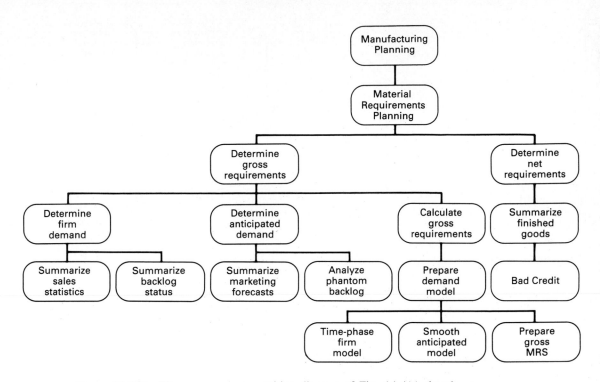

Figure 14.4(b) The process decomposition diagram of Fig. 14.4(a) shrunk to fit the screen. (Courtesy of KnowledgeWare.)

CARDINALITY

In the foregoing diagrams the dependent process is executed *once* after the preceding process. In some diagrams we want to show that it may be executed multiple times:

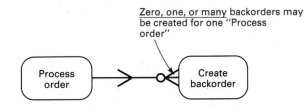

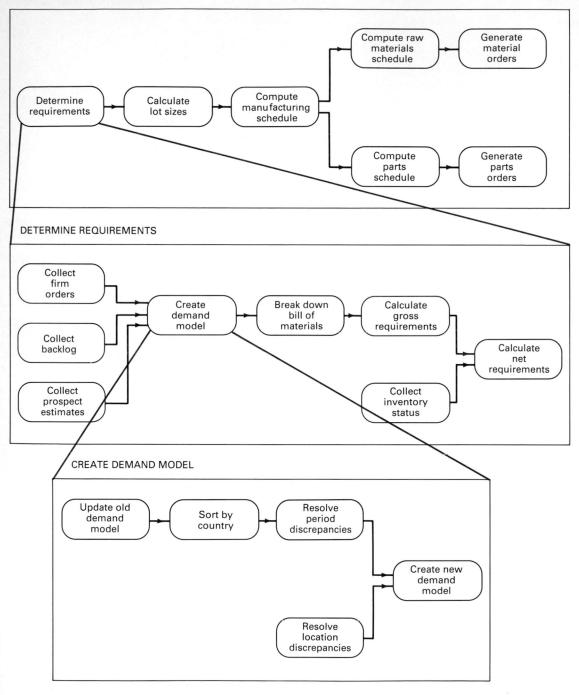

GENERATE PURCHASE ORDERS

Determine requirements → Calculate lot sizes → Compute manufacturing schedule

Compute raw materials schedule → Generate material orders

Compute parts schedule → Generate parts orders

DETERMINE REQUIREMENTS

Collect firm orders

Collect backlog

Collect prospect estimates

Create demand model → Break down bill of materials → Calculate gross requirements

Collect inventory status

Calculate net requirements

CREATE DEMAND MODEL

Update old demand model → Sort by country → Resolve period discrepancies

Resolve location discrepancies

Create new demand model

Figure 14.5   A dependency diagram broken into three layers.

Similarly, a dependent process may follow multiple executions of a preceding process:

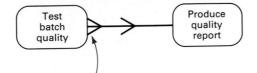

Multiple batch quality tests are
performed for each quality report

Less common is a one-to-many association at both ends of a link:

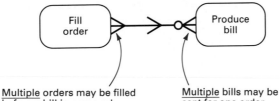

Multiple orders may be filled   Multiple bills may be
before a bill is prepared   sent for one order

MUTUAL EXCLUSIVITY

Sometimes one or the other of two activities must be performed, but not both. Sometimes one of several activities must be performed. These *mutually exclusive* choices of activity are shown by a solid circle on a branching line—the "OR" circle used earlier:

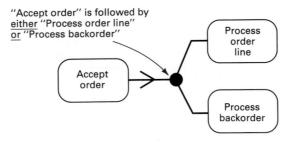

"Accept order" is followed by
either "Process order line"
or "Process backorder"

Conditions may be associated with the links from the mutual-exclusivity circle:

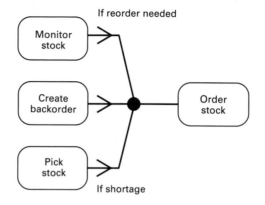

PARALLEL LINKS

Occasionally, two or more links join the same two activity blocks. If these go in the same direction, this might indicate that the processes have been insufficiently or incorrectly decomposed. Links going in opposite directions between two processes occur in feedback loops or control mechanisms:

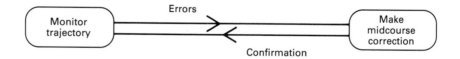

EVENTS

Some processes are triggered by other processes. This is often the case, but need not be so. Some are triggered by events. For example, the receipt of a payment may trigger a process. A process may be triggered by a customer telephoning to make a booking, a security alarm going off, the financial year ending, a bank's closing time being reached, a demand for information, and so on. They are all events external to the processes. We may talk about *event-triggered* processes and *process-triggered* processes. A large arrow on a diagram is used to show that an event occurs:

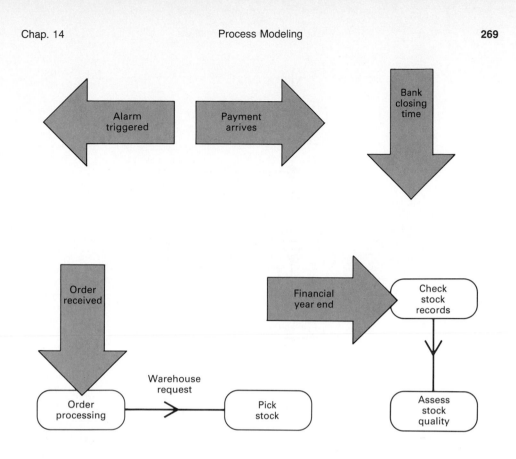

PROCESS DATA FLOW DIAGRAM

The process dependency diagram may now be expanded by adding data inputs and outputs to the process blocks. This makes it a process *data flow diagram*.

A *process* data flow diagram is different from data flow diagrams used for *design*. It describes the *fundamental* interactions that are necessary among processes. It does not show what documents pass from one process to another. It avoids the specific design of procedures, leaving open the many options for this. It does not show whether data passes from one process to another by direct transmittal or by one process updating an online database that the other process reads. It is concerned with logical interactions, not physical. Figure 14.6(a) shows a process dependency diagram; Fig. 14.6(b) shows the same diagram with data added to form a data flow diagram.

THE ENTITY/PROCESS MATRIX

When an analyst has described the processes in a business area and a data model has been built for that business area, a computerized workbench can auto-

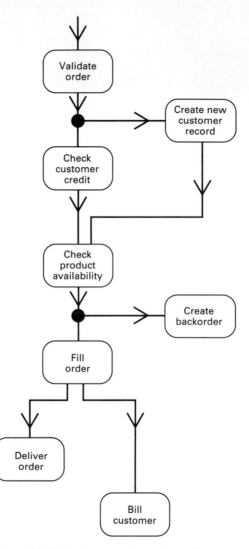

Figure 14.6(a)   A process dependency diagram.

matically produce an entity/process matrix for that business area. It shows only the elementary processes on the matrix.

The next step in business area analysis is to fill in this matrix. The analyst may first indicate what process *creates* each entity record. He does this for *every* entity type. Some entity records are not created by any process in that business area. In this case he will indicate that it is an externally created entity record.

When the computer agrees that it has a complete set of information about the *creation* of entity records, it may then ask the analyst to indicate what pro-

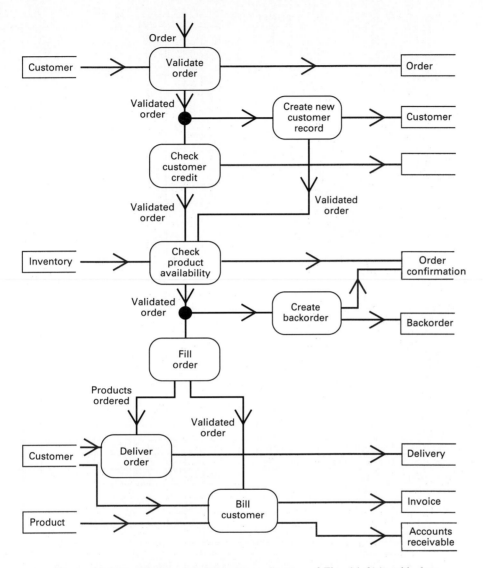

Figure 14.6(b)   The process dependency diagram of Fig. 14.6(a), with data added to make it into a data flow diagram.

cesses *update* what entity records, and then what processes *read* or *delete* what entity records.

Figure 14.7 shows a typical entity/process matrix. The entire matrix is too large to see all of it at one time on the workbench screen, so the analyst needs to be able to scroll the matrix both vertically and horizontally.

ENTITY TYPE

Key
C: Create
R: Delete
U: Update
D: Delete

PROCESS	Employee	Contract Employee	Applicant	HR Compensation Regs, Plans, etc.	HR Benefits Regs & Plans	HR StaffingRequirements & Plans	Job Requisition	Stockholder	Boardmember	Misc. Contacts/VIPs	Financial Plans	Accounting Regs, Practices	Ledger Accounts	Customer Purchase Order/Invoice	Customer Payments	Other Income
	1	2	3	4	5	6	7	8	9	10	11	12	13	14	15	16
1 Evaluate Financial Proposals																
2 Estimate Near- Term Earnings														R		
3 Budget Finances	R	R		R	R						CRUD	R	CRUD			
4 Receive Funds												R		R	CRUD	CRUD
5 Pay Funds	R											R				
6 Report Finances	R											R	RU	R	R	R
7 Administer Taxes												R	R		R	R
8 Maintain Financial Reg, Policies											R	CRUD				
9 Audit Finances												R	R		R	R
10 Manage Financial Investments								R				R				
11 Plan Humane Resources	R	R				CRUD	CRUD		R		R					
12 Acquire Personnel	CRU	CRU	CRUD			R	R		CRU							
13 Position People in Jobs			R			R	RU		R							
14 Terminate/Retire People	RUD	RUD							RUD							
15 Plan Carreer Paths	RU			R	R	R										
16 Develop Skills/Motivation	RU	RU			R	R										
17 Manage Individual Emp Relations	RU	RU			R											
18 Manage Benefits Programs				CRUD												
19 Comply with Govt HR Regulations	R			R												
20 Maintain HR Regs, Policies			CRUD		CRUD											
21 Determine Production Requirement														R		
22 Schedule Production	R	R														

Figure 14.7   A matrix mapping entity types against the processes that create or use those entities.

RELATIONS AMONG DIAGRAMS   The diagrams for business area analysis are strongly interrelated. The blocks on a process dependency diagram are the same blocks as on the equivalent decomposition diagram. The inputs and outputs of process blocks are on a data flow diagram data represented in the data model. The data used by the processes is shown on the entity/matrix diagram, and this must correlate with the data flow diagram.

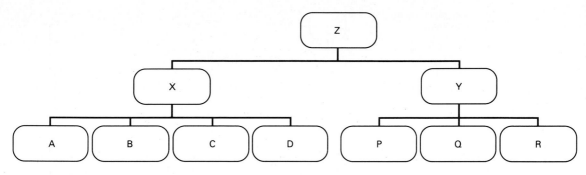

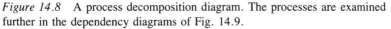

Figure 14.8 A process decomposition diagram. The processes are examined further in the dependency diagrams of Fig. 14.9.

We thus have a set of diagrams that are logically interrelated and form a *hyperdiagram*. Much computerized cross-checking should be done as the *hyperdiagram* is built and analyzed. The information on the various diagrams is validated and correlated by the workbench.

Figure 14.8 shows a process decomposition diagram; Fig. 14.9 shows dependency diagrams with the same processes. Figure 14.8 could be derived from Fig. 14.9. The workbench should check that they correspond exactly. If another process block is added to one of the diagrams in Fig. 14.9, it must appear *automatically* in Fig. 14.8. If another block is added to the decomposition of

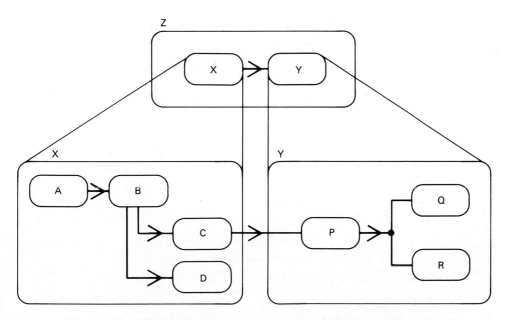

Figure 14.9 Process dependency diagrams corresponding to the decomposition diagram of Fig. 14.8.

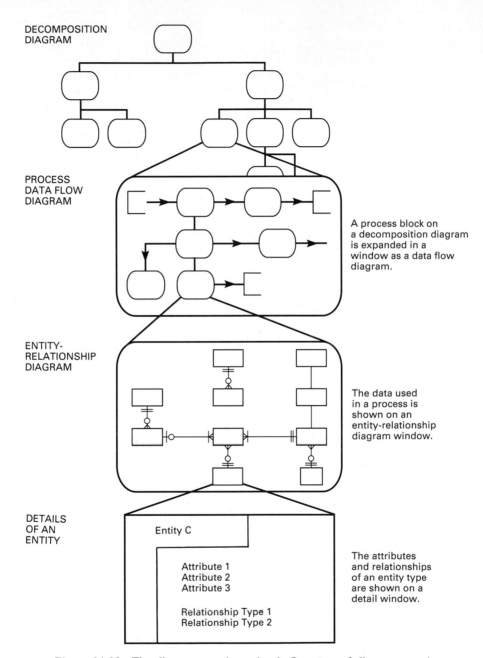

DECOMPOSITION
DIAGRAM

PROCESS
DATA FLOW
DIAGRAM

A process block on
a decomposition diagram
is expanded in a
window as a data flow
diagram.

ENTITY-
RELATIONSHIP
DIAGRAM

The data used
in a process is
shown on an
entity-relationship
diagram window.

DETAILS
OF AN
ENTITY

Entity C

Attribute 1
Attribute 2
Attribute 3

Relationship Type 1
Relationship Type 2

The attributes
and relationships
of an entity type
are shown on a
detail window.

Figure 14.10 The diagrams are interrelated. One type of diagram may be used in a window to show details of another type of diagram. (Courtesy of KnowledgeWare.)

process X in Fig. 14.8, a ghost of this block must appear on the dependency diagram of X on the left of Fig. 14.9. The computer asks how this new block should be connected to the rest of the dependency diagram.

From the collection of entities and processes that the analyst has identified in a business area, the workbench can automatically produce an empty entity/process matrix. As the analyst fills in this matrix, it can correlate this information with the data entering and leaving blocks on the data flow diagram. The cross-correlation often leads to the discovery of other interactions that must be added to the model.

We have stressed the importance of windows in diagramming tools. The user points to a block and displays details of it in a window. The window may display a different type of diagram, as shown in Fig. 14.10. The user asking to see details of a block may be given a choice. For example, if he points to a block on a data flow diagram, he may be able to see details of lower-level processes on another data flow diagram or a decomposition diagram, or he may see details of the data used in the block on an entity-relationship diagram. He may descend into further detail with a window that shows a listing of attributes from the data model. The encyclopedia stores the details of the objects and relationship and can display them in different ways as requested, enabling the user to explore the relations among the different facets of the perspective.

REUSABLE PROCESSES

A major objective of information engineering is to maximize the amount of design and code that is *reusable* in an enterprise, in order to minimize the work of design, coding, and maintenance. As we commented in Book I, Westpac, a large bank based in Sydney, applied information to all its activities to identify modules, and produced the processes it needed with 55 programs, whereas 1100 programs would have been needed if conventional software engineering had been done and the modules that were reusable across the bank had not been identified [1].

Entity-relationship analysis identifies the entity types that are common across an enterprise, such as CUSTOMER, EMPLOYEE, PAYMENT, and RESERVATION. Normalization organizes the attributes associated with those entity types into fourth-normal-form structures. An entity type has certain behavior associated with it. That behavior needs to be programmed no matter what department the entity type is being used in or what application it is participating in. There is certain information associated with a bank customer, for example, and certain validations that are applied, no matter whether the application is a loan application, savings, checking, mortgage, credit card, investment, or whatever.

Some processing routines are associated, not with one entity type, but with an association between two or more entity types: for example, when a CUSTOMER places an ORDER, when a PASSENGER makes or changes a RESER-

VATION, or when a WAREHOUSE ships a DELIVERY. Certain reports must be printed or certain information filed, or a given user dialog must occur; certain validation checks must be applied; and an audit trail must be maintained, regardless of the location, department, type of warehouse, or type of application. Procedures should be designed and programmed that are reusable across the enterprise (rather than being designed and programmed uniquely for each project).

An objective of I.E. is to identify commonality in both data and processes and consequently to minimize the redundant system development work. Data modeling makes it clear that the same entity types are used in numerous applications. Whenever they are used there may be certain routines that will be invoked, such as computing derived attributes, applying integrity checks, or creating summary data. A corporation may have many factories which to a large extent have the same entity types. Many of the data processing procedures can be the same from one factory to another. Some will be entirely different. The accounting and reporting should be the same in each factory so that higher-level management can make comparisons. Dialogs programmed for data entry, updating, reporting, and so on, should be common across applications and locations. HELP panels should be common. When process decomposition is done and processes are mapped against entity types, commonality among processes can be discovered.

When a code generator can generate code directly from a design representation, the focus of reusability is the analysis and design stages. Design modules may be stored in the encyclopedia and used when needed. The design workbench makes designs easy to modify. Being able to make adjustments to designs, and to add to them as needed, greatly extends the practicality of reusable design.

Standards for application design also extend the practicality of reusable design. These include standards established in the I.S. organization for access to networks, access to databases, standard document formats, standard user dialogs, IBM's SAA (Systems Application Architecture), and so on. Common use of such standards throughout an I.S. organization leads to increases in I.S. productivity. When a reusable block is decomposed, it should be decomposed once only, as shown in Fig. 14.11.

Sometimes the term *object-oriented* design or *object-oriented* database is used. An entity is described as an ''object,'' and the object has certain behavior associated with it, whenever the object is used. Certain screen panels, user dialogs, validation routines, and so on, may be needed whenever the object type is employed.

Often, the processing done on an object, or the dialog used, is not quite identical from one process to another, but is sufficiently close that the same code or dialog can be used with minor modifications. The user would like the different applications to look similar and use common dialog style, in order to increase familiarity and minimize the need for training. It is desirable to identify

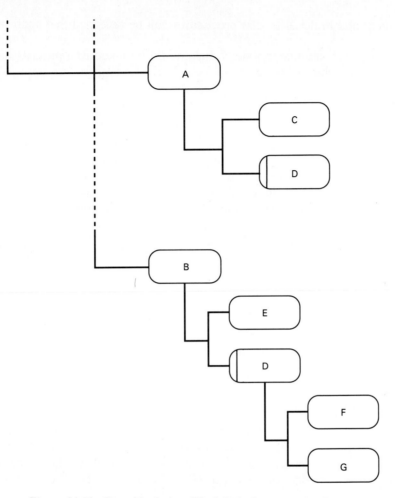

Figure 14.11　　Reusable design. Block D is decomposed only once.

similar processes as well as *identical* processes, in order to minimize the subsequent design, coding, and training requirements. The encyclopedia should be able to indicate blocks that arc similar.

　　It is recommended that data modeling and process modeling be applied to one business area at a time; otherwise, it becomes unwieldly and the team bogs down. Nevertheless, there will be entity types which are used outside that business area, and associated with these will be processes which are reusable outside that busincss area. The *enterprise-wide* entity types are discovered (at a summary level) during the ISP study and are recorded in the encyclopedia. During business area analysis the entity types and processes which appear to have applicability beyond that business area should be marked in the encyclopedia. When other business areas are analyzed, the common entity types and processes will be identified in detail so that procedures can be designed that span business areas.

Figure 14.11 summarizes steps that should be taken in a process model to help identify reusable processes.

CROSS-CHECKING AND ANALYSIS   The computer can cross-check and analyze the information given to it in a variety of ways. It can apply rules to enforce integrity among the types of information given to it, and to make suggestions to the analyst which cause him to discover other processes, entities, or relationships. Basic integrity checks should be applied whenever the user modifies or adds to a diagram. The user should be given real-time feedback of error information wherever possible. There are other types of integrity checks that can be performed only when a diagram or perspective is complete. Some of the analyses that provide these checks are as described below.

Data Flow Connectivity Analysis

In a completed data flow diagram the connectivity of the diagram can be analyzed to find any flows that are not continuous or not connected to valid sources or destinations.

Data Flow Course Analysis

Data flow diagrams are nested hierarchically. Only one level is displayed in one diagram. However, data flows through process blocks, which may be on multiple levels. Data flow course analysis displays to the path of data regardless of how many levels the data traverses, as shown in Fig. 14.12.

Data Conservation Analysis

The various blocks on a data flow diagram have different *views* of data that are represented in the data model. This analysis checks that all views are consistent with one another and that all blocks follow data conservation rules. When conservation is violated it means that data are, in effect, leaking into or out of the system. Data conservation analysis finds the leaks. When they are corrected it notifies the user that data is conserved properly.

Data conservation consists of four rules, each of which applies to a different type of data flow node:

- **Data Stores.** The contents of a data store must equal the contents of the flows entering the store and flows leaving it. Data stores conserve data; they cannot generate, transform, or lose data.

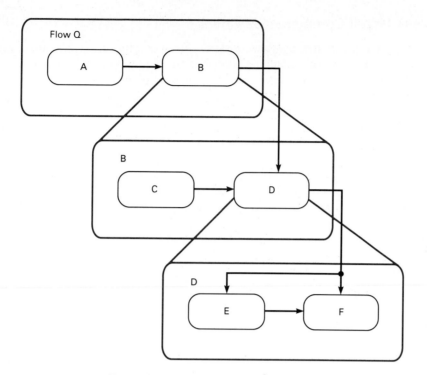

Figure 14.12   Data flow course analysis.

- **Junctions.** Total input must equal total output. Junctions transmit data; they cannot generate, transform, or lose data.

- **External Agents.** There is no input/output rule for external agents. They are ultimate sources and destinations of data and are not required to conserve. External agents send certain flows into the system and receive certain flows from it.

- **Activities.** An activity's view of the entity model equals all the data in all the data flows that are visible in the activity's data flow diagram. This includes flows entering the activity, flows leaving it, and flows between its children—the activities, data stores, and junctions immediately contained in it.

Data Model Completeness Analysis

To create the normalized data model many different views of data are synthesized. Each relates to a process. A check should be made that all processes have been considered in synthesizing the data models. There should be no processes without a data view, and no entity types (on the entity-relationship model) that do not exist on a detailed data view. A matrix mapping the views used in data synthesis against the processes may be generated automatically as an aid to the analyst to check that no views have been omitted.

Process Model Completeness Check

The entity/process matrix can be checked automatically to confirm that there is a process to create and terminate every entity type. One line on the matrix should be for *external* processes, as some entity records are created or deleted externally to the business area. The computer should also notify the analyst of any entity type that is not read or updated. There may be no reason to read or update an entity record after a process has created it, but this check sometimes causes the analyst to notice an omission in the process model.

In general, completeness checking and integrity checking is tedious to do by hand and is rarely done thoroughly. An automated workbench can apply rules that enforce completeness and integrity checks. A good workbench tool has a large number of such rules, some of them interrelating multiple-diagram types.

SUCCESSIVE REFINEMENT   During business area analysis the models of processes and data tend to grow a step at a time. They are refined and correlated successively until the representation of processes and data are thought to be complete. Computerized analysis and computer-aided checking are then applied to the overall business area. Box 14.1 is an action diagram of this kernel part of business area analysis.

PROCEDURE   Box 14.2 shows the overall procedure for process modeling.

REFERENCE

1. Information about CS90 in Westpac, Sydney, Australia, from Peter Horbituik, Manager of Research and Development for Westpac, 1989.

BOX 14.1 The kernel of business area analysis

Create a preliminary data model.
    Extract the entity-relationship model for this business area
      from the encyclopedia.
    Determine what events occur in this business area.
    Associate the events with entity types.
    Draw the lifecycle of each entity.
    Enter initial attributes of each entity.

Create a preliminary process model.
    Extract the business-function decomposition model for this
      business area from the encyclopedia.
    Decompose the functions into processes.

Successively refine the information
in the following stages until a complete representation of the
data and processes is achieved.
Create a detailed data model.

    | See BOX 12.1. |

Create a detailed process model.

    | See BOX 14.2. |

...Create a process decomposition diagram.
...Create a process dependency diagram.
...Generate an entity-type/process matrix.

Build matrices.
    Associate entity types, processes, and events with organizational
      units and locations.
    Associate entity types, processes, and events with goals and
      problems.

Analyze and correlate (automatically) the above information.
    Use a workbench tool which analyzes and correlates the above
      information with a knowledge coordinator.
    Use the knowledge coordinator of the design tool to ensure
      that the BAA is internally consistent, and consistent with
      other knowledge in the encyclopedia.

(Continued)

BOX 14.2 *(Continued)*

CREATE A DETAILED PROCESS MODEL

> Detailed process modeling is tackled in one business area at a time. Although described here as a self-contained activity, it needs to be an integral part of the Business Area Analysis procedure.

| See BOX 11.2 |

> The procedure given below may be modified with Action Diagrammer to meet the needs of the particular situation.

Preparation
- Appoint a professional to lead the activity.
  The person who leads the data modeling activity may also be responsible for the process model, the two being developed together.
  - If a skilled Business Area Analysis professional exists in house
    Make him responsible for completion of the model on time.
  - Else
    Employ a consultant skilled in BAA.
    Make him responsible for completion of the model on time.
    Appoint one or more in-house professionals to become BAA experts.
    Appoint an in-house professional to take over the work from the consultant and be responsible for the model.

- Ensure that the necessary tools are installed and working.
  Use an encyclopedia-based CASE tool (the one used in the earlier stages of information engineering) which enables the process decomposition diagram, process dependency diagram, and process/entity matrix to be built and changed easily, and which integrates the process model with the data model (BOX 12.3), and applies comprehensive integrity checking.

- Form an end-user committee.
  Determine which end users will help in developing the model.
  Establish a committee of end users and managers who will be responsible for making the BAA models correct and complete.
  This is likely to be the same committee that is described in the procedure for data modeling (BOX 12.3).
  Selected end-user participants may help with the data model and process model concurrently.
    End users selected should
        o be intelligent,
        o be creative,
        o have good human communication skills,
        o want to understand information-system techniques,
        o be highly knowledgeable about their own business areas.
  Give the participants a short course in the basic principles.

BOX 14.2 *(Continued)*

Create the initial model.
  Select and print the entity types and functions for this business
    area which were recorded in the ISP study.
  Print a decomposition diagram of the activities in the business area
  With the user committee, review the entities and functions to ensure
    that nothing has been forgotten.
  With the user committee, brainstorm the possible future processes
    which could improve the business. List these for further examination.
  Description
    Brainstorming means that a creative group of individuals
    attempt to produce a stream of ideas without inhibition.
    A rule of a brainstorming session is that there can be
    no implied criticism for making an impractical or stupid
    suggestion. The session is intended to generate as many
    ideas as possible. At the end of the session only certain
    of the ideas will be recorded for possible use.

Discuss the processes with end users.
  Three techniques may be used for communication with the end users:
  Interviewing
    The most common technique is end-user interviewing. The professional
      who is building the process model interviews appropriate users or
      managers to increase his understanding of the business area, and
      to validate the model as it evolves.
  End-user workshop
    An workshop may be conducted, similar to a JAD session (See Book III),
      with the end-user committee. A JAD leader may conduct it.
  Informal contact
    Informal contact suffices where in-depth expertise already exists
      within the team.

  Extend the process decomposition using the analyst's own knowledge
    and then discuss the model with users and managers to extend it
    and refine it further.
  Use fast computerized redesign after any changes are made to
    maintain the interest of the end users.
  Any problems which the end users are experiencing with their current
    systems should be recorded on the problem list for later analysis.

Decompose to the elementary process level.
  An elementary process is one which cannot be decomposed further
    without making design decisions which say HOW a procedure operates
    rather than WHAT a process does. An elementary process has been defined
    as "The smallest unit of activity of meaning to the end user, and which
    when complete leaves the information area in a self-consistent state."
  When events occur these cannot trigger a sub-elementary process.
  Decompose until elementary processes are derived.
  Check that each lowest-level is elementary; if not, decompose it further.
  Do not waste time perfecting the intermediate structure of the
    decomposition; it is the elementary processes that matter.
  Record a definition of each elementary process.

Draw process dependency diagrams.
  Develop a set of process dependency diagrams that show, between them,
    all the elementary processes.

(Continued)

BOX 14.2   *(Continued)*

Dependency diagrams will be created for higher-level process blocks,
  and these nested to lower levels, using the encyclopedia-based tool
  and its knowledge coordinator.
It is likely that errors will be found in the decomposition diagram
  while drawing the dependency diagrams; these should be corrected.
Do not waste time perfecting the intermediate structure of the
  dependency diagrams; it is the elementary processes that matter.

Develop the process/entity matrix.
  Create (automatically) a matrix mapping the elementary processes and
    entity types.
  Fill in the matrix with CREATE, READ, UPDATE, and DELETE codes (CRUDs).

Cluster the process/entity matrix to show natural systems.
  Use the clustering algorithm of the IE tool.
  Cluster on the basis of what processes CREATE what entity types.
  Assign all remaining processes and entity types to clusters.
  Refine the groupings manually to identify natural systems.
  Identify what data must flow from one system to another.
  Refine the dependency diagram to agree with the clustered matrix.
  Refine the clusterings to minimize the interaction among systems.

15 PREPARING FOR SYSTEM DESIGN

INTRODUCTION   Business area analysis is not an end in itself. It is desirable to progress as rapidly as possible to the design and construction of valuable systems. The pressure to build systems exists strongly while a BAA is being done, and in some cases it becomes so strong that the BAA is not completed or other BAAs are avoided. For this reason it is desirable to use BAA techniques that move fast and are not too complex. Some BAA methodologies are too much work.

We may divide system building into three categories:

- **Information Center Activities.** This refers to end users building their own systems with end-user tools. They range from simple database access and report generation, through spreadsheet computations, to the building of highly complex decision-support models.

- **Quick I.S. Projects.** These are projects done quickly by one or two skilled I.S. professionals using a fourth-generation language or code generator. The power of these tools makes it practical for *one person* to build systems that are not too complex. A system that would have required several person-years with COBOL and traditional methods can often be done in months by one person with design automation and fourth-generation tools. Sometimes two-person teams are more appropriate than solo projects. The high productivity comes from the avoidance of large teams as well as the use of power tools.

- **Major I.S. Projects.** These are projects done by I.S. professionals which take substantial time and planning.

While the BAA is progressing, the need for certain systems falling into the former two categories is usually made clear. It is often politic to proceed with these quickly to relieve the natural desire of end users to see results. Large-scale systems will normally be built faster and more satisfactorily when BAA information, thoroughly coordinated and cross-checked, exists in the encyclo-pedia linked to design automation tools. This is especially so when techniques discussed in Book III of this trilogy, such as I.E./JAD and prototyping, are used.

CHANGING THE ORGANIZATION

A major goal of business area analysis is not to ana-lyze *existing* procedures, but to be concerned with what the procedures *should* be. Business area analy-sis charts *what* processes must occur, rather than *how* the procedures *work*. It charts *what* data must be stored. It removes redundancy from the data by nor-malizing it, and removes redundancy from representation of processes. The an-alyst should have in mind constantly the thought that procedures with today's technology *ought to be entirely different* from procedures in an era of batch processing, or dumb terminals.

Senior management should regard ISP and BAA studies as a means not merely of modeling the *existing* organization, but of asking how the organiza-tion should be changed or is likely to be changed by external circumstances.

The user analysts have to be made to think creatively. It is easy for them to fall into the rut of documenting today's paper flow rather than the fundamen-tal needs of the business. They must not be constrained by today's documents. They must try to think: What data are important to us? What is it that we are going to need in the future? How could the enterprise be made to function better? What are the strategic technology-related opportunities? How can we attack competition by using technology better?

Thinking about the future is important for making the resulting databases as resilient as possible. It is often difficult for users to put themselves into this mode of thinking. It requires senior management to have some participation in the analysis. Senior managers know what their problems are now and have ideas about the kinds of actions they would like to take to fix them. They need a tool to express that. In some corporations this has made them take an enthusiastic interest in business area analysis.

Business area analysis will be more fruitful *if it is accepted from the be-ginning that it is likely to change the corporate procedures or organization*. If this is understood, top management is likely to take more interest in the study. The study will be staffed differently and its reporting procedures will be differ-ent.

COMPUTER-AIDED DECISIONS

The process diagrams described in Chapter 14 pro-vide a good model of how an enterprise functions. Along with the data models, they provide a frame-work that speeds up system design and makes separately built systems fit together in an overall architecture. They do not, however, say much about the decision-making processes needed. It is necessary to ask:

- What decisions need to be made to run the business area?
- Where is the optimum location for each decision to be made?
- Who should make it?
- What information is needed for making the decision?

The optimum place for a decision to be made may be different from where it was made in the past. In the past it was constrained by lack of availability of current information. In a computerized enterprise with efficient networking, data can be made available *anywhere* at *any time*. Given this instant networking of data, where should a decision be made?

In information-based enterprises, decisions tend to be made either by high-level management and their staff, or by people who are close to the action and who control operations. The middle layers of management, whose main purpose has been to collect, transform, summarize, and relay information, are not needed because information passes directly to the top, where it can be summarized or transformed with computerized tools. As we commented earlier, an information-based enterprise with computer networking should have fewer layers of management than a traditional enterprise with batch processing. An objective of today's system architectures should be to flatten the bureaucratic pyramid.

In highly automated factories such as the Nissan auto assembly plants or the GE locomotive plant in Erie, the first-level supervisor has a far bigger, far more demanding and more responsible job. The same is true with the flight controller who determines the number of discount seats and controls bookings on flights of a highly computerized airline. Staff members close to business operations use computers extensively to control operations, collect information, obtain information, and make decisions about the operations. From these first-level operations which are close to the action, information passes directly to the top-level planners and executives. The top level may manage widely dispersed operations and hence may be geographically distant from them. The information needed travels across this distance in a flash.

The middle-level personnel who coordinate or report rather than "do" are not levels of *authority* or *supervision*. Decision making takes place mainly at the first level of management or close to the top, where integrated planning is possible. The middle-level personnel collect, repackage, summarize, and send on information—all jobs that a computer can do better. In the information-based enterprise the operating units have far more capability and responsibility because of automation; the top levels have far more information and computer power to aid decision making. The information of the entire enterprise can be visible to top management.

The traditional business organization was modeled after the military. Command passes from the top to the bottom; information flows from the bottom to the top. A network-based organization can be very different. Information can pass horizontally from one operating unit to another. Many corporations that have grown up since the spread of networking technology are at least partially based on horizontal communications. Most knowledge workers have a workstation and send electronic messages to other knowledge workers, sometimes on a worldwide basis. Information resides in databases that are accessible anywhere. In principle any operating unit can extract information from the databases and repackage it for its own purposes.

The organization with this any-to-any communications pattern can work only if every operating unit knows its purpose and goals, and accepts responsibility for its own operations. It needs to know how it fits into the overall structure. A vital question for each operating unit is: What information does it need, when does it need it, and where does it come from? It needs to understand who in the organization it is dependent on and who depends on it. It is like a block in a dependency diagram asking about its neighbors. The overall dependency diagram needs to be drawn and has to be understood by all participants.

An organizational unit needs to understand what specialized skills and knowledge it requires. Who does it obtain specialized skills and knowledge from? In turn, who depends on it for those specialized skills and knowledge? Whom does it have to support, and who does it need to support it?

The corporation of the future might be thought about with the symphony-orchestra analogy used in Chapter 8 of Book I: Semiautonomous units are each performing excellently. Each knows its own role and objectives and how it interacts with other units. There are various ''soloists'' making complex computer-aided decisions. Different organizational units have to use the same overall data model, and the process model shows their roles and how they interrelate. Strong leadership is needed to ensure that the different efforts are orchestrated appropriately.

Some computing consists of routine systems, carefully preplanned; other computing consists of ad hoc information-center computation. Some computing is built as data-processing projects and some is created by end users for their own purposes. These types of computing need to be efficiently coordinated.

THREE LEVELS OF INFORMATION

A business area, like the entire enterprise, has three levels of information requirements: operations, control, and planning.

- **Operations** is concerned with *routine* processing and carrying out the minute-by-minute operations of the business. It requires human input of data but little human processing. Because it is routine, it can be largely automated.

- **Control** is concerned with the supervision of operations, the allocation and monitoring of operational tasks, and the short-term management of operations. Functions such as job-shop scheduling, purchasing, the setting of discounts, or airline flight control are being done with increasing levels of computerized support.

- **Planning** information is concerned with medium- or long-term planning. Decisions such as changing the products, setting priorities, increasing plant capacity, or changing marketing policy cannot be automated but need much information.

Business area analysis should identify these three types of information system. The procedure for designing and building *operations* systems is very different from that of building *planning* systems. In some cases information for planning can be extracted quickly from other systems and manipulated with spreadsheet tools or decision-support software.

Distance is almost immaterial to computer networks. Information can move over large distances quickly. Processes that interchange *information* rather than physical goods or paper *could* be far apart. Processes tend to exist in clusters where the work is done. A cluster of processes may be replicated in many locations, for example in every warehouse, every distribution center, or every branch office. Of the three types of processes, *operations* and *control* tend to be in the cluster where the work is done; *planning* is often remote from the cluster.

In general, decisions should be made where the work is done unless there is a good reason otherwise. The decision maker is more likely to know of subtle factors affecting the decision if he is where the action is. Examples of situations in which a decision *should* be made remotely are:

- The decision output affects multiple locations: for example, setting the price of goods in a chain of convenience stores.

- The input to the decision comes from multiple locations: for example, an airline reorganizing the crew schedules.

- The decision associates two or more processes that are geographically separate: for example, deciding whether to market a new product.

- The decision needs expertise which exists only at a distant location: for example, building an operation research model.

One sees many examples today of decisions being made remotely from the affected processes when on-the-spot decision making would be better. Sometimes this is because the procedure dates back to an earlier era when it was not possible to get the right information to the right people at the right time. Sometimes it relates to the power structure in a bureaucratic organization. Sometimes it is because of lack of training in the new decision-support tools. Too often it is because of lack of respect for the staff on the job; they are treated like mindless clerks when in fact they would do their job with more enthusiasm if given more responsibility.

In the earliest days of automation we treated many humans like robots, giving them boring, soul-destroying, repetitive tasks. Later it became clear that machines should do the boring repetitive tasks. Humans, even clerks and factory hands, are capable of common sense and craftsmanship. We build better systems if we respect and harness human ability. This may need substantial training, encouragement, and supervision. The best enterprises do this; the worst deserve the expression *mindless bureaucracy*.

The capability to make decisions remotely has sometimes caused the restructuring of local operations. The handling of money in a multinational corporation, for example, has in some corporations been changed from a country operation to a central worldwide operation, in order to use expertise in currency fluctuations and to minimize taxes. Purchasing has sometimes been moved from a local activity to a central activity in order to take advantage of bulk discounts or negotiations with vendors.

One large semiconductor manufacturer had many inventory locations around the world. Some countries had more than one inventory location. The inventory managers held enough chips to meet their customers' requests. The organization built a worldwide computer network and then the world chip inventory became visible at the head office. It became clear that the *world* inventory of chips was larger than it need be, which was expensive because last year's chips sell at a lower price. Chips rapidly become obsolete as newer versions are introduced. The corporation decided to close down many of its inventory locations. It is inexpensive to fly chips around the world on jets. In the inventory locations which remained inventory control changed so that a smaller inventory could be supplemented by chips flown in on demand from a central location. The *capability to make information* accessible worldwide caused a drastic corporate reorganization.

RECORDING DECISIONS NEEDED

To clarify what decisions have to be made, a window may be associated with process blocks on the process decomposition or dependency diagram. Figure 15.1 indicates what such a window may contain. Many processes have no such decision associated with them. Of those that do the information that helps in making the decision can be derived quickly with information center tools such as query languages, report generators, tools for extracting data from a database or file system, spreadsheet tools, graphics generators, financial modeling tools, and fourth-generation languages. Some decisions need a major decision-support tool. Operations research techniques may be needed for optimization. Multidimensional analysis of data may be needed. A fairly quick I.S. project may provide the decision-making help that is needed—often a one-person project. Less often the decision warrants a major I.S. project.

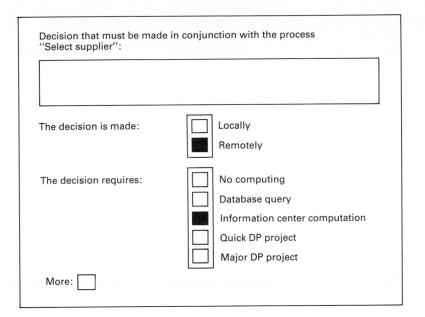

Figure 15.1   A DECISION window associated with certain process blocks.

The BAA study should constantly look out for improvements that can be made quickly and easily. Usually, many such improvements are possible. To make them as the study progresses helps to alleviate the end-user feeling that the study brings no immediate results. The software may generate a decision report for a business area, summarizing the information on the decision windows.

PRIORITIZATION OF SYSTEM BUILDING

As business area analysis progresses, the need for new systems becomes clear. Proposed systems may be described in terms of process blocks and/or decision windows to which they relate. System design starts by extracting the appropriate subset of BAA information from the encyclopedia. As a BAA progresses the proposed new systems should be listed. A final step of BAA is to prioritize the proposed projects to determine where system building effort should be spent.

Many factors that affect the prioritization of system building:

1. **Return on investment.** An estimate should be made of overall return on investment for project. Projects with the highest return on investment should be tackled first, subject to other constraints. Although this is an important general objective, it is sometimes difficult to assess overall return on investment realistically.

2. **Achievement of goals or critical success factors.** We have stressed the importance of critical success factor analysis. This is often more useful and practical than return-on-investment analysis. Proposed system projects may be related to the critical success factors, or to goals in general.

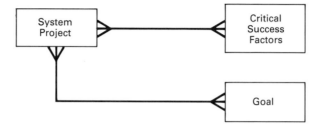

       A matrix mapping system projects against critical success factors may indicate how strongly the project is thought to affect the achievement of the critical success factor.

3. **Adequacy of current system.** A current system covering the processes in question may be doing a reasonably satisfactory job. On the other hand, it may badly need replacing. The operation of the enterprise may need restructuring for greater efficiency around the new system.

4. **Maintenance cost of current system.** The cost of maintaining a current system for the next four years or so should be estimated. It should be compared with the cost of building and maintaining a new system. The maintenance costs of a new system may be much lower if it is built with design automation and a code generator.

5. **Speed of implementation.** Many business needs for information can be met with a system that is quick and easy to implement—information-center projects or one-person I.S. projects. Such systems may be implemented immediately to satisfy worthwhile user needs. Lengthy projects, especially if they are technically difficult, need more careful justification.

6. **Manpower or resource availability.** Much needed systems are often deferred because all I.S. staff members, or certain critical staff members, are tied up on other projects. When manpower (or other resources such as mainframe capacity) are a bottleneck, careful prioritization of competing projects is needed.

7. **Urgent problems.** A system may be given high priority because it solves an urgent user problem. A concern here is that users who make the most noise tend to receive the most attention. The urgency of the problem should be assessed objectively and the cost and value of solving it should determine its ranking on the scale of system needs.

8. **Risk.** The degree of risk may be assessed. Very large systems with lengthy implementation cycles have a high failure rate. The probability of implementation being completed satisfactorily should be assessed. The degree of business acceptance of the system may also be estimated.

These factors may each be ranked on a scale of 1 to 7 to aid executives in deciding where the development money and talent should be applied. Other business areas are likely to be competing for the same development resources, so the decision of what to build first may be taken at a higher level than the business area.

PREPARING FOR SYSTEM DESIGN

Box 15.1 outlines a procedure for preparing for system design. The information collected in the encyclopedia can be used to clarify the opportunities for system design. The existing procedures and systems need to be mapped so that decisions can be made about how they fit into the new I.E. environment. Often, bridges must be built to take data from old systems into the new environment.

BOX 15.1   Transition from BAA to system design

```
┌  Prepare for system design.
│   ┌  Inventory BAA System Implementation.
│   │  ...Inventory Mechanisms.
│   │  ...Inventory Data Collections.
│   │  ...Associate Data Collections with Mechanisms.
│   │  ...Associate DCs with Entity Types & Mechanisms with Processes.
│   │  ...Associate DCs & Mechanisms with Organizational Units & Locations.
│   └  ...Approve BAA Data Collections & Mechanisms.

       Identify system design projects.
       Refine system design project boundaries.
│   ┌  Prioritize the system-building projects.
│   │     There are multiple factors which affect the prioritization
│   │     of system building.
│   │   ┌  Rank each of the factors below on a scale of 1 to 7:
│   │   │      o    Return on investment.
│   │   │      o    Achievement of critical success factor.
│   │   │      o    Achievement of goal.
│   │   │      o    Solution to serious problem.
│   │   │      o    Adequacy of current system.
│   │   │      o    Maintenance cost of current system.
│   │   │      o    Speed of implementation.
│   │   │      o    Manpower or resource availability.
│   │   └      o    Risk.

│   │     Other business areas are likely to be competing for the
│   │        same development resources, so the decision of what to build
│   └        first may be taken at a higher level than the business area.

       Schedule the system-building projects.
└      Obtain approval for system projects.

    Present the results to the executive sponsor.
```

In large enterprises a vast mass of old systems exists. A decision must be made about which systems to convert or rebuild. The term *reverse engineering* is used to describe the automated capturing of old systems and modifying them with the help of a CASE toolset. This subject is important because of the vast investment in old systems. Reverse engineering and reengineering are discussed in Book III of the trilogy.

CONCLUSION

As commented earlier, the ISP and BAA studies described in this book create a framework within which different systems can be built by different teams in different places at different times. The ISP and BAA knowledge resides in an encyclopedia, and the same encyclopedia is used for the design of individual systems and generation of their code.

Within this framework the building of individual systems can be fast if the techniques used include prototyping, reusable design, end-user design workshops (JAD), a code generator, a database generator, and a documentation generator. These need to be an integrated part of an I.E. toolkit.

Design, construction, cutover, and migration are discussed in Book III (Fig. 15.2).

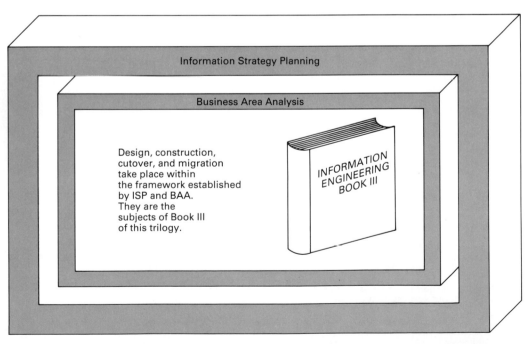

Figure 15.2

PART **III** APPENDICES

Appendix

▌ **DIAGRAMMING STANDARDS**

INTRODUCTION   Information engineering depends heavily on its use of diagramming. Diagrams showing facets of highly complex designs need to be as easy to understand as possible. Diagrams, and their associated windows for displaying details, need to have precision so that a computer can use them as a basis for design automation and code generation. A complex design is often represented by multiple diagram types in such a way that the computer can interrelate the diagrams (a hyperdiagram). This subject is examined in more detail in the author's book *Recommended Diagramming Standards for Analysts and Programmers* [1]. The standards in that book have been the basis for most of the computer industry's leading CASE (computer-aided systems engineering) tools for information engineering.

To gain control of its computing, an enterprise must establish a set of standards for I.S. diagrams. The standards should be the basis of the training given to both data processing professionals and end users. Enterprisewide standards are essential for communication among all persons involved with computers, for establishing corporate or interdepartmental data models and procedures, and for managing the move into CASE tools.

Many corporations have adopted diagramming conventions from methodologies of the past which today are inadequate because they are narrowly focused, ill-structured, unaware of database techniques, unaware of fourth-generation languages, too difficult to teach to end users, clumsy and time consuming, inadequate for automation, or as is usually the case, tackle only part of problems that should be tackled.

This appendix summarizes the constructs that we need to be able to draw. Similar symbols are needed on many different types of diagrams. A consistently drawn set of symbols can be used on the following basic tools:

- Decomposition diagrams
- Dependency diagrams
- Data flow diagrams
- Action diagrams
- Program structure diagrams, for which we employ action diagrams
- Data analysis diagrams
- Entity-relationship diagrams
- Data structure diagrams
- Data navigation diagrams
- Decision trees and tables
- State transition diagrams and tables
- Dialog diagrams

All of these types of diagrams should be drawn from the same small set of blocks and symbols. These blocks and symbols are described in this appendix.

CHANGING METHODS

Diagramming techniques in computing are still evolving. This is necessary because when we examine techniques in common use today, many of them have *serious* deficiencies. Flowcharts are falling out of use because they do not give a structured view of a program. Some of the early structured diagramming techniques need replacing because they fail to represent some important ideas. *Indeed, one of the remarkable deficiencies of the early structured techniques is their use of diagrams that cannot represent many of the important constructs.* We are inventing more rigorous methods for creating better specifications. Vast improvements are needed and are clearly possible in the specification process. These improvements bring new diagramming methods.

One of the problems with computing is that it is so easy to make a mess. Very tidy thinking is needed about the complex logic, or the result is a rat's nest. Today's structured techniques are an improvement over earlier techniques. However, we can still make a mess with them. Most specifications for complex systems are full of ambiguities, inconsistencies, and omissions. More precise mathematically based techniques are evolving so that we can use the computer to help create specifications without these problems. As better, more automated techniques evolve, they need appropriate diagramming methods.

Sometimes the advocates or owners of a particular diagramming technique defend it more like pagan priests defending a religion than like computer scientists seeking to advance their methods. It is very necessary to look objectively at the changes needed for full *automation* and *integration* of diagramming techniques, and to speak openly about the defects of earlier techniques.

Many of the diagramming techniques in common use are old and obsolete. The IBM diagramming template, which most analysts use, is two decades old. It contains symbols for "magnetic drum," "punched tape," and "transmitted tape." It was created before database systems, display terminals, or structured techniques were in use.

BOX I.1 Principles of diagramming standards

Principles of Diagramming Standards

- Analysts, programmers, and end users should be provided with a set of diagramming techniques which are aids to clear thinking about different aspects of analysis, design, and programming.
- The multiple diagramming tools should use the minimum number of icons.
- They should be as easy to learn as possible.
- Conversion between diagrams should be automatic whenever possible.
- The diagramming techniques should be a corporatewide standard, firmly adhered to.

Automation of Diagramming

- The diagrams should be the basis of computer-aided analysis and design—the basis of CASE tools.
- Higher-level design diagrams should convert automatically to action diagrams where relevant.
- The family of diagrams should be a basis for code generation.
- The diagrams should be easy to change and file at the computer screen.
- The diagrams should relate to data models.
- The diagrams convey *meaning* which is stored in a system encyclopedia. The encyclopedia often stores more detail than is shown on any one screen.
- The diagrams and associated encyclopedia should *be* the system documentation.

We need an integrated set of diagramming standards with which we can express all of the constructs that are necessary for the automation of system design and programming. The old techniques *must* give way to techniques that can draw all the concepts we need in an integrated fashion appropriate for computer-aided design and code generation. Box I.1 lists principles that should apply to diagramming standards.

STRUCTURED PROGRAM DESIGN Structured programs are organized hierarchically. There is only one root module. Execution must begin with this root module. Any module can pass control to a module at the next lower level in the hierarchy—a parent module passes control to a child module. Program control enters a module at its entry point and must leave at its exit point. Control returns to the invoking (parent) module when the invoked (child) module completes execution.

A tree-structured diagram is used to draw the program modules that obey this orderly set of rules. Tree structures can be drawn in various ways. It is common to draw them as a set of blocks with the root block at the top, and each parent above its children. A neater way to show the flow of control is to draw them with brackets. Children are within, and to the right of, their parent bracket:

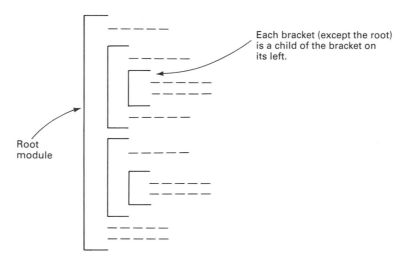

In creating structured programs, four basic constructs are used.

- SEQUENCE   Items are executed in the stated sequence.
- CONDITION   A set of operations are executed only if a stated condition applies.
- CASE   One of several alternative sets of operations are executed.

- REPETITION   A set of operations is repeated, the repetition being terminated on the basis of a stated test. There are two types of repetition control, one (DO WHILE) where the termination test is applied *before* the set of operations is executed, the other (DO UNTIL) where the terminated test is applied *after* the set of operations is executed.

Amazingly, some of the diagramming techniques used for representing structured programs cannot show these four basic constructs. The four constructs can be shown very simply with brackets:

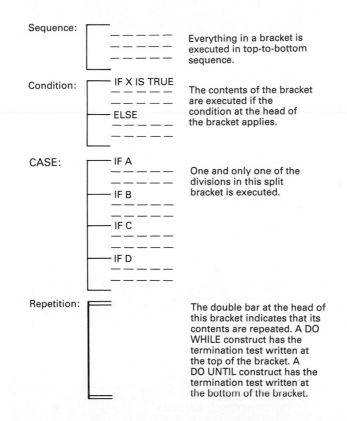

Sequence: Everything in a bracket is executed in top-to-bottom sequence.

Condition: IF X IS TRUE   The contents of the bracket are executed if the condition at the head of the bracket applies.   ELSE

CASE: IF A   One and only one of the divisions in this split bracket is executed.   IF B   IF C   IF D

Repetition: The double bar at the head of this bracket indicates that its contents are repeated. A DO WHILE construct has the termination test written at the top of the bracket. A DO UNTIL construct has the termination test written at the bottom of the bracket.

The words used in fourth-generation languages can be appended to the brackets. The diagram is thus edited until it becomes an executable program. Figure I.1 shows an executable program drawn in this way. This type of diagram is called an action diagram. At its initial stage it can be a tree structure representing a high-level overview or decomposition. It is successively extended until it becomes an executable program. This can be done in a computer-aided fashion, with software ending the words of a particular computer language. Action diagrams can be generated automatically from decomposition diagrams, de-

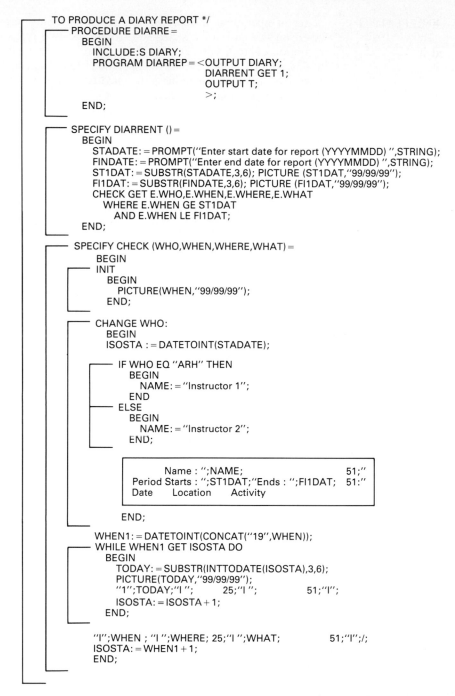

```
TO PRODUCE A DIARY REPORT */
    PROCEDURE DIARRE =
        BEGIN
            INCLUDE:S DIARY;
            PROGRAM DIARREP = <OUTPUT DIARY;
                                DIARRENT GET 1;
                                OUTPUT T;
                                >;
        END;

    SPECIFY DIARRENT () =
        BEGIN
            STADATE: = PROMPT("Enter start date for report (YYYYMMDD) ",STRING);
            FINDATE: = PROMPT("Enter end date for report (YYYYMMDD) ",STRING);
            ST1DAT: = SUBSTR(STADATE,3,6); PICTURE (ST1DAT,"99/99/99");
            FI1DAT: = SUBSTR(FINDATE,3,6); PICTURE (FI1DAT,"99/99/99");
            CHECK GET E.WHO,E.WHEN,E.WHERE,E.WHAT
                WHERE E.WHEN GE ST1DAT
                    AND E.WHEN LE FI1DAT;
        END;

    SPECIFY CHECK (WHO,WHEN,WHERE,WHAT) =
        BEGIN
        INIT
            BEGIN
                PICTURE(WHEN,"99/99/99");
            END;

        CHANGE WHO:
            BEGIN
            ISOSTA : = DATETOINT(STADATE);

                IF WHO EQ "ARH" THEN
                    BEGIN
                        NAME: = "Instructor 1";
                    END
                ELSE
                    BEGIN
                        NAME: = "Instructor 2";
                    END;
```

Name : ";NAME;	51;"
Period Starts : ";ST1DAT;"Ends : ";FI1DAT;	51;"
Date Location Activity	

```
            END;

        WHEN1: = DATETOINT(CONCAT("19",WHEN));
        WHILE WHEN1 GET ISOSTA DO
            BEGIN
                TODAY: = SUBSTR(INTTODATE(ISOSTA),3,6);
                PICTURE(TODAY,"99/99/99");
                "1";TODAY;"I ";        25;"I ";            51;"I";
                ISOSTA: = ISOSTA + 1;
            END;

        "I";WHEN ; "I ";WHERE; 25;"I ";WHAT;            51;"I";/;
        ISOSTA: = WHEN1 + 1;
        END;
```

Figure I.1   A complete MIMER PG program in action diagram format.

302

pendency diagrams, data flow diagrams, data navigation diagrams, decision trees, state transition diagrams, and dialog diagrams. Action diagrams are discussed in Appendix II.

BOXES

The foregoing family of diagramming tools use blocks to represent activities or data. To distinguish between activities and data, activities are drawn as round-cornered blocks, data are drawn as square-cornered boxes:

ARROWS

Many types of diagrams have lines connecting boxes. An arrow on a line is used to mean *flow* or *sequence*. Flow implies that activities are performed in sequence:

Arrows are drawn in the middle of a line connecting boxes rather than at the end, because the ends of the line are used for cardinality symbols.

High-level decomposition diagrams are usually unconcerned with sequence. They use a tree structure to show how a function is composed of lower-level functions. Lower-level decomposition diagrams may need to show sequence. They may show how an activity is composed of subactivities which are executed in a given sequence. To show this, an arrow is used pointing in the direction of the sequence. This direction should be drawn top to bottom on a *vertical tree* or left to right on a *horizontal tree*.

It is usually better to show sequence on a dependency diagram than on a decomposition diagram:

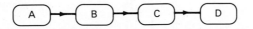

CROW'S FOOT

The term *cardinality* refers to how many of one item is associated with another. There can be one-with-one and one-with-many cardinality. Sometimes numbers may be used to place upper or lower limits on cardinality.

A crow's-foot connector from a line to a box is drawn like this:

It means that one or more than one instances of *B* can be associated with one instance of *A*. It is referred to as a *one-with-many association*.

ONE-WITH-ONE CARDINALITY

On a diagram of data, one-with-one cardinality is drawn with a small bar like a ''1'' across the line:

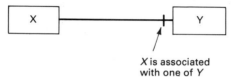

X is associated with one of *Y*

ZERO CARDINALITY

A zero as part of the cardinality symbol means that there may be zero of that block in the association:

CUSTOMER has zero, one, or many TRANSACTIONS

EMPLOYEE has zero or one WIFE

A line may have cardinality indicators in both directions:

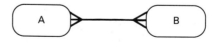

One B is associated with one or many of A.

One A is associated with one or many of B.

On data diagrams it is recommended that a line representing a relationship between data entities should *always* have the cardinality symbols drawn at both ends. It is sloppy diagramming to draw a line connecting to a data box with no cardinality symbol. On activity diagrams the cardinality is usually one-with-one;

because of this the one-with-one symbol is often omitted. A line with no cardinality symbol implies one-with-one (as on a typical data flow diagram, for example).

MAXIMUM AND MINIMUM

The cardinality indicators express a maximum and a minimum:

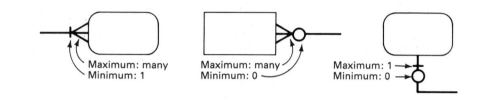

The maximum is always placed next to the box it refers to.

There may be more detailed information about cardinality stored in the encyclopedia associated with the diagram. It might say, for example that the maximum is 25, or that the maximum and minimum are both 3.

Where the minimum and maximum are both 1, two bars may be placed on the line:

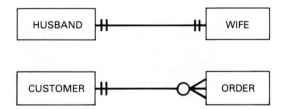

This may be read as meaning "one and only one." Often, a single bar is used to mean "one and only one."

CONDITIONS

Zero cardinality has a special role to play. It means that something may or may not exist. With activities it means that an activity may or may not be performed. On activity diagrams a *condition* is associated with zero cardinality. The condition may be shown on the link. In some cases a complex network of conditions is required between two blocks. These may be shown on a different diagram.

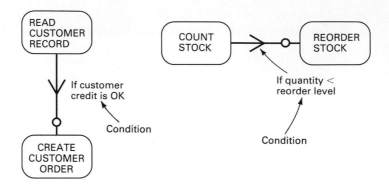

ALTERNATIVE PATHS

The zero cardinality symbol could be at either end of a line with an arrow on it:

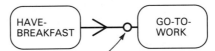

HAVE-BREAKFAST may be followed by GO-TO-WORK

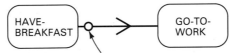

GO-TO-WORK may occur without HAVE-BREAKFAST

In each case the zero is placed against the box that may not exist.

When an activity may be triggered by many different activities, a zero may be placed on the paths from these activities:

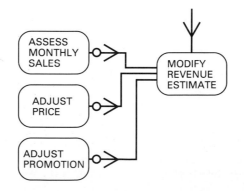

The diagram above says that neither ASSESS MONTHLY SALES, nor ADJUST PRICE, nor ADJUST PROMOTION has to exist for MODIFY REVENUE ESTIMATE to occur.

The case structure of action diagrams is similar in shape to the branching mutual-exclusivity line:

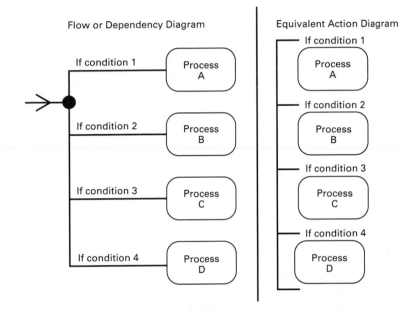

MUTUAL EXCLUSIVITY

Sometimes a block is associated with *one* of a group of blocks. This is indicated with a branching line with a filled-in circle at the branch:

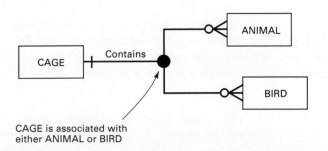

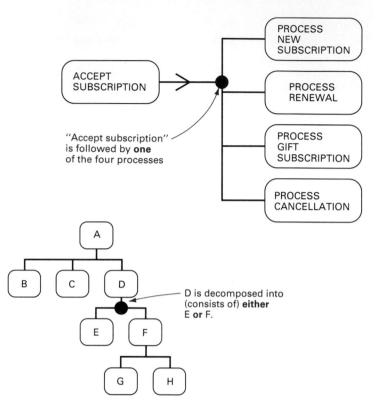

The reader may think of the solid circle as being a small letter "o" for "or".

A mutual-exclusivity circle, like a cardinality circle, has conditions associated with it. These conditions are written on, or associated with, the lines leaving the circle:

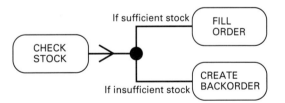

When we convert dependency diagrams, data navigation diagrams, or other diagrams into action diagrams ready for creating executable code, the condition statement will appear on the action diagrams. Figure I.2 shows the possible combinations of two activities and their translation to action diagrams.

LABELING OF LINES

One some types of diagrams the lines connecting boxes should be labeled. Lines between *activity*

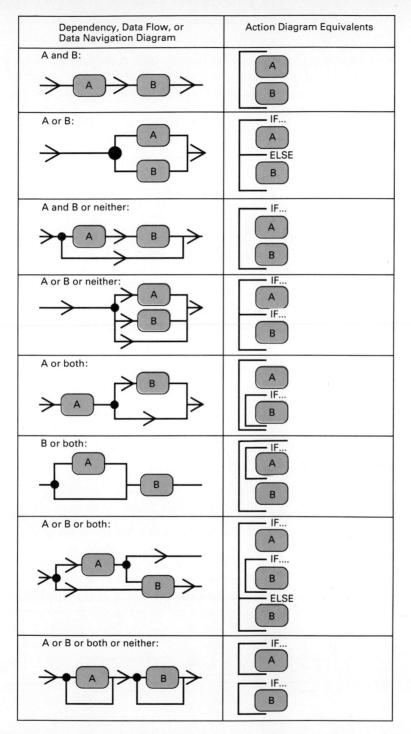

Figure I.2 Diagrams showing activities, such as dependency diagrams, data flow diagrams, or data navigation diagrams.

boxes are unidirectional. There may be lines in both directions between activity boxes, but these should be separate lines each with its own particular meaning. Lines between *data* boxes, on the other hand, are bidirectional. The line could be read in either direction:

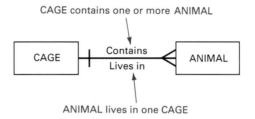

It is usually necessary to label only one direction of such a line.

A label *above* a horizontal line is the name of the relationship when the line is read from left to right. A label *below* a horizontal line is the name when the line is read from right to left. As the line is rotated the label remains on the same side of the line:

Thus the label to the right of a vertical line is read when going *down* the line. The label on the left of a vertical line is read when going *up* the line.

READING LINKS LIKE SENTENCES Lines between boxes give information about the relationship between the boxes. This information ought to read like an English sentence. For example:

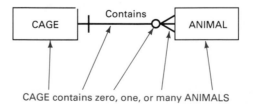

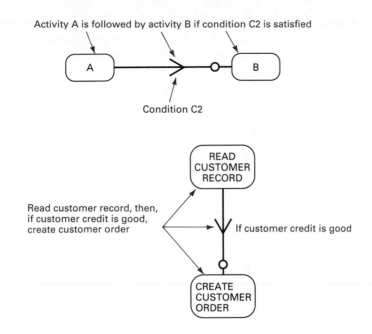

LARGE ARROWS

A large arrow on a diagram is used to show that an event occurs:

This may be used on a dependency diagram, data flow diagram, or state transition diagram:

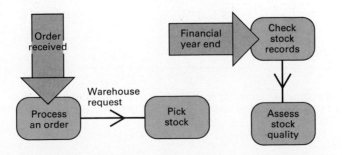

CONCURRENCY

For the first four decades of computing, almost all computers performed their operations sequentially. A major difference between the fourth and fifth generations of computers is likely to be that a fifth-generation machine will have multiple processors and will execute operations in parallel where this is possible. Where parallel processing is possible we need a construct on our diagrams which indicates that specified activities can happen concurrently.

The language OCCAM* is a tight programming language that can express concurrency. It is used for writing programs for multi-microprocessor configurations, or transputer systems. To control the order of execution of processes, OCCAM uses three fundamental mechanisms in addition to the conventional WHILE and IF constructions. These are:

- SEQ   indicating that operations are carried out in *sequence*.
- ALT   indicating that one and only one operation is carried out of several *alternate* operations.
- PAR   indicating that operations can be carried out in *parallel*.

SEQ and ALT are represented in the brackets discussed earlier, ALT being a *case* structure. PAR requires a new diagramming construct. We will indicate that brackets can be executed concurrently by linking them with a semicircular arc:

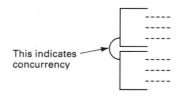

The reader might think of the arc as being a "C" for concurrency.

The basic constructs SEQ, ALT, and PAR are then drawn as follows:

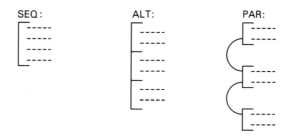

*OCCAM manuals are available from INMOS at: INMOS Ltd., Whitefriars, Lewins Mead, Bristol, England BS1 2NP.   Tel: (0272) 290861; or INMOS Corp., P.O. Box 16000, Colorado Springs, CO 80935, U.S.A.   Tel: 303-630-4000.

Whereas OCCAM is designed for machine programming at a low level, the HOS specification language is designed for systems analysts who begin with a high-level overview of the systems they are designing [2]. This specification language has three forms of decomposition: JOIN, OR, and INCLUDE. These again express *sequence, alternates,* and *concurrency.* Where they are binary decompositions, they can be drawn as follows:

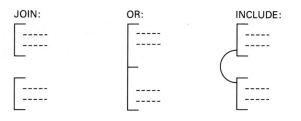

A decomposition can be drawn with diagram symbols rather than with the words JOIN, INCLUDE, and OR:

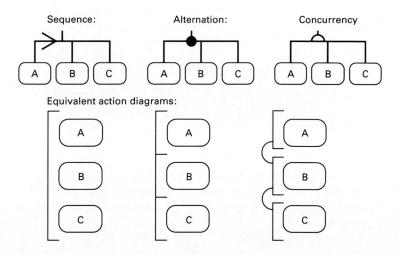

In some cases the concurrency symbol is on one bracket or block only, indicating that this bracket or block relates to parallel activities. This one subroutine may initialize and use a parallel array of processors. In OCCAM, for example, we may have the following:

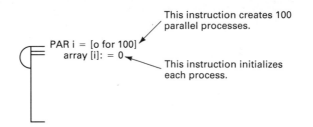

While the other types of constructs in the book have been used extensively in practice, the concurrency indicator has not as yet because of the essentially serial nature of today's programming. Concurrency will be vitally important in future system design.

DIAGRAM CONNECTORS

A pentagon arrow is used as a connector to connect lines to a distant part of a diagram:

The connector symbol may be used to connect to other pages. This is often unnecessary with computerized graphics because the user scrolls across large complete diagrams.

THREE DOTS

Three dots in front of a name on a box or a line of an action diagram indicate that that item can be expanded with the EXPAND command.

When a large diagram is contracted, the three dots are inserted automati-

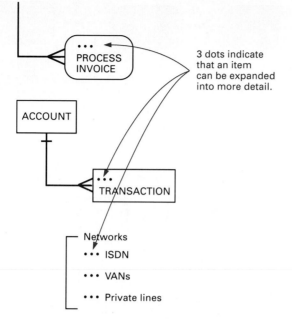

cally to show the view that it may be expanded to its original form. Expansion and contraction are illustrated in Fig. I.3.

ENTITY-RELATIONSHIP DIAGRAM

An entity-relationship diagram shows entity types as square-cornered boxes. (An entity is any person or thing about which data is stored.) The entity types are associated with one another; for example, a PRODUCT entity *is purchased by* a CUSTOMER entity. Lines linking the boxes show these associations. The lines have cardinality indicators. Figure I.4 shows an example of an entity-relationship diagram.

CONVERSION OF DIAGRAMS TO EXECUTABLE CODE

There is a correspondence among the differing diagramming types. They need to be associated in order to automate as fully as possible the tasks of the analyst and programmer. It is this drive toward computer-aided design that makes it so important to have consistent notation among the different types of diagrams.

A data navigation diagram is drawn using an entity-relationship diagram. A data navigation diagram can be converted automatically into an action diagram. Similarly, decomposition diagrams, dependency diagrams, data flow diagrams, decision trees, state transition diagrams, and dialog diagrams can be

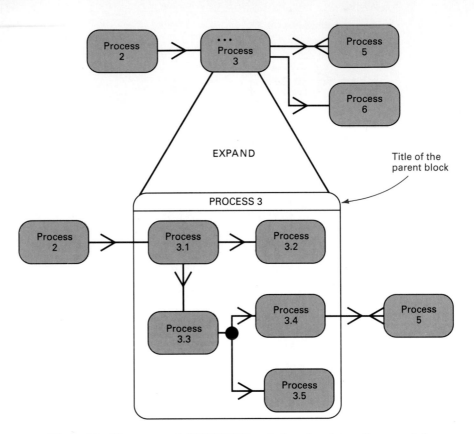

Figure I.3   The command "EXPAND" explodes a box into a diagram *of the same type*. The converse command is "CONTRACT."

automatically converted to action diagrams if drawn rigorously (see the author's *Recommended Diagramming Standards for Analysts and Programmers* [1]). An action diagram is edited in computer-aided fashion until it becomes executable code. This computer-aided progression from high-level overview diagrams or data administrator's data models to executable code makes it possible to increase the productivity of the systems analyst by a large amount.

Figure I.5 shows the relationship between diagramming techniques and the forms of conversion to action diagrams. Code generation can occur from action diagrams and representations of data, screens, and reports.

HAND-DRAWN DIAGRAMS   The diagrams of this report are intended to be created with a modern workstation or a dot-matrix printer. When they are drawn by hand, a template like that in Fig. I.6 should be used.

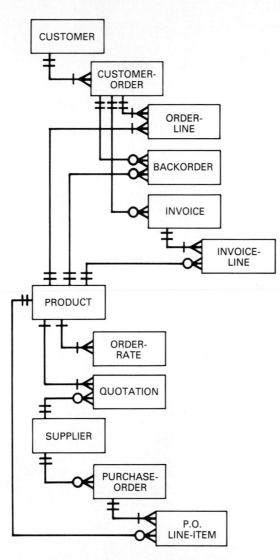

Figure I.4   An entity-relationship diagram for a wholesale distributor

ASCII CHARACTER DIAGRAMS

Sometimes diagrams have to be drawn on a line printer or printer with an ASCII character set. In this case the crow's foot has only two toes and is represented with $<$, $>$, $\vee$, or $\wedge$:

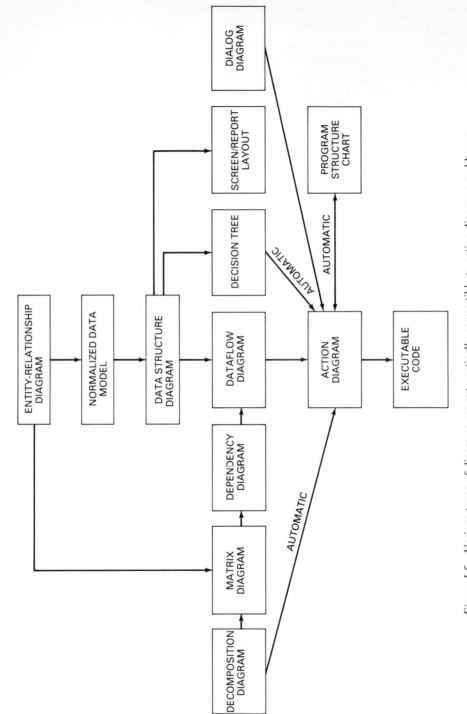

Figure I.5 Various types of diagrams are automatically convertible to action diagrams and hence to executable code.

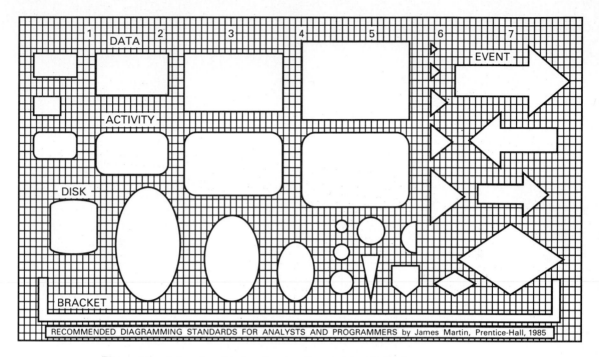

Figure I.6   A template for drawing the diagrams in this book.

Square-cornered and round-cornered boxes can be represented as boxes with a + or o, respectively, at their corners:

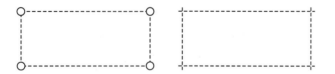

ASCII diagrams are not likely to be as elegant as drawings done with a graphics screen and dot-matrix printer.

REFERENCES

1. James Martin, *Recommended Diagramming Standards for Analysts and Programmers,* Savant Technical Report 38. Carnforth, Lancashire, England: Savant, April 1985.

2. James Martin, *System Design from Provably Correct Constructs.* Englewood Cliffs, N.J.: Prentice-Hall, 1985.

Appendix

II ACTION DIAGRAMS

OVERVIEW VERSUS DETAILED LOGIC DIAGRAMMING Of the diagramming techniques that evolved in the 1970s and earlier, some are usable for the *overview* of program structure and some are usable for the *detailed* program logic. Structure charts, HIPO diagrams, Warnier-Orr diagrams, and Michael Jackson charts draw overall program structures, but not the detailed tests, conditions, and logic. Their advocates usually resort to structured English or pseudocode to represent the detail. Flowcharts and Nassi-Shneiderman charts show the detailed logic of a program, but not the structural overview.

There is no reason why the diagramming of the *overview* should be incompatible with the diagramming of the *detail*. Indeed, it is highly desirable that these two aspects of program design should employ the same type of diagram because complex systems are created by successively filling in detail (top-down design) and linking together blocks of low-level detail (bottom-up design). The design needs to move naturally between the high levels and low levels of design. The low level should be a natural extension of the high level. *Action diagrams* achieve this. They give a natural way to draw program overviews such as structure charts, HIPO or Warnier-Orr diagrams, *and* detailed logic such as flowcharts or Nassi-Shneiderman charts. They were originally designed to be as easy to teach to end users as possible and to assist end users in applying fourth-generation languages. Most of the leading CASE tools use action diagrams.

Glancing ahead, Figs. II.2 and II.3 show simple examples of action diagrams. Figure II.8 shows an extension of Fig. II.2. They are useful for showing, and modifying, human agendas and procedures, and are used in the procedure boxes throughout this trilogy. They are particularly useful because of the ease with which they can be expanded, contracted, and edited on the screen of a personal computer.

BRACKETS

A program module is drawn as a bracket:

```
 ┌ ─ ─ ─ ─ ─
 │ ─ ─ ─ ─ ─
 │ ─ ─ ─ ─ ─
 └ ─ ─ ─ ─ ─
```

Brackets are the basic building blocks of action diagrams. The bracket can be of any length, so there is space in it for as much text or detail as is needed.

Inside the bracket is a sequence of operations. A simple control rule applies to the bracket. You enter it at the top, do the things in it in a top-to-bottom sequence, and exit at the bottom.

Inside the bracket there may be other brackets. Many brackets may be nested. The nesting shows the hierarchical structure of a program. Figure II.1 shows the representation of a hierarchical structure with brackets.

Some brackets are *repetition* brackets. The items in the bracket are executed many times. The repetition bracket has a double line at its top:

When one of several processes is to be used (mutually exclusive selection), a bracket with multiple divisions is used:

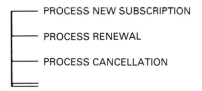

This is the programmer's multiple-option structures, called a "case structure." One, and only one, of the divisions in the bracket above is executed.

ULTIMATE DECOMPOSITION

Figure II.2 illustrates an action diagram overview of a program structure. It can be extended to show conditions, case structures, and loops of different types—it can show detailed program logic. Figure II.3 expands the process in Fig. II.2 called VALIDATE SUB ITEM. Figures II.2 and II.3 could be merged into one chart.

Glancing ahead, Fig. II.7 shows *executable* program code written in a

Decomposition Diagram, Structure Chart, HIPO Chart, etc.

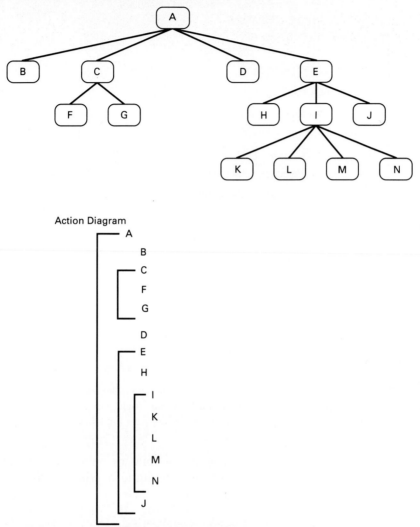

Figure II.1   A hierarchical block structure and the equivalent action diagram.

fourth-generation language. This diagramming technique can thus be extended all the way from the highest-level overview to working code in a fourth-generation language. When it is used on a computer screen the developers can edit and adjust the diagram and successively fill in detail until they have working code that can be tested interpretively. We refer to this as *ultimate decomposition*.

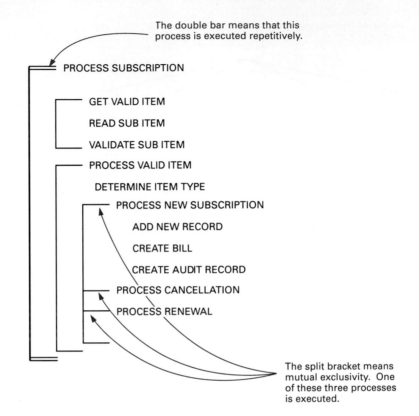

Figure II.2   A high-level action diagram. This action diagram can now be expanded into a chart showing the detailed program logic. VALIDATE SUB-ITEM from this chart is expanded into detailed logic in Fig. II.3.

CONDITIONS

Often a program module or subroutine is executed only IF a certain condition applies. In this case the condition is written at the head of a bracket:

A condition bracket should normally have an "ELSE" partition:

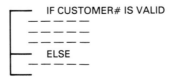

```
─── VALIDATE SUB ITEM
    CHECK GENERAL FORMAT
    ┌── IF ERROR
    │   WRITE ERROR MESSAGE
    ┌── WHEN NEW SUB
    │   CHECK NAME AND ADDRESS
    │   CHECK FOR NUMERIC ZIP
    │   CHECK FOR VALID TERMS
    │   CHECK FOR PAYMENT
    │   ┌── IF ERRORS
    │   │     SET INVALID INDICATOR
    │   ┌── ELSE
    │   │     SET VALID INDICATOR
    ├── WHEN RENEWAL
    │   CHECK FOR VALID TERMS
    │   CHECK FOR PAYMENT
    │   ┌── IF ERRORS
    │   │     SET INVALID INDICATOR
    │   ┌── ELSE
    │   │     SET VALID INDICATOR
    ├── WHEN CANCEL
    │   SET CANCEL FLAG
    ├── DEFAULT
    │     .
    │     .
    ┌── IF INVALID INDICATOR IS SET
        WRITE ERROR MESSAGE
```

Figure II.3 An action diagram showing the detailed logic inside the process VALIDATE SUBITEM. This diagram showing detailed logic is an extension of the overview diagram of Fig. II.2.

This has only two mutually exclusive conditions, an IF and an ELSE. Sometimes there are many mutual-exclusive conditions, as follows:

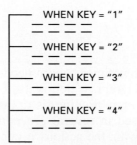

LOOPS

A loop is represented with a repetition bracket with the double line at its top. When many people first start to program, they make mistakes with the point at which they test a loop. Sometimes the test should be made *before* the actions of the loop are performed, and sometimes the test should be made *after*. This difference can be made clear on brackets by drawing the test at either the top or bottom of the bracket:

If the test is at the head of the loop as with a WHILE loop, the actions in the loop may never be executed if the WHILE condition is not satisfied. If the test is at the bottom of the loop, as with an UNTIL loop, the actions in the loop are executed at least once. They will be executed more than once if the condition is fulfilled.

SETS OF DATA

Sometimes a procedure needs to be executed on all of the items in a set of items. It might be applied to all transactions or all records in a file, for example:

```
╔═══ FOR ALL TRANSACTIONS
║    — — — — —
║    — — — — —
║    — — — — —
╚    — — — — —
```

Action diagrams are used with fourth-generation languages such as NO-MAD, MANTIS, FOCUS, RAMIS, and IDEAL. They are a good tool for teaching end users to work with these languages. Some such languages have a FOR construct with a WHERE clause to qualify the FOR. For example:

```
╔═══ FOR EACH TRANSACTION WHERE CUSTOMER# >5000
║    — — — — —
║    — — — — —
╚    — — — — —
```

SUBPROCEDURES

Sometimes a user needs to add an item to an action diagram, which is itself a procedure that may contain actions. This subprocedure, or subroutine, is drawn with a round-cornered box. A subprocedure might be used in several procedures. It will be exploded into detail, in another chart, showing the actions it contains.

SUBPROCEDURES NOT YET DESIGNED

In some cases the procedure designer has sections of a procedure that are not yet thought out in detail. He can represent this as a box with rounded corners and a right edge made of question marks:

COMMON PROCEDURES

Some procedures appear more than once in an action diagram because they are called (or invoked) from more than one place in the logic. These procedures are called *common procedures*. They are indicated by drawing a vertical line down the left-hand side of the procedure box:

The use of procedure boxes enables an action diagrammer to concentrate on those parts of a procedure with which he is familiar. Another person may, perhaps, fill in the details in the boxes. This enables an elusive or complex procedure formation problem to be worked out a stage at a time.

The use of these boxes makes action diagrams a powerful tool for designing procedures at many levels of abstraction. As with other structured techniques, top-down design can be done by first creating a gross structure with such boxes, while remaining vague about the contents of each box. The gross structure can then be broken down into successive levels of detail. Each explosion of a box adds another degree of detail, which might itself contain actions and boxes. Similarly, bottom-up design can be done by specifying small procedures as action diagrams whose names appear as boxes in higher-level action diagrams.

TERMINATIONS

Certain conditions may cause a procedure to be terminated. They may cause the termination of the bracket in which the condition occurs, or they may cause the termination of multiple brackets. Terminations are drawn with an arrow to the left through one or more brackets, as follows:

It is important to note than an escape structure allows only a forward skip to the exit point of a bracket. This restriction keeps the structure simple and does not allow action diagrams to degenerate into unstructured "spaghetti" logic.

An escape is different from a GO TO instruction. It represents an orderly close-down of the brackets escaped from. Some fourth-generation languages have an escape construct and no GO TO instruction. The escape command has names such as EXIT, QUIT, and BREAK.

GO TO

When a language has a well-implemented *escape,* there is no need for GO TO instructions. However, some languages have GO TO instructions and no escape. Using good structured design, the GO TO would be employed to emulate an escape. Any attempt to branch to a distant part of the program should be avoided.

It has, nevertheless, been suggested that a GO TO should be included in the action diagram vocabulary. This can be done by using a dashed arrow to replace the solid escape arrow, thus:

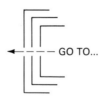

In the interests of structured design we have not included this construct in our recommended list of action diagram features.

NEXT ITERATION

In a repetition bracket a *next-iteration* construct is useful. With this, control skips the remaining instructions in a repetition bracket and goes to the next iteration of the loop. A next-iteration construct (abbreviated "NEXT") is drawn as follows:

IF...

The arrow does not break through the bracket as with an escape construct.

FOURTH-GENERATION LANGUAGES

When fourth-generation languages are used the wording on the action diagram may be the wording that is used in coding programs with the language. Examples of this are as follows:

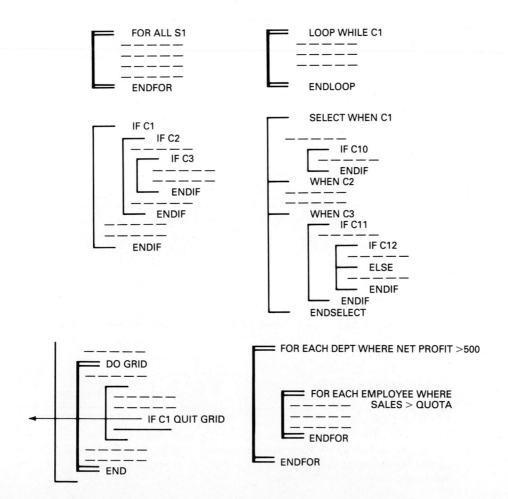

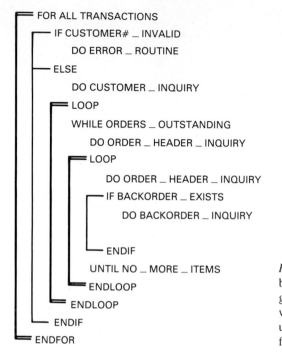

```
┌─ FOR ALL TRANSACTIONS
│   ┌── IF CUSTOMER# _ INVALID
│   │       DO ERROR _ ROUTINE
│   ├── ELSE
│   │       DO CUSTOMER _ INQUIRY
│   │   ┌─ LOOP
│   │   │   WHILE ORDERS _ OUTSTANDING
│   │   │       DO ORDER _ HEADER _ INQUIRY
│   │   │   ┌─ LOOP
│   │   │   │       DO ORDER _ HEADER _ INQUIRY
│   │   │   │   ┌─ IF BACKORDER _ EXISTS
│   │   │   │   │       DO BACKORDER _ INQUIRY
│   │   │   │   │
│   │   │   │   └── ENDIF
│   │   │   │       UNTIL NO _ MORE _ ITEMS
│   │   │   └─ ENDLOOP
│   │   └─ ENDLOOP
│   └── ENDIF
└─ ENDFOR
```

Figure II.4 Action diagrams can be labeled with the control statement of fourth-generation language and form an excellent way to teach such languages. This example uses statements from the language IDEAL from ADR.

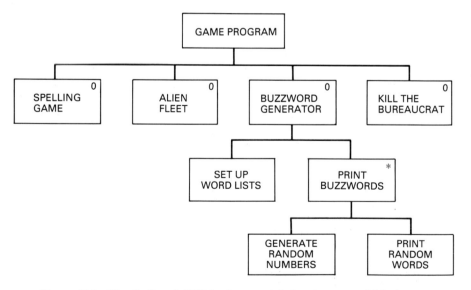

Figure II.5 The ''o'' and ''*'' in the top right-hand corner of blocks on charts such as this do not have obvious meaning. The form of the diagram should be selected to make the meaning as obvious as possible to relatively uninitiated readers.

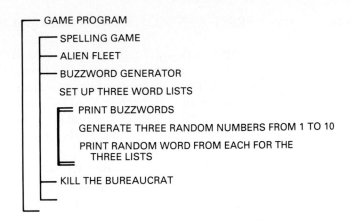

Figure II.6   An action diagram equivalent to the Jackson diagram of Fig. II.5.

Figure II.4 shows an action diagram for a procedure using control statements from the language IDEAL for ADR [1].

DECOMPOSITION TO PROGRAM CODE

Figure II.5 shows a Jackson diagram of a game program. With action diagrams we can decompose this until we have program code. Figure II.6 shows an action diagram equivalent to Figure II.5. The action diagram gives more room for explanation. Instead of saying "PRINT RAN-

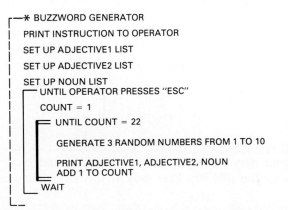

Figure II.7   An expansion of the buzzword generator portion of Fig. II.6.

DOM WORDS'' it says ''PRINT RANDOM WORD FROM EACH OF THE THREE LISTS.''

Figure II.7 decomposes the part of the diagram labeled BUZZWORD GENERATOR. The inner bracket is a repetition bracket that executes 22 times. This is inside a bracket that is terminated by the operator pressing the ESC (escape) key. The last statement in this bracket is WAIT, indicating that the system will wait after executing the remainder of the bracket until the operator presses the ESC key. This gives the operator as much time as he wants to read the printout.

Figure II.8 decomposes the diagram further into an executable program. This program is written in the fourth-generation language MANTIS, from CIN-COM INC.†

TITLES VERSUS CODE STRUCTURE   At the higher levels of the design process, action diagram brackets represent the *names* of processes and subprocesses. As the designer descends into program-level detail, the brackets become *program constructs:* IF brackets, CASE brackets, LOOP brackets, and so on. To show the difference, different colors may be used. The *name* brackets may be red and the *program-construct* brackets black. If a black-and-white copier or terminal is used, the *name* brackets may be dotted or gray and the *program-construct* brackets black. The program-construct brackets may be labeled with appropriate control words. These may be the control words of a particular programming language or they may be language-independent words.

A bracket that shows a title rather than an action to be implemented, or a program instruction, may be drawn as a dotted or dashed line. It may have a character preceding the title, such as an *, &, or C, to indicate that the title line should be treated as a comment by the compiler. Different compilers use different characters for this purpose.

Title brackets may be single ''if else,'' case structure, or repetition brackets.

The designer may use a mix of title brackets and program brackets such that by displaying the title brackets only (with action diagramming software),

---

†The example in Figs. II.7 and II.8 is adapted from a program in the *MANTIS User's Guide,* Cincom Systems Inc., Cincinnati, Ohio, 1982.

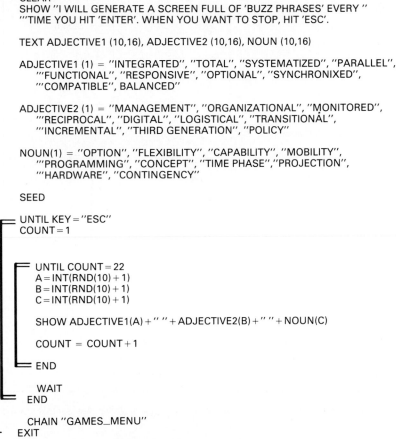

```
┌─ENTER BUZZWORD GENERATOR

    CLEAR
    SHOW "I WILL GENERATE A SCREEN FULL OF 'BUZZ PHRASES' EVERY "
    "'TIME YOU HIT 'ENTER'. WHEN YOU WANT TO STOP, HIT 'ESC'.

    TEXT ADJECTIVE1 (10,16), ADJECTIVE2 (10,16), NOUN (10,16)

    ADJECTIVE1 (1) = "INTEGRATED", "TOTAL", "SYSTEMATIZED", "PARALLEL",
        "'FUNCTIONAL", "RESPONSIVE", "OPTIONAL", "SYNCHRONIXED",
        "'COMPATIBLE", BALANCED"

    ADJECTIVE2 (1) = "MANAGEMENT", "ORGANIZATIONAL", "MONITORED",
        "'RECIPROCAL", "DIGITAL", "LOGISTICAL", "TRANSITIONAL",
        "'INCREMENTAL", "THIRD GENERATION", "POLICY"

    NOUN(1) = "OPTION", "FLEXIBILITY", "CAPABILITY", "MOBILITY",
        "'PROGRAMMING", "CONCEPT", "TIME PHASE","PROJECTION",
        "'HARDWARE", "CONTINGENCY"

    SEED

┌═ UNTIL KEY = "ESC"
│   COUNT = 1
│
│  ┌═ UNTIL COUNT = 22
│  │   A = INT(RND(10) + 1)
│  │   B = INT(RND(10) + 1)
│  │   C = INT(RND(10) + 1)
│  │
│  │   SHOW ADJECTIVE1(A) + " " + ADJECTIVE2(B) + " " + NOUN(C)
│  │
│  │   COUNT = COUNT + 1
│  └═ END
│
│     WAIT
└═ END

    CHAIN "GAMES_MENU"
└─  EXIT
```

Figure II.8 An expansion of the action diagram of Fig. II.7 into program code. This is an executable program in the fourth-generation language, MANTIS. Successive decomposition of a diagram until it becomes executable code is called *ultimate decomposition*.

an overview structure of the program is seen. He may also use comments to clarify his design. The comment line starts with an asterisk. The software may be instructed to display or to hide the comments.

Figure II.9 shows the program constructs with language-independent control words. Figure II.10 shows the same constructs with the words of the fourth-generation language IDEAL. It is desirable that any fourth-generation language should have a set of clear words equivalent to Fig. II.9, and it would help if standard words for this existed in the computer industry. In these two illustra-

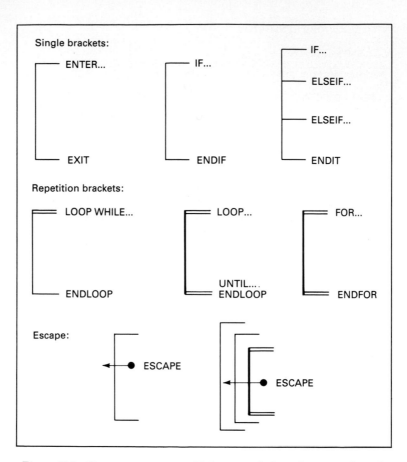

Figure II.9 Program constructs with language-independent control words.

tions, the control words are shown as in bold italic print. The other statements are in normal print.

CONCURRENCY

As discussed in Appendix I, where brackets may be executed concurrently, they are to be joined with a semicircular link:

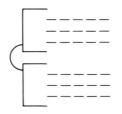

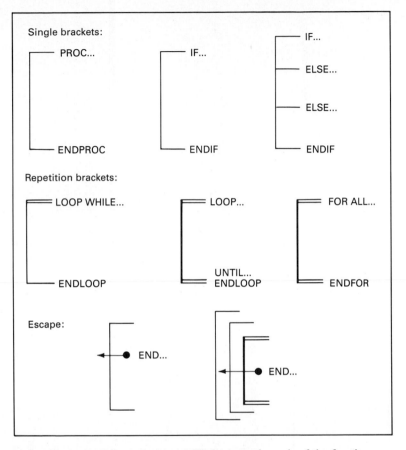

Figure II.10   Program constructs with the control words of the fourth-generation language IDEAL.

**INPUT AND
OUTPUT DATA**

The brackets of the action diagram are quick and easy to draw. If the user wants to show the data that enters and leaves a process, the bracket is expanded into a rectangle as shown in Fig. II.11. The data entering the process is written at the top right corner of the block. The data leaving is written at the bottom right corner.

This type of functional decomposition is designed for computerized checking to ensure that all the inputs and outputs balance. Figure II.12 shows nested blocks and the arrows represent checks that inputs are used and the outputs come from somewhere. Some CASE tools show the inputs to a bracket at its top and the outputs at its bottom.

A diagramming technique, today, should be designed for both quick manual manipulation and for computerized manipulation. Users and analysts will

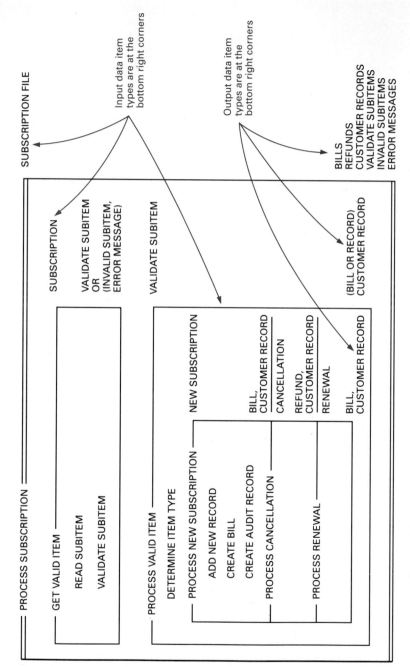

Figure II.11 The bracket format of Fig. II.2 is here expanded into the rectangular format used to show the data item types that are input and output to each process. In some CASE tools the inputs are shown at the top and the outputs at the bottom of an action diagram bracket. The computer should perform the checking illustrated in Figure II.12.

want to draw rough sketches on paper or argue at a blackboard using the technique. They will also want to build complex diagrams at a computer screen, using the computer to validate, edit, and maintain the diagrams, possibly linking them to a dictionary, database model, and so on. The tool acts rather like a word processor for diagramming, making it easy for users to modify their diagram. Unlike a word processor, it can perform complex validation and cross-checking on the diagram. In the design of complex specifications the automated correlation of inputs and outputs among program modules is essential if mistakes are to be avoided.

In showing input and output data, Fig. II.11 contains the information on a data flow diagram. It can be converted into a layered data flow diagram as in Fig. II.13. Unlike a data flow diagram, it can be directly extended to show the program structure, including conditions, case constructs, and loop control.

It is highly desirable that a programmer should sketch the structure of programs with action diagram brackets. Often the coder has made a logic error in the use of loops, END statements, CASE structures, EXITs, and so on. When he is taught to draw action diagram brackets and fit the code to them, these structure errors become apparent. Control statements can be automatically placed on brackets by a CASE tool. The CASE tool should do all the cross-checking that is possible.

SAMPLE DATABASE ACTIONS

Most of the action diagrams drawn for commercial data-processing systems relate to databases or on-line files. A common action of these diagrams is the database or file operation. It is desirable that these operations relate to the dictionary and data model employed.

We will distinguish between simple and compound database actions. A simple database action is an operation applied to *one instance of one record type*. There are four types of simple actions:

- CREATE
- READ
- UPDATE
- DELETE

The memorable acronym CRUD is sometimes used to refer to these and to help remember them.

On an action diagram, a simple database action is represented by a rectan-

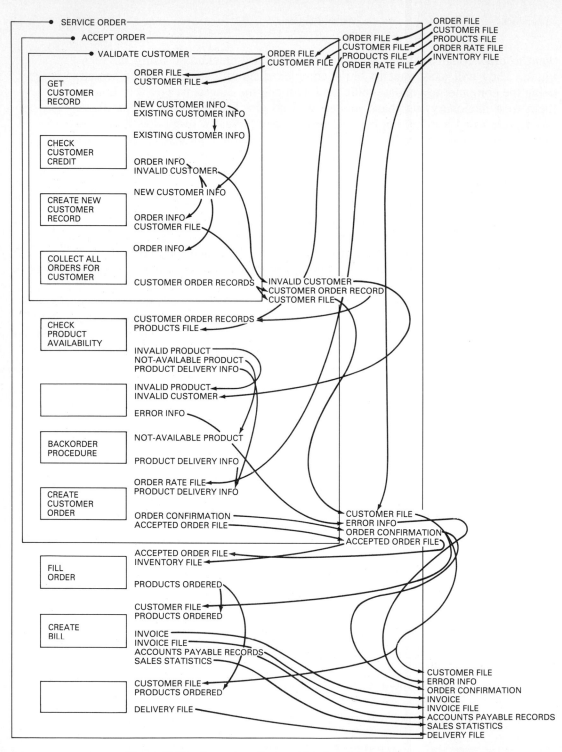

Figure II.12 An action diagram showing inputs and outputs. The arrows indicate a check that the graphics tool should make on the usage of inputs and outputs.

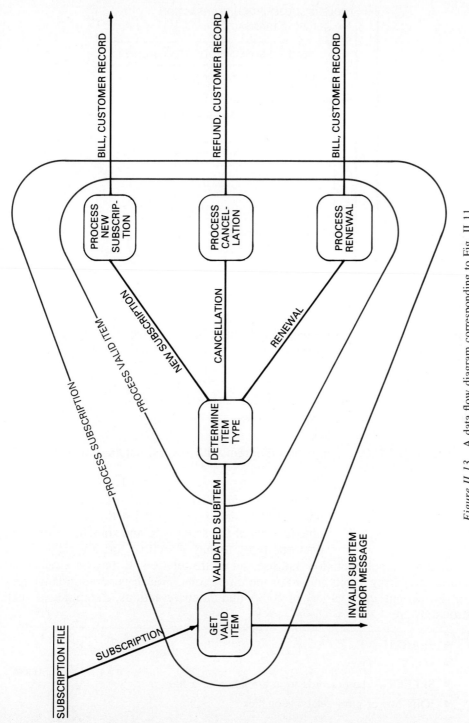

Figure II.13   A data flow diagram corresponding to Fig. II.11.

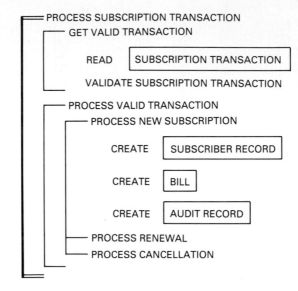

Figure II.14   An action diagram showing four simple database actions.

gular box. The name of the record is written inside the box; the type of action is written on the left side of the box:

Figure II.14 shows an action diagram with several database actions.

COMPOUND DATABASE ACTIONS

A *compound database action* also takes a single action against a database, but the action may use multiple records of the same type and sometimes of more than one type. It may search or sort a logical file. It may be a relational operation that uses an entire relation. It may be a relational operation requiring a join on two or more relations. Fourth-generation languages have instructions for a variety of compound database actions. Examples of such instructions are:

- SEARCH
- SORT
- SELECT certain records from a relation or a file
- JOIN two or more relations or files

- PROJECT a relation or file to obtain a subset of it
- DUPLICATE

CREATE, READ, UPDATE, and DELETE may also be used for compound-database actions. For example, DELETE could be used to delete a whole file.

Most of the database actions in traditional data processing are simple database actions. As relational databases and nonprocedural languages spread, *compound* database actions will become more common. A compound database action is represented as a double rectangular box. The name of the record is written inside the box; the database action is written on the left-hand side of the box:

SORT   ‖ SUBSCRIBER ‖

Often a compound database action needs a qualifying statement associated with it to describe how it is performed. For example:

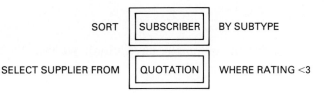

SORT   ‖ SUBSCRIBER ‖   BY SUBTYPE

SELECT SUPPLIER FROM   ‖ QUOTATION ‖   WHERE RATING <3

AUTOMATIC NAVIGATION

A compound database action may require automatic navigation by the database management system. Relational databases and a few nonrelational ones have this capability. For a database without automatic navigation, a compiler of a fourth-generation may generate the required sequence of data accesses. With a compound database action, search parameters or conditions are often an integral part of the action itself. They are written inside a bracket containing the access box.

SIMPLE VERSUS COMPOUND DATABASE ACCESSES

There are many procedures that can be done with either simple database accesses or compound accesses. If a traditional DBMS is used, the programmer navigates through the database with simple accesses. If the DBMS or language compiler has automatic navigation, higher-level statements using compound database accesses may be employed.

Suppose, for example, that we want to give a $1000 bonus to all employees who are salespeople in the Southeast region. In IBM's database language SQL, we would write:

```
UPDATE EMPLOYEE
SET SALARY = SALARY + 1000
WHERE JOB = 'SALESMAN'
AND REGION = 'SOUTHEAST'
```

We can diagram this with a compound database action as follows:

```
    ┌
    │
    │    UPDATE  ║ EMPLOYEE ║
    │
    │    WHERE JOB IS SALESMAN
    │    AND REGION IS SOUTHEAST
    │    INCREASE SALARY BY 1000
    │
    └
```

With simple actions (no automatic navigation), we can diagram the same procedure as follows:

```
    ┌─ For All Employees
    │
    │    READ  ║ EMPLOYEE ║
    │    ┌─ If Job Is SALESMAN
    │    │    and REGION Is SOUTHEAST,
    │    │    INCREASE SALARY BY 1000
    │    │
    │    │    UPDATE  ║ EMPLOYEE ║
    │    └
    └
```

RELATIONAL JOINS

A relational join merges two relations (logical files or tables) on the basis of a common data item. For example, the EMPLOYEE relation and the REGION relation for a company may look like this:

REGION

REGION-ID	LOCATION	REGION-STATUS	SALES-YTD
001	NEW YORK	1	198,725
004	CHICAGO	7	92,615
006	LA	3	156,230

EMPLOYEE

SSN	NAME	SALARY	JOBCODE	LOCATION
337-48-2713	SMITH	42000	07	CHICAGO
341-25-3340	JOHNSON	39000	15	LA
391-62-1167	STRATTON	27000	05	LA

These relations are combined in such a way that the LOCATION data item of the EMPLOYEE relation becomes the same as the LOCATION data item of the REGION relation. We can express this with the statement

REGION.LOCATION = EMPLOYEE.LOCATION

The result is a combined record as follows:

SSN	NAME	SALARY	JOB-CODE	LOCATION	REGION-ID	REGION-STATUS	SALES-YTD
337-48-2713	SMITH	42000	07	CHICAGO	004	7	92,615
341-25-3340	JOHNSON	39000	15	LA	006	3	156,230
391-62-1167	STRATTON	27000	05	LA	006	3	156,230

The database system may not combine them in reality but may join the appropriate data in response to the request. A join is shown on an action diagram by linking the boxes with an access operation applying to the combination:

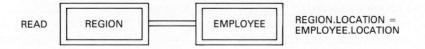

A statement may follow the joined records showing how they are joined. Often this is not necessary because the joined records contain one common data

item which is the basis for the join. For example, the EMPLOYEE record probably contains the data item LOCATION, in which case we can simply show:

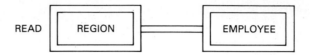

We might, for example, constrain the join operation by asking for employees whose job code is 15, whose salary exceeds $35,000, and whose region status is 3. The result would then be

SSN	NAME	SALARY	
341-25-3340	JOHNSON	39000	

From the join of EMPLOYEE and REGION, we might say SELECT SSN, NAME, REGION-STATUS, LOCATION. With the data base language SQL from IBM, and others, this operation would be expressed as follows:

```
SELECT SSN, NAME, REGION-STATUS, LOCATION
FROM REGION, EMPLOYEE
WHERE REGION.LOCATION = EMPLOYEE.LOCATION
AND JOB-CODE = 15
AND SALARY > 35000
```

This can be written on an action diagram as follows:

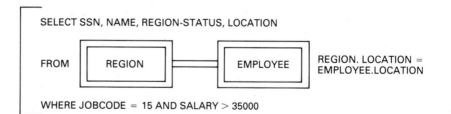

For a simple query such as this, we do not need a diagram representation. The query language itself is clear enough. For a complex operation, we certainly need to diagram the use of compound data actions.

Similarly, a relational join can be represented with either a sequence of single actions or one compound action, as shown in Fig. II.15. In this example, there are multiple projects in an EMPLOYEE PROJECT record showing how employees were rated for their work on each project to which they were assigned. They were given a salary raise if their average rating exceeded 6.

Data used in this example:

EMPLOYEE

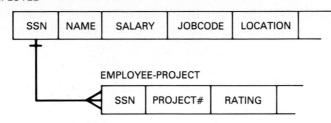

A procedure for giving employees an increase in salary, using simple database action:

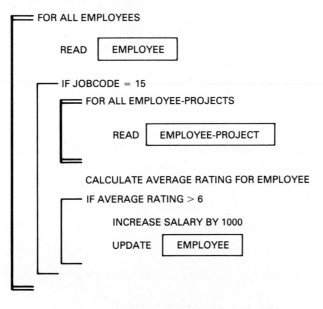

The same procedure using a compound database action:

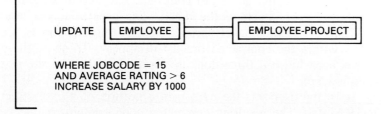

Figure II.15 Illustration of a procedure that may be done with either three simple database access commands or one compound access command.

THREE-WAY JOINS In some cases, three-way joins are useful. Suppose an accountant is concerned that accounts receivable are becoming too high. He wants to telephone any branch manager who has a six-month-old debt outstanding from a customer. The following record structures exist:

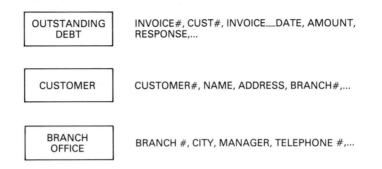

He enters the following query:

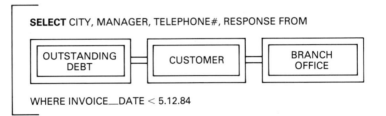

The three-way join is shown in a similar fashion to two-way joins.

CONTRACT AND EXPAND A very useful feature of an action diagram editor is the ability to *contract* large action diagrams, hiding much of the detail. The user selects a bracket and says "CONTRACT." The bracket shrinks so that only its top is seen. Any nested brackets within the contracted bracket disappear. To show the user that information has been hidden, three dots are inserted in front of the text line of the contracted bracket.

In Fig. II.16 the user sets the cursor on a portion of a case structure and says "CONTRACT." The resulting contracted code contains a line beginning with three dots. In Fig. II.17 the user selects this line and says "EXPAND."

"CONTRACT" may be used multiple times to create hierarchies of contraction. "EXPAND" then reveals lines which themselves can be expanded. Contracting and expanding permits large programs to be manipulated with ease.

ACTION DIAGRAM EDITORS AND CASE TOOLS

Action diagram editors exist for personal computers and are also part of most of the good quality CASE tools. The control words of diverse programming languages can be added to the action diagrams by the computer.

The brackets used can be selected from a menu and can be stretched, edited, cut and pasted, and duplicated. The computer can apply a variety of integrity checks. Large programs can be displayed in overview form. Code can be contracted to hide the details and then reexpanded at will.

Experience with action diagram editors has shown that end users can employ them to sketch the systems and procedures they need. When this occurs, action diagrams form a useful communication vehicle between users and systems analysts. The design so created has successively greater detail added to it until it becomes executable code.

AUTOMATIC DERIVATION OF ACTION DIAGRAMS

Action diagrams can be derived automatically from correctly drawn decomposition diagrams, dependency diagrams, decision trees, or state transition diagrams (see Fig. I.5). If a computer algorithm is used for doing this, it needs to check the completeness or integrity of the dependency diagram or navigation diagram. This helps to validate or improve the analyst's design.

CONVERSION OF ACTION DIAGRAMS TO CODE

Different computer languages have different commands relating to the constructs drawn on action diagrams. If the action diagram is being edited on a computer screen, a menu of commands can be provided for any particular language. Using the language IDEAL, for example, the designer might select the word LOOP for the top of a repetition bracket, and the software automatically puts ENDLOOP at the bottom of the bracket and asks the designer for the loop control statement. The designer might select IF and the software creates the following bracket:

```
IF
ELSE
ENDIF
```

The user is asked to specify the IF condition.

Such structures with the commands for a given language may be generated

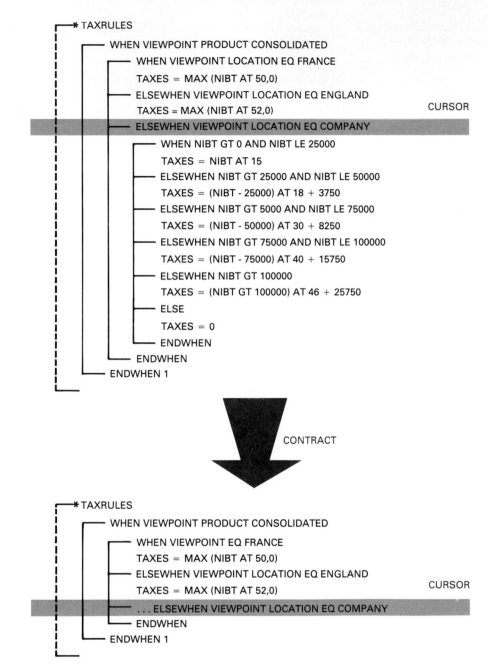

Figure II.16 The CONTRACT command that hides the contents of a bracket. To show that there is hidden information, three dots are placed at the start of the contracted line.

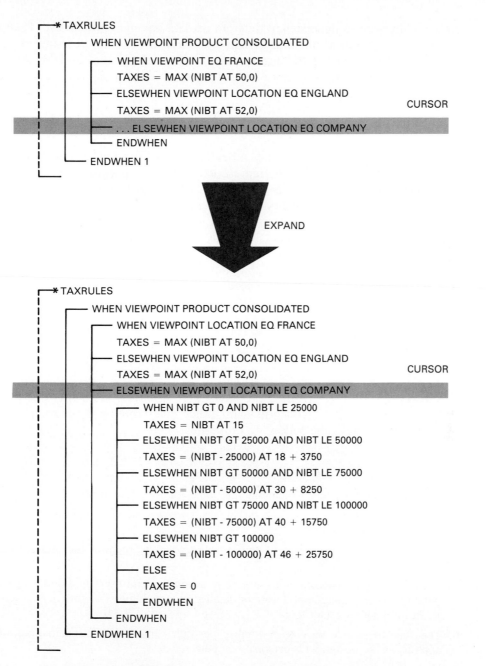

Figure II.17 The EXPAND command can be applied to lines beginning with three dots. It reveals their hidden contents. This and Fig. II.16 show the use of CONTRACT and EXPAND. With these commands, large designs can be reduced to summary form. These commands are very useful in practice.

automatically from a dependency diagram or data navigation diagram. The objective is to speed up as much as possible the task of creating error-free code.

With different menus of commands for different languages, a designer may switch from one language to another if necessary. This facilitates the adoption of different languages in the future.

ACTION DIAGRAMS FOR MANAGEMENT PROCEDURES

Like any other procedure, a management procedure can be represented with an action diagram. It is convenient to represent fourth-generation computer methodologies with action diagrams, because such methodologies are likely to be customized to fit the circumstances in question. A fourth-generation development lifecycle is not a fixed unchangeable lifecycle.

Throughout this book action diagrams are used to represent the methodologies of information engineering. These methodology action diagrams are found in boxes in the chapters that describe the methodology in question. Such procedures can quickly be adjusted with an action diagram editor to fit the circumstances in question.

ADVANTAGES

Action diagrams were designed to solve some of the concerns with other diagramming techniques. They were designed to have the following properties:

1. They are quick and easy to draw and to change.

2. They are good for manual sketching and for computerized editing.

3. A single technique extends from the highest overview down to coding-level detail (ultimate decomposition).

4. They draw all the constructs of traditional structured programming and are more graphic than pseudocode.

5. They are easy to teach to end users; they encourage end users to extend their capability into examination or design of detailed process logic. They arc thus designed as an information center tool.

6. They can be printed on normal-width paper rather than wall charts, making them appropriate for design with personal computers.

7. Various types of diagrams, if drawn with precision, can be converted *automatically* into action diagrams.

8. Action diagrams are designed to link to a data model.

BOX II.1 Summary of notation used in action diagrams

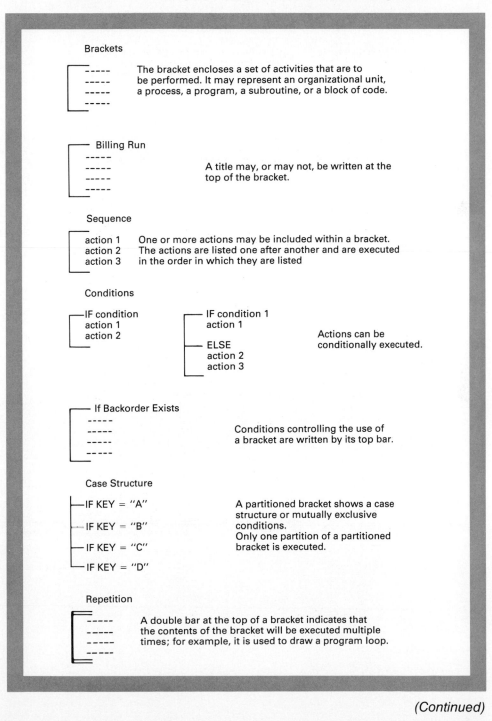

Brackets

The bracket encloses a set of activities that are to
be performed. It may represent an organizational unit,
a process, a program, a subroutine, or a block of code.

Billing Run

A title may, or may not, be written at the
top of the bracket.

Sequence

action 1 One or more actions may be included within a bracket.
action 2 The actions are listed one after another and are executed
action 3 in the order in which they are listed

Conditions

IF condition   IF condition 1
action 1   action 1   Actions can be
action 2   conditionally executed.
                    ELSE
                    action 2
                    action 3

If Backorder Exists

Conditions controlling the use of
a bracket are written by its top bar.

Case Structure

IF KEY = "A"   A partitioned bracket shows a case
                    structure or mutually exclusive
IF KEY = "B"   conditions.
                    Only one partition of a partitioned
IF KEY = "C"   bracket is executed.

IF KEY = "D"

Repetition

A double bar at the top of a bracket indicates that
the contents of the bracket will be executed multiple
times; for example, it is used to draw a program loop.

(Continued)

BOX II.1 *(Continued)*

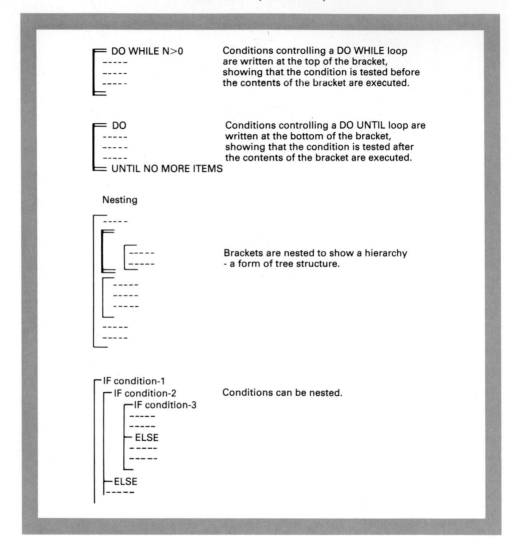

DO WHILE N>0
- - - - -
- - - - -
- - - - -

Conditions controlling a DO WHILE loop
are written at the top of the bracket,
showing that the condition is tested before
the contents of the bracket are executed.

DO
- - - - -
- - - - -
- - - - -
UNTIL NO MORE ITEMS

Conditions controlling a DO UNTIL loop are
written at the bottom of the bracket,
showing that the condition is tested after
the contents of the bracket are executed.

Nesting

- - - - -
    - - - - -
    - - - - -
- - - - -
- - - - -
- - - - -
- - - - -
- - - - -

Brackets are nested to show a hierarchy
- a form of tree structure.

IF condition-1
IF condition-2
IF condition-3
- - - - -
- - - - -
ELSE
- - - - -
- - - - -
ELSE
- - - - -

Conditions can be nested.

BOX II.1 *(Continued)*

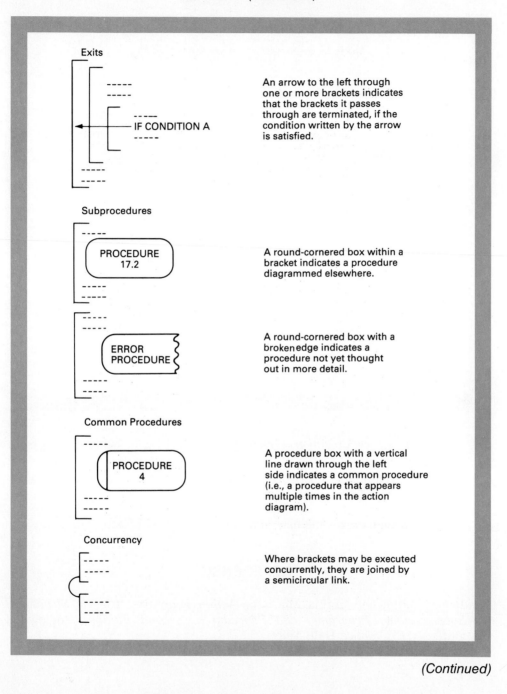

Exits

An arrow to the left through one or more brackets indicates that the brackets it passes through are terminated, if the condition written by the arrow is satisfied.

IF CONDITION A

Subprocedures

PROCEDURE 17.2

A round-cornered box within a bracket indicates a procedure diagrammed elsewhere.

ERROR PROCEDURE

A round-cornered box with a broken edge indicates a procedure not yet thought out in more detail.

Common Procedures

PROCEDURE 4

A procedure box with a vertical line drawn through the left side indicates a common procedure (i.e., a procedure that appears multiple times in the action diagram).

Concurrency

Where brackets may be executed concurrently, they are joined by a semicircular link.

(Continued)

BOX II.1 *(Continued)*

The Following Relate to Database Action Diagrams

Simple Data Action:

READ CUSTOMER

A rectangle containing
the name of a record type
or entity type is preceded
by a simple data access
action: CREATE, READ,
UPDATE, or DELETE.

Compound Data Action:

SELECT SUPPLIER from   QUOTATION

SORT CUSTOMER BY SUPPLIER

A double rectangle
containing the name
of a record type or
entity type is preceded
by a compound data access
action, such as SORT,
JOIN, PROJECT, SELECT.
Words of a nonprocedural
language may accompany
the double rectangle.

9. They work well with fourth-generation languages and can be tailored to a specific language dialect.

10. They are designed for computerized cross-checking of data usage on complex *specifications*.

   Box II.1 summarizes the diagramming conventions of action diagrams.

REFERENCE

1. James Martin and Carma McClure, *Action Diagrams: Clearly Structured Specifications, Programs, and Procedures, Second Edition.* Englewood Cliffs, N.J.: Prentice-Hall, 1989.

E. F. Codd
IBM Research Laboratory
San Jose, California

▐▐▐ FURTHER NORMALIZATION OF THE DATA BASE RELATIONAL MODEL

This definitive paper on third normal form, published by Ted Codd in 1972, is included here for the convenience of the reader. The full reference is E. F. Codd, ''Further Normalization of the Data Base Relational Model,'' in *Data Base Systems,* Randall Rustin, ed. © 1972, pp. 65–98. Reprinted by permission of Prentice-Hall, Inc., Englewood Cliffs, N. J.

In an earlier paper, the author proposed a relational model of data as a basis for protecting users of formatted data systems from the potentially disruptive changes in data representation caused by growth in the data base and changes in traffic. A first normal form for the time-varying collection of relations was introduced. In this paper, second and third normal forms are defined with the objective of making the collection of relations easier to understand and control, simpler to operate upon, and more informative to the casual user. The question, ''Can application programs be kept in a viable state when data base relations are restructured?'' is discussed briefly and it is conjectured that third normal form will significantly extend the life expectancy of application programs.

1. INTRODUCTION

1.1 Objectives of Normalization

In an earlier paper [1] the author proposed a relational model of data as a basis for protecting users of formatted data systems from the potentially disruptive changes in data representation caused by growth in the variety of data types in the data base and by statistical changes in the transaction or request traffic. Using this model, both the application programmer and the interactive user view the data base as a time-varying collection of normalized relations of assorted degrees. Definitions of these terms and of the basic relational operations of projection and natural join are given in the Appendix.

The possibility of further normalization of the database relational model was mentioned in [1]. The objectives of this further normalization are:

1. To free the collection of relations from undesirable insertion, update and deletion dependencies;
2. To reduce the need for restructuring the collection of relations as new types of data are introduced, and thus increase the life span of application programs;
3. To make the relational model more informative to users;
4. To make the collection of relations neutral to the query statistics, where these statistics are liable to change as time goes by.

The rules or conventions upon which the second and third normal forms are based can be interpreted as guidelines for the data base designer. They are also of concern in the design of general purpose, relational data base systems.

1.2 Functional Dependence

When setting up a relational database, the designer is confronted with many possibilities in selecting the relational schema itself, let alone its representation in storage. A fundamental consideration is that of identifying which attributes are functionally dependent on others (see Appendix for definition of "attribute"). Attribute B of relation R is *functionally dependent* on attribute A of R if, at every instant of time, each value in A has no more than one value in B associated with it under R. In other words, the projection $\Pi_{A,B}(R)$ is at every instant of time a function from $\Pi_A(R)$ to $\Pi_B(R)$ (this function can be, and usually will be, time-varying). We write $R.A \rightarrow R.B$ if B is functionally dependent on A in R, and $R.A \nrightarrow R.B$ if B is not functionally dependent on A in R. If both $R.A \rightarrow R.B$ and $R.B \rightarrow R.A$ hold, then at all times R.A and R.B are in one-to-one correspondence, and we write $R.A \longleftrightarrow R.B$.

The definition given above can be extended to collections of attributes. Thus, if D,E are distinct collections of attributes of R, E is functionally dependent on D if, at every instant of time, each D-value has no more than one E-value associated with it under R. The notation $\rightarrow$, $\nrightarrow$ introduced for individual attributes is applied similarly to collections of attributes. A functional dependence of the form $R.D. \rightarrow R.E$ where E is a subset of D will be called a *trivial dependence*.

As an example to illustrate functional dependence (both trivial and non-trivial), consider the relation

$$U(E\#, D\#, V\#)$$

where E# = employee serial number; D# = serial number of department to which employee belongs; and V# = serial number of division to which employee belongs.

Suppose that an employee never belongs to more than one department, that a department never belongs to more than one division, and an employee belongs to the division to which his department belongs. Then, we observe that

$$U.E\# \rightarrow U.D\# \tag{1}$$

$$U.D\# \rightarrow U.V\# \tag{2}$$

$$U.E\# \rightarrow U.V\# \tag{3}$$

$$U.(E\#,D\#) \rightarrow U.V\# \tag{4}$$

where (4) is a consequence of (3) and (3) is a consequence of (1) and (2) together.

Suppose we are also given the following additional facts: normally, there are many employees belonging to a given department and many departments belonging to a given division. Then, we may observe that

$$U.D\# \nrightarrow U.E\#$$

and

$$U.V\# \nrightarrow U.D\#$$

An example of a trivial dependence is:

$$U.(E\#,D\#) \rightarrow U.E\#$$

since E# is included in (E#,D#).

1.3   Candidate Keys

Each *candidate key* K of relation R is, by definition, a combination of attributes (possibly a single attribute) of R with properties P_1 and P_2:

P_1: *(Unique Identification)* In each tuple of R the value of K uniquely identifies that tuple; i.e., $R.K \rightarrow R.\Omega$ where Ω denotes the collection of all attributes of the specified relation;

P_2: *(Non-redundancy)* No attribute in K can be discarded without destroying property P_1.

Obviously, there always exists at least one candidate key, because the combination of *all* attributes of R possesses property P_1. It is then a matter of looking for a subset with property P_2.

Two properties of candidate keys can be deduced from P_1 and P_2:

P_3: Each attribute of R is functionally dependent on each candidate key of R;

P_4: The collection of attributes of R in a candidate key K is a maximal functionally independent set (i.e., every proper subset of the attributes of K is functionally independent of every other proper subset of attributes of K, and no other attributes of R can be added without destroying this functional independence).

It is left to the reader to show that

1. P_1 is logically equivalent to P_3.
2. $P_1 \wedge P_2$ implies P_4.
3. A maximal functionally independent set of attributes is not necessarily a candidate key.

For each relation R in a data base, one of its candidate keys is arbitrarily designated as the *primary key* of R. The usual operational distinction between the primary key and other candidate keys (if any) is that no tuple is allowed to have an undefined value for any of the primary key components, whereas any other components may have an undefined value. This restriction is imposed because of the vital role played by primary keys in search algorithms. The statement ''B functionally depends on A in R'' may be expressed in the alternative form ''A identifies B in R'', since in this case A satisfies condition P_1 for $\Pi_{A,B}(R)$.

2. SECOND NORMAL FORM

2.1 Introductory Example

The basic ideas underlying the second and third normal forms are simple, but they have many subtle ramifications. The author has found that numerous examples are needed to explain and motivate the precise definitions of these normal forms. Accordingly, we begin with the simplest case of a relation in first normal form but not in second (i.e., a relation of degree 3):

$$T(\underline{S\#},\underline{P\#},SC)$$

where   S# = supplier number

                            P# = part number

                            SC = supplier city

A triple (x,y,z) belongs to T if the supplier with serial number x supplies the part with serial number y, and supplier x has his base of operations in city z. A given part may be supplied by many suppliers, and a given supplier may supply many parts. Thus, the following time-independent conditions hold:

$$T.S\# \nrightarrow T.P\#$$

$$T.P\# \nrightarrow T.S\#$$

In other words, although the attributes $S\#$, $P\#$ are related under T, they are functionally independent of one another under T. Now, each supplier has (in this example) only one base of operations and therefore only one city. Thus,

$$T.S\# \rightarrow T.SC$$

Intuitively, we can see that the only choice for the primary key of T is the attribute combination $(S\#,P\#)$.

Looking at a sample instantaneous tabulation of T (Fig. III.1), the undesirable properties of the T schema become immediately apparent. We observe for example that, if supplier u relocates his base of operations from Poole to Tolpuddle, more than one tuple has to be updated. Worse still, the number of tuples to be updated can, and usually will, change with time. It just happens to be three tuples at this instant.

Now suppose supplier v ceases to supply parts 1 and 3, but may in the near future supply some other parts. Accordingly, we wish to retain the information that supplier v is located in Feistritz. Deletion of one of the two tuples does not cause the complete disappearance of the association of v with Feistritz, but deletion of both tuples does. This is an example of a deletion dependency which is a consequence of the relational schema itself. It is left to the reader to illustrate a corresponding insertion dependency using this example.

Conversion of T to second normal form consists of replacing T by two of its projections:

$$T_1 = \Pi_{S\#,P\#}(T)$$

$$T_2 = \Pi_{S\#,SC}(T)$$

We thus obtain the relations tabulated in Fig. III.2.

Note how the undesirable insertion, update and deletion dependencies have disappeared. No essential information has been lost, since at any time the original relation T may be recovered by taking the natural join (see Section A.3) of T_1 and T_2 on $S\#$.

```
T(S#,P#,SC)
     u     1     'POOLE'
     u     2     'POOLE'
     u     3     'POOLE'
     v     1     'FEISTRITZ'
     v     3     'FEISTRITZ'
```

Figure III.1   A relation not in second normal form.

$$T_1(\underline{S\#},\underline{P\#})$$

u	1
u	2
u	3
v	1
v	3

$$T_2(\underline{S\#},SC)$$

u	'POOLE'
v	'FEISTRITZ'

Figure III.2   Relations in second normal form.

2.2   More Probing Examples

Unfortunately, the simple example above does not illustrate all of the complexities which can arise. For expository purposes we now consider five possible relations in a data base concerning suppliers, parts, and projects. In a crude sense these relations represent five alternative possibilities—it is not intended that they coexist in a single data base. Note, however, that some contain more information (in the form of additional attributes) than others. In each case the primary key is underlined.

$$R_1(\underline{S\#,P\#,J\#})$$

$$R_2(\underline{X\#},S\#,P\#,J\#)$$

$$R_3(\underline{X\#},S\#,P\#,J\#,Q)$$

$$R_4(\underline{X\#},S\#,P\#,J\#,Q,SC)$$

$$R_5(\underline{S\#,P\#,J\#},Q,SC)$$

where

$$S\# = \text{supplier number}$$

$$P\# = \text{part number}$$

$$J\# = \text{project number}$$

$$X\# = \text{serial number}$$

$$Q = \text{quantity supplied}$$

$$SC = \text{supplier city}$$

A triple (x,y,z) belongs to R_1 if supplier x supplies part y to project z. The same interpretation holds for $\Pi_{S\#,P\#,J\#}(R_i)$ for $i = 2,3,4,5$. In each of the five relations, a given combination of supplier and part may be associated with more than one project, a given combination of part and project may be associated with more than one supplier, and a given combination of project and supplier may be associated with more than one part. Thus, for all i

$$R_i \cdot (S\#, P\#) \nrightarrow R_i \cdot (J\#)$$
$$R_i \cdot (P\#, J\#) \nrightarrow R_i \cdot (S\#)$$
$$R_i \cdot (J\#, S\#) \nrightarrow R_i \cdot (P\#)$$

In each of the relations that have the attribute Q, there is only one value of Q for a given value of the attribute combination $(S\#, P\#, J\#)$. Thus,

$$R_i \cdot (S\#, P\#, J\#) \rightarrow R_i \cdot Q \text{ for } i = 3, 4, 5.$$

However, the value of Q is not uniquely determined by any proper subset of these attributes. Thus, for $i = 3, 4, 5$

$$R_i \cdot (S\#, P\#) \nrightarrow R_i \cdot Q$$
$$R_i \cdot (P\#, J\#) \nrightarrow R_i \cdot Q$$
$$R_i \cdot (J\#, S\#) \nrightarrow R_i \cdot Q$$

In each of the relations that have the attribute SC, there is only one value of SC for a given value of S#. Thus, for $i = 4, 5$

$$R_i \cdot S\# \rightarrow R_i \cdot SC$$

In three of the relations a serial number key X# has been introduced and selected as the primary key, even though there is already an attribute combination $(S\#, P\#, J\#)$ capable of acting as the primary key. Thus, for $i = 2, 3, 4$

$$R_i \cdot X\# \leftrightarrow R_i \cdot (S\#, P\#, J\#).$$

This is not at all unusual in practice (consider a purchase order number, for instance).

In what follows, we shall suppose that in the given relations there are no functional dependencies other than those itemized above together with those that

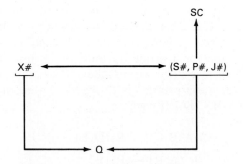

Figure III.3   Attribute dependencies in *R*.

can be formally deduced from them. Figure III.3 summarizes the non-trivial dependencies (but not the non-dependencies) in a parent relation R from which R_1, R_2, R_3, R_4, R_5 can be derived by projection.

In all five sample relations above, (S#,P#,J#) is a candidate key. In R_1 and R_5 it is the primary key also. X# is both a candidate key and the primary key in relations R_2, R_3, R_4.

2.3   Prime Attributes

We have observed that in a given relation there may be several distinct candidate keys (although distinct, they need not be disjoint) and, in this case, one is arbitrarily designated as the primary key. Let us call any attribute of R which participates in at least one candidate key of R a *prime attribute* of R. All other attributes of R are called *non-prime*. In sample relations R_1, R_2 all attributes are prime. In R_3 the only non-prime attribute is Q, while in R_4, R_5 both Q and SC are non-prime.

2.4   Full Functional Dependence

Suppose D,E are two distinct subcollections of the attributes of a relation R and

$$R.D \rightarrow R.E$$

If, in addition, E is not functionally dependent on any subset of D (other than D itself) then E is said to be *fully dependent* on D in R. Intuitively, E is functionally dependent on the whole of D, but not on any part of it. An example of full dependence is:

$$R_3 \cdot (S\#,P\#,J\#) \rightarrow R_3 \cdot Q$$

2.5   Definition of Second Normal Form

A relation R is in *second normal form* if it is in first normal form and every non-prime attribute of R is fully dependent on each candidate key of R. Although each prime attribute is dependent on each candidate key *of which it is a component,* it is possible for a prime attribute to be non-fully dependent on a candidate key of which it is not a component. Thus, this definition is changed in meaning if the term ''non-prime'' is dropped. An example which illustrates this distinction is R(A,B,C,D,E,F) where

$$R.(A,B,C) \leftrightarrow R.(D,E) \rightarrow R.F$$

$$R.(A,B) \rightarrow R.D$$

$$R.E \rightarrow R.C$$

Prime attribute C is not fully dependent on candidate key (D,E); neither is D on (A,B,C). This definition rules out both kinds of undesirable dependence of the attribute SC in the example above.

1. The obvious functional dependence of SC in R_5 on a portion S# of the primary key
2. The less obvious functional dependence of SC in R_4 on a portion S# of a candidate key that is not the primary key

Thus, R_4 and R_5 are not in second normal form.

Two special cases of the definition are worth noting. Suppose R is in first normal form and one or both of the following conditions hold:

C1: R has no non-prime attribute;

C2: Every candidate key of R consists of just a single attribute.

Then, without further investigation, we can say that R is in second normal form. Observe that both R_1 and R_2 are in second normal form, because special case C1 applies. Relation R_3 is an example of a relation in second normal form, but not as a result of the special conditions C1,C2 above.

2.6   Optimal Second Normal Form

In Section 1, a simple example of conversion from first to second normal form was discussed. The operation of projection, employed twice in that example, is adequate for the general case. However, to keep the user from being confused by unnecessary relation names (and to keep the system catalog from getting clogged by such names), projection should be applied sparingly when normalizing.

$$\text{Consider the relation } T(\underline{S\#,P\#},SN,SC)$$

where

$$S\# \rightarrow SN \text{ (supplier name)}$$
$$S\# \rightarrow SC \text{ (supplier city)}$$

If we apply projection sparingly in converting to second normal form, we obtain collection C_1, say:

$$\Pi_{S\#,P\#}(T), \ \Pi_{S\#,SN,SC}(T)$$

On the other hand, we could apply projection liberally and obtain collection C_2 say:

$$\Pi_{S\#,P\#}(T), \ \Pi_{S\#,SN}(T), \ \Pi_{S\#,SC}(T).$$

Both C_1 and C_2 are in second normal form and both retain all the essential information in the original relation T. However, collection C_1 contains the fewest possible relations, and is accordingly said to be in *optimal second normal form*. C_2 is in non-optimal second normal form.

3. THIRD NORMAL FORM

3.1 Transitive Dependence

Suppose that A,B,C are three distinct collections of attributes of a relation R (hence R is of degree 3 or more). Suppose that all three of the following time-independent conditions hold:

$$R.A \rightarrow R.B, \qquad R.B \nrightarrow R.A,$$
$$R.B \rightarrow R.C$$

From this we may conclude that two other conditions must hold:

$$R.A \rightarrow R.C \qquad R.C \nrightarrow R.A$$

and we may represent the entire set of conditions on A,B,C as shown in Fig. III.4. Note that $R.C \rightarrow R.B$ is neither prohibited nor required.

In such a case we say that C is *transitively dependent* on A under R. In the special case where $R.C \rightarrow R.B$ also, both B and C are transitively dependent on A under R.

To illustrate transitive dependence, consider a relation W concerning employees and their departments:

$$W(\underline{E\#},JC,D\#,M\#,CT)$$

where   E# = employee serial number

JC = employee jobcode

D# = department number of employee

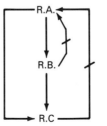

Figure III.4   Transitive dependence of *C* on *A* under *R*.

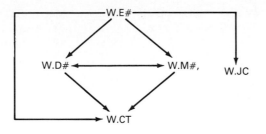

Figure III.5   Example of several transitive dependencies.

M# = serial number of department manager

CT = contract type (government or non-government)

Suppose that each employee is given only one jobcode and is assigned to only one department. Each department has its own manager and is involved in work on either government or non-government contracts, not both. The non-trivial functional dependencies in W are as shown in Fig. III.5 (the non-dependencies are implied). If M# were not present, the only transitive dependence would be that of CT on E#. With M# present, there are two additional transitive dependencies: both D# and M# are transitively dependent on E#. Note, however, that CT is not transitively dependent on either D# or M#.

Looking at a sample instantaneous tabulation of W (Fig. III.6) the undesirable properties of the W schema become immediately apparent. We observe, for example, that, if the manager of department y should change, more than one tuple has to be updated. The actual number of tuples to be updated can, and usually will, change with time. A similar remark applies if department x is switched from government work (contract type g) to non-government work (contract type n).

Deletion of the tuple for an employee has two possible consequences: deletion of the corresponding department information if his tuple is the sole one remaining just prior to deletion, and non-deletion of the department information otherwise. If the data base system does not permit any primary key to have an

W(E#,	JC,	D#,	M#,	CT)
1	a	x	11	g
2	c	x	11	g
3	a	y	12	n
4	b	x	11	g
5	b	y	12	n
6	c	y	12	n
7	a	z	13	n
8	c	z	13	n

Figure III.6   A relation not in third normal form.

W_1(E#,	JC,	D#)	W_2(D#,	M#	CT)
1	a	x	x	11	g
2	c	x	y	12	n
3	a	y	z	13	n
4	b	x			
5	b	y			
6	c	y			
7	a	z			
8	c	z			

Figure III.7   Relations in third normal form.

undefined value, then D# and CT information for a new department cannot be established in relation W before people are assigned to that department. If, on the other hand, the primary key E# could have an undefined value, and if a tuple were introduced with such a value for E# together with defined values for D# (a new department) and CT, then insertion of E# and JC values for the first employee in that department involves no new tuple, whereas each subsequent assignment of an employee to that department does require a new tuple to be inserted.

Conversion of W to third normal form consists of replacing W by two of its projections:

$$W_1 = \Pi_{E\#,JC,D\#}(W)$$

$$W_2 = \Pi_{D\#,M\#,CT}(W)$$

We thus obtain the relations tabulated in Fig. III.7.

Note how the undesirable insertion, update and deletion dependencies have disappeared with the removal of the transitive dependencies. No essential information has been lost, since at any time the original relation W may be recovered by taking the natural join of W_1 and W_2 on D#.

3.2 Keybreaking Transitive Dependence

It is not always possible to remove all transitive dependencies without breaking a key or losing information. This is illustrated by a relation R(A,B,C) in which

$$R.(A,B) \rightarrow R.C, \quad R.C \nrightarrow R.(A,B)$$

$$R.C \rightarrow R.B$$

Thus, B is transitively dependent on the primary key (A,B).

3.3   Definition of Third Normal Form

A relation R is in *third normal form* if it is in second normal form and every non-prime attribute of R is non-transitively dependent on each candidate key of R. Relations T_1, T_2, R_1, R_2, R_3 of Section 2.1 are in third normal form. Relations R_4, R_5 are not in third normal form, because they are not even in second. Relation U of section 1.2 is in second normal form, but not in third, because of the transitive dependence of V# on E#.

Any relation R in third normal form has the following property:

P_5: 'Every non-prime attribute of R is both fully dependent and non-transitively dependent on each candidate key of R.

This property is an immediate consequence of the definition given above. Note that the definition has been so formulated that it does not prohibit transitive dependence of a prime attribute on a candidate key of R, as in Section 3.2.

3.4   Optimal Third Normal Form

Suppose C_2 is a collection of relations in optimal second normal form and projection is applied to convert to third normal form. The resulting collection of relations C_3 is in optimal third normal form relative to C_2 if both of the following conditions hold:

1. C_3 must contain the fewest possible relations (as in the case of the optimal second normal form) each in third normal form;
2. Each relation in C_3 must not have any pair of attributes such that one member of the pair is strictly transitively dependent on the other in some relation of C_2 (this condition forces attributes which are "remotely related" to be separated from one another in the normalized collection of relations).

(*Note:* Attribute C is *strictly transitively dependent* on attribute A under R if there is an attribute B such that

$$R.A \rightarrow R.B \quad , \quad R.B \nrightarrow R.A$$
$$R.B \rightarrow R.C \quad , \quad R.C \nrightarrow R.B$$

This is a special case of transitive dependence.)

Application of these conditions is illustrated in Figs. III.8(a) and III.8(b) using the relation W of Section 3.1. Figure III.8(a) treats the normalization of W_0 (obtained from W by dropping manager number M#). Figure III.8(b) treats the normalization of W itself, and shows how one-to-one correspondences are forced to occur between candidate keys of the projections (instead of between non-prime attributes). Note also the non-uniqueness of the optimal third normal form in Fig. III.8(b).

W_0(E#, JC, D#, CT)					
Collection of Projections of W_0			**TNF**	**Optimal**	**Violates**
E# → JC	E# → D#	E# → CT	Yes	No	1, 2
E# → JC E# → D#	E# → CT		Yes	No	2
E# → JC E# → D#	D# → CT		Yes	Yes	NIL

Figure III.8(a) Conversion of W_0 to third normal form.

W(E#, JC, D#, M#, CT)					
Collection of, Projections of W			**TNF**	**Optimal**	**Comments**
E# → JC E# → D# E# → M#	E# → CT OR M# → CT OR D# → CT		No	—	D# and M# are transitively dependent on E#
E# → JC	E# → D#	D# ↕ M# D# → CT M# → CT	Yes	No	Violates 1
E# → JC E# → D#	D# ↕ M# D# → CT M# → CT		Yes	Yes	Violates NIL
E# → JC E# → M#	D# ↕ M# D# → CT M# → CT		Yes	Yes	Violates NIL

Figure III.8(b) Conversion of W to third normal form.

4. ADMISSIBLE STATES

When converting a time-varying data base from first normal form to second, or from second to third, certain new insertion and deletion possibilities are introduced. Let us look at the example in Section 2.1 again.

In first normal form the data base B_1 consists of the single time-varying relation denoted by the schema

$$T(\underline{S\#,P\#},SC)$$

In second normal form the corresponding data base B_2 consists of two relations denoted by the schema

$$T_1(\underline{S\#,P\#}) \qquad T_2(\underline{S\#},SC)$$

where, for any time

1. $T_1 = \Pi_{S\#,P\#}(T)$
2. $T_2 = \Pi_{S\#,SC}(T)$

As usual, the primary keys are underlined.

A data base state (i.e., instantaneous snapshot) is *admissible* relative to a given schema if

1. each relation named in the schema has tuples whose components belong to the specified domains;
2. all tuples of a relation named in the schema are distinct;
3. no tuple has an undefined value for its primary key (and thus no *component* of the primary key may have an undefined value).

The last condition makes an operational distinction between that candidate key selected to act as the primary key of a relation and all other candidate keys of that relation.

Given any admissible state for B_1, we can produce a corresponding admissible state for B_2 by applying the operation of projection as in the example above. The original B_1 state can be recovered by taking the natural join (see Appendix for definition) of T_1 and T_2 on $S\#$.

We now observe that the schema for B_2 has more admissible states than that for B_1. Thus, in B_2 it is perfectly admissible to have a $S\#$ value appearing in T_2 which does not appear at all in T_1, or vice versa, as in the B_2-state exhibited in Fig. III.9.

If we now take the natural join of T_1 and T_2 on $S\#$, we obtain the state (or tabulation) of T exhibited in Fig. III.10. Although this state is admissible for B_1, essential information has been lost.

$$T_1(S\#, P\#)$$
u	1
u	2
v	1
z	3

$$T_2(S\#, SC)$$
u	'POOLE'
v	'FEISTRITZ'
w	'SWANAGE'

Figure III.9   An admissible state for B_2.

An obvious property of the class of admissible states for a given data base schema is that by means of the operations of tuple insertion and tuple deletion all the admissible states are reachable from any given admissible state. Clearly, the schema for B_2 permits insertions and deletions not permitted by the schema for B_1. It is accordingly reasonable to say that these schemata are not *insertion-deletion equivalent*.

5. QUERY EQUIVALENCE

A useful notion of *query equivalence* of data base states can be based on the algebraic view of queries.

In this view retrieval of data is treated as the formation of a new relation from the data base relations by some operation of a relational algebra (see [2]).

If θ is a relational algebra, B is a collection of relations and R is a relation which is derivable from B using operations of the algebra θ only, then we say (as in [1]) that R is θ-*derivable* from B. Suppose now that we have two data bases A,B which at time t are in states A_t, B_t respectively. We say that the data base states A_t, B_t are *query-equivalent* providing they are each θ-dcrivable from the other and θ is a relationally complete algebra (see [2]). The reasonableness of this definition stems from the fact that, if each of the data-base states A_t, B_t is θ-derivable from the other, then any relation R which is θ-derivable from one must be θ-derivable from the other.

Figure III.11 summarizes the observations made in Section 4 on admissible states. It also illustrates the fact that the set S of all admissible states for a data base cast in first normal form is query-equivalent to a subset T_1 of all admissible states when this data base is cast in second normal form. Similarly, the set $T_1 u T_2$ of all admissible states for this data base cast in second normal form is query-equivalent to a subset U_1 of all admissible states when the same data base is cast in third normal form.

$$T(\underline{S\#, P\#}, SC)$$
u	1	'POOLE'
u	2	'POOLE'
v	1	'FEISTRITZ'

Figure III.10   The natural join of relations in Fig. III.9.

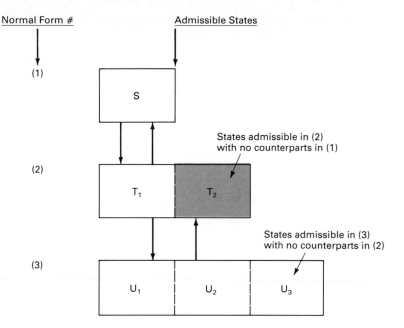

Figure III.11   Admissible states for a database cast in normal forms 1, 2, and 3.

6. GROWTH AND RESTRUCTURING

One of the principal reasons for making application programs interact with an abstract collection of relations instead of their storage representations is to keep these programs from being logically impaired when the storage representations change. Now we wish to consider (but only briefly) what happens to the application programs when the collection of relations is itself changed to conform to a new schema. Simple additions of new data base domains and new relations have no effect. Outright removal of a relation R obviously cripples those programs that previously made use of R. Replacement of a relation by *one* of its projections will cripple those programs that previously made use of the attributes now dropped.

The really interesting type of change is replacement of a relation R by two or more of its projections such that R may be recovered by taking the natural join of these projections. We discussed this type of change in sections 2 and 3 in the context of conversion to second and third normal forms respectively. In the present context of data base growth we call this phenomenon *attribute migration*.

Some of the reasons why attribute migration may accompany data base growth are as follows:

1. Through continued acquisition of additional attributes a relation has become too cumbersome in size and fuzzy in meaning;

2. New controls (e.g., ownership of data, access authorization, recovery, etc.) are being introduced;

3. There has been a change in that part of the real world which the data base reflects or models.

To illustrate the effect of attribute migration on application programs, consider the splitting of data base relation $U(E\#,JC,D\#,M\#,CT)$ into the two projections:

$$U1 = \Pi_{E\#,JC,D\#}(U)$$

$$U2 = \Pi_{D\#,M\#,CT}(U)$$

(See Section 3.1 for the interpretation of U and its attributes.)

We first examine a query and then an insertion. Each is expressed in the data base sublanguage ALPHA [3].

**Find the contract type (CT) for the employee whose serial number (E#) is 1588. Place result in workspace W.

GET   W   U.CT:(U.E# = 1588)

When U is replaced by the two projections U1, U2, queries on U must undergo a transformation to make them work as before. If the data base system were supplied with a suitable set of substitutions it could make this transformation automatically. We do not propose to go into the details here, but merely state that the resulting transformed query would be:

GET   W   U2.CT: $\exists$U1((U1.D# = U2.D#)$\wedge$(U1.E# = 1588))

The real difficulty arises with insertion and deletion.

**Insert from workspace W into the data base relation U a tuple for a new employee with serial number 1492 and contract type non-government (n). Values for his jobcode, department number, and manager number are not yet available.

PUT   W   U

When data base relation U is replaced by U1, U2 and we attempt to transform this insertion to make it work on these projections, we find that the insertion of two new tuples is necessary: one into U1, and one into U2. The insertion into U1 presents no problem, because we have a value (1492) for its primary key component (E#). In the case of U2, however, we do not have a value for its primary key component (D#). To cope with this difficulty, the system could temporarily insert a fictitious (but defined) value to represent a department (as yet undetermined) which is assigned to non-government work. Unfortunately, when the total data base is considered together with all the possible partially defined associations which may have to be temporarily remembered, the system may require a very large pool of fictitious values to call upon.

We have seen that attribute migration can logically impair an application program. Further, it may be feasible to systematically re-interpret the data base requests made by a program P so as to make P work correctly again. This problem is simpler for those programs that avoid insertion and deletion on the relations affected by attribute migration. Whether or not this special case holds, the re-interpretation is likely to cause significant system overhead. Avoidance of attribute migration is accordingly desirable. It is this author's thesis that, by casting the data base in third normal form at the earliest possible time and by keeping it that way, an installation will reduce the incidence of attribute migration to a minimum, and consequently have less trouble keeping its application programs in a viable state.

7. CONCLUSION

In Section 1 we introduced the notion of functional dependence within a relation—a notion that is fundamental in formatted data base design. Using this notion, two new normal forms were defined. Figure III.12 summarizes the relationship between the three normal forms introduced by this author. Notice that as a collection of relations is translated from first normal form to second, and then to third, the conditions applied are progressively more stringent.

In the past, design of records (computerized or not) for commercial, industrial and government institutions has been oriented in an ad hoc way to the needs of particular applications. For the large integrated data bases of the future, application-independent guidelines for logical record design are sorely needed. This paper is intended to provide such guidelines.

It is also conjectured that physical records in optimal third normal form will prove to be highly economical in space consumed. In some cases a further saving in space can be obtained by factoring (see [2]) relations in third normal form.

Although the three normal forms are query-equivalent in the sense that the set of queries answerable by a collection C in first normal form is transformable into queries yielding the same information from the second and third normal

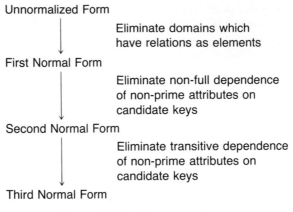

Unnormalized Form

Eliminate domains which
have relations as elements

First Normal Form

Eliminate non-full dependence
of non-prime attributes on
candidate keys

Second Normal Form

Eliminate transitive dependence
of non-prime attributes on
candidate keys

Third Normal Form

Figure III.12   Three normal forms.

forms of C, there is a difference in information content of the three forms. The second is more informative than the first, and the third is more informative than the second. The increased information lies in the data description (rather than in the data described) as a consequence of the underlying conventions. Like the declarations of redundancies and combinational possibilities within the relational model (see [1]), the normal forms described above tend to capture some aspects of the semantics (minor, of course). Thus, a relational model in second normal form, and more especially, one in third normal form is likely to be more readily understood by people who are not everyday users of the data. It is also likely to be better tuned to the authorization requirements of installations.

Compared with first normal form, the second and third do carry with them the penalty of extra names. In the many data bases that have relations of high degree, this name penalty will not be nearly as severe as that associated with a complete conversion to nested binary relations.

Some queries will also need to employ more join terms for cross-referencing between relations than might otherwise be the case. This potential burden on the user can be eased by user-declared (and possibly pooled) cross-referencing for heavily used types of queries.

ACKNOWLEDGMENTS   The author is indebted to Claude Delobel of the Conservatoire National des Arts et Metiers, Paris for indicating an inadequacy in the treatment of one-to-one correspondences in an early draft of this paper. Working from this draft, C. J. Date, I. J. Heath and P. Hopewell of the IBM Development Laboratory in Hursley, England have developed some theoretical and practical applications of the third normal form, which will be published soon [4,5]. Their interest in and enthusiasm for the third normal form encouraged the author to produce a more detailed paper than the original version. Thanks are also due to F. P. Palermo and J. J. Rissanen of IBM Research, San Jose for suggesting changes which improved the clarity.

REFERENCES

1. E. F. Codd, A relational model of data for large shared data banks, *CACM 13*(6), 377–387, June 1970.

2. E. F. Codd, Relational completeness of data base sublanguages, *this volume*.

3. E. F. Codd, *A Data Base Sublanguage Founded on the Relational Calculus, IBM Research Report RJ893,* July 1971.

4. I. J. Heath, Unacceptable file operations in a relational data base, Proc. 1971 ACM-SIGFIDET Workshop on Data Description, Access and Control, to be available from ACM HQ, 1972.

5. C. J. Date, P. Hopewell, File definition and logical data independence, Proc 1971 ACM-SIGFIDET Workshop on Data Description, Access and Control, to be available from ACM HQ, 1972.

APPENDIX

A1. Basic Definitions

Given sets $D_1,D_2,\ldots,D_n$ (not necessarily distinct), R is a *relation* on these n sets if it is a set of elements of the form $(d_1,d_2,\ldots,d_n)$ where $d_j \epsilon D_j$ for each $j=1,2,\ldots,n$. More concisely, R is a subset of the Cartesian product $D_1 x D_2 x \ldots x D_n$. We refer to D_j as the jth *domain* of R. The elements of a relation of degree n are called *n-tuples* or *tuples*. A relation is in *first normal form* if it has the property that none of its domains has elements which are themselves sets. An *unnormalized relation* is one which is not in first normal form.

   A data base B is a finite collection of time-varying relations defined on a finite collection of domains, say $D_1,D_2,\ldots,D_p$. Suppose relation R is one of the relations in B, and is of degree n. To declare R to a data base system we need to cite n of the p data base domains as those on which R is defined.

   Now, not all these n cited domains need be distinct. Instead of using an ordering to distinguish these n citations from one another (as is common in mathematics), we use a distinct name for each citation and call this the *attribute name* for that particular use of a data base domain. Each distinct use (or citation) of a data base domain in defining R is accordingly called an *attribute* of R. For example, a relation R of degree 3 might have attributes (A_1, A_2, A_3) while the corresponding data base domains are (D_5, D_7, D_5). Attribute names provide an effective means of protecting the user from having to know domain positions.

A2. Projection

Suppose r is a tuple of relation R and A is an attribute of R. We adopt the notation r.A to designate the A-component of r. Now suppose A is instead a list $(A_1, A_2, \ldots, A_k)$ of attributes of R. We extend the notation r.A so that, in this case:

$$r.A = (r.A_1, r.A_2, \ldots, r.A_k)$$

When the list A is empty, r.A = r.

Let $C = (C_1, C_2, \ldots, C_n)$ be a list of all the attributes of R. Let A be a sublist (length k) of C and r a tuple of R. Then, we adopt the notation $r.\bar{A}$ to designate the (n-k)-tuple r.B where B is the complementary list of attributes obtained by deleting from C those listed in A.

The *projection* of R on the attribute list A is defined by

$$\Pi_A(R) = \{r.A: r\epsilon R\}$$

A more informal definition is given in [1].

A3. Natural Join

Suppose R,S are two relations and

$$A = (A_1, \ldots, A_k), \quad B = (B_1, \ldots, B_k)$$

are equal-length lists of the attributes of R,S respectively. Suppose that for i = 1,2, . . .,k attributes A_i, B_i are comparable: that is, for every $r\epsilon R$, $s\epsilon S$

$$r.A_i = s.B_i$$

is either true or false (not undefined). We say that

$$r.A = s.B$$

if $(r.A_1 = s.B_1)\hat{} \ldots \hat{}(r.A_k = s.B_k)$

Then, the *natural join* of R on A with S on B is defined by:

$$R*S = \{(r,s.\bar{B}): r\epsilon R \hat{} s\epsilon S \hat{} (r.A = s.B)\}$$

This definition is the same as that given in [1] except that there is no requirement that

$$\Pi_A(R) = \Pi_B(S)$$

for relations R,S to be joinable. This condition was imposed in [1] solely for the purposes of treating redundancy and consistency.

Appendix

IV BUBBLE CHARTS FOR DATA ANALYSIS

Bubble charts provide a valuable way to teach users and analysts about data structures. The most elemental piece of data the *data item* (sometimes also called a *field* or a *data element*) is the atom of data, in that it cannot be subdivided into smaller data types and retain any meaning to users of the data. You cannot split the data item called SALARY, for example, into smaller data items which by themselves are meaningful to end users. In a bubble chart each *type* of data item is drawn as an ellipse:

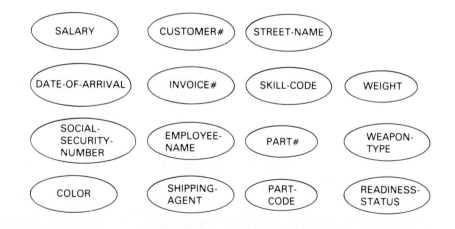

ASSOCIATIONS BETWEEN DATA ITEMS

A data item by itself is not of much use. For example, a value of SALARY by itself is uninteresting. It becomes interesting only when it is associated with another data item, such as EMPLOYEE-NAME:

A database, therefore, consists not only of data items but also of associations among them. There are a large number of different data-item types and we need a map showing how they are associated. This map is sometimes called a *data model*.

ONE-TO-ONE AND ONE-TO-MANY ASSOCIATIONS
There are two kinds of links that we shall draw between data items: a one-to-one association and a one-to-many association. A one-to-one association from data item type A to data item type B means that *at each instant in time, each value of A has one and only one value of B associated with it*. There is a one-to-one mapping from A to B. If you know the value of A, you can know the value of B.

There is only one value of SALARY associated with a value of EMPLOYEE# at one instant in time; therefore, we can draw a one-to-one link from EMPLOYEE# to SALARY. It is drawn as a small bar across the link:

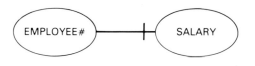

It is said that EMPLOYEE# *identifies* SALARY. If you know the value of EMPLOYEE#, you can know the value of SALARY.

A one-to-many link from A to B means that *one value of A has one or many values of B associated with it*. This is drawn with a crow's foot. While an employee can only have one salary at a given time, he might have one or many girlfriends. Therefore, we would draw

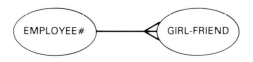

For one value of the data item type EMPLOYEE# there can be one or many values of the data item type GIRLFRIEND.

We can draw both of the foregoing situations on one bubble chart:

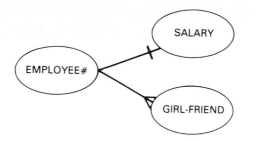

This *synthesizes* the two preceding charts into one chart. From this one chart we could derive either of the two preceding charts. The two preceding charts might be two different user views, one user being interested in salary and the other in girlfriends. We have created one simple data structure which incorporates these two user views. This is what the data administrator does when building a database, but the real-life user views are much more complicated than the illustration above and there are many of them. The resulting data model sometimes has hundreds or even thousands of data-item types.

Note:

    Some analysts draw the one-to-one and one-to-many associations as single-headed and double-headed arrows. Thus:

—————————————|—— is drawn as —————————————→

—————————————⊰ is drawn as —————————————⇶

    The author has used the single-headed and double-headed arrows in earlier books. These are avoided here because arrows tend to suggest a flow or time sequence, and are used extensively for this in other types of diagrams. The one-to-one symbol is extremely important in the processes of normalizing and synthesizing data—the basis of data analysis.

TYPES AND INSTANCES

The terms with which we describe data can refer to *types* of data or to *instances* of that data. "EMPLOYEE-NAME" refers to a type of data item. "FRED SMITH" is an *instance* of this data-item type. "EMPLOYEE" may refer to a type of record. There are many instances of this record type, one for each person employed. The diagrams in this chapter show *types* of data, not instances. A data model shows the associations among *types* of data.

    The bubble chart shows data-item types. There are many occurrences of each data-item type. In the example above, there are many employees, each with a salary and with zero, one, or many girlfriends. The reader might imagine a third dimension to the bubble charts, showing the many values of each data-item type, thus:

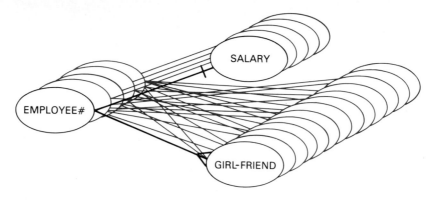

In discussing data we ought to distinguish between types and instances. Sometimes, abbreviated wording is used in literature about data. The words "DATA ITEM" or "RECORD" are used to mean "DATA ITEM TYPE" or "RECORD TYPE."

REVERSE ASSOCIATIONS

Between any two data item types there can be a mapping in both directions. This gives four possibilities for forward and reverse association. If the data-item types are MAN and WOMAN, and the relationship between them represents *marriage,* the four theoretical possibilities are:

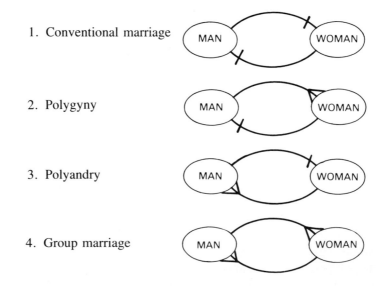

The reverse associations are not always of interest. For example, with the following bubble chart:

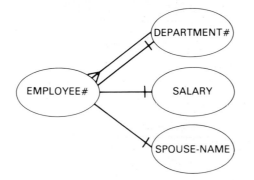

we want the reverse association from DEPARTMENT# to EMPLOYEE# because users want to know what employees work in a given department. However, there is no link from SPOUSE-NAME to EMPLOYEE# because no user wants to ask: "What employee has a spouse named Gertrude?" If a user wanted to ask "What employees have a salary over $25,000?" we might include a crow's-foot link from SALARY to EMPLOYEE#.

KEYS AND ATTRIBUTES

Given the bubble chart method of representing data, we can state three important definitions:

1. Primary key
2. Secondary key
3. Attribute

A primary key is a bubble with one or more one-to-one links going to other bubbles. Thus, in Fig. IV.1, *A, C,* and *F* are primary keys.

A primary key may uniquely identify many data items. Data items that are not primary keys are referred to as *nonprime attributes*. All data items, then, are either *primary keys* or *nonprime attributes*.

In Fig. IV.1, *B, D, E, G, H,* and *I* are nonprime attributes. Often the word "attribute" is used instead of "nonprime attribute." Strictly, the primary key data items are attributes also. EMPLOYEE# is an attribute of the employee.

The names of data-item types that are primary keys are underlined in the bubble charts and drawings of records. We can define a nonprime attribute as follows:

A nonprime attribute is a bubble with no one-to-one links going to another bubble.

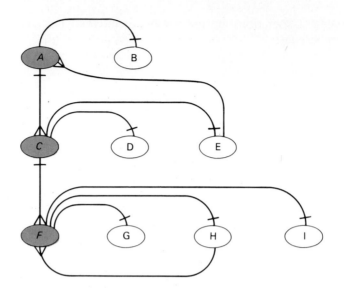

Figure IV.1   A bubble chart showing one-to-one (————+) and one-to-many
(————<) associations among data item types.

Each primary key uniquely identifies one or more data items. Those which are not other primary keys are attributes.

A *secondary key* does not uniquely identify another data item. One value of a secondary key is associated with one or many values of another data item. In other words, there is a crow's-foot link going from it to that other item.

> A secondary key is a nonprime attribute with one or more crow's-foot links to other data items.

In Fig. IV.1, *E* and *H* are secondary keys.

For emphasis, the following box repeats these three fundamental definitions.

A *PRIMARY KEY* is a bubble with one or more one-to-one links going to other bubbles.

A *NONPRIME ATTRIBUTE* is a bubble with no one-to-one link going to another bubble.

A *SECONDARY KEY* is an attribute with one or more one-to-many links going to other bubbles.

DATA-ITEM GROUPS

When using a database, we need to extract multiple different views of data from one overall database structure. The bubble charts representing these different views of data can be merged into one overall chart. In the bubble chart that results from combining many user views, the bubbles are grouped by primary key. Each primary key is the unique identifier of a group of data-item types. It has one-to-one links to each nonprime attribute in that group.

The data-item group needs to be structured carefully so that it is as stable as possible. We should not group together an ad hoc collection of data items. There are formal rules for structuring the data-item group, which are part of the normalization process (Chapter 9).

RECORDS

The data-item group is commonly called a *record,* sometimes a *logical record* to distinguish it from whatever may be stored physically. A record is often drawn as a bar containing the names of its data items, as in Fig. IV.2. The record in Fig. IV.2 represents the following bubble chart:

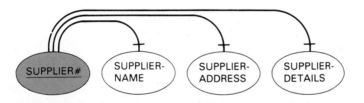

It may be useful to split the SUPPLIER ADDRESS data item into component data items:

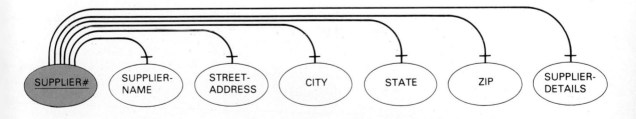

This is useful only if the components may be individually referenced.

Figure IV.3 shows the record redrawn to show that STREET-ADDRESS, CITY, STATE, and ZIP are referred collectively to as SUPPLIER-ADDRESS but are not by themselves a record with primary key.

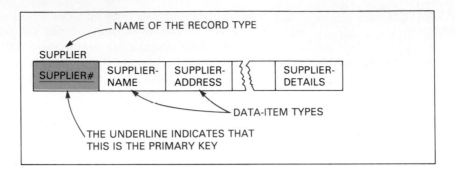

Figure IV.2   A drawing of a record.

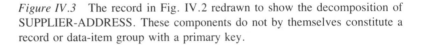

Figure IV.3   The record in Fig. IV.2 redrawn to show the decomposition of SUPPLIER-ADDRESS. These components do not by themselves constitute a record or data-item group with a primary key.

CONCATENATED KEYS

Some data-item types cannot be identified by any single data-item type in a user's view. They need a primary key (unique identifier) which is composed of more than one data-item type in combination. This is called a concatenated key.

Several suppliers may supply a part and each charge a different price for it. The primary key SUPPLIER# is used for identifying information about a *supplier*. The key PART# is used for identifying information about a *part*. Neither of those keys is sufficient for identifying the *price*. The price is dependent on both the supplier and the part. We create a new key to identify the price, which consists of SUPPLIER# and PART# joined together (concatenated). We draw this as one bubble:

The two data items from which the concatenated key is created are joined with a "+" symbol.

The concatenated key has one-to-one links to the keys SUPPLIER# and PART#. The resulting graph is as follows:

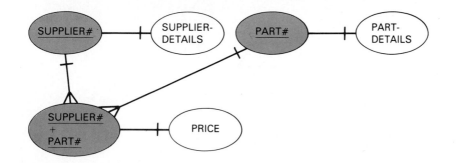

By introducing this form of concatenated key into the logical view of data, we make each data item dependent on one key bubble.

Whenever a concatenated key is introduced, the designer should ensure that the items it identifies are dependent on the whole key, not on a portion of it only.

In practice it is sometimes necessary to join together *more than two* data item types in a concatenated key. For example, a company supplies a product to domestic and industrial customers. It charges a different price to different *types of customers,* and the price varies from one *state* to another. There is a *discount* giving different price reductions for different quantities purchased. The *price* is identified by a combination of CUSTOMER-TYPE, STATE, DISCOUNT, and PRODUCT:

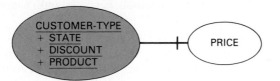

The use of concatenated keys gives each data item group in the resulting data model a simple structure in which each nonprime attribute is fully dependent on the key bubble and nothing else:

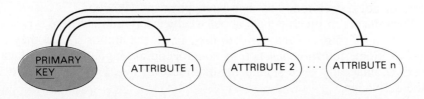

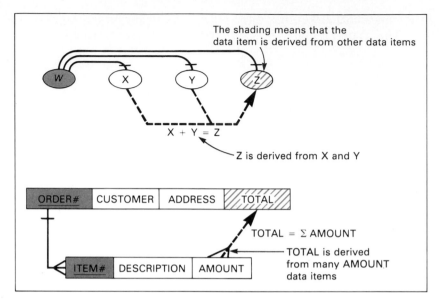

Figure IV.4   Derived data-item types shown on diagrams of data.

DERIVED DATA   Certain data items are derived by calculation from
                       other data items. For example, TOTAL-AMOUNT
on an invoice may be derived by adding the AMOUNT data items on individual
lines. A derived data-item type may be marked on a bubble chart by shading its
ellipse. Boldfaced lines or colored lines may be drawn to the derived data-item
type from the data-item types from which it is derived. Figure IV.4 illustrates
this.

Where possible the calculation for deriving a data item should be written
on the diagram, as in Fig. IV.4. Sometimes the computation may be too complex and the diagram refers to a separate specification. It might refer to a decision tree or table that shows a derived data item.

Derived data items may or may not be stored with the data. They might
be calculated whenever the data is retrieved. To store them requires more storage; to calculate them each time requires more processing. As storage drops in
cost, it is increasingly attractive to store them. The diagrams initially drawn are
logical representations of data that represent derived data without saying
whether or not it is stored. This is a later, physical decision.

There has been much debate about whether derived data-item types should
be shown on diagrams of data or data models. In the author's view they should
be shown. Some fourth-generation or nonprocedural languages cause data to be
derived automatically once statements like those in Fig. IV.4 are made describing the derivation.

THE HOUSE OF MUSIC INC.

A Collins Corporation
Main Office
108 Old Street, White Cliffs, IL 67309
063 259 0003

SALES CONTRACT

Contract No. 7094

SOLD BY	Mike	DATE	6/10/83

Name   Herbert H. Matlock

Address   1901 Keel Road

City   Ramsbottom, Illinois   Zip   64736

Phone   063 259 3730   Customer #   18306

REMARKS:

10 yrs. parts and labor on the Piano
1 yr. parts and labor on pianocorder

Delivery Address:

DESCRIPTION	PRICE	DISCOUNT	AMOUNT
New Samick 5'2" Grand Piano model G-1A			
# 820991 with Marantz P-101 # 11359			9500.00
		TOTAL AMOUNT	9500.00
		TRADE IN ALLOWANCE	2300.00
		SALES TAX	
		DEPOSIT	1000.00
		FINAL BALANCE	6200.00

PLEASE NOTE: All sales pending approval by management and verification of trade-in description.

If this contract is breached by the BUYER, the SELLER may take appropriate legal action, or, at its option, retain the deposit as liquidated damages.

Buyer's Signature _____

Figure IV.5   A sales contract. The data-item types on this document and their associations are diagrammed in Figs. IV.6 and IV.7.

OPTIONAL DATA ITEMS

Sometimes a data-item type may or may not exist. For one value of *A* there may be zero or one value of *B*. This is indicated by putting a "O" on the cardinality indicator:

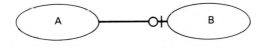

For example:

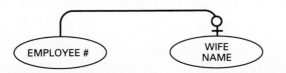

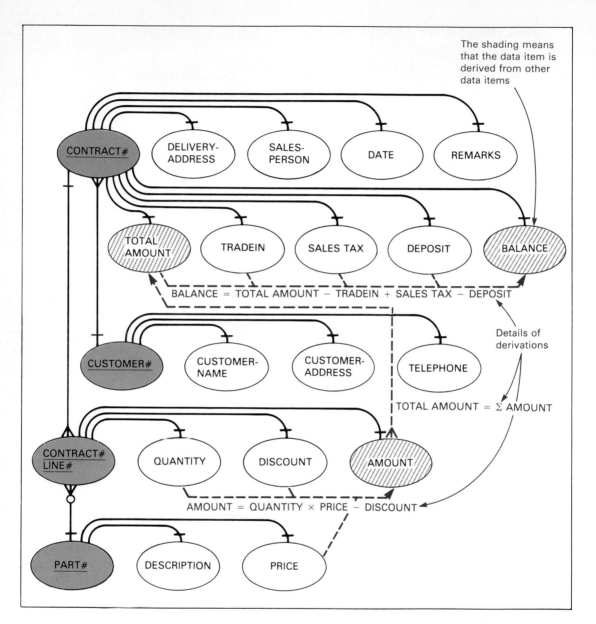

The shading means that the data item is derived from other data items

BALANCE = TOTAL AMOUNT − TRADEIN + SALES TAX − DEPOSIT

Details of derivations

TOTAL AMOUNT = Σ AMOUNT

AMOUNT = QUANTITY × PRICE − DISCOUNT

Figure IV.6 A data analysis diagram showing the data items on the sales contract of Fig. IV.5 and the associations among them. The diagram is drawn in a more formal style than the others in the chapter for ease of computer representation.

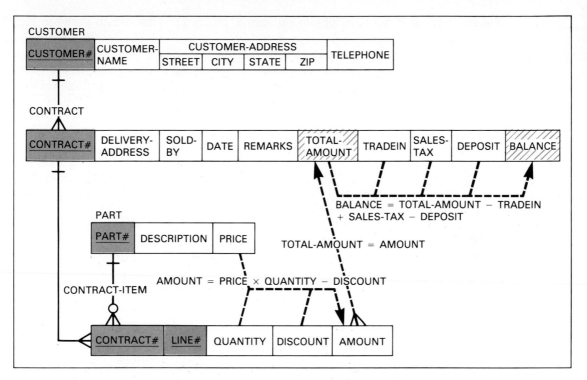

Figure IV.7 A record diagram of the data in Fig. IV.6. The derivation
expressions could be recorded separately.

If the optional bubble is a nonprime attribute (rather than a primary key),
it may be treated like any other nonprime attribute when synthesizing the data
model.

Optionality applies to one-to-many associations also:

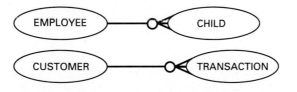

DATA ANALYSIS

When data analysis is performed, the analyst examines the data-item types that are needed and draws a
diagram of the dependencies among the data items. The one-to-one and one-to-

many links that we have drawn on bubble charts are also drawn between records, as in Fig. IV.4.

Figures IV.5 through IV.7 illustrate data analysis. Figure IV.5 shows a sales contract. The data-item types on this contract are charted in Figure IV.6. The bubble chart of Figure IV.6 is redrawn as a record diagram in Figure IV.7.

V CANONICAL SYNTHESIS

This appendix describes the use of synthesis to build a canonical data model—a minimal, nonredundant, fully normalized representation of the data in an enterprise. We have emphasized that this representation of data needs to be as stable as possible because it is the foundation stone of most future systems. It is the use of a common data model that enables separately built systems to work together.

SYNTHESIZING VIEWS OF DATA

The data modeling process takes many separate views of data and *synthesizes* them into a structure that incorporates all of them. The synthesis is done in such a way that redundant data items are eliminated where possible. The same data item does not generally appear twice in the final result. Also, redundant *associations* are eliminated where possible. In other words, a minimal number of lines connects the bubbles in the resulting bubble chart.

The synthesis process is a formal procedure following a formal set of rules. It should be done by computer. This eliminates errors in the process, provides formal documentation which is a basis for end-user discussion, and permits any input view to be changed or new views to be added and immediately reflects the effect of the change in the resulting data model.

SYNTHESIS ILLUSTRATION

As a simple illustration of the synthesis process, consider the four user views of data shown in Fig. V.1. We want to combine those into a single data model.

To start, here is view 1:

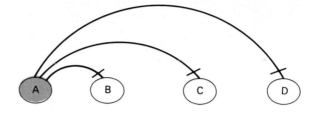

We will combine view 2 with it:

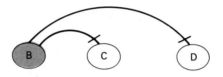

None of the data items above appear twice in the result:

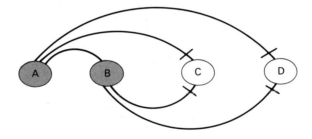

There are, however, some redundant links.

     A identifies *B;*
     And *B* identifies *C;*
     Therefore, *A must* identify *C*.
     Therefore, the link *A*———┤*C* is redundant.

     Similarly, *A* identifies *B* and *B* identifies *D;* therefore, *A must* identify *D*. Therefore, the link A———┤D is redundant. The redundant links are removed and we have

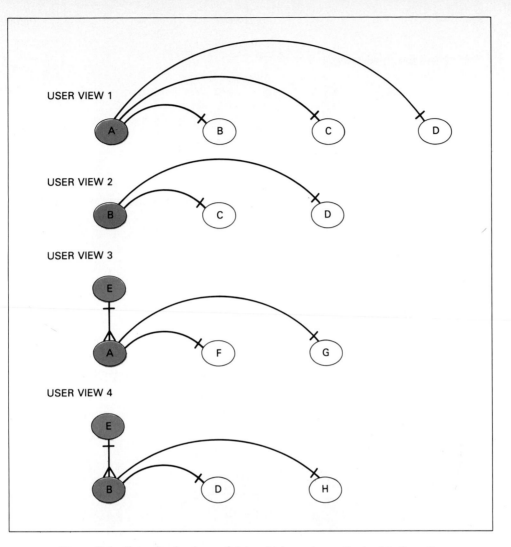

Figure V.1 Four simple views of data which can be synthesized to form the structure in Fig. V.2.

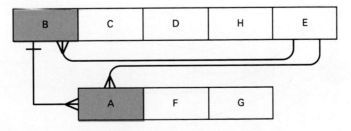

Figure V.2 The synthesis of the data views in Fig. V.1. (Here, *E* is a secondary key pointing to *B* and *A*. These secondary paths could be represented *physically* in a variety of possible ways.)

Now the third view:

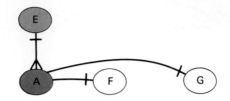

This contains three data items, *E, F,* and *G.* When it is merged into the model, we get

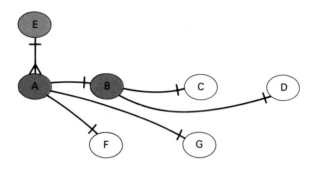

There are no new redundancies, so we will merge in the fourth view:

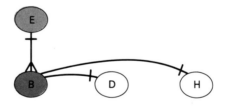

This adds one new data item to the model, *H:*

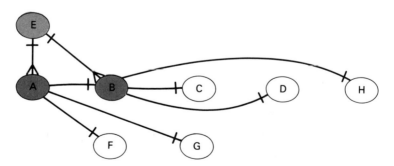

There is now one redundant link.

A identifies *B; B* identifies *E;* therefore, *A must* identify *E*. We can remove the *A*———┼*E* link (we cannot change the one-to-many link from *E* to *A*):

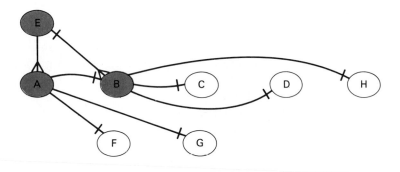

In this resulting structure there are two primary keys: *A* and *B*. (A primary key is a bubble with one or more one-to-one links going to other bubbles.)

We can associate each primary key with the attributes it identifies:

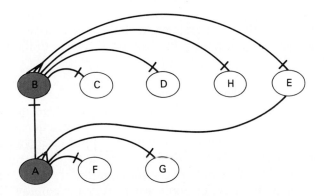

On each linkage between primary keys it is desirable to put the reverse linkage. We should therefore ask: Is the link from *B* to *A* a one-to-one or one-to-many link?

Suppose that it is a one-to-many link. Figure V.2, shows the entity records that result from this synthesis. *E*, here, is a secondary key pointing to both *A* and *B*. In old punched-card or batch-processing systems, secondary keys, such as *E,* were the *sort* keys. In on-line systems secondary key paths such as those from *E* to *A* or *B* are followed by such means as pointers or indices.

CANONICAL DATA STRUCTURES

If we have a given collection of data items and we identify their functional dependencies, we can combine them into a nonredundant model. We combine redundant data items and redundant associations so that no redundancy remains.

There is one and only one nonredundant model of a given collection of data. We call this the *canonical model*— the simplest, standard model. Secondary keys may be added to the model later as the need to search the data is identified. If we consider only primary keys and the grouping of the data items in entity records, the resulting model is *independent of how the data are used. We can structure the data independently of its usage.* The structure is inherent in the properties of the data themselves.

We have stressed that procedures—the way people use data—change rapidly in a typical enterprise. The data themselves have a structure that will not change unless new types of data are added. As new types of data are added the model can grow in a fashion that does not necessitate the rewriting of existing programs (if the database management system has good data independence).

Most structured techniques have analyzed procedures first and then decided what file or database structures are necessary for these procedures. This has resulted in high maintenance costs because the procedures change. In information engineering we analyze the data first and apply various steps to make it stable. Then we look for techniques which enable users to employ that data with as little programming effort as possible—techniques that give results *as fast as possible,* and techniques that permit fast and easy change to the procedures.

CANONICAL SYNTHESIS

The technique we describe takes any number of user views of data and combines them into a minimal set of canonical records with the requisite links between records. We will represent the user views, or application views of data, by means of bubble charts and will combine them, a step at a time, eliminating redundancies. We will not include every possible link between the data items, but only those which end users or application programs employ. The method is tedious to do by hand but is easy to do by computer. The input to the process must correctly identify the associations among data items in each user view. *The output is then automatically in fourth normal form.*

The technique can be applied to the narrow perspective of databases designed for a specific set of applications, or to the broader perspective of building enterprise data models. In doing *enterprise* data modeling the data administrator tries to create a structure representing the inherent properties of the data independently of any one application. This is a big task and needs assistance from many types of end users. It requires multiple reiterations in which the data administrator and the users examine the data to determine whether the model meets their needs now and, as far as they can anticipate, in the future.

ELIMINATION OF REDUNDANCIES   In the following grouping of data items, the link from X to Z is *probably* redundant:

If we know that X———$+Y$ and Y———$+Z$, this implies that X———$+Z$ (i.e., there is one value of Z for each value of X). In other words, X identifies Y; Y identifies Z; therefore, X identifies Z.

Why did we say that the link from X to Z is "probably" redundant? Is it not *always* redundant? Unfortunately, we cannot be absolutely sure unless we know the meaning of the association. As we have illustrated earlier, it is possible to have more than one association between the same two data items:

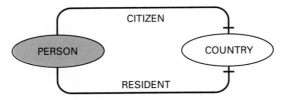

Therefore, before we delete X———$+Z$, we must examine the meaning of the associations to be sure that X———$+Z$ is *really* implied by X———$+Y$ and Y———$+Z$.

In the following case we could not delete it. An employee has a telephone number:

The employee reports to a next of kin:

The next of kin also has a telephone number:

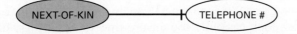

Combining these gives us

It would not be valid to assume that EMPLOYEE——⊢TELEPHONE# is redundant and delete it. The employee's telephone number is different from the next of kin's and we want both:

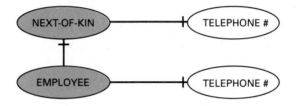

Because TELEPHONE# is an attribute, we can have a separate data item with this name associated with both EMPLOYEE and NEXT-OF-KIN.

The same pattern of associations could have occurred if all the data items in question had been keys.

In this case the links between the three key data items would be left as shown. Nevertheless, the situation when we have

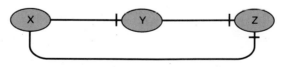

and cannot delete X——⊢Z is the exception rather than the rule. We will use the rule that one-to-one redundancies can be removed, but each time we use this rule we must look carefully too ensure that we have a genuine redundancy.

Sometimes redundancies can be removed in longer strings of links. Thus in the case

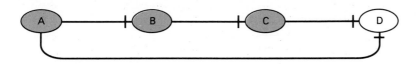

$A\text{———}+D$ is a candidate for removal.

It should be noted that crow's-feet links cannot be removed. There is nothing necessarily redundant in the following:

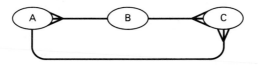

CANDIDATE KEYS

We defined a primary key as a *bubble with one or more one-to-one links leaving it*. There is one exception to this definition—the situation in which we have more than one *candidate key;* more than one data item identifies the other data items in a group:

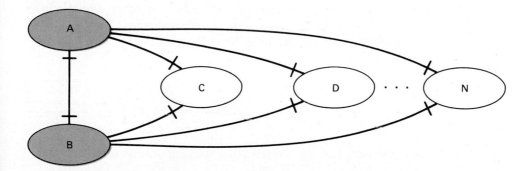

A and *B* in this case are equivalent. Each identifies the other; hence both identify *C, D, . . ., N*. There is redundancy in this diagram. We could remove $A\text{———}+C$, $A\text{———}+D$, . . ., $A\text{———}+N$. Alternatively, we could remove $B\text{———}+C$, $B\text{———}+D$, . . ., $B\text{———}+N$.

The designer might decide that *A* is the candidate key that he wants to employ. *A*, for example, might be EMPLOYEE# and *B* is EMPLOYEE-

NAME. The designer then deletes the links $B \longrightarrow\!\!\!+ C$, $B \longrightarrow\!\!\!+ D$, . . ., $B \longrightarrow\!\!\!+ N$:

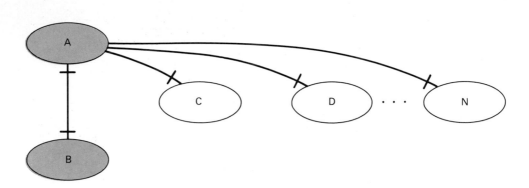

Candidate keys are not as common as this example might suggest. EM-PLOYEE-NAME would not normally be represented as identifying EM-PLOYEE# because two employees could have the same name. EMPLOYEE# is the unique identifier. Occasionally, there is a genuine $A \longrightarrow\!\!\!+ B$ relationship that should be left in the graph: for example, EMPLOYEE# $\longrightarrow\!\!\!+$ SOCIAL SECURITY#. The designer must make a decision about which redundant links are deleted.

TRANSITIVE DEPENDENCIES

The input views to the synthesis process should contain no *hidden* primary keys. In other words, there should be no *transitive dependencies*. The following purchase-order master record contains a transitive dependency:

ORDER#	SUPPLIER#	SUPPLIER-NAME	SUPPLIER-ADDRESS	ORDER-DATE	DELIVERY-DAY	$-TOTAL

ORDER# is the key. It might be tempting to diagram this record as

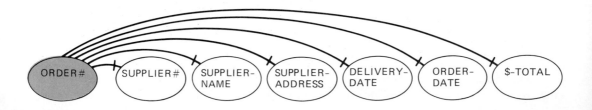

However, SUPPLIER-NAME and SUPPLIER-ADDRESS are identified by SUPPLIER#. The record should therefore be diagrammed as follows:

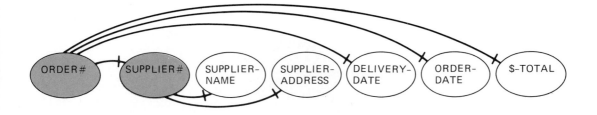

This process of removing transitive dependencies is essentially equivalent to the conversion to *third normal form* discussed in Chapter 12.

  In the design technique discussed in this appendix, transitive dependencies will be removed from a user's view when they are diagrammed, making all the user's attributes directly, not transitively, dependent on a key. This is done before they are fed into the synthesis process.

CONCATENATED KEYS

As discussed earlier, concatenated keys may be necessary. Price, for example, may be identified by a combination of CUSTOMER-TYPE, STATE, DISCOUNT, and PRODUCT.

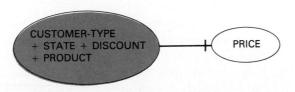

  When the modeling process encounters a concatenated key such as this, it *automatically* makes the component data items of the key into data item bubbles in their own right in the model. In other words, it explodes the concatenated key:

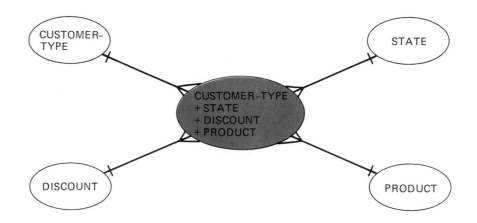

Some of these data items might become keys themselves, for example PRODUCT; others may remain attributes.

In the final synthesis, those which still remain merely attributes may be deleted because they already exist in the concatenated key. They are deleted if they are not used as a separate data item.

INTERSECTION DATA

In some types of database software, data can be related to the *association* between data items. A part, for example, may be supplied by several vendors, who each charge a different price for it. The data item PRICE cannot be associated with the PART record alone or with the SUPPLIER record alone. It can only be associated with the combination of the two. Such information is sometimes called *intersection data*—data associated with the association between records.

Figure V.3 shows a more complex example of intersection data. Products made by a factory are composed of subassemblies and parts. In the factory database are records called PRODUCT, SUBASSEMBLY, and PART. These records are different in composition. They might be linked as shown in the schema of Fig. V.3. Associated with each link is a number that tells how many of a given part is in a given subassembly or product, and how many subassemblies are in a product. For example, product 1001 contains 1 of subassembly X, 2 of subassembly Y, and 4 of part 610. In general, a structure something like that in Fig. V.3 gives a *bill of materials* showing a breakdown of the products for manufacturing purposes.

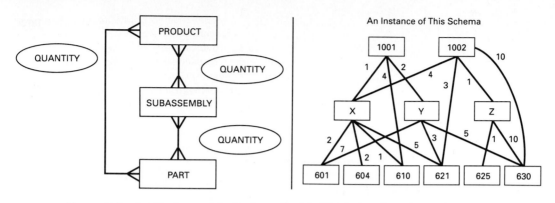

Figure V.3　A bill-of-materials database. In this illustration there is much intersection data. Extra records (segments) can be created to store intersection data, as in Fig. V.5.

Many-to-many associations are encountered several times in this book. They are common in the encyclopedia structure, as discussed in Chapter 4. For example:

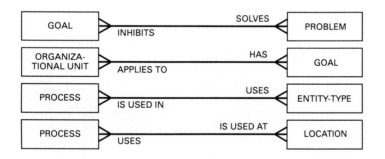

The tools for planning and analysis produce a matrix mapping the two types of data in these cases, as in Fig. IV.4. The boxes in the matrix contain intersection data. Sometimes, as in Fig. V.4, the intersection data consists of only one attribute:

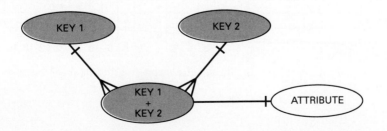

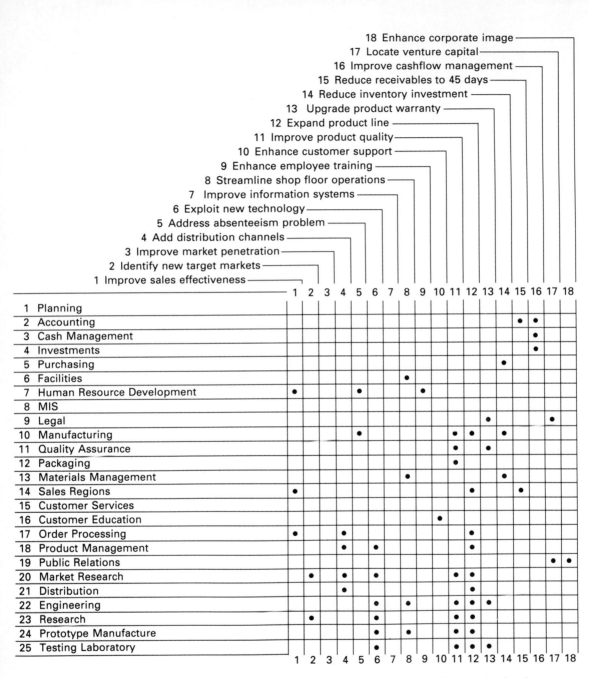

Figure V.4 Tactical goals of an enterprise mapped against its organizational units.

Two examples of intersection data:

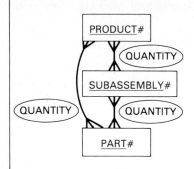

Intersection data could be handled by creating
an exta record (segment) containing the intersection
data and the concatenated key of the records (segments)
associated with it. The keys are shown in red.

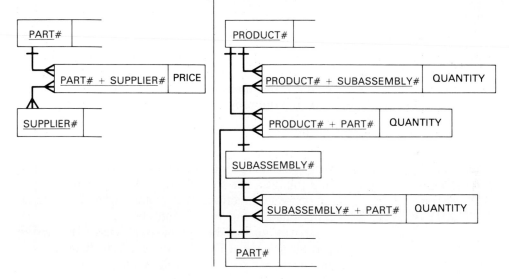

Figure V.5   Two examples of intersection data.

It is necessary to be cautious with many-to-many associations. Usually, there will be intersection data associated with the pair of data items, sooner or later. If there is no intersection data to start with, they are likely to be added later as the database evolves. If intersection data are associated with records having keys *A* and *B,* those data are identified by a concatenated key *A* + *B.* Figure V.5 shows two examples of intersection data and how they might be handled.

A data modeling tool may take any many-to-many link and insert a con-catenated key:

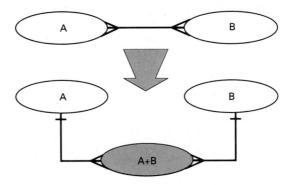

It might ask the analyst to identify possible attributes of the $A + B$ key.

Canonical modeling is an attempt to find the most *stable* data model. It therefore adds to the $A + B$ key rather than risking it being added later with a possible need to restructure and rewrite programs.

TWO-WAY MAPPING BETWEEN PRIMARY KEYS

When the modeling identifies a mapping *between keys* the designer should *always* add the mapping in the opposite direction. This is done when building an entity-relationship model and should be done in the same way during the synthesis process. The design tool should ask the designer to fill in a panel like that in Fig. V.6. If the answer indicates that a many-to-many relationship exists, a follow-on window may ask about intersection data.

INTERSECTING ATTRIBUTES

A problem that sometimes exists in the synthesized structure is that an *attribute* may be attached to more than one primary key. In other words, it has more than one one-to-one link pointing to it. This is sometimes called an intersecting attribute. It cannot remain in such a state in the final synthesis. An attribute in a canonical model can be owned by only one key. Box V.1 illustrates an inter-secting attribute and shows three ways of dealing with it. There should be no intersecting attributes on the final canonical graph.

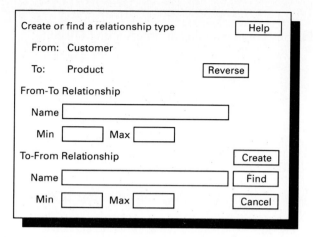

Figure V.6 A window for the designer to fill in, asking for details of the association between entities or primary keys. The same window is used to find or display a relationship.

ISOLATED ATTRIBUTES

An isolated attribute is an attribute that is not identified by a primary key. It is a bubble with no one-to-one links entering or leaving it, although there will be one-to-many links.

An isolated attribute should be treated in one of the following ways:

1. It may be implemented as a repeating attribute in a variable-length record.
2. It may be treated as a solitary-key—a one-data-item record.

Often, it results from an error in interpretation of the user's data, so the meaning related to it should be carefully checked.

RECORD SEQUENCE

In certain user views the *sequence* in which the data is presented to the application program, or displayed on a terminal, is critical. However, the canonical model does not indicate the sequence in which records are stored. *In general, it is undesirable to state a record sequence in the model because different applications of the data might require the records in a different sequence.*

In a database of book titles, for example, one application might want a logical file of book titles in alphabetical order, another might want them ordered by author, another by Library of Congress number. The different sequencing

BOX V.1 Intersecting attributes must be reorganized

The following graph contains an intersecting attribute:

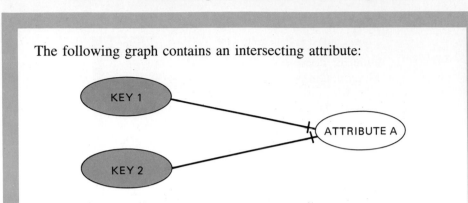

An intersecting attribute can be avoided in one of the following three ways:

1. All but one link to it may be replaced with equivalent links via an existing key:

2. Redundant versions of it may be connected to each associated key:

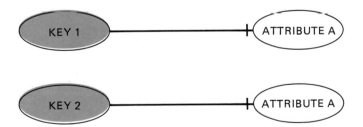

3. It may be made into a key with no attributes:

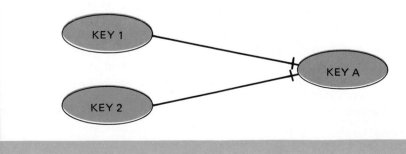

can be indicated by secondary keys: bubbles with a one-to-many link to BOOK-TITLE.

When the model is converted to a physical representation, it is necessary to state the record sequencing. This is a statement that should be part of the physical rather than the logical description of data. Some *logical* data description languages require statements about the order of records. This information must then be added when the canonical model is converted to the software schema. The enthusiasts of *relational* databases stress that the sequencing of the tuples should not be part of the *logical* data description.

SHIPPING
EXAMPLE

Now we will examine an example selected to illustrate how intelligent human attention is needed to the *meaning* of the links when they are candidates for deletion. The application relates to the movement of cargo by sea. A company operates a fleet of cargo ships that visit many ports. Box V.2 shows views of

BOX V.2   A shipping example: seven input views

Input View 1

Information is stored about each ship. The key is VESSEL#, and access is also required by OWNER.

VESSEL #	VESSEL-NAME	TONNAGE	DETAILS	COUNTRY-OF-DESTINATION	OWNER	LENGTH	VOYAGE

Input View 2

A ship goes on many voyages and stops at many ports. It is necessary to print its itinerary.

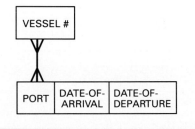

VESSEL #

PORT	DATE-OF-ARRIVAL	DATE-OF-DEPARTURE

(Continued)

BOX V.2 *(Continued)*

Input View 3

A shipper may have many consignments of goods in transit. They are given a consignment identification number. A list can be obtained, when requested, of what consignment a shipper has in each shipment. Information is also required of shipments to each consignee.

SHIPPER

CONSIGNMENT #	CONSIGNEE	VESSEL #	DELIVERY-DATE	DESTINATION-PORT	SHIPPING-AGENT

Input View 4

The fourth user view is the BILL-OF-LADING. A BILL-OF-LADING relates to a given consignment of goods. Large containers are used for shipping the goods. A BILL-OF-LADING relates to goods in one container. If a shipper's goods fill more than one container, a separate BILL-OF-LADING is used for each container.

BILL-OF-LADING #	SHIPPER	CONSIGNEE	CONSIGNMENT #	SHIPPING AGENT
	BILL-OF-LADING-DATE	SAILING-DATE	CONTAINER #	
	ORIGINATION-PORT	DESTINATION-PORT	TOTAL-CHARGE	

ITEM #	NO-OF-PIECES	COMMODITY-CODE	WEIGHT	CHARGE

BOX V.2 *(Continued)*

Input View 5

A shipping agent wants a list of what containers he has in shipment, and what consignments of goods they contain.

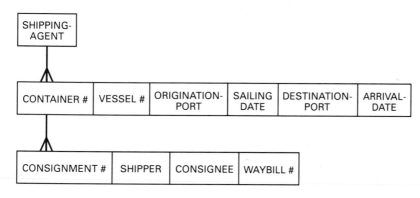

CONTAINER #	VESSEL #	ORIGINATION-PORT	SAILING DATE	DESTINATION-PORT	ARRIVAL-DATE

CONSIGNMENT #	SHIPPER	CONSIGNEE	WAYBILL #

Input View 6

Details of the containers are required.

CONTAINER #	OWNER	TYPE	SIZE	VESSEL-NAME	DESTINATION-PORT	ARRIVAL-DATE

Input View 7

For a given voyage of each vessel, a list is required of what containers are to be loaded at each port. Details of the container size, type, and handling instructions are needed for loading purposes. Similarly, a list of what containers should be taken *off* the vessel is needed.

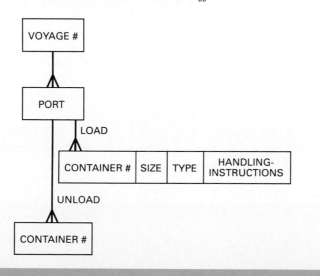

CONTAINER #	SIZE	TYPE	HANDLING-INSTRUCTIONS

BOX V.3 Inputs of the seven views that were loosely drawn in Box V.2

Input View 1

Input view 1 appears simple, but VOYAGE should not be in the same data group as the other data items. A vessel can go on many voyages. A one-to-many link from VESSEL to VOYAGE is needed.

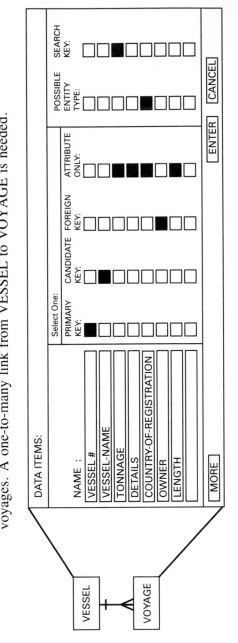

Owner is marked here as a *foreign key*, so the tool requests that it be linked to VESSEL on the entity-relationship diagram.

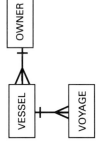

Input View 2

In input view 2 we need to ask: What identifies DATE-OF-AR-RIVAL and DATE-OF-DEPARTURE? The stopping of a ship at a port. Is VESSEL # + PORT an adequate key? If you know VES-SEL# + PORT, does that identify DATE-OF-ARRIVAL? Not com-pletely, because the vessel stops at the same port many times. VES-SEL# + PORT + DATE-OF-ARRIVAL would be a complete key for identifying the itinerary records. In practice, the shipping com-pany gives each voyage a number. The itinerary entries can therefore be identified by VOYAGE# + PORT. VOYAGE# identifies VES-SEL#. The view is redrawn as follows:

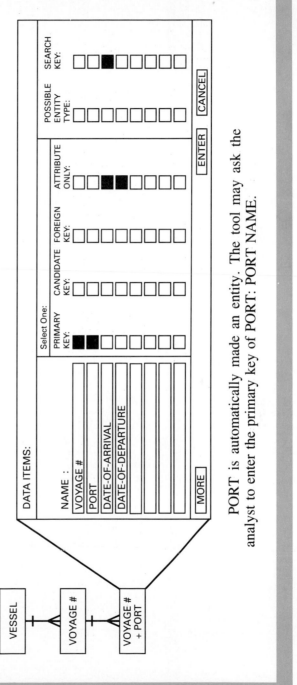

PORT is automatically made an entity. The tool may ask the analyst to enter the primary key of PORT: PORT NAME.

(Continued)

415

BOX V.3 *(Continued)*

Input View 3

Input view 3 is straightforward except that we need to ask whether DESTINATION-PORT is the same as PORT in view 2. It is. Again, is DELIVERY-DATE the same as DATE-OF-ARRIVAL in view 2? The data administrator decides that these are different dates. DATE-OF-ARRIVAL is the scheduled docking date of the vessel, and DE-LIVERY-DATE is the estimated date of delivery to the customer.

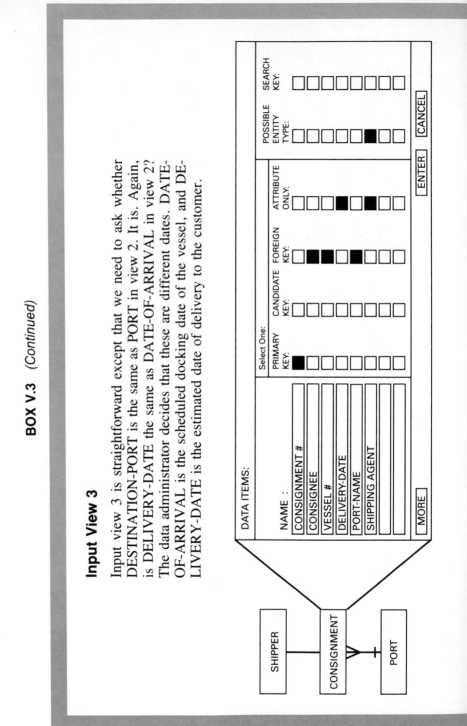

The analyst has marked CONSIGNEE as a foreign key here. The tool requests that the CONSIGNEE be linked to CONSIGN-MENT.

Input View 4

In input view 4 there is a hidden transitive dependency. CONSIGN-MENT# identifies CONSIGNEE, SHIPPER, SHIPPING-AGENT, CONTAINER#, ORIGINATION-PORT, DESTINATION-PORT, and SAILING-DATE. It is necessary to ask whether *one* consignment has *one* bill of lading, and vice versa. It is decided that if the con-signment is split, there would be more than one bill of lading. Again does one consignment always relate to one container? It is decided that a consignment could be split into two or more containers, and a container can contain multiple consignments.

Both ORIGINATION-PORT and DESTINATION-PORT are the same as PORT in view 2. They can be handled by labeled asso-ciations to the entity PORT:

(Continued)

BOX V.3 *(Continued)*

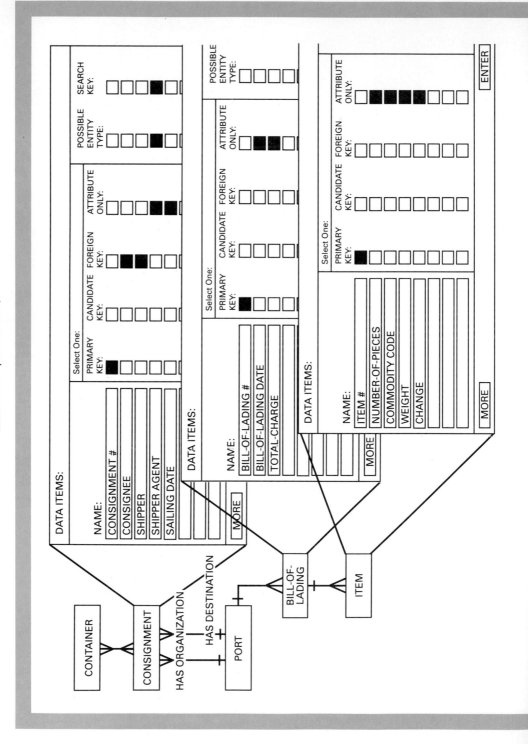

418

Input View 5

View 5 contains the data item WAYBILL #. It is realized that this is called BILL-OF-LADING# in view 4. It is therefore changed to BILL-OF-LADING#.

There is another problem in view 5. CONTAINER # does not, by itself, identify any of the data items that are linked to it. The same container can go on many voyages. To identify VESSEL #, SAIL-ING-DATE, and so on, we need a concatenated key CONTAINER # + VOYAGE #, as follows:

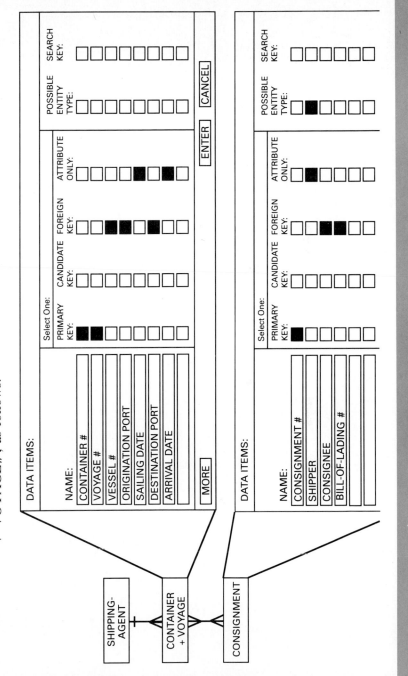

(Continued)

419

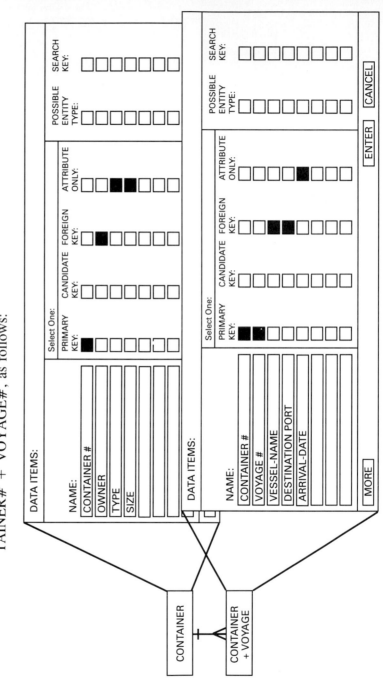

BOX V.3 (Continued)

Input View 6

View 6 mixes up two types of data. Some data are properties of the container, regardless of where it is. Some are properties of the container on this particular voyage. View 6 is split into data items identified by CONTAINER# and data items identified by CONTAINER# + VOYAGE#, as follows:

Input View 7

View 7 also has a problem. A vessel stops at the same port many times. We need VOYAGE# + PORT to identify what containers are to be loaded and unloaded.

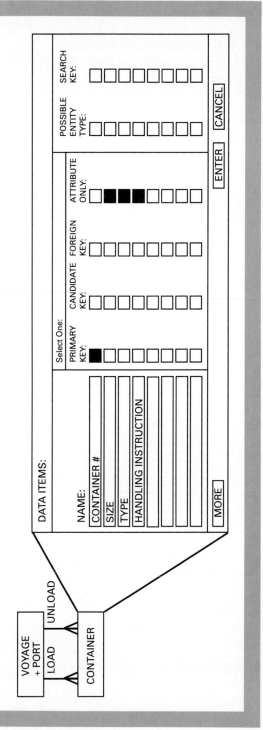

**BOX V.4   Synthesis of the views
(produced by Data Designer II)**

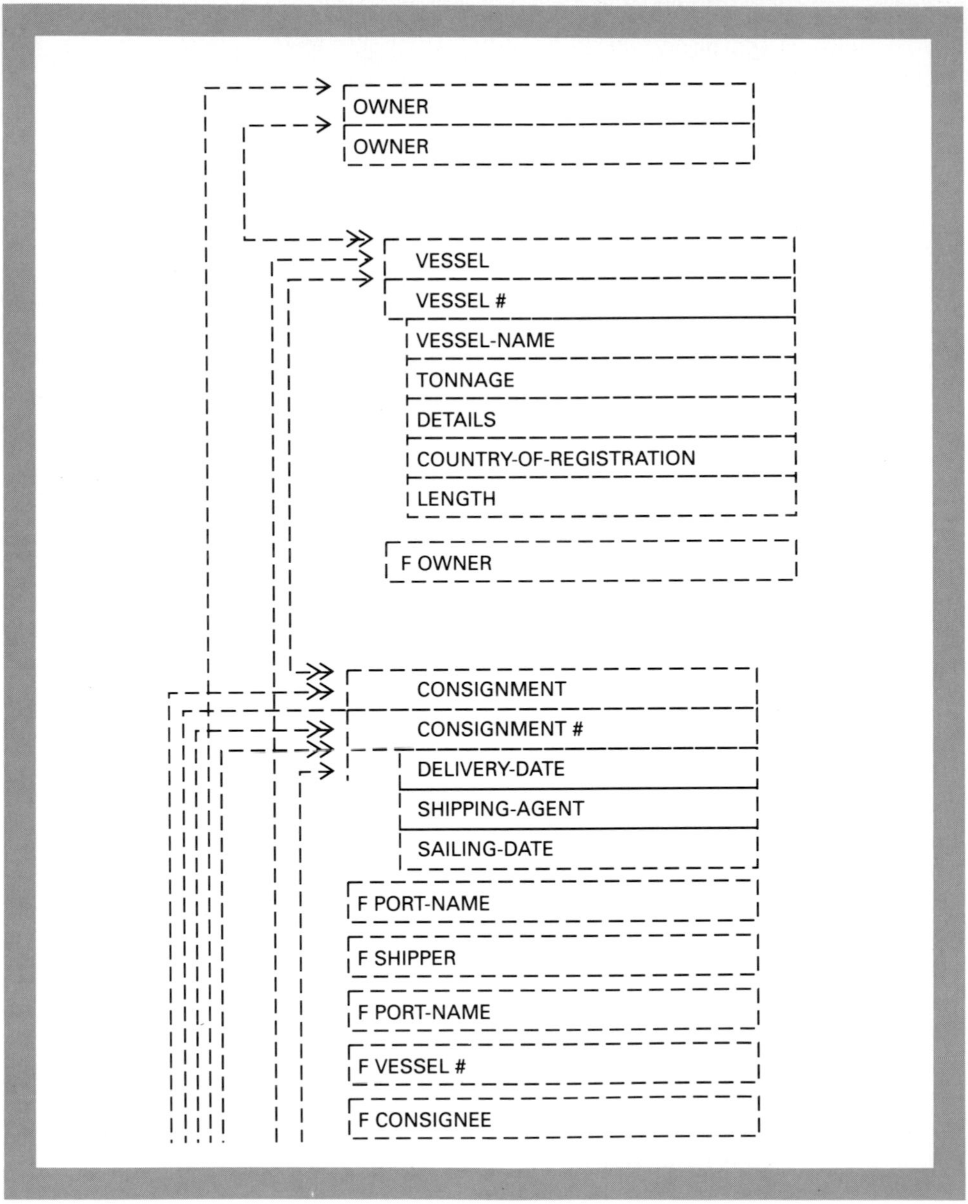

OWNER

OWNER

VESSEL

VESSEL #

I VESSEL-NAME

I TONNAGE

I DETAILS

I COUNTRY-OF-REGISTRATION

I LENGTH

F OWNER

CONSIGNMENT

CONSIGNMENT #

DELIVERY-DATE

SHIPPING-AGENT

SAILING-DATE

F PORT-NAME

F SHIPPER

F PORT-NAME

F VESSEL #

F CONSIGNEE

BOX V.4 *(Continued)*

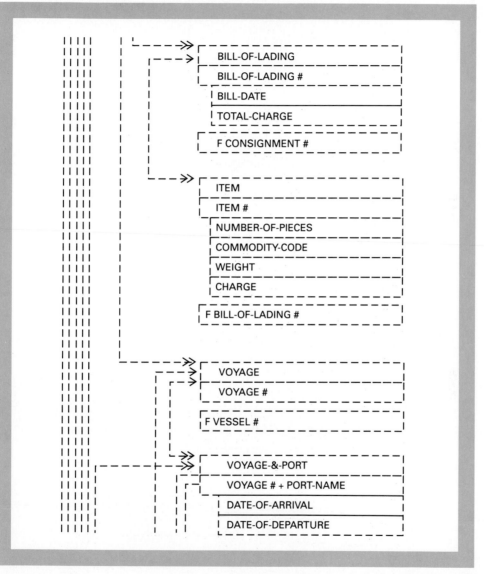

(Continued)

BOX V.4 *(Continued)*

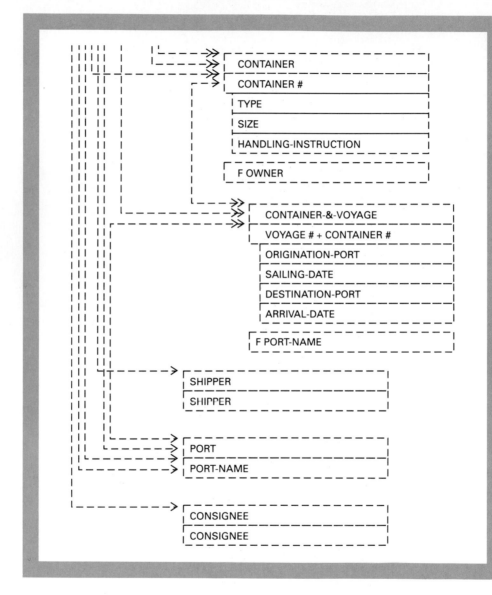

the data that various application designers require. The example is *highly* simplified from reality. For ease of tutorial diagramming, many *attributes* have been combined or omitted, and the number of views is small. A real bill of lading typically contains about 65 data items, not the 15 shown here.

CLARIFICATION OF USER VIEWS Before attempting to synthesize the views in Box V.2, we need to clarify their structure. As is often the case, they are drawn loosely in Box V.2 (although not as loosely as often in real life!). The drawings of Box V.2 contain various traps for the unwary. Some of them are incorrect representations of data. Before reading further we suggest that the reader examine Box V.2 looking for misrepresentations of data. We gave Box V.2 to one senior systems analyst, and after trying for a week, he was unable to find some of the misrepresentations in it.

To clarify the input views, they may be drawn as bubble charts. The data administrator or analyst needs to ask the following question for each data item that is synthesized into a data model: On what is it functionally dependent? In different words: What data item (or items) identifies it? The single-headed arrow links between the data items *must* be correct.

Box V.3 shows a cleaned-up version of the views being entered into a synthesis tool. In practice, an entity-relationship diagram should exist from an ISP study before the entry of the views, as in Box V.3. The views are shown synthesized in Box V.4.

Appendix

VI STABILITY ANALYSIS

INTRODUCTION   There are three main objectives of data modeling:

- To create databases that are as stable as possible (this has a major impact on maintenance costs)
- To ensure that diverse end users can automatically derive information they need
- To help ensure that separately developed systems will work together

The structures of databases in use will change in the future, but an objective of their design should be to *minimize those types of change that will cause existing application programs to be rewritten*. It is expensive to rewrite programs—often so expensive that it is avoided or postponed. The data model needs to be a *stable* foundation which serves as the basis for future system design.

The logical structures of data in an enterprise can be made *stable,* whereas the procedures change constantly. Various considerations are needed in data modeling to achieve stable data models. In this appendix we discuss these considerations.

The first step is to employ a computerized tool that synthesizes the views of data into a fully normalized model and makes the coordinated model available to all analysts, developers, and information centers. Given an automated synthesis tool, careful attention is needed to the inputs, and imaginative discussion is needed for the outputs.

The inputs need to come from as many sources as possible to help ensure completeness. Each input needs to be examined to ensure that it represents the data items and functional dependencies correctly. The output needs to be examined to ensure that it contains no anomalies and that it represents future uses of the data as effectively as possible.

The synthesis of views of data is used in conjunction with the entity-relationship diagram established in information strategy planning. The start of the detailed data modeling process is to establish primary keys for the entity types involved in the business area.

SUCCESS IN DATA MODELING

There are five important rules for success in data modeling:

- Involve the end users at every step in the data-modeling process.
- Employ canonical synthesis with an automated design tool, and ensure that the model is fully normalized.
- Ensure that the users understand and review the data model and data definitions.
- Apply the stability analysis steps listed in this appendix when the data models are being created and reviewed.
- Respond *rapidly* to all end-user criticisms and suggestions about the data models. Fast redesign feedback is essential to keep the end users interested.

Probably the best way to involve end users is to set up committees of interested users to review the inputs and outputs of the modeling process, as described in Chapter 13. Meetings of the user committees should employ a graphics workbench tool with a large-screen projector. As subjects come up for discussion, the relevant portion of the model should be displayed and suggested modifications either entered into the model or recorded for further study. Often there are many last-minute changes to data definitions or associations. These can be appropriately entered into the model ready for the meeting.

Data modeling is done a small step at a time. Views of data are discovered and synthesized into the overall model. The data modeling and process modeling parts of business area analysis often proceed hand-in-hand with the process modeling, helping to discover views of data that are added to the overall synthesis. The data model should be accessible online at different locations so that coordination of the data across the enterprise steadily grows. The organization's data is steadily cleaned up, removing and documenting the many inconsistencies.

THINKING ABOUT THE FUTURE

When the output from the modeling process is reviewed, this is the time to think about the future. If future requirements can be understood at this stage, a better logical design will result with a lower probability of expensive maintenance later.

The users, systems analysts, and data administrator should examine the output and ask themselves: How might this data be used in the future? Any potential future use should be incorporated provisionally in the model to see whether that use causes changes in the structure of the data-item groups.

Sometimes end users are better at thinking about the future than I.S. professionals because they know their possible applications better. This is not always the case. Sometimes imaginative systems analysts, or a data administrator, are best at thinking up future uses for the data. Often the best way to do it is with a user group meeting with the users, analysts, and data administrator, all trying to brainstorm future uses of the data.

The user team is asked to play games with the model. They think of things that have not happened, or things that were not inputs to the model. Suppose, for example, that a supplier's factory burns down and information is needed for rescheduling. What could be the characteristics of future products? Suppose that new government legislation is enacted. Can the model adapt to change that can be foreseen without enforcing massive rewrites of existing programs? If the model is resiliant to most future changes, it is a *stable* model. We can build stability into the data when there is little or no stability in the business procedures.

The attributes of each entity type should be examined to ask whether the users or analysts can think of possible future attributes. The links between primary keys should be questioned to assess whether a link with "one" cardinality could have "many" cardinality in the future. Thought about future requirements may cause an entity type to be added to the entity-relationship model. Every entity type in the entity-relationship model should be examined to ensure that none are forgotten in the detailed data modeling.

Many enterprises change their organizational structure. The data analysis groups should consider whether possible organizational changes could cause a change in the data model. It is not possible to achieve a data model that will never change, but by applying the steps in the appendix, it can be made as resiliant as possible. To achieve resiliancy, a set of checks should be applied to each input to the synthesis process, and a set of checks should be applied to the output. We discuss these in the remainder of this appendix. Box VI.1 summarizes the steps.

**INPUT
TO THE MODEL**
Each input data item should be checked to make sure that no data item already in the model has the same name but a different meaning. In some cases an input data item may already exist in the model under a different name: for example, SAILING-DATE and DATE-OF-DEPARTURE. In some cases it may exist in a slightly different form; for example, ETD, EXPECTED-TIME-OF-DEPARTURE, may incorporate the intended SAILING-DATE. Avoiding these situations is part of the process of cleaning up the data.

In some cases the input data can be simplified. For example, it contains DATE-OF-VOYAGE, but this already exists in effect as the first of many dates

BOX VI.1 Steps in creating stable data models

The data models are a foundation stone on which so much will be built. The foundation needs to be as stable as possible (i.e., it should not change in ways that force application programs to have to be rewritten). The following steps are needed to achieve this:

Strategy

- Select an encyclopedia/data modeling tool to form the corporatewide repository and coordination tool.
- Determine in an information strategy planning study the information needs of the enterprise. Establish an enterprisewide overview in the form of an entity-relationship model.
- For each business area establish user committees with key persons representing each use of data.

Data Analysis

- Capture all documents that will be derived from the database or will serve as inputs to the database.
- Determine by discussion with the end users what types of data they want to obtain from the database, now and in the future.
- Determine from the systems analysis process whether any new record or document requirements are emerging.
- Examine any existing databases, files, or dictionaries that relate to this data.
- Plan whether existing files or databases will coexist with the new database or be converted. If they will coexist, plan the bridge between the old system and the new.
- Employ a data dictionary to document a description of the meaning of each data item.

Creating the Data Model

- Employ canonical synthesis, with an automated design tool, and ensure that the model is fully normalized.
- Inspect each input to see whether it can be simplified.
- Do any of the input data items already exist in the model under a different name or in a slightly different form?

BOX VI.1 *(Continued)*

- For each input data item, check that no different item in the model has the same name.

- Employ naming convention standards for selecting data-item names.

- Be sure that concatenated keys are correctly represented in the input to the synthesis process.

- Be sure that all attributes entered as input are dependent on the *whole* of the key that identifies them.

- Be sure that the data groups entered as input contain no transitive dependencies (see Box VI.2).

- Question the validity of all links that represent business rules, as opposed to the natural inherent properties of the data (see the text). Could these rules be changed in the future?

- Question any link between keys with ''one'' cardinality to ask whether it could become ''many'' cardinality in the future.

Inspecting the Output of the Data Model

- With the user group, review the data dictionary to ensure that all users agree about the definitions of data items.

- With the user group, review the model to ensure that their data requirements can be derived from it.

- With the user group, brainstorm the possible future uses of the data. For any uses that the model does not serve, create new input to the synthesis process.

- Examine every attribute data item in the model to determine whether it could possibly become a primary key in the future.

- Complete the reverse mapping of any links between keys to identify any possible many-to-many links ($\gg$———$\ll$). The synthesis tool will create an extra concatenated key in the model to take care of any future intersection data (see Box VI.3). This can be changed if no intersection data is possible.

- Examine any links that the synthesis process deletes, to ensure that they are truly redundant.

- Examine the effect of exploding any concatenated keys, to see whether the resulting single-field data items need to exist separately in the database.

(Continued)

BOX VI.1   *(Continued)*

- If candidate keys exist in the resulting model, check that they are in fact likely to remain candidate keys in the future.

- Check the treatment of any intersecting attributes to ensure that it is the best of the three possible treatments (Box V.1). Could the intersecting attribute become a primary key in the future?

- Inspect any cycles in the modeling output. Check whether a further link should be added to break the cycle (Box VI.4).

- Use fast (computerized) redesign after any changes are made, in order to maintain the interest of the users.

   Note: Further considerations for stability are necessary when the database schema and physical representation are designed.

---

in the voyage itinerary. There may be no need to have VOYAGE# identifying DATE-OF-VOYAGE when VOYAGE# + PORT already identifies DATE-OF-DEPARTURE.

It *is* desirable to have conventions for naming the data items. This can improve the uniformity of the names, and can often help to avoid the situation where the same data item has different names in different inputs.

CAUTION WITH CONCATENATED KEYS

Certain circumstances are necessary in creating *input* to the modeling process. First, caution is needed with concatenated keys. There is a big difference between

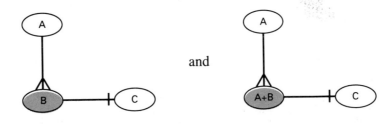

and

It would be incorrect to draw the following:

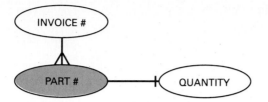

If you know the value of PART#, you do not know the value of QUAN-TITY. PART# alone does not identify QUANTITY. To know the value of QUANTITY, you need to know both INVOICE# and PART#. QUANTITY therefore needs to be pointed to by a concatenated key INVOICE# + PART#. The following is correct:

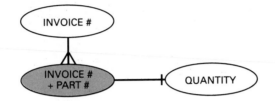

On the other hand,

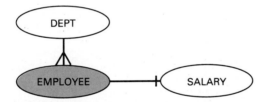

is correct, because EMPLOYEE# does (by itself) identify SALARY.

REVERSE MAPPING BETWEEN KEYS   For all associations between primary keys the cardinality in both directions should be entered. For example, in the following case:

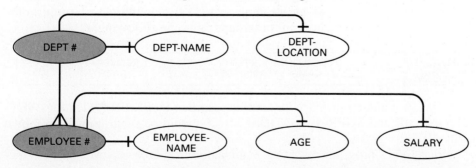

DEPT# and EMPLOYEE# are primary keys. The reverse mapping between them should be entered:

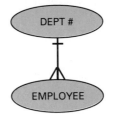

DEPENDENCE ON THE WHOLE KEY

When attributes are drawn the user should make sure that they are identified correctly by the primary key which points to them (as above), but they are also dependent on the *entire* concatenated key. Thus the following is incorrect:

PART-DESCRIPTION is identified by only a portion of the concatenated key: PART#. Therefore, a separate key PART# should be drawn:

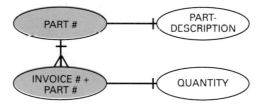

AVOIDANCE OF HIDDEN PRIMARY KEYS

When a data-item group is entered, there may be a hidden primary key in the group. One item entered as an attribute may in fact identify some other data item in the group, as in the following:

ORDER #	SUPPLIER #	SUPPLIER-NAME	SUPPLIER-ADDRESS	ORDER-DATE	DELIVERY-DATE	TOTAL

There is a hidden primary key in this record. SUPPLIER# identifies SUP-PLIER-NAME and SUPPLIER-ADDRESS. It should be diagrammed as shown in Box VI.2.

What forces program rewriting is a change in the basic structure of a rec-

BOX VI.2   The avoidance of hidden transitive dependencies
in the representation of user views of data

The record below, taken from a user's view of data, contains a hidden transitive dependency:

ORDER#	SUPPLIER#	SUPPLIER-NAME	SUPPLIER-ADDRESS	DELIVERY-DATE	ORDER-DATE	$-TOTAL

It might be tempting to diagram it thus:

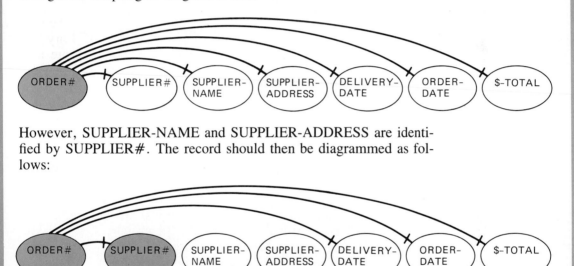

However, SUPPLIER-NAME and SUPPLIER-ADDRESS are identified by SUPPLIER#. The record should then be diagrammed as follows:

ord. The most common cause of this is that a data item that is an attribute in the record *now* becomes a primary key *later*. It is easy to spot any such data items in the output of a data modeling tool.

The data administrator, systems analysts, and user committee should examine each attribute data item in turn and ask: Could this possibly be used as a primary key in the future? If data items are found which are potential future primary keys, the decision should be made whether to make them primary keys *now* by giving the modeling tool new input views. If they are made into primary keys now, this will possibly save future redesign with extensive program rewriting.

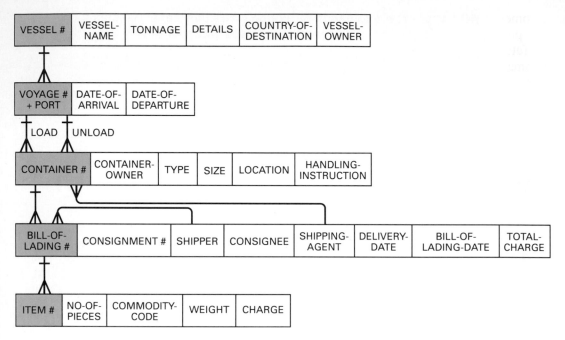

Figure VI.1   The canonical structure for the shipping example developed in Appendix V.

Let us reexamine our highly simplified model of data for a shipping company. For convenience it is drawn again in Fig VI.1, in a simplified format.

We can take each data item that is not by itself a primary key and ask whether it could be used as a primary key in the future:

VESSEL-NAME	This is equivalent to VESSEL#. VESSEL# is used to identify vessels, so there would never be a *separate record* with VESSEL-NAME as its primary key. VESSEL-NAME is a candidate key and may be used for accessing the vessel record.
TONNAGE	No. This would not be used as a primary key at any time. (It could conceivably be used as a secondary key. That does not matter.)
DETAIL	No.
COUNTRY-OF-REGISTRATION	This is an entity type, but no attributes are stored about it.

The data administrator, systems analysts, and end-user group should examine each data item in this way. It is generally easy to spot those that might become primary keys in the future. If they are made primary keys now, that will prevent having to restructure that data and rewrite the programs using it in the future. It could save much money and disruption. The modeling process will automatically take care of this if views of data using the key in question are fed to it.

DICTIONARY
CHECK

When the foregoing checks are taking place, the dictionary definitions of the data items should be used in conjunction with the model. Users should double check that they really represent the true meaning of the data as it is employed by the users.

INTERSECTION
DATA

With a good database management system, it is possible to add new *attributes* to an existing record without forcing the rewriting of application programs, provided that there is no change in primary keys. It is possible, however, that a new attribute might be needed which relates to an existing *link* rather than to a single key. This is *intersection data,* which we illustrated in Fig. V.5.

If a one-to-many link exists between the primary keys, new data can be identified by one or other of the existing primary keys. It can therefore be added to an existing record. If a many-to-many link exists between the primary keys, intersection data cannot be identified by either of the primary keys alone. It needs a concatenated key. This is illustrated in Box VI.3.

The synthesis process should detect any many-to-many links between primary keys and automatically create a concatenated key which combines them, deleting the many-to-many link. This is illustrated in the bottom half of Box VI.3

Suppose, for example, that a college database was created that recorded information about classes and information about teachers. It contained the following many-to-many link:

It did not consider textbooks.

Sometime later it is necessary to record what textbooks are used. However, the textbook for a class is selected by the teacher. It cannot therefore be identified by the primary key CLASS-TITLE alone. It is identified by the concatenation of CLASS-TITLE and TEACHER:

BOX VI.3   Intersection data

The following are examples of intersection data:

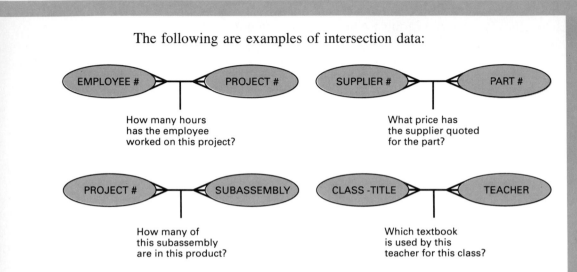

When a many-to-many link exists between two primary keys, it is likely that intersection data will need to be stored which is keyed by the concatenation of both primary keys. The synthesis process automatically creates these concatenated keys, as follows:

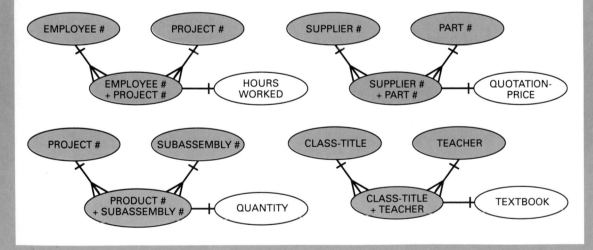

In anticipation of such changes the modeling process should automatically change each many-to-many link between primary keys and insert the appropriate concatenated key:

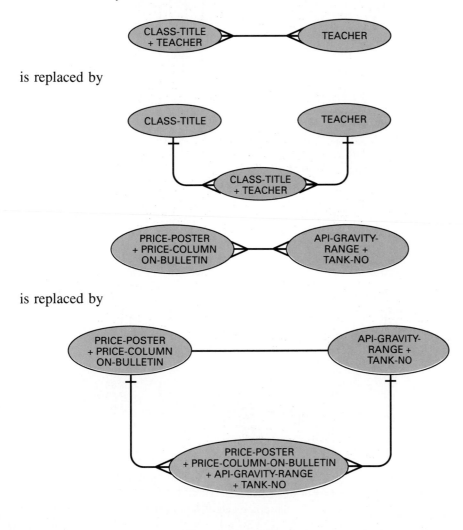

is replaced by

is replaced by

CANDIDATE KEYS   The model may contain some links with a "one" cardinality in both directions. These indicate a *candidate key*. If A identifies B and B identifies A (A ⊢———⊣ B), then A and B are functionally equivalent.

Any such situations should be inspected carefully and the question asked: Are A and B *really* functionally equivalent and likely to remain so in the future?

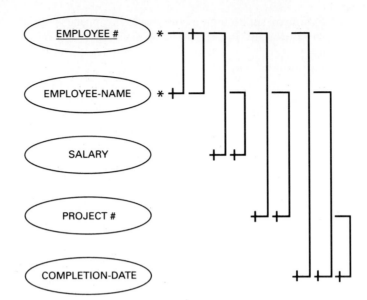

An instance of this record:

EMPLOYEE #	EMPLOYEE NAME	SALARY	PROJECT #	COMPLETION DATE
120	JONES	2000	X	17.7.84
121	HARPO	1700	X	17.7.84
270	GARFUNKAL	1800	Y	12.1.87
273	SELSI	3600	X	17.7.84
274	ABRAHMS	3000	Z	21.3.86
279	HIGGINS	2400	Y	12.1.87
301	FLANNEL	1800	Z	21.3.86
306	McGRAW	2100	X	17.7.84
310	ENSON	3000	Z	21.3.86
315	GOLDSTEIN	3100	X	17.7.84
317	PUORRO	2700	Y	12.1.87
320	MANSINI	1700	Y	12.1.87
321	SPOTO	2900	X	17.7.84
340	SCHAFT	3100	X	17.7.84
349	GOLD	1900	Z	21.3.86

Figure VI.2 Functional dependencies in the record EMPLOYEE (EM-PLOYEE#, EMPLOYEE-NAME, SALARY, PROJECT#, COMPLETION-DATE). The asterisks indicate the prime data items (members of candidate keys).

It is easy to illustrate candidate keys in textbooks, but in practice they are rare because:

1. In the future A may identify a slightly different set of data items from B.
2. Two values of A may be identical, whereas the equivalent values of B are not. For example, EMPLOYEE# and EMPLOYEE-NAME, shown as functionally equiva-

lent in Fig. IV.2, are not really equivalent candidate keys because two employees might have the same name. Only EMPLOYEE# should be used as the primary key.

The model might contain situations such as the following:

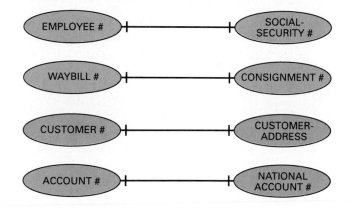

CYCLES
IN THE MODEL

The one-cardinality links in the model may form a cycle as in the following case:

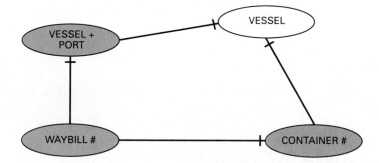

There is often a redundancy in such cycles. They can be simplified by the addition of a cross-link which causes two or more of the links in the cycle to be deleted, thus simplifying the structure. This is illustrated in Box VI.4 The data administrator should examine all such cycles.

HOW LARGE
SHOULD USER
VIEWS BE?

When preparing data for the synthesis process, users and analysts have sometimes worried about how complex one user view should be. They have sometimes had difficulty deciding where one user view starts and where it ends. The answer is: It doesn't matter.

BOX VI.4   Cycles in the model

The one-cardinality in the model may form a cycle as in the following cases:

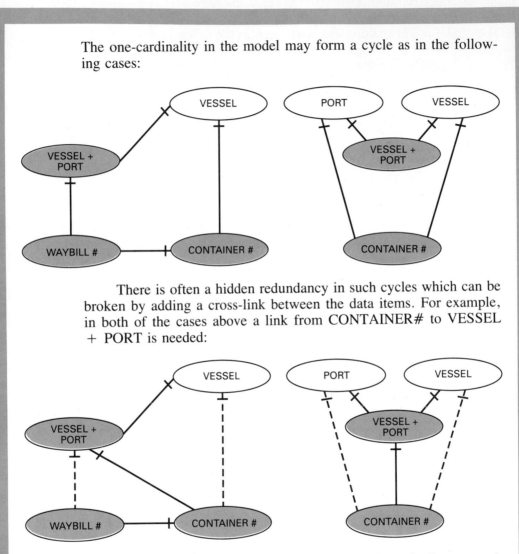

There is often a hidden redundancy in such cycles which can be broken by adding a cross-link between the data items. For example, in both of the cases above a link from CONTAINER# to VESSEL + PORT is needed:

The dashed links are then redundant and automatically removed. A simpler structure results.

The modeling process combines them into a synthesized structure. A complex user view can be entered as multiple separate user views and the end result will be the same. It is often a good idea to do this because it lessens the likelihood of making an error. *Keep the inputs simple.*

For example, the following bubble chart represents the data on the bills which I receive from a nearby hardware store:

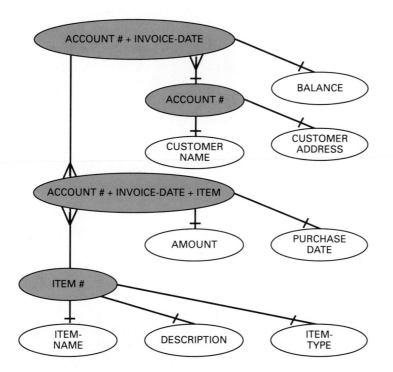

This could be entered in three separate pieces, as follows:

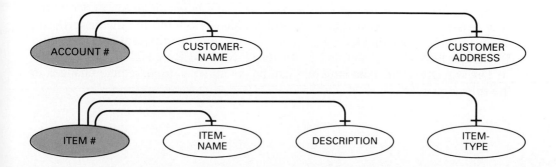

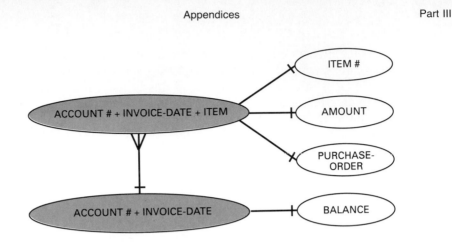

In both cases, ACCOUNT# + INVOICE-DATE + ITEM# would be linked *automatically* to its component data items: ACCOUNT#, INVOICE-DATE, and ITEM#. ACCOUNT# + INVOICE-DATE would be linked *automatically* to ACCOUNT# and INVOICE-DATE. The resulting model would be the same in each case. INVOICE-DATE would not appear as a primary key and hence could be deleted.

INHERENT PROPERTIES OF DATA

The intent of the data model is to represent the *inherent* properties of the data. There are two types of inherent characteristics of the links on the bubble chart—those which are *naturally* inherent, and those which represent *business rules*.

The *naturally* inherent characteristics include such properties as the following: a branch office can have *many* salespeople; an employee has *one* pension record; a supplier can supply *many* parts; a part has only *one* description.

The business rules include such properties as the following: a particular policyholder will be sent all his bills on the same day regardless of how many policies he has; a given flight number is always the same type of plane; a person may have two addresses, but not three.

The data administrator should distinguish between the *naturally* inherent properties and the business rules. In the case of the latter, he needs to determine how feasible the assumed rule is. Could it change? Should the database be set up so that the policyholder bills *could* be sent out on different days? Should TYPE-OF-PLANE be identified by FLIGHT-NUMBER or FLIGHT-NUMBER + DATE? Often, the data structure can be set up so as to anticipate changes in the rules.

GLOSSARY

Note 1: References to Other Entries

Items in **bold** type in the Glossary are defined elsewhere in the Glossary.

Note 2: Types and Instances

Words describing data can either refer to a type of data or an instance (or occurrence) of data. Thus we have:

Entity type	Entity instance (or occurrence)
Attribute type	Attribute instance (or occurrence)
Data item type	Data item instance (or occurrence)
Field type	Field instance (or occurrence)
Association type	Association instance (or occurrence)
Link type	Link instance (or occurrence)
Record type	Record instance (or occurrence)

Type refers to a category of data representation, independent of time or value. *Instance* (or occurrence) refers to a specific example of that data type. The instances of a given type differ from one another in their value. To describe an instance fully, one must provide both the information that defines its type and the values that define this particular instance.

The flight information board at an airport is designed to show certain *types* of data, such as flight number, destination, departure time, and gate. If we look at the board at one instant, it shows values *(instances)* of these data types.

A data model consists exclusively of *type* information. Logical database design is a process of discovering and defining the *types* of entities, attributes, records, associations, and so on. Only when the database is operational are *instances* created (as with the flight information board).

We often refer to data loosely without saying whether we mean a *type* or an *instance*. Thus we say "record," "entity," or "attribute." *Record* is a shorthand word that could mean either *record type* or *record instance*. It might mean employee record (a *type*) or the record for John Jones (an *instance*). This shorthand is useful in that it avoids cluttered descriptions. It should not be used unless that context makes clear whether it refers to *types* or *instances* of data.

Note 3: Items That Are in the Encyclopedia

Some items in this glossary are objects in an IE encyclopedia. These are noted by "(KB)," for knowledge base, at the end of the definition.

ACCEPTANCE TEST. A test, executed by **users** or operators, of the functionality of **procedures** and **programs** against predetermined criteria, to formally accept a new or modified **application system.**

ACCESS. The operation of **seek**ing, reading, or writing **data** on a storage unit.

ACCESS CONTROL SCHEME. A **security technique** by which the use of specific **modules** and **data object types** is restricted to authorized **persons.**

ACCESS MECHANISM. A mechanism for moving one or more reading and writing heads to the position at which certain **data** are to be read or written. Alternatively, the data medium may be moved to the read/write head.

ACCESS METHOD. 1. A **technique** for moving **data** between a computer and its peripheral devices: for example, serial access, **random access, virtual** sequential access method **(VSAM),** hierarchical indexed-sequential access method **(HISAM), access via secondary indices,** and relational accesses such as joins, projects, or other **relational algebra** operations. The word is often used to describe the **type** of file organization that facilitates the accessing technique. 2. A method of retrieving **records** which implies that the records have a particular type of file organization. The word is often used to describe the file organization.

ACCESS TIME. The time that elapses between an instruction being given to **access** some **data** and those data becoming available for use.

ACTION. 1. Something accomplished by a single **program access** command when using the **database.** A *simple action* is a command that creates, reads, updates, or deletes an **instance** of a single **record.** A *compound action* is a command that requires multiple instances of records because it performs a **sort, search,** join, projection, or other relational operation. 2. A **type of activity** by which an **entity** of a given type or a value of a given predicate is involved in some specific way during the execution of a **process,** or by which a record or **linkage** or **field,** is involved in some specific way during the execution of a **procedure.**

ACTION DIAGRAM.   diagram using nested brackets to show a hierarchy or to show the structure of a **program** or specification. An *action diagram* shows loops, **condi-**

tions, case structures, escapes, **database** accesses, subroutine calls, and programming structures in general. Several other types of diagrams can be converted automatically to *action diagrams,* and *action diagrams* can be set to the code of any procedural language. *The use of action diagrams* are the preferred way of representing programming structures and specification structures.

ACTION DIAGRAM EDITOR. A **tool,** usually on a personal computer, with which to build and edit **action diagrams.** The tool helps to enforce good structuring of **programs** and specifications.

ACTION LIST. A selection **list** in which each entry has a defined **action** to be performed upon one or more **objects** in the **encyclopedia.**

ACTION ON ATTRIBUTE. A **type** of **action** performed on a value of an **attribute** during the execution of an action on an **entity** of a given type.

ACTION ON ENTITY TYPE. A **type** of **action** performed on one or more **entities** of an **entity type** at a particular point during the execution of an **elementary process.**

ACTION ON PAIRING. A **type** of **action** on one or more **pairings** of a given **relationship** by an **elementary process** following an action on an **entity.**

ACTION ON PREDICATE. *See* **Action on Attribute; Action on Pairing.**

ACTION STATEMENT. A representation of a minimal unit of a procedural **activity.**

ACTIVITY. 1. Something which is carried out in order to achieve a stated purpose. An *activity* may be a **function, process, procedure,** or **program module.** 2. A collection of **tasks** within the **methodology.**

ACTIVITY ARCHITECTURE. A **model** of the **activities** of the **enterprise** consisting of an **activity decomposition** model and an **activity dependency** model. *See also* **Business Systems Architecture.**

ACTIVITY DECOMPOSITION DIAGRAM. A structure showing the breakdown of **activities** into progressively increasing detail. *See also* **Function Decomposition Diagram; Process Decomposition Diagram; Procedure Decomposition Diagram.**

ACTIVITY RATIO. The percentage of **records** in a file or **data set** which have **activity** (are updated or inspected) in a given period or during a given run.

AD HOC FACILITY. A **set** of **tools** and **techniques** allowing individual **users** to set up their own **systems** and to query databases on a random basis.

ADDRESS. An identification (number, name, **label**) for a **location** in which **data** is stored.

ADDRESSING. The means of assigning **data** to storage **locations,** and subsequently retrieving it, on the basis of the **key** of the data.

AFFINITY. A measure of the strength of the association between two objects.

AFFINITY ANALYSIS. A **technique** for identifying the degree of association between two **objects.**

ALGORITHM. A computational **procedure** containing a finite sequence of steps.

ALTERNATE TRACK. A **track** that is automatically substituted for a damaged track on a disk or other storage device.

ANALYSIS PHASE. A phase of information engineering in which a detailed analysis of business elements is carried out within a defined **business area** in preparation for the design of systems to support that area.

ANTICIPATORY STAGING. The movement of blocks of **data** from one storage device to another device with a shorter **access** time, in anticipation of their being needed by the computer **programs.** This is to be contrasted with **demand staging,** in which the blocks of data are moved *when* programs require them, not *before*.

APPLICATION FLOW DIAGRAM. A schematic representation of the sequence of **application programs.**

APPLICATION PACKAGE. A vendor-supplied, reusable **application system.**

APPLICATION PROGRAM. A **program** included in a specific **application system.** *(KB)*

APPLICATION SYSTEM. The automated and related manual **procedures** within an information system that support a set of **business processes.** One or more applications comprise an information system. *Applications* are defined in the **analysis phase** of the methodology as a result of studying **business area.** *(KB)*

ASSEMBLE. To convert a routine coded in nonmachine language into actual machine language instructions. To perform some or all of the following **functions:** (1) translation of symbolic operation codes into machine codes; (2) allocation of storage, to the extent at least of assigning storage **locations** to successive instructions; (3) computation of absolute or relocatable **addresses** from symbolic addresses; (4) insertion of **library** routines; (5) generation of sequences of symbolic instructions by the insertion of specific parameters into macroinstructions.

ASSOCIATION. A meaningful link between two objects (e.g., **entities,** processes, goals, or **critical success factors**). Associations are used to capture **data** about the relationship between two objects.

ASSOCIATION MATRIX. The summary, in tabular form, of the associations between elements of the same **object type.**

ASSOCIATION RELATION. A **relation** or **record** containing **information** about the association. The association name is sometimes stored. In more advanced forms of **data modeling** information is stored about the *meaning* of the association or the rules which are applied when using the association. *Synonym:* association record.

ASSOCIATIVE ENTITY. An **entity** that exists primarily to interrelate other **entity types.** *See also* **Intersection Entity.**

ASSOCIATIVE STORAGE (MEMORY). Storage that is **addressed** by content rather than by **location,** thus providing a fast way to **search** for **data** having certain contents. (Conventional storage has addresses related to the **physical** location of the data.)

ATTRIBUTE. 1. A **type** of characteristic or property describable in terms of a value that **entities** of a given type possess. *(KB)* 2. A **data item** containing a single piece of **information** about an entity instance. **Records** are composed of *attributes* relating to a given entity. An *attribute* is often atomic; that is, it cannot be broken into parts that have meaning of their own. The term *attribute* is a shorthand meaning of either *attribute type* or *attribute value* (see Note A). All *attributes* of a given type have the same **format,** interpretation, and range of acceptable values. An **instance** of a record has its own (not necessarily unique) value of this *attribute.* 3. A property of an **entity type.** For a specific entity the *attribute* usually has a value that is stored in an **entity record.**

ATTRIBUTE INVOLVEMENT MATRIX. A matrix that shows, for all **attributes** of an **entity type,** the **process**es in which each is involved and by which **actions.**

ATTRIBUTE SOURCE. The categorizing of an **attribute** as to whether its values are basic, derived, or designed. *See also* **Basic Attribute; Derived Attribute; Designed Attribute.**

ATTRIBUTE VALUE. The number, character string, or other element of **information** assigned to a given **attribute** of a given **record instance** at a given time. The name, **format,** interpretation, and range of acceptable values of an attribute are determined by its **attribute type.** Within these constraints, *attribute values* are free to vary from time to time and from one record instance to another. The shorter term ''attribute'' may be used to mean *attribute value,* but only when the context suffices to distinguish it from attribute type. **Attribute instances** can have nulls instead of values. These are of two types: (a) value not yet known (but there can potentially be a value) and (b) value not applicable (the given **entity instance** will *never* have a value for this attribute).

ATTRIBUTIVE ENTITY. An **entity** serving mainly as an **attribute** of another **entity type.**

AUDIT TRAIL. The recording of additions, updates, and deletions to a **data collection,** including time occurred and person responsible.

A means of interaction to transfer **information** between **applications, programs,** or **modules.** *(KB)*

AUTOMATED SYSTEM. A collection of related **programs** performing a routine or repetitive **task.**

AUTOMATIC NAVIGATION. The ability to use high-level **relational algebra** commands, which are automatically executed in the use of a **database,** rather than **accessing records** one at a time.

AVAILABILITY. A measure of system reliability expressed as the fraction of time as agreed. *Availability = time the function is performed as intended/total time during which the function should have been performed.*

BACK UP. The **process** of making copies of files to enable **recovery** of their contents in the event the originals are damaged or lost.

BACKUP COPY. A copy of a **database** or file taken at a known point in time.

BACKUP PROCEDURE. A **procedure** devised to take copies of **data,** transactions, or both to be used in case of loss or corruption of the **database.**

BASIC ATTRIBUTE. An **attribute** whose values cannot be deduced or calculated and hence must be collected during the execution of a **process.**

BATCH PROCESS. A group of **programs** and instructions that accumulates all input before it is run.

BATCH WINDOW. A fixed period of time in which **batch procedures** must be executed.

BEHAVIOR MODEL. The **set** of rules and integrity constraints that determine the combinations of values of **attributes** of different **entity types** in an **information system.**

BEHAVIOR RULE. A rule that must be applied when an **entity, attribute,** or **relationship** is created, **retrieved,** updated, or deleted. It is implemented by invoking a **procedure** that verifies the integrity of the **data structure** and initiates any additional **processing** that may be required. *(KB)*

BENCHMARKING. The execution of a predefined **set** of test cases under **production conditions** in order to evaluate a **system's** performance.

BENEFIT. An effect produced directly or indirectly, by an intervention or **action** upon an **enterprise,** that is helpful, favorable, or profitable to the enterprise. *See also* **Tangible Benefit; Intangible Benefit.**

BENEFIT ANALYSIS. The study of the potential advantages to the **enterprise** resulting from the automation of selected **process**es.

BENEFIT ANALYSIS MATRIX. A matrix containing estimates of the achievable **benefit** from a number of benefit sources resulting from the automation of various **activities.**

"BEST-GUESS" CLUSTERING. A **heuristic** approach to defining **business areas** within an **entity type/process** matrix, based on substantial industry knowledge and experience.

BINARY SEARCH. A method of **search**ing a sequenced **table** or file. The **procedure** involves **select**ing the upper and lower half based on an examination of its midpoint value. The selected portion is then similarly halved, and so on until the required item is found.

BLACK BOX FUNCTION. A reusable **module** developed during the **construction and implementation phase.**

BUFFER. An area of storage that holds **data** temporarily while it is being received, transmitted, read, or written. It is often used to compensate for differences in the speed or timing among devices. *Buffers* are used in terminals, peripheral devices, storage units, and in the CPU.

BUSINESS AREA. A **set** of highly cohesive **process**es and **entity types. Technique**s such as **clustering** or **factor analysis** with an entity type/process matrix are used to identify business areas. A business area is typically the scope of the **analysis phase.**

BUSINESS AREA ANALYSIS. *See* **Analysis Phase.**

BUSINESS AREA ANALYSIS PROJECT. A **project** to analyze a **business area** and produce a **business area information model.** *Synonym:* analysis phase project.

BUSINESS AREA INFORMATION MODEL (BAIM). A product of an **analysis phase.** A *business area information model* is expressed through **data** and **activity models** and represents the **process**es and **information** needed within a **business area** by an organization.

BUSINESS AREA PARTITION. A subdivision of a **business area,** consisting of closely related groups of **process**es and **data** which is created for the purpose of subdividing the effort within an **analysis phase** of a **project.** The **models** pertaining to the **partitions** are progressively consolidated through this **phase.**

BUSINESS EVENT. A significant occurrence, initiated by **external agents** or by the passage of time, which triggers a process that must be recognized and responded to. *(KB)*

BUSINESS FUNCTION. A group of business **activities** which together completely support one aspect of furthering the **mission** of the **enterprise.**

BUSINESS FUNCTION DECOMPOSITION. A **decomposition** of a **business function** into more detailed business functions.

BUSINESS FUNCTION DEPENDENCY. A dependency between two **business functions** which exists because **information** provided by one is required by the other.

BUSINESS PLAN. A high-level, strategic plan used by senior management to direct the **enterprise.** The plan should reference the role of the information systems department within the organization and its expected contribution to business strategies.

BUSINESS PROCESS. A **task** or group of tasks carried out as part of a **business function.**

BUSINESS REQUIREMENT. A formal written statement specifying what the **information system** must do or how it must be structured to support the business.

BUSINESS SEGMENT. A group of **function**s within an organization that provide a family of products or services which relates to a specific market sector. *(KB)*

BUSINESS STRATEGY PLANNING. The **activity** in which the **objective**s and strategies of the **enterprise** are set. This provides prime input to the **information strategy planning stage.**

BUSINESS SYSTEM. *See* **Application System.**

BUSINESS SYSTEM DESIGN (BSD). *See* **Design Phase.**

BUSINESS SYSTEMS ARCHITECTURE. A structure that represents the dependencies between the business **system**s of an **enterprise.**

BUSINESS TRANSACTION. 1. A series of manual steps and computer **process**ing that enables an **elementary process** to be executed successfully. *(KB)* 2. A **logical** unit of work that must be completed as a whole and has a discrete input, defined **procedure,** and specific output or result.

CANDIDATE KEY. A **key** that uniquely identifies **normalized record instance**s of a given **type.** A *candidate key* must have two properties: (a) Each instance of the **record** must have a different value on the key, so that given a key value one can locate a single instance. (b) No **attribute** in the key can be discarded without destroying the property. In a bubble chart, a *candidate key* is a bubble with one or more single-headed arrows leaving it.

CANONICAL MODEL. A **model** of **data** which represents the inherent structure of that data and hence is independent of individual **application**s of the data and also of the software or hardware mechanisms which are employed in representing and using the data. The minimal nonredundant model is a given collection of **data item**s. Neither redundant data items nor redundant associations exist in the *canonical model.* The *canonical model* should correctly represent all **functional dependencies** among the data items in the model. When this is done, the model contains third-normal-form groupings of data items.

CANONICAL SYNTHESIS. The **construction** of a normalized **data model** by integrating separate views of **data** such as inputs, outputs, and **user** views. The views are represented formally and their integration often builds an overall **canonical model.** *Canonical synthesis* is used in conjunction with top-down **entity relationship modeling** to help ensure that a data model is complete.

CARDINALITY. The number of **instance**s of one **object type** associated with an instance of another type. *Cardinality* is a property of an association. *See* **Association.**

CATALOG. A **directory** of all files available to a computer.

CELL. Contiguous storage **location**s referred to as a group in an **addressing** or file **search**ing scheme. The *cell* may be such that it does not cross mechanical boundaries in the storage unit; for example, it could be a **track** or **cylinder.**

CELLULAR CHAINS. **Chain**s that are not permitted to cross **cell** boundaries.

CELLULAR MULTILIST. A form of **multilist organization** in which the **chain**s cannot extend across **cell** boundaries.

CELLULAR SPLITTING. A **technique** for handling **record**s added to a file. The records are organized into **cell**s and a cell is split into two cells when it becomes full.

CHAIN. An organization in which **record**s or other items of **data** are strung together by means of **pointer**s.

CHANNEL. A **subsystem** for input to and output from the computer. **Data** from storage units, for example, flows into the computer via a *channel.*

CHECKPOINT/RESTART. A means of restarting a **program** at some point other than the beginning, used after a failure or interruption has occurred. *Checkpoints* may be used at intervals throughout an **application program;** at these points **record**s are written given enough **information** about the status of the program to permit its being re-started at that point.

CHILD. An **object** in a **decomposition diagram** that is immediately below a specified object.

CIRCULAR FILE. An organization for a file of high volatility, in which new **record**s being added replace the oldest records.

CLUSTER ANALYSIS. A formal **technique** for analyzing the associations of one **object type** to another object type based on their commonality of involvement. Data to activity cluster is specifically used to defining the scope of a phase project. *Synonym:* Clustering.

CODASYL. Conference of Data Systems Languages. The organization that specified the programming language COBOL. It now has specified a **set** of manufacturer-in-dependent, application-independent languages designed to form the basis of **database** management.

COHERENCE. The extent to which components of a **function** or **process** are more closely associated with each other than with components of other functions or pro-cesses.

COMMON LOGIC MODULE. A **module** of a **procedure** or **program** that is used in more than one **function** or **process.**

COMMUNICATIONS NETWORK. A **system** that facilitates the transfer of **information** between the components of computer systems. *(KB)*

COMPACTION. A **technique** for reducing the number of bits in **data** without destroying any **information** content.

COMPILER. A computer **program** that in addition to performing the **function**s of an assembler has the following characteristics: (a) it makes use of **information** on the overall **logical** structure of the program to improve the efficiency of the resulting machine program; (b) its language does not parallel the actual form of the machine language, but rather is oriented toward a convenient **problem** or **procedure** state-ment; (c) it usually generates more than one machine instruction for each symbolic instruction.

COMPOSITE IDENTIFIER. Two or more **attribute**s whose values taken in combination uniquely identify the **entities** of one **type.**

CONCATENATE. To **link** together. A *concatenated* **data set** is a collection of **logically** connected data sets. A *concatenated* **key** is composed of more than one **data item.**

CONCEPTUAL MODEL. The overall **logical** structure of a **database,** which is indepen-dent of any software or **data storage structure.** A *conceptual model* often contains data objects not yet implemented in **physical database**s. It gives a formal represen-tation of the **data** needed to run an **enterprise,** even though certain **system**s in the enterprise may not yet conform to the **model.** Some organizations prefer the term *logical model* rather than *conceptual model,* because "conceptual" might imply that the model may never be implemented.

CONCEPTUAL SCHEMA. A term used to mean the same as **conceptual model.** The word **schema** often refers to the **logical** representation of **data** which is used by a particular class of **database management systems** (e.g., **CODASYL**). *(James Martin: I recommend that the word* model *be used for software-independent data structures, and schema be used for these linked to a specific class of software.)*

CONDITION. 1. A rule expressed in the form "If *P*, then *Q*," which describes one aspect of the behavior of a business. 2. A specified circumstance that causes a particular set of **actions** to be invoked.

CONDITION EVENT. A specific situation in the **enterprise,** occurrences of which trigger the execution of one or more **process**es.

CONDITION LOGIC. A rule expressed in the form of "If *P*, then *Q*." *P* is known as the **condition.**

CONDITION TABLE. A **table** specifying all the valid combinations of **attribute value**s that constitute the **condition.**

CONDITION TREE. A diagram representing an execution **condition** as a hierarchy of all the valid combinations of **attribute values** that constitute the condition.

CONDITIONAL SUBPROCESS. A **process** whose execution depends on **attribute value**s established by prior processes.

CONNECTIVITY ANALYSIS. A **technique** for checking that all **data flow**s in a **process model** or **procedure** are connected to valid source and destination **object**s.

CONSERVATION ANALYSIS. A **technique** for checking that all references made to the use of **data object**s in a **process** or **procedure** are satisfied by the **data flow model** and that there is no redundancy in this model.

CONSTRUCTION. *See* **Construction and Implementation Phase.**

CONSTRUCTION AND IMPLEMENTATION PHASE. A **phase** of **information engineering.** The period in the **systems** life cycle in which the systems, to support a defined area, are coded and proven according to the detailed design specifications produced during the **design phase.** It is also a **set** of work **activities** that implements the **application system** design. Major products of this phase are the coded and tested system; system documentation **package;** a training package; system operating instructions; an operational **database;** and the installed application system.

CONTINGENCY PLAN. A **set** of provisions to ensure that an application **system function**s when something occurs that interrupts or destroys the **information process**ing capability.

CONTINUOUS ATTRIBUTE. An **attribute** whose values cannot be precisely matched against any defined collection. Contrast with **discrete attribute.**

CONTRACT. To contract means to hide **information** and cause **ellipses** to be placed in an item to show that more information is available. It should be possible to *contract* within *contract* within *contract*.

CONTROL REQUIREMENT. A requirement to control the integrity of an **application** (e.g., audit control, **access, security, backup,** and **recovery**). *(KB)*

CONVERSION. The one-time setting up of **data store**s, by transfer of **data** from existing data stores, that will be required by a new **system,** or the translation of existing **program**s to run with new data stores. More generally, it is the **process** of changing **information** from one form of representation to another.

CONVERSION ALGORITHM. A method by which **data** for a field in a current system is transferred to the equivalent field(s) in a new system, and vice versa, for **conversion** and bridging, respectively.

COOPERATING PROCESSES. Two **process**es such that each is dependent on **attribute**s being passed from the other.

COOPERATIVE PROCESSING. A **program** that is split between a personal computer or intelligent workstation and a larger computer to obtain the good human-factoring and low-cost **process**ing of the small machine combined with the power and shared **data** of the large machine.

CORPORATE CULTURE. The collective sense of traditions, conventions, and behavioral **standard**s characteristic of a given **enterprise.** It is determined by **organizational structure** and by formal and informal human resources **policies, procedure**s, and practices.

CORPORATE INFORMATION MODEL. A description of the **entity type**s, **function**s, and **process**es that define an organization and of their inter**relationships.** It consists of a corporate data model, a corporate activity model, and a corporate organizational model.

COURSE ANALYSIS. A **technique** for checking that the paths through a **data flow model** are complete, consistent, and without redundancy.

CRITICAL ASSUMPTIONS. A group of assumptions about a **business segment,** competitor, or industry that supports or validates an organization's **critical success factors.**

CRITICAL DECISIONS. The decisions that must be made by an organization to have an impact on its **critical success factors.**

CRITICAL INFORMATION. The **information** that is required by an organization's operational **system** to enable them to support the organization's **critical success factors.**

CRITICAL SUCCESS FACTOR. An internal or external business-related result that is measurable and that will have a major influence on whether a **business segment** meets its **goals.** *(KB)*

CRITICAL SUCCESS FACTOR ANALYSIS. A **process** for extracting and reconciling **critical success factors.**

CRUD MATRIX. A tabular representation of the **relationship** between **process**es and **entities** with an indication as to whether the type of involvement is created, **retrieve**d, updated, deleted, or a combination of these.

CULTURAL CHANGES. Changes in the business's **organizational structure, skill** and staffing levels, **job functions,** or **policies** and **procedures.**

CURRENT APPLICATION. *An* **application** *presently in use.*

CURRENT PROCESSING CONFIGURATION. A **process***ing configuration presently in use.*

CYLINDER. That area of a storage unit which can be read without the movement of an **access mechanism.** The term originated with disk files, in which a *cylinder* consisted of one **track** on each disk surface such that each of these tracks could have a read/ write head positioned over it simultaneously.

DASD. *See* **Direct Access Storage Device.**

DATA. Facts or figures from which conclusions can be inferred.

DATA ACCESS DIAGRAM. *See* **Logical Access Map (LAM).**

DATA ADMINISTRATOR. A person with an overview understanding of an organization's **data.** The function is responsible for the most cost-effective organization and use of an **enterprise's** data resources. The *data administrator* is ultimately responsible for designing the **data model** and obtaining agreement about the definitions of data which are maintained in the **data dictionary.**

DATA AGGREGATE. A named collection of **data item**s within a **record.** There are two types: vectors and repeating groups. A vector is a one-dimensional, ordered collection of data items, all of which have identical characteristics. A repeating group is a collection of **data** that occurs an arbitrary number of times within a record occurrence. The collection may consist of data items, vectors, and repeating groups. (CODASYL)

DATA ANALYSIS. A disciplined approach to analyzing the meaning and properties of the **data element**s in existing clerical forms and computer files, independently from the **system**s that produce and use this **data.**

DATA ARCHITECTURE. A structure that **model**s the **data** of the **enterprise.**

DATA BANK. A collection of **online data.** The term **database** is more precise than *data bank. Database* implies the formal **technique**s of database management. *Data bank* refers to any collection of data, whether in the form of files, databases, or an **information retrieval** system.

DATA COLLECTION. A repository of **data** maintained by an **enterprise,** usually in the form of manual or electronic files. *(KB)*

DATA CONSERVATION ANALYSIS. *See* **Conservation Analysis.**

DATA DEPENDENCY. The situation where a **process** creates or modifies some **data,** which is subsequently used by some other process.

DATA DESCRIPTION LANGUAGE. A language for describing **data** (in some software for describing the **logical,** not the **physical,** data; in other software for both).

DATA DICTIONARY. A **catalog** of all **data type**s, giving their names and structures, and **information** about **data** usage. Advanced *data dictionaries* have a **directory**

function that enables them to represent and report on the cross-references between components of data and business **model**s.

DATA DIVISION (COBOL). That division of a COBOL **program** which consists of entries used to define the nature and characteristics of the **data** to be **process**ed by the procedure division of the program.

DATA ELEMENT. The **physical** representation of an **attribute.** A *data element* has a specified size and **format.** The smallest unit of **data** that has meaning in describing information; the smallest unit of named data. *(KB)*

DATA FLOW. The movement of a **data view** between two objects, each being a **process, procedure, data store,** or **external agent.** *(KB)*

DATA FLOW COURSE ANALYSIS. *See* **Course Analysis.**

DATA FLOW DIAGRAM. A diagram of the **data flows** through a set of **process**es or **procedure**s. It shows the **external agent**s that are sources or destinations of data, the **activities** that transform the data, and the **data stores** or **data collections** where the data is held.

DATA FLOW EXPRESSION. A precise definition of the **data** content of a **data flow,** expressed using a formal syntax and notation.

DATA INDEPENDENCE. The property of being able to change the overall **logical** or **physical** structure of the **data** without changing the **application program**'s view of the data.

DATA INDEPENDENCE, LOGICAL. The property of being able to change the overall **logical** structure of the **data** without changing the **application program**'s view of the data.

DATA INDEPENDENCE, PHYSICAL. The property of being able to change the **physical** structure of the **data** without changing the **application program's logical** structure.

DATA ITEM. *See* **Data Element.**

DATA MANAGEMENT. A general term that collectively describes those **function**s of the **system** that provide creation of and **access** to stored **data,** enforce data storage conventions, and regulate the use of input/output devices.

DATA MANIPULATION LANGUAGE. The language that the programmer uses to cause **data** to be transferred between his **program** and the **database.** The *data manipulation language* is not a complete language by itself. It relies on a host programming language to provide a framework for it and to provide the procedural capabilities required to manipulate data.

DATA MODEL. A **logical map** of **data** which represents the inherent properties of the data independently of software, hardware, or machine performance considerations. The **model** shows **data items** grouped into **third-normal-form record**s, and shows the associations among those records. The term *model* may be contrasted with the term **schema.** A schema also shows a logical representation of data, but it is usually related to a type of software representation (e.g., **CODASYL,** hierarchical, or relational). *(James Martin: I recommend that the term* model *be reserved for data representation that are independent of which class of software is used for implementation. The software choice may change, but the model remains a fundamental description of the data.)*

DATA SET. A named collection of **logically** related **data item**s, arranged in a prescribed manner, and described by control **information** to which the programming **system** has access. Also, a part of the storage provided on a storage device, the extent of which is defined in terms of **physical** characteristics of that device and which is used as a container for specific files or parts of files.

DATA SHARING. The situation where one **type** of **data** is used to support more than one **activity.**

DATA STORAGE STRUCTURE. The way in which **data** is organized in storage, which determines the performance of the business **system**s in their use of data, but which is not known to **program**s. **It is a type of data structure. The data storage structures are defined records, relations, and interface files.**

DATA STORE. A repository of **data,** possibly temporary, of which **user**s are aware, and from which data may be read repeatedly and nondestructively. *(KB)*

DATA STRUCTURE. A designed and defined collection of **record types, linkages, field**s, entry points, and **integrity rule**s required to support one or more business **system**s.

DATA STRUCTURE DESIGN. A way of organizing the **data** required to support one or several business **system**s, which assumes the constraints of a given **data management** system.

DATA STRUCTURE DIAGRAM. A representation of a **data structure.**

DATA TYPE. The size and type of a **data element.** An interpretation applied to a string of bits, such as integer, real, or character.

DATA USAGE ANALYSIS. A disciplined approach to documenting the ways and frequencies by which **data element**s are used in each **location** in existing **system**s and will be used in future systems.

DATA USAGE MATRIX. A matrix that shows, for each **record, field** or **linkage type,** the **procedure**s in which it is involved, and by which **action**s.

DATA VIEW. 1 An organized collection of **field**s or layouts that is meaningful to a **procedure,** business **system,** or **organizational unit.** *(KB)* 2. A subset of the **data model** which specifies a grouping of **entities, attributes,** and **relationships** which is used by a **process, procedure, data store,** or **external agent.**

DATABASE. 1. A collection of interrelated **data** stored together with controlled redundancy to serve one or more **application**s; the data is stored so that it is independent of **program**s that use the data; a common and controlled approach is used in adding new data and in modifying and retrieving existing data within a *database.* A **system** is said to contain a collection of *databases* if they are disjoint in structure. *(IE)* 2. A *database* consists of all the **record** occurrences, **set** occurrences, and areas that are controlled by a specific **schema.** If an **installation** has multiple *databases,* there must be a separate schema for each *database.* Furthermore, the content of different *databases* is assumed to be disjoint. (CODASYL)

DATABASE ADMINISTRATOR. A person with an overview of one or more **databases,** who controls the physical design and use of these databases. It is often better to use two people: a **data administrator,** who manages the architecture and logical model, and a database administrator, who designs the **physical** aspects of the database.

DATABASE MANAGEMENT SYSTEM. The collection of software required for using a **database,** and presenting multiple different views of the **data** to the **user**s and programmers. The **system** software manages the database, provides for **logical** and **physical data independence,** controls redundancy, and enforces integrity constraints, privacy, and **security.**

DATA/PROCESS INVOLVEMENT MODEL. A **model** of the associations between **type**s of **data (entities)** and the **process**es that use them, which are constructed as a series of **data views** from the processes.

DB/DC. **Database**/data communication.

DECISION TABLE. A diagram that consists of a **condition table,** together with a list of the **process**es that are executed for each combination of **attribute value** in the **table.**

DECOMPOSITION. The step-by-step breakdown into increasing detail either of **function**s, eventually into **process**es, or of subject areas into subject areas, organizational units.

DECOMPOSITION DIAGRAM. A structure that shows the breakdown of **object**s of a given **type** into progressively increasing detail.

DEFAULT VALUE. The value that represents an **attribute** when no specific value is supplied by the **process**es establishing occurrences of the attribute.

DELIVERABLE. A subset of the **knowledge base** which is presented and approved.

DEMAND STAGING. Blocks of **data** are moved from a storage device to another device with a shorter **access time** (possibly including main memory); when **program**s request them and they are not already in the faster **access** storage. Contrast with **anticipatory staging.**

DEPENDENCY. *See* **Process Dependency; System Dependency; Business Function Dependency; Data Dependency.**

DERIVED ATTRIBUTE. An **attribute** whose values can each be calculated or deduced from the values of other attributes.

DESIGN AREA. A collection of closely related **process**es and **entity types for** which an application system is designed.

DESIGN PHASE. The period in the **systems lifecycle** in which a complete and detailed specification is produced of the **application system** needed to support a defined area within the **enterprise.**

DESIGNED ATTRIBUTE. An **attribute** that has been invented in order to overcome constraints or to simplify the operation of a **system.**

DEVICE/MEDIA CONTROL LANGUAGE. A language for specifying the **physical** layout and organization of **data.**

DIALOG. 1. A generic word for a preplanned human-machine interaction; it encompasses formal programming languages, languages for interrogating **databases,** and innumerable nonformal conversational interchanges, many of which are designed for one specific **application.** *(KB)* 2. A series of exchanges in which a **user,** through the use of **screen** components, either makes an inquiry or provides **information** to an application.

DIALOG FLOW DIAGRAM. A representation of the steps within a **dialog,** their sequence, and the **screen** layouts used by each step.

DICTIONARY. *See* **Data Dictionary.**

DIRECT ACCESS. Retrieval or storage of **data** by a reference to its **location** on a **volume,** rather than relative to the previously **retrieved** or stored data. The **access mechanism** goes directly to the data in question, as is normally required with **online** use of data.

DIRECT ACCESS STORAGE DEVICE (DASD). A **data** storage unit on which data can be **access**ed directly at random without having to progress through a serial file such as tape. A disk unit is a *direct access storage device.*

DIRECTORY. A **table** giving the **relationships** between items of **data.** Sometimes a table **(index)** giving the **address**es of data.

DISCRETE ATTRIBUTE. An **attribute** whose values are restricted to a defined collection of values. Contrast with **continuous attribute.**

DISTRIBUTED FREE SPACE. Space left empty at intervals in a **data** layout to permit the possible insertion of new data.

DISTRIBUTION ANALYSIS. A **technique** for assessing the **location** of **data** repositories and **process**ing **system**s across the locations of an **enterprise.**

DL/1. IBM's Data Language/1, for describing **logical** and **physical data** structures.

DOMAIN. 1. The collection of **data item**s **(field**s) of the same **type,** in a **relation (flat file).** 2. A **named set** of values that an **attribute** can assume.

DYNAMIC STORAGE ALLOCATION. The allocation of storage space to a **procedure** based on the instantaneous or actual demand for storage space by the procedure, rather than allocating storage space to a procedure based on its anticipated or predicted demand.

ELEMENTARY PROCESS. The smallest unit of **decomposition** in the **process model** for a **business area.** An *elementary process* is executed in response to a single triggering **event** and consists of a simple sequence of business **procedure**s. It is the smallest unit of business **activity** of meaning to a **user,** which when complete leaves the business area in a self-consistent **state.**

ELEMENTARY STEP. A step that is the smallest unit of **activity** within a **procedure** which has meaning to a **user** or operator.

ELLIPSIS. A symbol consisting of three dots (. . .) which indicates that more **information** is available. With **tools** that use this symbol the additional information may be displayed by pointing to the line or block containing the three dots and giving the command **"Expand."**

EMBEDDED POINTERS. Pointers in the **record**s used for addressing the records rather than a directory.

ENCYCLOPEDIA. A repository of knowledge about the **enterprise,** its **goals, entities, records, organizational units, functions, processes, procedure**s, and **application and information systems.** It is populated progressively during each **stage** of **information engineering.** A **dictionary** contains names and descriptions of **data item**s, processes, variables, etc. An *encyclopedia* contains complete coded representations of plans, **model**s, and designs with **tool**s for cross-checking, correlation analysis, and validation. Graphic representations are derived from the *encyclopedia* and are used to update it. The *encyclopedia* contains many rules relating to the knowledge it stores, and employs rule processing, the artificial intelligence **technique,** to help achieve accuracy, integrity, and completeness of the plans, models, and designs. The *encyclopedia* is thus a **knowledge base** which not only stores development **information** but helps to control its accuracy and validity. The *encyclopedia* should be designed to drive a code generator. The toolset helps the **system**s analyst build up in the *encyclopedia* the information necessary for code generation. The *encyclopedia* "understands" the **module**s and designs; a dictionary does not.

ENTERPRISE. An organization that exists to perform a **mission** and to achieve **objectives.** This information is typically stored in the **encyclopedia.** *(KB)*

ENTERPRISE KNOWLEDGE BASE. A formally controlled and approved collection of **information** used to develop, support, maintain, and operate **information systems.**

ENTERPRISE MODEL. A description of the **entity type**s, **function**s, and **process**es that define an **enterprise** and the inter**relationship**s.

ENTERPRISE STRATEGY. A plan or **action** of an **enterprise** to achieve a stated **goal** or **objective.**

ENTITY. 1. A **person,** place, thing or concept that has characteristics of interest to the **enterprise.** *(KB)* 2. An *entity* is something about which we store **data.** Examples of *entities* are: Customer, Part, Employee, Invoice, Machine Tool, Salesperson, Branch Office, Sales TV Area, Warehouse, Warehouse Bin, Shop Order, Shift **Report,** Product, Product Specification, Ledger Account, Payment, Debtor, and Debtor Analysis Record. An *entity* has various **attributes** which we wish to record, such as Color, Size, Monetary Value, Percentage Utilization, or Name. For each **entity type** we have at least one **record type.** Sometimes more than one record type is used to store the data about the *entity* type (because of **normalization**). An *entity* type has one **data item type** or a group of data item types which uniquely identifies it. *Entity* is a shorthand word meaning either *entity type* or *entity instance* (*see* Note A).

ENTITY ANALYSIS. A disciplined approach to understanding and documenting the things of interest to the **enterprise**, independently from the **activities** that take place in the enterprise. *See also* **Data Analysis.**

ENTITY IDENTIFIER. A **key** that uniquely identifies an **entity.**

ENTITY LIFECYCLE. A description of the sets of processes and events that can act on an entity in each of the states that are possible in the lives of the entities of that type. A description of what happens during the lives of entities of one type. The lifecycle is analyzed for the entity from the time it becomes of interest to an enterprise to the time it ceases to be of interest to the enterprise.

ENTITY LIFECYCLE ANALYSIS. A technique for analyzing the transition of an entity between its possible states (defined in terms of changes to the values of its attributes) to identify any missing processes.

ENTITY LIFECYCLE DIAGRAM. A diagram showing all the possible states in the lives of the **entities** of one type and processes that cause changes in their states.

ENTITY LIFECYCLE MATRIX. A matrix showing for each state, applicable to the **entities** of one type, the processes that are valid and those which cause a change in state.

ENTITY MODEL. A **model** of the **entity type**s, their **attribute type**s, and the **relationship** between entity types that represent the kind of **information** needed to **support an enterprise.**

ENTITY-RELATIONSHIP DIAGRAM. A diagram representing **entity type**s and the **relationship**s between them, and certain properties of the relationship, especially its **cardinality** and name.

ENTITY-RELATIONSHIP MODEL. A detailed and structured representation of all the results of **entity analysis.** It contains the diagram and all the released definitions.

ENTITY STATE. A definable, discrete period in the life of an **entity.** *(KB)*

ENTITY STATE MATRIX. A tabular representation of an **entity lifecycle.**

ENTITY STATE TRANSITION DIAGRAM. A pictorial representation of an **entity lifecycle.**

ENTITY SUBTYPE. A collection of **entities** of the same **type** but to which a narrower definition and additional attributes and/or relationships apply.

ENTITY TYPE. *See* **Entity.**

ENTITY-TYPE LIFECYCLE. *See* **Entity Lifecycle.**

ENTITY-TYPE LIFECYCLE ANALYSIS. *See* **Entity Lifecycle Analysis.**

ERROR HANDLING. Computer instructions to detect errors in input **information** and provide a response to a **user** and/or an alternative logic path.

EVENT. *See* **Business Event.**

EVENT MODEL. A diagram illustrating the valid **state**s of a **system** and the **transition**s between states.

EVENT TRIGGER. A value of an **attribute** or a set of attributes that causes a **process** to execute or to cease execution.

EVOLUTION PROPOSAL. A proposal prepared during the end of the **construction and implementation phase** which outlines continued development of **application system**s to meet changes in underlying business needs.

EXECUTION CONTROL SOFTWARE. A **set** of instructions to the computer that control the order of execution of computer **program**s and specify the **data collection**s they will use. *(KB)*

EXISTENCE DEPENDENCY. An **integrity condition** constraining two **attribute**s, such that each value of the first attribute determines whether or not for each **entity** it is meaningful for a value of the second attribute to exist.

EXPAND. A command used to display hidden **information** by pointing to an item containing an **ellipsis** (. . .). It should be possible to *expand* multiple times to reveal successive levels of detail.

EXTENT. A contiguous area of **data** storage.

EXTERNAL AGENT. The persons, **application system**s, or organizations outside the **project scope** with whom a **process** must interact and exchange **information.** *(KB)*

EXTERNAL EVENT. A change in the external environment affecting the area under study. The change is recognized by a flow of incoming **data.**

EXTERNAL SCHEMA. A **user**'s or programmer's view of the **data.** A **set** of similarly constructed **record**s. *Synonym:* **subschema.** *See also* **Data Element.**

FACILITY. A collective term for the accommodation, equipment, services, and supplies necessary to support the development and use of **application system**s. *(KB)*

FACTOR ANALYSIS. A **technique** for defining **business area**s by using a statistical approach to surface correlations between **process**es and **entity types.**

FALLBACK PROCEDURE. A **procedure** that allows business **activities** to continue while a computer **system** is unavailable.

FAN-OUT. The **process** by which a new **system** is first installed in one or a small number of groups of business **user**s and then expanded to involve all potential users within the organization.

FIELD. A physical container for **data elements,** representing part of a screen, report, or form layout.

FILTER. A **selec**tion **condition** expressed in terms of values, property **type**s, and **association type**s which restricts a view of **information** from the **encyclopedia.**

FILTERED MODEL. A diagram that represents only those elements **select**ed to be supported by one or more integrated **systems.**

FIXED ATTRIBUTE. An **attribute** whose values, once established for any given **entity,** remain unchanged for the life of that entity.

FIXED CARDINALITY. A type of **cardinality condition** in which the cardinality of a **dependency, relationship,** or subprocess is always the same number.

FIXED EVENT. An event that occurs at fixed time intervals and so is completely predictable.

FLAT FILE. A sequential file of **data elements.**

FLOW EXPRESSION. *See* **Data Flow Expression.**

FOCUS. Arthur Young's strategic management service that is used as a guideline in assisting clients in evaluating their current situation and future developments, developing creative strategies, and implementing their resulting plans through achieving change.

FOREIGN KEY. An **attribute** of an **entity type** that is an **identifier** of a second entity type.

FORM. A pro forma document used for collecting **information** for later storage in a **data collection.** *(KB)*

FORMAT. The way in which the digits and characters are displayed for occurrences of **field.**

FUNCTION. A **logical** collection of **process**es within a **business segment.** *See also* **Business Function.** *(KB)*

FUNCTION ANALYSIS. A disciplined approach to understanding and documenting the detailed **activities** in the **enterprise,** independently from its organization structure.

FUNCTION DECOMPOSITION. 1. The breakdown of the **activities** of an **enterprise** into progressively increasing detail. 2. The breakdown of the **function**s of an enterprise into progressively increasing detail.

FUNCTION DECOMPOSITION DIAGRAM. A structure that shows the breakdown of **function**s into progressively increasing detail.

FUNCTION DEPENDENCY. *See* **Business Function Dependency.**

FUNCTION DEPENDENCY DIAGRAM. A diagram that shows how each **function** depends on other functions.

FUNCTION MODEL. A representation of one or more **activities** that a **system** performs.

FUNCTIONAL DEPENDENCE. 1. **Attribute** B of a **relation** R is *functionally dependent* on attribute A or R if, at every instant in time, each value of A has no more than one value of B associated with in relation R (equivalent to saying that A identifies B). An attribute or collection of attributes, B, of a relation, R, is said to be *fully functionally dependent* on the whole of A but not on any subset of A. 2. A **dependency** between two **field**s, such that the value of the first determines the value of the second.

FUNCTIONAL REQUIREMENT. A functional-level capability or business rule identified by an organization which is necessary to solve a **problem** or achieve an **objective.**

FUNDAMENTAL ENTITY TYPE. An **entity type** whose instances are each not dependent on any other entities for their existence.

GLOBAL MODEL. A diagram that represents all of the **enterprise** or that part of the enterprise so far analyzed.

GOAL. 1. A statement of an organization's medium- to long-term target or direction of development. A *goal* is achieved when all **objective**s relating to it have been achieved. Typically, *goals* do not have exact timetables or achievement measures associated with them. *(KB)* 2. Specific targets that a **business segment** intends to meet within a specified time frame to further the achievement of more general objectives.

HARDWARE COMPONENT. A physical device in a computer **system.** *(KB)*

HASH TOTAL. A total of the values of a certain **field** in a file, maintained for control purposes to ensure that no items are lost or changed invalidly, and thus having no meaning of its own.

HASHING. A **direct access**ing **technique** in which the **key** is converted to a pseudo-random number from which the required **address** is derived.

HEADER RECORD OR HEADER TABLE. A **record** containing common, constant, or identifying **information** for a group of records that follows.

HEURISTIC. Pertaining to trial-and-error methods of obtaining solutions to **problems.**

HIERARCHICAL FILE. A file in which some **record**s are subordinate to others in a **tree structure.**

HIERARCHICAL STORAGE. Storage units **link**ed together to form a storage **subsystem,** in which some forms are fast but small and others are large but slow. Blocks of **data** are moved from the large, slow **level**s to the small, fast levels when required.

HIT RATE. A measure of the number of **record**s in a file which are expected to be **access**ed in a given run. Usually expressed as a percentage: *number of records accessed* × *100%/number of records in the file.*

HOME ADDRESS. 1. The **address** of a **physical** storage **location** (e.g., a home bucket) into which a **data record** is assigned; as opposed to **overflow** address. 2. A **field** that contains the physical address of a **track,** recorded at the beginning of a track.

HOMONYM. A name that is used ambiguously to denote two or more different **objects.**

HUFFMAN CODE. A code for **data compaction** in which frequently used characters are encoded with a smaller number of bits than are infrequently used characters.

HYPERCHART. *See* **Hyperdiagram.**

HYPERDIAGRAM. A collection of diagrams relating to a **process** or **procedure** with

logical links and **relationship**s between the diagrams so that they constitute an integrated whole. Changing one of the diagrams that constitute a *hyperdiagram* may result in other diagrams changing automatically in order to preserve consistency among the diagrams. *Synonym:* **hyperchart.**

HYPERVIEW. A **user** view consisting of related diagrams joined into a **hyperdiagram.**

IDENTIFIER. An **attribute** or **relationship** or combination of attributes and relationships that identifies **instance**s of an **entity type.**

IMPLEMENTATION AREA. A functional area within the **enterprise** where a new **application,** or parts of it, may be implemented in a coherent fashion. A new application may be phased in over time in a series of *implementation areas.*

INDEPENDENCE, DATA. *See* **Data Independence.**

INDEPENDENCE, DEVICE. **Data** organization that is independent of the device on which the data is stored.

INDEX. A **table** used to determine the **location** of a **record.**

INDEX CHAINS. **Chain**s within an **index.**

INDEX POINT. A hardware reference mark on a disk or drum; used for timing purposes.

INDEX, SECONDARY. *See* **Secondary Index.**

INDEXED-SEQUENTIAL STORAGE. A file structure in which **record**s are stored in ascending sequence by **key. Indices** showing the highest key on a **cylinder, track,** bucket, and so on, are used for the **select**ed **retrieval** of records.

INDICATIVE DATA. **Data** that identify or describe; for example, in a stock file, the product number, description, and pack size. Normally, *indicative data* does not change on a regular, frequent basis during **process**ing (as in, for example, an account balance).

INDIRECT ADDRESSING. Any method of specifying or locating a storage **location** whereby the **key** (directly or through calculation) does not represent an **address:** for example, locating an address through **indices.**

INDUSTRY MODEL. A generic business information model that is applicable to a range of **enterpris**es within a given industry. *Industry models* are maintained (as templates awaiting customizing) in the **information engineering encyclopedia.**

INFORMATION. Any formal, structured **data** that is required to support a business and can be stored in or **retrieve**d from a computer.

INFORMATION ARCHITECTURE. A structure expressed in terms of an **entity-relationship model** and a **function** or **process dependency model,** based on which individual business **system**s can be developed, in the knowledge that these may be readily integrated and share **data** at a future time.

INFORMATION ENGINEER. An **information system**s professional who has been trained in and who practices **information engineering.**

INFORMATION ENGINEERING. 1. An interlocking **set** of formal **technique**s in which business **models**, **data model**s, and **process** models are built up in a comprehensive **knowledge base** and are used to create and maintain **information systems.** 2. An interlocking set of automated techniques which apply structured planning, analysis, and design to the **enterprise** as a whole rather than merely to one **project.** 3. A **methodology** that creates a corporatewide architectural framework for information systems. 4. An interlocking set of computerized techniques in which **enterprise models**, data models, process models, and system designs are built up in an **encyclopedia** (a knowledge base) and used to create and maintain more effective DP **system**s. 5. An enterprisewide set of disciplines for getting the right **information** to the right people at the right time and providing them with **tool**s to use the information.

INFORMATION ENGINEERING/JOINT SESSION TECHNIQUES (IE/JST). A strategy for rapid product development through end **user** and **system** professional participation in thorough, well-structured group sessions under the control of a facilitator. Ideas are captured in computerized **model**s through automated diagramming **tool**s.

INFORMATION FLOW EVENT. *See* **Business Event.**

INFORMATION MODEL. A high-level **data model,** describing **key** business **entities** and their **relationship**s, but without full **attribute information,** reference, or **intersection** entities.

INFORMATION NEED. A specific **information requirement** of a particular **person** or **organizational unit** to make a decision or complete a **task.** *Information needs* provide an input to **entity modeling.** *(KB)*

INFORMATION REQUIREMENT. *See* **Information Need.**

INFORMATION STRATEGY PLANNING (ISP). The period in the **systems lifecycle** in which an **information architecture,** a **business systems architecture,** and a **technical architecture** are first produced and under which a consistent and integrated set of business systems will be developed. *See also* **Planning Phase.**

INFORMATION SYSTEM. (?) 1. A **system** of **data** and **process**es that can be used to record and maintain **information.** Contrasted with **production system,** to mean a system in which the data stored will be used in ways that are not fully predictable in advance. *(KB)* 2. A **logical partition** of data and processes that can be analyzed independently to collect, store, and **retrieve** information to satisfy a portion of a **business segment**'s **information need**s. **Business area** is often used interchangeably with the **scope** of an *information system*.

INFORMATION SYSTEMS ENVIRONMENT. The technologies, applications portfolio, human resources, and management practices that constitute an organization's **information system**s capability.

INFORMATION SYSTEMS GROUP. A generic name for an enterprise's information systems organizational units.

INFORMATION SYSTEMS REQUIREMENT. A condition or capability that must be met by a **system** or system component to satisfy a contract, standard, specification, or other formal document.

INFORMATION TECHNOLOGY. The merging of computing and high-speed communication **link**s carrying **data,** sound, and video.

INFRASTRUCTURE. The basic **installation**s and **facilities** on which continuance and growth of an organization depend.

INHIBITOR. A factor that could prevent the **enterprise** from achieving its **objective**s or **goals.**

INSPECTION. A **technique** of quality control which detects and records defects in **deliverables.**

INSTALLATION. 1. The **process** of making an application's system operative to end users. 2. The process of turning the developed system into a production status.

INSTANCE. See Note A.

INTANGIBLE BENEFIT. A **benefit** to which a direct monetary value cannot be applied. *See also* **Benefit.**

INTEGRATION TEST. A test that is conducted to prove that a group of interfacing modules operates as expected and that the programming language statements ("code") perform as defined in the module specification. An iterative **process** involving the multiple levels of testing.

INTEGRITY CONDITION. *See* **Integrity Rule.**

INTEGRITY RULE. A rule expressed in terms of **logical data** constructs and/or layouts and/or constants, which states a constraint upon the data values and/or **linkage memberships** of a business **system.**

INTERNAL EVENT. An **event** that results from the execution of some **process** within the **enterprise.**

INTERNAL SCHEMA. The **physical** structure of the **data.** A description of the data described in the **schema** as represented on storage media. *Synonym:* **data storage structure.**

INTERPRETIVE ROUTINE. A routine that decodes instruction written as pseudocodes and immediately executes those instructions, as contrasted with a **compiler,** which decodes the pseudocodes and produces a machine language routine to be executed at a later time.

INTERSECTION. **A form of entity identification requiring of two or more relationship members.**

INTERSECTION DATA. **Data** associated with the conjunction of two or more **entities** or **record type**s, but which has no meaning if associated with only one of them.

INTERSECTION ENTITY. Some characteristics represented in **attributes** belong not to individual **entity instance**s but to specific combinations of two or more entity instances. Such cases require a separate **data** grouping called **intersection data.** The

intersection is represented in a **logical data model** by a **normalized record type** whose **primary key** is the concatenation of the **keys** that identify the entities involved, and whose other attributes represent characteristics belonging to the intersection. Usually, an intersection relates to entities of different types (e.g., Supplier and Part). Less commonly it relates to entities of the same type (e.g., Subassembly and Subassembly, when a product or subassembly contains multiple other subassemblies). *Synonym:* **associative entity.**

INVERTED FILE. A file structure that permits fast spontaneous **search**ing for previous unspecified **information.** Independent **list**s or **indices** are maintained in **record**s **keys** that are accessible according to the values of specific **fields.**

INVERTED LIST. A **list** organized by a **secondary key,** not a **primary key.**

INVOLUTED DEPENDENCY. The situation where the execution of a **process** may lead to a further execution of the same process.

INVOLUTED RELATIONSHIP. A **relationship** in which the two **entities** of every **pairing** are from the same **entity type.**

INVOLVEMENT MATRIX. The summary of the involvement of **process**es with **entity type**s, or **procedure**s with **record types.**

IS FUNCTION. A subtype of **function** specific to IS which provides a service to support **application systems** (e.g., **data** center operations, technical support, data resource management). *(KB)*

IS ORGANIZATIONAL UNIT. A subtype of an **organizational unit** that develops, implements, operates, and maintains **application system**s. *Synonym:* **information systems group.** *(KB)*

IS STRATEGY. A **set** of plans aimed at successful achievement of **goal**s in terms of developing application **systems.** *(KB)*

ISAM. Indexed-sequential **access method.**

ISOLATED ENTITY TYPE. An **entity type** that does not participate in any **relationship.**

JOB. A sequence of one or more **job step**s that is activated as a unit. *Synonyms:* batch job; **run unit.**

JOB FUNCTION. A set of **skill**s of a **person** to fill a role in an organization. *(KB)*

JOB STEP. One main **program** that has (optionally) a hierarchy of one or more subprograms and is activated by an **operating system.** *It is a component of a job.*

JUNCTION. The point at which a **data flow** divides or combines with another flow or crosses a **level** in the data flow **model.**

KEY. A **data item** or combination of data items used to identify or locate a **record instance** (or other **data** groupings).

KEY, CANDIDATE. *See* **Candidate Key.**

KEY COMPRESSION. A **technique** for reducing the number of bits in **key**s; used in making **indices** occupy less space.

KEY, PRIMARY. A **key** that is used to uniquely identify a **record instance** (or other **data** grouping).

KEY, SEARCH. *Synonym:* **secondary key.**

KEY, SECONDARY. An alternative key to the primary key. It is not used to uniquely identify a **record instance;** that is, more than one record instance can have the same key value. A key that contains the value of an **attribute (data item)** other than the unique **identifier.** *Secondary keys* are used to **search** a file or extract subsets of it (e.g., ''all the engineers'' or ''all employees living in Boston''.)

KNOWLEDGE BASE. A **data** repository that contains both **information** and knowledge about applying this information within a particular context. The latter is usually expressed in the form of rules.

KNOWLEDGE COORDINATOR. The portion of the **information engineering** toolkit responsible for applying the rules of information engineering to ensure the consistency and correctness of any **information** that will be saved in the **encyclopedia.**

LABEL. A **set** of symbols used to identify or describe an item, **record,** message, or file. Occasionally, it may be the same as the **address** in storage.

LATENCY. The time taken for a storage **location** to reach the read/write heads on a rotating surface. For general timing purposes, average *latency* is used; this is the time taken by one half-revolution of the surface.

LEVEL. The number of times the **object** of broadest **scope** has been progressively decomposed to arrive at the object being described.

LFU. Least Frequently Used. A replacement **algorithm** in which when new **data** has to replace existing data in an area of storage, the least frequently used items are replaced. Contrast with **LRU.**

LIBRARY. 1. The room in which **volumes** (tapes and disk packs) are stored. 2. An organized collection of **program**s, source statements, or **object module**s maintained on a **direct access storage device** accessible by the **operating system.**

LIFECYCLE ANALYSIS. *See* **Entity Lifecycle Analysis.**

LIFECYCLE DIAGRAM. *See* **Entity Lifecycle Diagram.**

LIFECYCLE MATRIX. *See* **Entity Lifecycle Matrix.**

LINK. An association or **relationship** between **entities** or **records**. A *link* is drawn as a line connecting entities or records on an entity chart or **data model.** The word *link* is more visual than *association* or *relationship* and so is sometimes preferred when referring to such lines drawn on charts. The word *link* sometimes refers to **link relation** or **link record.** A distinction should be made between **link type**s and **link instance**s (see Note A). This is important when the **attribute instance**s associated with a *link* can change as they might in an intelligent **database.**

LINK RELATION OR LINK RECORD. A **relation** or **record** containing **information** about the **link.** *See also* **Association Relation.**

LINKAGE. A connection between two related **record**s by which records may be **ac-cess**ed, but of which **module**s need have no knowledge.

LINKAGE MEMBERSHIP. The participation of a **record layout** in a **linkage type.**

LINKAGE TYPE. A type of connection between two or more related **record types.**

LIST. An ordered **set** of **data item**s. A **chain.**

LOAD MATRIX. A matrix that summarizes the usage of **record type**, **linkages,** and entry points of the preliminary **data structure** by those **procedure**s included within the **design area.**

LOCAL ENCYCLOPEDIA. A subset of the central **encyclopedia** for a **project** together with **information** pertaining to the project but not yet accepted by the central encyclopedia. A *local encyclopedia* is the responsibility of the project leader.

LOCAL MODEL. A diagram that is a subset of a **global model,** which represents a specific view of part of the **enterprise.**

LOCATION. A geographic place where **process**es are performed and/or **data** are recorded or maintained for an organization. *(KB)*

LOCATION MODEL. A representation of **locations.**

LOGICAL. An adjective describing the form of **data** organization, hardware, information systems, or **application system** that is perceived by an analyst, programmer, or **user;** it may be different from the real **(physical)** form. Indicates independence from physical constraints and considerations.

LOGICAL ACCESS MAP (LAM). A chart showing the sequence of **logical access**es to a **data model** used by an **application** system. *LAMs* give guidelines to the designer of the **program** structure which employs the **database.** A collection of *LAMS,* annotated with suitable numbers, form the input to the **physical database** design **process.**

LOGICAL DATABASE. 1. A **database** as perceived by its accessing modules; it may be structured differently from the **physical database** structure. 2. A tree-structured collection of **segment**s derived from one or more physical databases by means of **pointer linkage**s. (DL/1)

LOGICAL DATABASE DESCRIPTION. A **schema.** A description of the overall logical **database** structure. It is dependent on the database management software.

LOGICAL FILE. A file as perceived by an **application program;** it may be in a completely different form from that which it is stored on the storage unit.

LRU. Least Recently Used. A replacement **algorithm** in which when new **data** has to replace existing data in an area of storage, the least recently used items are replaced. Contrast with **LFU.**

MACHINE INDEPENDENT. An adjective used to indicate that a **procedure** or **program** is conceived, organized, or oriented without specific reference to the **system.** Use of this adjective usually implies that the procedure or program is oriented or organized in terms of the **logical** nature of the **problem** or **process**ing, rather than in terms of the characteristics of the machine used in handling it.

MACROINSTRUCTION. One line of source **program** code which generates a program routine rather than one program instruction.

MAINTENANCE OF A FILE. Periodic reorganization of a file to accommodate, more efficiently, items that have been added or deleted. (Sometimes this term is used to refer to the **process** of updating a file.)

MANAGEMENT, DATABASE. *See* **Database Management System.**

MAPPING. A definition of the way **record**s are associated with one another.

MENU. A type of **screen** used to traverse an online dialog. *(KB)*

METADATA. Data about data; that is, the **information** about data which is stored in **data dictionaries, data model**s, **schemas, encyclopedias,** and their computerized representation.

METHODOLOGY. A guideline identifying how to develop an application **system.** A methodology describes the managerial and technical **procedure**s that facilitates development of an application system.

MIGRATION. 1. The **process** whereby an **enterprise** transfers **data** and **procedure**s from an existing **information system** to a new **system** and organizes **business function**s to make best use of the new system. 2. The process of conversion, installation, and transition.

MIGRATION ANALYSIS. The study of how the **business area** is supported by existing systems and how they may be converted or incorporated into new, more comprehensive systems.

MIGRATION DESIGN. The specifying of how existing business systems and files will be gradually replaced by or interfaced with new systems.

MIGRATION PLAN. 1. A **user**-oriented plan for realigning **organizational unit**s, **job** descriptions, and staffing levels to mesh effectively with a new **information system** and to move **data** and **procedure**s to a new **system.** 2. A plan encompassing conversion, installation, and transition.

MILESTONE. A point within the duration of a **project** which is clearly definable and is of interest to management.

MISSION. A general statement of the purpose and nature of the **enterprise.**

MISSION STATEMENT. A broad description of an **enterprise**'s purpose, **policies,** and long-range strategy and vision.

MODEL. A representation for some aspect of an organization. A *model* built using **information engineering technique**s is stored in the **encyclopedia.**

MODELING SOURCE. A **person,** group, or document that provides the **information** used to **model** some aspect of the organization.

MODULE. 1. The section of storage hardware that holds one **volume,** such as one spindle, of disks. *(KB)* 2. A collection of **program** code that can be compiled by itself. 3. A collection of program statements which are designed as reusable and possess four **basic attribute**s: discrete input and output, single **function, standard** mechanics, and internal **data.**

MODULE STRUCTURE DIAGRAM. A diagram which shows the logic of the source code which constitutes the **module.**

MULTILIST ORGANIZATION. A chained file organization in which the **chain**s are divided into fragments and each fragment **indexed,** to permit faster **search**ing.

MULTIPLE ASSOCIATION. An association between two **field**s such that for each value of one field it is possible to know one or more values of the associated field. A type of behavior rule. *Synonym:* **multivalued dependence.**

MULTIPLE-KEY RETRIEVAL. **Retrieval** that requires **search**es of **data** based on the values of several **key field**s (some or all of which may be **secondary keys**).

MULTIVALUED ATTRIBUTE. An **attribute** where more than one value can describe an **entity** at any given time. Not valid in an entity type normalized to first normal.

MULTIVALUED DEPENDENCE. *See* **Multiple Association.**

NATURAL BUSINESS SYSTEM. A collection of **procedure**s which, together, support a particular functional area of an **enterprise.**

NETWORK STRUCTURE. *See* **Plex Structure.**

NONPRIME ATTRIBUTE. An **attribute** that is not part of the **primary key** of a **normalized record.** Attributes that are part of the primary key are called **prime attributes.**

NORMAL FORM, FIRST. **Data** in two-dimensional form, without repeating groups.

NORMAL FORM, SECOND. A **relation** R is in *second normal form* if it is in **first normal form** and every **nonprime attribute** of R is fully **functionally dependent** (q.v.) on each **candidate key** of R *(E.F. Codd's definition).*

NORMAL FORM, THIRD. 1. A **relation** R is in *third normal form* if it is in **second normal form** and every **nonprime attribute** of R is nontransitively dependent on each **candidate key** of R *(E.F. Codd's definition).* 2. A **record, segment,** or **tuple** which is **normalized** (i.e., contains no repeating groups) and in which every **nonprime data item** is nontransitively dependent and fully **functionally dependent** on each candidate key. In other words, the entire **primary key** or candidate key is needed to identify each other **data item** in the tuple, and no data item is identified by a data item that is not in the primary key or candidate key.

NORMALIZATION. The simplification of more complex **data structure**s according to E.F. Codd's rules which are designed to produce simpler, more stable structures. **Third normal form** (q.v.) is usually adequate for stable data structures.

NORMALIZED RECORD. A named **set** of **attributes** representing some or all of the characteristics of some **entity** or **intersection of entities.** One entity is represented by one or more **record**s in **third normal form,** and an **intersection** of two or more entities (if that intersection has **nonprime attributes**) is represented by one *normalized record*. Every *normalized record* has a **primary key. Record** may be used as a shorthand for *normalized record* in contexts where there is no possible confusion with other uses of record that are prevalent in the **field** (e.g., IMS **logical** records or **physical record**s). Moreover, the term *normalized record* is itself a shorthand meaning either *normalized record* **type** or *normalized record* **instance** (see Note 2).

OBJECT. A component of a **logical database description** that represents a real-world **entity** about which **information** is stored.

OBJECTIVE. An end or target **state** that is achieved by accomplishing all **critical success factor**s related to it. *Objectives* are short-term targets (12 to 24 months or less), with defined achievement measures.

ONLINE. An *online* **system** is one in which the input **data** enters the computer directly from the point of origin and/or output data is transmitted directly to where it is used. The intermediate **stage**s, such as punching data, writing tape, loading disks, or offline printings, are avoided.

ONLINE CONVERSATION. A particular path through a set of screens to support a single instance of a **business transaction.** *(KB)*

ONLINE STORAGE. Storage devices, especially the storage media they contain, under the direct control of a computing **system,** not offline or in a **volume library.**

OPERATING SYSTEM. Software that enables a computer to supervise its own operations, automatically calling in **program**s, routines, language, and **data** as needed for continuous throughput of different types of jobs.

OPPORTUNITY/PROBLEM. An identification of the possibilities, constraints, and other factors that assist or hinder an organization's ability to achieve its **goal**s and **critical success factor**s. *(KB)*

OPTIONALITY. The characteristic of an **entity relationship** that describes whether it exists for all occurrences of the **entity type** pair or only for some.

ORGANIZATIONAL ROLE. The primary set of **function**s that an organization performs.

ORGANIZATIONAL STRUCTURE. A representation of the interrelationships between the organization units.

ORGANIZATIONAL UNIT. An administrative subdivision of a **business segment,** which is **partition**ed to reflect reporting lines and which performs one or more **process**es. *(KB)*

ORGANIZATIONAL UNIT TYPE. A classification of **organizational unit** which performs a **standard set** of processes within a **business segment.** *(KB)*

OVERFLOW. The **condition** when a **record** (or **segment**) cannot be stored in its **home address,** that is, the storage **location logically** assigned to it on loading. It may be stored in a special *overflow* location, or in the home address of other records.

PACKAGE. A reusable **program** or collection of programs to be used by more than one business and/or **organizational unit.** *(KB)*

PAGE. A subdivision of a file or program, which is the minimum amount of information that may be transferred from the control of the **operating system** to the control of the **data management** software.

PAGE FAULT. A **program** interruption that occurs when a **page** that is referred to is not in main memory and has to be read in.

PAGING. In **virtual** storage **system**s, the **technique** of making memory appear larger than it is by transferring **pages** of **data** or **program**s into memory from external storage when needed.

PAIRING. Two **entity** instances of one or two **type**s associated by virtue of a defined **relationship.**

PAIRING MEMBERSHIP. The participation of an **entity** in a **pairing.**

PARALLEL DATA ORGANIZATIONS. Data organizations that permit multiple **access** arms to **search,** read, or write **data** simultaneously.

PARALLEL DEPENDENCY. A situation where there is more than one **dependency** between two **process**es, any one of which can apply to a given execution of the processes.

PARALLEL RELATIONSHIPS. Two or more **relationship**s associating two entity types.

PARENT. An **object** in a **decomposition diagram** that is immediately above at least one specified object.

PARTIAL IDENTIFIER. A constituent **attribute** of a composite **identifier.**

PARTITION. *See* **Business Area Partition.**

PARTITIONING. The **technique** for identifying **partitions.**

PERFORMANCE ASSESSMENT. The prediction, within reasonable bounds, of the performance of an application system.

PERFORMANCE MEASURE. An indicator that shows the progress of an **action** against a plan. It indicates to what extent the **goal** has been reached.

PERFORMANCE TEST. An evaluation of how well a **system** performs its **functions**, including speed maximum volume, accuracy, and use of resources such as memory space.

PERSON. An individual who plays a role in an **enterprise.** *(KB)*

PERSPECTIVE. A **user**'s view of an organization or of a portion of one; it is obtained by considering multiple diagrams (e.g., **decomposition** view, **data view,** or **process** view diagrams).

PHASE. A series of **stages** within the **methodology.**

PHYSICAL. An adjective, contrasted with **logical,** which refers to the form in which **data** or **system**s exist in reality. Data is often converted by software from the form in which they are *physically* stored to a form in which a **user** or programmer perceives them.

PHYSICAL DATABASE. A **database** in the form in which it is stored on the storage media, including **pointers** or other means of interconnecting it. Multiple **logical databases** may be derived from one or more *physical databases*.

PHYSICAL RECORD. A collection of bits that are *physically recorded* on the storage medium and which are read or written by one machine input/output instruction.

PLANNING HORIZON. A planning range of the **tactical IS project plan** that can vary from six to nine months to two to three years based on what is being planned (e.g., technology, new applications, organizational changes).

PLANNING PHASE. A **phase** of **information engineering.** A high-level study of an organization (or of a portion of one) that identifies **information needs,** assesses existing **information system**'s capabilities, identifies appropriate technologies and architectures, and defines **business area**s. A **corporate information model,** information needs **report,** existing information systems profile report, and information systems plan (which includes a **tactical IS project plan** and a long-term information systems plan) are produced.

PLEX STRUCTURE. A **relationship** between **record**s (or other groupings) in which a **child record** can have more than one **parent** record. *Synonym:* **network structure.**

POINTER. The **address** of a **record** (or other **data** groupings) contained in another record so that a **program** may **access** the former record when it has **retrieve**d the latter record. The address can be absolute, relative, or symbolic, and hence the *pointer* is referred to as absolute, relative, or symbolic.

POLICY. A principle, plan, or course of **action** pursued by an organization.

PRIMARY KEY. *See* **Key, Primary.**

PRIME ATTRIBUTE. An **attribute** that forms all or part of the **primary key** of a **record.** Other attributes are called **nonprime attributes.**

PROBLEM. An obstacle to achieving a **goal** or **critical success factor;** a situation or issue that presents uncertainty, complication, complexity, or difficulty.

PROBLEMS AND ISSUES LIST. A record of the **problem**s and issues raised during a **structured interview.**

PROCEDURE. 1. A method by which one or more processes may be carried out. Contrast with **process.** *(KB)* 2. A sequence of detailed instructions that performs specific **physical task**s to support a lowest-**level logical** process. *Synonym:* functional primitive.

PROCEDURE ACTION DIAGRAM. A representation of the logic of a **procedure** in terms of the **action**s carried out on each **data object** involved and the **condition**s constraining them.

PROCEDURE CONDITION. A rule expressed in terms of **logical data** constructs and/or layouts and/or constants which constrains the behavior of the business **system.**

PROCEDURE DECOMPOSITION DIAGRAM. A form of **activity decomposition diagram** showing the hierarchical breakdown of **procedure**s.

PROCEDURE DEPENDENCY DIAGRAM. A diagram which shows how for each **procedure,** and execution may depend upon the prior execution of other procedures.

PROCEDURE DESIGN. The **task** of specifying the steps, **data** input and output, and the detailed logic of a **procedure.**

PROCESS. 1. A low-level **activity** that starts and stops, and is executed repeatedly. The execution of the *process* produces a specific kind of effect on **entities** or **information** about entities of a specified **type.** *Processes* are determined by successively decomposing the **business functions.** The word *process* relates to ''what'' is to be done but not ''how'' it is done. The word **procedure** relates to ''how'' something is accomplished. *(KB)* 2. A repetitive, well-defined **set** of **logical task**s that support one **function,** are repeatedly executed in a **business segment,** can be defined in terms of inputs and outputs, and have a definable beginning and end. *Processes* can be decomposed into *processes* and are triggered by an **event** and carried out by a business segment to achieve a stated purpose. A low-level *process* may be replicated across the business segment.

PROCESS ACTION DIAGRAM. A representation of the logic of a **process** in terms of the **action**s carried out on each **entity analysis object** involved and the **condition**s constraining these actions.

PROCESS DECOMPOSITION DIAGRAM. A structure that shows the breakdown of **process**es into progressively increasing detail.

PROCESS DEPENDENCY. An association between **process**es such that an execution of a process produces an **information** view that must be or may be required as input to an execution of another process. The **dependency** may be between executions of the same process.

PROCESS DEPENDENCY ANALYSIS. The analysis of the sequences in which **process**es can be executed and the **attribute**s that are passed from one process to another.

PROCESS DEPENDENCY DIAGRAM. A diagram that shows how each **process** depends on the prior execution of other processes.

PROCESS FILTER. The elimination, prior to the **design phase,** of any **process**es that do not at this time warrant computer support.

PROCESS HIERARCHY. *See* **Process Decomposition Diagram.**

PROCESS LOGIC An analysis of the inherent logic of a **process** in terms of the **entity type**s, **relationship**s, and **attribute**s involved, the **condition**s constraining the execution of its subprocesses, and the algorithms used.

PROCESS LOGIC DIAGRAM. A diagram showing the inherent logic of a **process,** in terms of the sequence in which **entity type**s and **relationship**s are involved.

PROCESS LOGIC FORM. A pro forma on which all the details from the logic analysis of a **process** are documented.

PROCESS NETWORK DIAGRAM. A diagram that shows the breakdown of **process**es into progressively increasing detail, but such that each process appears only once in the diagram.

PROCESS PURPOSE. The categorization of a **process** according to whether it contributes to the operational, tactical, or strategic **activities** of the **enterprise.**

PROCESS SCHEDULING. The extent to which the timing of the executions of a **process** can be controlled.

PROCESS SELECTION CRITERION. A characteristic of a **process** that is used to judge whether or not a process should be **select**ed for computerization.

PROCESS SELECTION SCORE. A relative value assigned to a **process** according to the degree to which the process meets a **select**ion criterion.

PROCESS STIMULUS. The categorization of a **process** according to whether or not its execution directly follows the execution of some process.

PROCESS-DRIVEN PROCESS. A **process** that follows the completion of some other process.

PROCESSING CYCLE. A period during the **production stage** for a business **system,** which provides a basis for control.

PROCESSOR CONFIGURATION. A combination of the hardware and systems software on which an **application system** is **process**ed. *(KB)*

PRODUCTION. The period in the **systems developed lifecycle** during which application systems provide support to the areas of the **enterprise** for which they were designed.

PRODUCTION SYSTEM. The execution of debugged **program**s that routinely accomplishes its purpose.

PROGRAM GROUP DEPENDENCY DIAGRAM. A diagram that shows the **dependency** of **program** groups on one another for testing purposes.

PROGRAM STRUCTURE DIAGRAM. A diagram that shows the **module**s from which the **program** is constructed and the **field**s by which they communicate.

PROGRESSIVE OVERFLOW. A method of handling **overflow** in a randomly stored file which does not require the use of **pointer**s. An overflow **record** is stored in the first available space and is **retrieve**d by a forward serial **search** from the **home address.**

PROJECT. A related group of work **activities,** organized under the direction of a *project* manager using a *project* plan, which when carried out will allow the *project* **goal**(s) to be achieved. Examples are **analysis phase** *projects,* **infrastructure** *projects,* and **design phase** *projects. (KB)*

PROJECT BASELINE. *See* **Project Knowledge Base.**

PROJECT CHARTER. An approved **project** definition that outlines the purpose, **scope,** and **objective**s of an I.E. project.

PROJECT CONTROL FILE (PCF). The collection of all documentary material from a **project.**

PROJECT KNOWLEDGE BASE. A subset of the **enterprise knowledge base** that is being utilized by an **I.E. project.**

PROJECT MANAGEMENT. The administration of a **project** to ensure enforcement of its **goal**s.

PROJECT SCOPE. A definition of what is and is not included in a **project.** A **business area** is equivalent to an analysis *project scope*.

PROJECT TASK. A unit of work contained within a **project** to be performed by a person to achieve a specific result.

PROTOTYPE. A representation of a **system** that simulates the main **user** interfaces so that users can understand and critique the system. Software **tool**s are used which enable the *prototype* to be built quickly and modified quickly to adapt it to end-user needs. This provides an important means for user needs and capabilities. In some cases tools are used that enable the *prototype* to be successively added to until it becomes the full working system.

PURGE DATE. The date on or after which a **storage area** is available to be overwritten. Used in conjunction with a file **label,** it is a means of protecting file **data** until an agreed release date is reached.

QUALITY ASSURANCE. The development of standards and the formal monitoring to ensure that standards are being enforced.

QUALITY CONTROL. A technique for evaluating the quality of a product being processed, by checking it against a predetermined standard and taking the proper corrective action if the product does not meet the standard.

QUALITY PLAN. A **project management** plan used to indicate key **milestone**s and deliveries in a **project** that will be examined in the quality control review. It is constructed in the preparation **stage** of a project and adjusted during the duration of the project.

RANDOM ACCESS. To obtain **data** directly from any storage **location** regardless of its position with respect to the previously referenced **information.** *Synonym:* **direct access.**

RANDOM ACCESS STORAGE. A storage **technique** in which the time required to obtain **information** is independent of the **location** of the information most recently obtained. This strict definition must be qualified by the observation that we usually mean relatively random. Thus magnetic drums are relatively nonrandom **access** when compared to magnetic cores for main memory, but relatively **random access** when compared to magnetic tapes for file storage.

RANDOMIZING. *See* **Hashing.**

REAL TIME. 1. Pertaining to actual time during which a **physical process** transpires.
2. Pertaining to the performance of a computation during the actual time that the related physical process transpires so that results of the computation can be used in guiding the physical process.
3. Pertaining to an **application** in which response to input is fast enough to effect subsequent input, as when conducting the **dialog**s that take place at terminals on interactive **system**s.

RECORD. 1. A group of related **data elements** treated as a unit by an **application program.** *(KB)* 2. A collection of occurrences of **field**s which is read or written as a single unit, during the execution of a **module.** *(IE)* 3. A named collection of zero, one, or more data items or **data aggregates.** There may be an arbitrary number of occurrences in the **database** of each *record* type specified in the **schema** for that database. For example, there would be one occurrence of the *record* type "payroll *record*" for each employee. This distinction between the actual occurrences of a *record* and the **type** of *record* is an important one. **(CODASYL)** 4. A **logical database** *record* consists of a named hierarchy (tree) of related **segment**s. There may be one or more segment types, each of which may have a different length and **format.** (DL/1)

RECORD LAYOUT. A collection of related **field**s which represent **data** in a structure visible to both **module**s and the **data management system.**

RECOVERY. The **process** to allow the continuance of **program** execution after a failure.

RECURSION. The dependence of an **activity** or **action** on itself. An activity calling itself.

REDUNDANT ATTRIBUTE. A superfluous **attribute** that already appears elsewhere.

REDUNDANT DEPENDENCY. A **process dependency** that exists only because each of its **process**es have a dependency, directly or indirectly, with some third process.

REDUNDANT RELATIONSHIP. A **relationship** where each of its **pairing**s can be derived from pairings under other, more basic relationships.

RELATION. A two-dimensional array of **data** elements. A file in **normalized** form.

RELATIONAL ALGEBRA. A language providing a **set** of operators for manipulating **relation**s. These include "project," "join," and **"search"** operators.

RELATIONAL CALCULUS. A language in which the **user**s state the result they require from manipulating a **relational database.**

RELATIONAL DATABASE. A **database** made up of **relation**s (as defined above) that uses a **database management system** has the capability to recombine the **data item**s to form different relations, thus giving great flexibility in the usage of **data.** If the database management system does not provide the **function**s of or equivalent to a **relational algebra,** the term *relational database* should not be used.

RELATIONAL VIEW. A representation of part or all of an **enterprise**'s **data architecture** in terms of **relation**s.

RELATIONSHIP. A reason (of relevance to the **enterprise**) why **entities** from one or from two **entity type**s may be associated. *(KB)* A named connection or association between entity types that embodies some relevant **information** of value to an organization.

RELATIONSHIP INVOLVEMENT MATRIX. A matrix which shows for **relationship**s the **process**es in which they are involved and by which **action**s.

RELATIONSHIP MODEL. *See* **Entity-Relationship Diagram.**

RELATIONSHIP ROLE. A business reason whereby **entities** of a specific **type** may participate in groupings under a **relationship,** either as plural members or as single members.

REPORT. A preparation of **information** generated by an **application system** which may be sent to a printer. *(KB)*

RESPONSE TIME. The time taken for a **system** to respond to a **user** input. It is usually measured from the point at which the last character is input at the terminal to the point at which the first character is output.

RETRIEVE. An **action** by which a **record** is made available for use during the execution of a **module.**

REUSABLE COMPONENT. A **construct** developed and used in multiple applications.

RING STRUCTURE. **Data** organized with **chain**s such that the end of the chain points to its beginning, thus forming a ring.

RISK FACTOR. A feature of the environment in which a business **system** is to be developed which can be assessed as contributing to the likely success or failure of the development **project.**

RISK MANAGEMENT PLAN. A plan to address the risks involved in a **project** and the measures to be taken to control and reduce them.

ROLL BACKWARD. A method of **database recovery** in which, after corruption, before images are applied to the database until it is returned to the last known point of consistency.

ROLL FORWARD. A method of **database recovery** in which, after corruption, after-images are applied to a backup copy of the database until it is brought up to the last known point of consistency.

ROOT. The base node of a **tree structure. Data** in the tree may be **access**ed starting at its *root*.

ROOT ENTITY TYPE. An **entity type** that does not participate as the plural entity type in any one-to-many **relationship.**

ROOT FUNCTION. A **function** that is not itself a **subfunction** of any other function.

ROOT IDENTIFIER. The identifying **attribute**s of a **root entity type.**

ROUTINE EVENT. An **event** which occurs with such regularity that the number in a given time period can be estimated but cannot be known precisely.

ROUTINE PROCESS. A **process** which is executed with such regularity that the number in a given time period may be estimated accurately but not precisely.

RUN UNIT. A collection of **batch programs** to be executed as a group based on **process**ing **location**s, processing type **(online** vs. **batch),** and timing. *(KB)*

RUN-TIME INCLUDE. An alternative to copy compile where code is copied into a **program** at *runtime* and then interpreted.

SCHEDULE. A plan for the performance of **task**s within a **project,** detailing the time and resource requirements.

SCHEMA. 1. A **map** of the overall **logical** structure of a **database.** Contrast with **data model.** *(KB)* 2. A *schema* consists of DDL **(data description language)** entries and is a complete description of all the area, **set** occurrences, **record** occurrences, and associated **data item**s and **data aggregate**s as they exist in the database. (CODASYL)

SCHEMA LANGUAGE. Logical database description language.

SCOPE. A defined subset of **object**s which are the subject of a specific **project.**

SCREEN. A presentation of **information** generated by an **application system** and sent to a video display device. *(KB)*

SEARCH. To examine a series of items for any that have a desired property or properties.

SEARCH KEY. *See* **Key, Secondary.**

SECONDARY INDEX. An **index** composed of **secondary key**s rather than **primary key**s.

SECONDARY KEY. *See* **Key, Secondary.**

SECONDARY STORAGE. 1. Storage **facilities** forming not an integral part of a computer but directly **link**ed to and controlled by the computer (e.g., disks, magnetic tapes, etc.) The smallest **address** portion of storage on some disk and drum storage units. 2. A hardware product that can be used to store **data** for indefinite periods of time.

SECURITY CLASSIFICATION. The extent to which specific **module**s or **information object type**s need to be protected from unauthorized use.

SECURITY CONTROL. A measure by means of which a form of protection is given to a business **system** or computing environment.

SECURITY SYSTEM. Hardware, software, or control data designed to prevent damage, theft, or corruption of data application.

SEEK. To position the **access mechanism** of a **direct access storage device** at a specified **location.**

SEEK TIME. The time taken to execute a **seek** operation.

SEGMENT. A named fixed-**format** quantum of **data** containing one or more **data items.** A *segment* is the basic quantum of data that is passed to and from the **application program**s when IBM Data Language/1 is used. (DL/1)

SELECT. An **action** by which a value of an **attribute** is used to *select,* or to assist in *selecting,* an **entity** for involvement in the execution of a **process,** or by which a **data** value is used to *select,* or assist in *selecting,* a **record** for use during the execution of a **module.**

SENSITIVITY. A programmer may view only certain of the **data** in a **logical database.** His **program** is said to be *sensitized* to those data.

SEQUENCE SET INDEX. The lowest **level** in a **tree-structured index.** The **entities** in this level are in sequence. **Search**es and other operations may be carried out in the *sequence set index;* those are called *sequence set operations.*

SEQUENTIAL PROCESSING. **Access**ing **record**s in the sequence in which they were stored.

SERIAL ACCESS STORAGE. Storage in which **record**s must be read serially one after the other (e.g., tape).

SERIAL PROCESSING. **Access**ing **record**s in their **physical** sequence. The next record accessed will be the record in the next physical position/**location** in the **field.**

SERVICE-LEVEL BENCHMARK. A point of reference from which measurements can be made.

SERVICE-LEVEL OBJECTIVE. The measurable level of service provided by an **IS organization unit** for an **application system** which has been agreed to with the **user** (e.g., end-user support, **response time,** turnaround). *(KB)*

SET. A *set* is a named collection of **record type**s. As such, it establishes the characteristics of an arbitrary number of occurrences of the named *set.* Each *set* type specified in the **schema** must have one record type declared as its "Owner" and one or more record types declared as its "Member" records. Each occurrence of a *set* must contain one occurrence of its owner record and may contain an arbitrary number of occurrences of each of its member record types. *(CODASYL)*

SET, SINGULAR. A **CODASYL set** without owner **record**s; the owner is declared to be "**System.**" A *singular set* is used to provide simple non**hierarchical file**s such as a file of customer records.

SKELETON PROGRAM. A partially constructed **program** that performs a small but useful subset of the **function**s of the complete program.

SKILL. The ability or proficiency of a **person.** *(KB)*

SKIP-SEARCHED CHAIN. A **chain** having **pointer**s that permit it to be **search**ed by skipping, not examining every **link** in the chain.

SOFTWARE COMPONENT. **Program**s or instructions that tell a computer what to do.

SORT. Arrange a file in the sequence of a specified **key.**

STAGE. A collection of **activities** within the **methodology.**

STAGING. Blocks of **data** are moved from one storage device to another with a shorter **access time,** either before or at the time they are needed.

STAKEHOLDER. A key member of an **organizational unit** who defines and has a personal stake in achieving the **goal** of the unit.

STANDARD. An approved rule and required practice for controlling the technical performance and methods of personnel involved in **system**s development, modification, and maintenance.

STATE. The **condition** of the **system** at a point in time. **Information** about the *state* of a system, together with new **event**s, determines the system's response.

STORAGE AREA. An area that supports a **logical** view of the **physical** storage structures used to hold **data.** *(KB)*

STORAGE HIERARCHY. Storage units **link**ed together to form a storage **subsystem,** in which some are fast but small and others are large but slow. Blocks of **data** are moved (**stage**d) from the large slow **level**s to the small fast levels as required.

STORAGE SCHEMA. *See* **Internal Schema.**

STRATEGIC INFORMATION SYSTEMS PLAN. A plan that sets out the overall **objective**s for **information system**s development over a three- to five-year period.

STRUCTURED ENGLISH. Statements written in a subset of English within a disciplined organization, such that they may be readily translated into a computer language.

STRUCTURED INTERVIEW. An interview session with (normally) a single businessperson which aims to achieve a specific **information**-gathering **objective** through the use of defined, formal **technique**s and a **format** planned in advance.

STRUCTURED WALK-THROUGH. A symbol-by-symbol verbal explanation of a diagram by the analyst or designer responsible, with the **objective** of eliminating errors and inconsistencies.

SUBJECT AREA. A major, high-level classification of **data.** A group of **entity type**s that pertains directly to a **function** or major topic of interest to the **enterprise.** *(KB)*

SUBSCHEMA. A **map** of a **program**'s view of the **data** used. It is derived from the global **logical** view of the data—the **schema.** *(KB)*

SUBSYSTEM. A complete, self-contained subdivision of an **information system** that performs one discrete **function.**

SYSTEM. An interrelated **set** of components that are viewed as a whole. *Synonym:* **application system.**

SYSTEM ARCHITECTURE. The composite of specific components, and the way in which they interact, that form a computer **system.**

SYSTEM DEPENDENCY. An association between two **system**s which exists because **information** originating in one is required by the other.

SYSTEM DEVELOPMENT METHODOLOGY. A defined way of developing a business **system.** *Synonym:* **methodology.**

SYSTEM SOFTWARE COMPONENT. Software other than the **application programs**

which is required to operate, maintain, or support the **processor configuration, communications network,** and the **application** (e.g., TP monitor, **operating system**s, utilities, **compiler**s). *(KB)*

SYSTEM STRUCTURE DIAGRAM. A representation of the designed and defined collection of **procedure**s, **data store**s, **data flow**s, **data view**s, and **terminator**s which, when implemented, will make up a **system.**

SYSTEM TEST. A test carried out on a business **system** to verify that as a whole, it **function**s as specified in the **business system design** specification. *Synonym:* **data flow program.**

SYSTEM VARIANT. A business **system** modified for certain **function**s of a specific (**set of**) **location**(s) or **organizational unit**(s). It is based on a business system designed for the functions of another location or organizational unit within the same **business area.**

SYSTEMS LIFECYCLE. The **stage**s and **task**s in the development and productive use of a **system** from its inception to its demise.

TABLE. 1. A collection of **data** suitable for quick reference, each item being uniquely identified either by a **label** or by its relative position. 2. A rectangular grid of data values each identifiable by the labels applied to the rows and columns.

TACTICAL DECISION. A decision concerning changes in the allocation of resources or in the ways in which an **enterprise** operates.

TACTICAL IS PROJECT PLAN. A plan that describes in detail which **project**s are to be carried out in the first one to three years of the **planning horizon.**

TACTICAL PROCESS. A **process** concerned with the allocation and efficient utilization of the resources of an **enterprise.**

TANGIBLE BENEFIT. A **benefit** to which a direct monetary value can be applied.

TASK. A defined, low-level unit of work for one or more **person**s within a **project.**

TASK RESULT. The creation, update, or deletion of a **project** management, **deliverable,** and/or **knowledge base** component.

TECHNICAL ARCHITECTURE. A structure that summarizes the mixture of hardware, system software, and communication **facilities** which supports or will support the information systems within an **enterprise.**

TECHNICAL COMPONENT OR FACILITY. A hardware, systems software, or communication facility object within the **technical architecture.**

TECHNICAL CONTEXT. A subset of the **technical architecture** within the context of which a **design project** will proceed.

TECHNICAL DESIGN. That part of the **design phase** during which a **system** is refined to achieve the most economic and efficient performance using the chosen technology. *Synonym:* internal design.

TECHNICAL REQUIREMENTS. The technological requirements and constraints identified in planning and analysis that will be considered in depth by the design project.

TECHNIQUE. A **set** of interrelated **procedure**s which together describe how a **task** in the **methodology** can be accomplished.

TECHNOLOGY IMPACT ANALYSIS. A **methodology** for the effects or potential of the adoption of new enabling technologies on an organization's business opportunities.

TEMPORAL EVENT. The triggering of one or more **process**es at a predetermined time. These processes use only **data** that has previously been saved within the **system.**

TERMINATION STATE. A final **state** in the life of an **entity.**

TERMINATOR. An **organizational unit,** lying outside the boundary of a **system,** that originates or receives one or more of the system's **data view**s.

TEST. A formally organized execution of **modules, programs,** and/or **procedure**s to prove the integrity of part of the business **system.**

TEST CASE. A collection of input **data** and expected output data designed to ascertain whether a **test condition** is met correctly. A **set** of **select**ed **data element** test values and expected results which is used during various types of testing (e.g., unit, integration, performance, acceptance).

TEST CONDITION. A rule that must be tested to ensure the correct operation of a **procedure** step, **action statement,** or statement block.

TEST CYCLE. A collection of **test case**s which are applied in sequence to verify the correct operation of all the **test condition**s tested by the test case.

TEST HARNESS. Software needed to adequately test components of an **application.**

THIRD NORMAL FORM. *See* **Normal Form, Third.**

TIME EVENT. The passage of a specific time period which triggers the execution of one or more **processes.**

TOOL. A software product used by **information systems** personnel to manage and support information systems.

TRACK. The circular recording surface transcribed by a read/write head on a drum, disk, or other rotating mechanism.

TRANSACTION SCREEN. A **screen** that accepts **business transactions** as input to an **application.** *(KB)*

TRANSITION. 1. The period in the **systems lifecycle** in which the new business **systems,** to support a defined area within the **enterprise,** gradually replace or are interfaced to the existing system. 2. The **process** by which a new system is first installed with one or a small number of groups of business **users** and then expanded to involve all potential users within the organization.

TRANSITION ALGORITHM. *See* **Conversion Algorithm.**

TRANSITION ANALYSIS. *See* **Migration Analysis.**

TRANSITION DESIGN. *See* **Migration Design.**

TRANSITIVE DEPENDENCY. A **dependency** between two elements, which is due to the first element being dependent on some other element, which in turn is dependent on the second.

TRANSPARENT DATA. Complexities in the **data structure** are hidden from the programmers or **users** (made transparent to them) by the systems software.

TREE INDEX. An **index** in the form of a **tree structure.**

TREE STRUCTURE. A hierarchy of groups of **data** such that (a) the highest **level** in the hierarchy has only one group, called a **root;** (b) all groups except the root are related to one and only one group on a higher level than themselves. A simple master/detail file is a two-level tree. *Syn:* Hierarchical Structure.

TRIAL RUN. A period in which the **user** can engage the new **system** to perform actual business **procedures** in the working environment, but in which there is still an option to return to the former business system if serious **problems** are encountered when operating the new system.

TUPLE. A group of related **fields.** *N* related fields are called an *N-tuple.*

TYPE. *See* Note 2, p. 445.

UNIT TEST. A test performed on an atomic unit, typically **modules** and **programs,** in order to test detailed logic.

USER. A staff member in a **business area** who will make use of an **information system.**

VIRTUAL. Conceptual or appearing to be, rather than actually being. An adjective which implies that **data,** structures, or hardware appear to the **application** programmer or **user** to be different from what they are in reality, the **conversion** being performed by software.

VIRTUAL MEMORY. Memory that can appear to the **programs** to be larger than it really is because blocks of **data** or program are rapidly moved to or from **secondary storage** when needed.

VOLATILE FILE. A file with a high rate of additions and deletions.

VOLATILE STORAGE. Storage that loses its contents when the power supply is cut off. Solid-state (LSI) storage is volatile; magnetic storage is not.

VOLUME. Demountable tapes, disks, and cartridges are referred to as *volumes.* The word also refers to a nondemountable disk or other storage medium. It has been defined as ''that portion of a single unit of storage medium which is **access**ible to a single read/write mechanism''; however, some devices exist in which a volume is accessible with two or more read/write mechanisms.

VOLUME TABLE OF CONTENTS (VTOC). A **table** associated with a **volume** which describes each file or **data set** on the volume.

VSAM. Virtual Sequential **Access Method.** An IBM **volume**-independent indexed-sequential **access method.**

VTOC. *See* **Volume Table of Contents.**

Work Plan. A plan prepared for each **phase** detailing **tasks,** resource estimates, and time **schedules.**

Working Storage. A portion of storage, usually computer main memory, reserved for the temporary intermediate results of processing.

INDEX

The Conceptual Prism of
Information Systems:

THE JAMES MARTIN BOOKS

Information Systems Management and Strategy	Methodologies for Building Systems	Analysis and Design	CASE
AN INFORMATION SYSTEMS MANIFESTO	STRATEGIC INFORMATION PLANNING METHODOLOGIES (second edition)	STRUCTURED TECHNIQUES: THE BASIS FOR CASE (revised edition)	STRUCTURED TECHNIQU THE BASIS FOR CASE (revised edition)
INFORMATION ENGINEERING (Book I: Introduction)	INFORMATION ENGINEERING (Book I: Introduction)	DATABASE ANALYSIS AND DESIGN	INFORMATION ENGINEER (Book I: Introduction)
INFORMATION ENGINEERING (Book II: Planning and Analysis)	INFORMATION ENGINEERING (Book II: Planning and Analysis)	DESIGN OF MAN-COMPUTER DIALOGUES	**Languages and Program**
STRATEGIC INFORMATION PLANNING METHODOLOGIES (second edition)	INFORMATION ENGINEERING (Book III: Design and Construction)	DESIGN OF REAL-TIME COMPUTER SYSTEMS	APPLICATION DEVELOPME WITHOUT PROGRAMMER
SOFTWARE MAINTENANCE: THE PROBLEM AND ITS SOLUTIONS	STRUCTURED TECHNIQUES: THE BASIS FOR CASE (revised edition)	DATA COMMUNICATIONS DESIGN TECHNIQUES	FOURTH-GENERATION LANGUAGES (Volume I: Principles)
DESIGN AND STRATEGY FOR DISTRIBUTED DATA PROCESSING	**Diagramming Techniques**	DESIGN AND STRATEGY FOR DISTRIBUTED DATA PROCESSING	FOURTH-GENERATION LANGUAGES (Volume II: Representative 4(
CORPORATE COMMUNICATIONS STRATEGY	DIAGRAMMING TECHNIQUES FOR ANALYSTS AND PROGRAMMERS	SOFTWARE MAINTENANCE: THE PROBLEM AND ITS SOLUTIONS	FOURTH-GENERATION LANGUAGES (Volume III: 4GLs from IBN
Expert Systems	RECOMMENDED DIAGRAMMING STANDARDS FOR ANALYSTS AND PROGRAMMERS	SYSTEM DESIGN FROM PROVABLY CORRECT CONSTRUCTS	ACTION DIAGRAMS: CLEA STRUCTURED SPECIFICATI PROGRAMS, AND PROCEDU (second edition)
BUILDING EXPERT SYSTEMS: A TUTORIAL	ACTION DIAGRAMS: CLEARLY STRUCTURED SPECIFICATIONS, PROGRAMS, AND PROCEDURES (second edition)	INFORMATION ENGINEERING (Book II: Planning and Analysis)	
KNOWLEDGE ACQUISITION FOR EXPERT SYSTEMS		INFORMATION ENGINEERING (Book III: Design and Construction)	